The Cambridge Handbook of
The Just War

What makes a war just? What makes a specific weapon, strategy, or decision in war just? The tradition of Just War theory has provided responses to these questions since at least A.D. 400, yet each shift in the weapons and strategies of war poses significant challenges to Just War theory. This book assembles scholars from around the world to reflect on the most pressing problems and questions in Just War theory. The volume will be important for students and scholars of the philosophy of war as well as for others interested in contemporary ethical issues arising from the changing shape of warfare.

Larry May is W. Alton Jones Professor of Philosophy, Law, and Political Science at Vanderbilt University. He has published more than thirty books, including *War Crimes and Just War* (Cambridge, 2007), *After War Ends* (Cambridge, 2012), and *Contingent Pacifism* (Cambridge, 2015).

Cambridge Handbooks in Philosophy

Cambridge Handbooks in Philosophy are explorations of philosophical topics for both students and specialists. They offer accessible new essays by a range of contributors, as well as a substantial introduction and bibliography.

Titles published in this series

The Cambridge Handbook of Information and Computer Ethics
Edited by Luciano Floridi

The Cambridge Handbook of Cognitive Science
Edited by Keith Frankish and William Ramsey

The Cambridge Handbook of Artificial Intelligence
Edited by Keith Frankish and William Ramsey

The Cambridge Handbook of Evolutionary Ethics
Edited by Michael Ruse and Robert J. Richards

The Cambridge Handbook of the Just War
Edited by Larry May

The Cambridge Handbook of
The Just War

EDITED BY

Larry May

Vanderbilt University, Tennessee
**With the assistance of Shannon Fyfe and
Eric Ritter**

CAMBRIDGE
UNIVERSITY PRESS

University Printing House, Cambridge CB2 8BS, United Kingdom

One Liberty Plaza, 20th Floor, New York, NY 10006, USA

477 Williamstown Road, Port Melbourne, VIC 3207, Australia

314–321, 3rd Floor, Plot 3, Splendor Forum, Jasola District Centre,
New Delhi – 110025, India

79 Anson Road, #06–04/06, Singapore 079906

Cambridge University Press is part of the University of Cambridge.

It furthers the University's mission by disseminating knowledge in the pursuit of
education, learning, and research at the highest international levels of excellence.

www.cambridge.org
Information on this title: www.cambridge.org/9781107152496
DOI: 10.1017/9781316591307

First published 2018

Printed in the United Kingdom by Clays, St Ives plc

A catalogue record for this publication is available from the British Library.

Library of Congress Cataloging-in-Publication Data
Names: May, Larry, editor.
Title: The Cambridge handbook of the just war / edited by Larry May, Vanderbilt University,
Tennessee ; with the assistance of Shannon Fyfe and Eric Ritter.
Description: New York : Cambridge University Press, 2017. | Includes bibliographical
references and index.
Identifiers: LCCN 2017040736 | ISBN 9781107152496 (alk. paper)
Subjects: LCSH: Just war doctrine – Handbooks, manuals, etc. | War – Moral and ethical
aspects – Handbooks, manuals, etc. | War (Philosophy)
Classification: LCC U22 .C354 2017 | DDC 172/.42–dc23
LC record available at https://lccn.loc.gov/2017040736

ISBN 978-1-107-15249-6 Hardback
ISBN 978-1-316-60662-9 Paperback

Contents

Contributors

Saba Bazargan-Forward is Associate Professor of Philosophy at the University of California, San Diego, and coeditor, with Samuel C. Rickless, of *The Ethics of War: Essays* (2017).

Yitzhak Benbaji teaches philosophy in the law faculty at Tel-Aviv University. He is the author of "Legitimate Authority in War" in Helen Frowe and Seth Lazar (eds.), *The Oxford Handbook of Ethics of War* (forthcoming).

Jovana Davidovic is Assistant Professor of Philosophy at the University of Iowa working on issues relating to Just War theory, international criminal law, and human rights.

Shannon E. French is Inamori Professor of Ethics at Case Western Reserve University, and author of *The Code of the Warrior: Exploring Warrior Values, Past and Present* (2003).

Shannon Fyfe is PhD Candidate in Philosophy at Vanderbilt University, where she previously obtained her JD. She recently published (with Larry May) *International Criminal Tribunals: A Normative Defense* (Cambridge University Press, 2017).

Adil Ahmad Haque is Professor of Law and Judge Jon O. Newman Scholar at Rutgers Law School and the author of *Law and Morality at War* (2017).

Elizabeth Lanphier is PhD Candidate in the Philosophy Department at Vanderbilt University.

Steven Lee is Professor of Philosophy at Hobart and William Smith Colleges; his most recent book is *Ethics and War: An Introduction* (Cambridge University Press, 2012).

John Mark Mattox is Senior Research Fellow at National Defense University, Washington, D.C. He is the author of *Saint Augustine and the Theory of Just War* (2006).

Larry May is W. Alton Jones Professor of Philosophy, Professor of Law, and Professor of Political Science at Vanderbilt University. His recent publications include *Necessity in International Law*, with Jens David Ohlin (2016).

Jeff McMahan is White's Professor of Moral Philosophy at the University of Oxford and author of *Killing in War* (2009).

Lionel K. McPherson is Associate Professor of Philosophy at Tufts University; his recent publications include "Legalism, Justice, and the War on Terrorism" in *Who Should Die? The Ethics of Killing in War*, edited by Bradley Strawser, Ryan Jenkins, and Michael Robillard (forthcoming).

Jens David Ohlin is Professor of Law at Cornell Law School; his most recent books include *The Assault on International Law* (2015) and (with Larry May) *Necessity in International Law* (2016).

Johan Olsthoorn holds a PhD in Philosophy from KU Leuven and currently holds a postdoctoral research fellowship from FWO-Flanders. He has published widely on early modern theories of justice, rights, and property.

Eric Joseph Ritter is PhD Candidate in the Philosophy Department at Vanderbilt University.

Henry Shue is Senior Research Fellow Emeritus at Merton College, Oxford, and the author of *Fighting Hurt: Rule and Exception in Torture and War* (2016).

Uwe Steinhoff is Associate Professor in the Department of Politics and Public Administration at the University of Hong Kong. His most recent single-authored book is *On the Ethics of Torture* (2013).

Suzanne Uniacke is Professor in Philosophy at Charles Sturt University, Canberra, Australia. Her most recent publication is "The Value of Applied Philosophy," in K. Lippert-Rasmussen et al. (eds.), *A Companion to Applied Philosophy* (2017).

Foreword

Jeff McMahan

Since the end of the Korean War, the nature of war has changed in many ways. The most obvious change is that wars are now less often between the organized military forces of opposing states. Even when wars begin as conflicts between states, they frequently devolve, as in the wars in Afghanistan and Iraq, into protracted conflicts between the military forces of a state and a loosely organized network of fighters whose ultimate aims may be opposed but who are at least temporarily united in their unwillingness to capitulate to the state. Many recent wars have been fought by people seeking independence from a colonial power that had held them in subjugation. In some instances, such as in Angola, wars that began as anti-colonial struggles later became, or led to, civil wars between factions that had cooperated in the successful war of independence. Many wars have also been fought by people seeking freedom from the tyranny of a local despot, often imposed on them and sustained with the assistance of an ostensibly benevolent foreign power, such as the United States or the former Soviet Union.

While civil wars can be understood as struggles for political control between or among groups within a state, there have also been wars of secession in which one group has attempted, not to control the other groups, but to achieve political independence from the others as well as legal sovereignty over some territory hitherto controlled by the state. In both civil and secessionist wars, one side, or indeed both sides, may commit atrocities that precipitate yet another form of war: humanitarian intervention by a third-party state to protect innocent potential victims in the original domestic conflict.

These various forms of war, whether they pit state against state or state against rebel group, are often "asymmetrical" in that one side has vastly greater military power than the other. In such conflicts, the weaker group cannot hope to achieve its aims through reliance on conventional military tactics. It must instead use various tactics of guerrilla warfare, which sometimes include terrorist attacks against members of the opposed group who are both morally innocent and uninvolved in the fighting. And the fighters on the weaker side also typically, and often deliberately, fail to distinguish themselves from ordinary members of the civilian population, thereby making it more difficult, and more dangerous, for soldiers on the more powerful, state-controlled side to discriminate in their military action between combatants and noncombatants. Because the weaker side in some asymmetrical wars has aims that are just, these wars challenge the traditional theory of the just war, which holds that the central moral principle governing the conduct of war is that while combatants are always permitted to attack enemy combatants, they are not permitted to attack noncombatants, at least not intentionally.

The challenges do not, however, all derive from problems that confront the weaker side. In asymmetrical wars, the forces of the more powerful side almost always fight outside their home territory, so that their civilian populations usually face no immediate threat of harm and may thus be averse to sacrificing their state's soldiers for the sake of what they perceive to be the interests of foreigners. Their government may therefore follow the practice known as "force protection," which often involves reducing the risks to its forces by means that may increase the risks to innocent bystanders in the area in which the war is being fought. One means by which states seek to avoid exposing their soldiers to risk is to engage in what is known as "targeted killing," which, as currently practiced, involves killing specific individuals with weapons carried by remotely piloted aircraft. This practice is morally problematic in various respects, one of which is that it consists in killing people who are not actively engaged in combat and may indeed be living in a civilian community in a state with which the attacking state is not at war.

Also, in asymmetrical wars, including civil wars, the stronger side may have weapons of mass destruction, such as nuclear, chemical, or biological weapons, or autonomous weapons systems, all of which raise questions for traditional ways of understanding the morality of war.

While the nature of war has thus changed in ways that challenge the traditional theory of the just war, Just War theory has changed as well, and over a relatively short period, starting around the beginning of the new century. The controversies between traditional Just War theorists and their challengers are discussed in many of the chapters in this volume and some of the ways in which Just War theory has evolved (or devolved, depending on one's point of view) are exemplified in some of these same chapters.

It is natural to suppose that the theory has been undergoing change in direct response to challenges from the practice of war. But this seems to me, as one who has participated in the debates about the morality of war over the relevant period, not to be true. The different ways in which many Just War theorists now think about the morality of war arose more in response to developments internal to philosophy than in response to changes in the practice of war.

For much of the twentieth century, moral philosophers were, like other philosophers, obsessed with language and tended to be dismissive of the idea that philosophy had anything to contribute to the understanding of practical moral issues. According to A.J. Ayer, for example, moral philosophy explains "what people are doing when they make moral judgements; it is not a set of suggestions as to what moral judgements they are to make ... All moral theories ... in so far as they are philosophical theories, are neutral as regards actual conduct."[1] C.D. Broad expressed a similar view when he wrote, "It is no part of the professional business of moral philosophers to tell people what they ought or ought not to do … Moral philosophers, as such, have no special information not available to the general public, about what is right and what is wrong."[2] Moral philosophers themselves seem to have agreed and thus resolutely confined their work to issues in metaethics and to certain issues in normative ethics, such as the nature of the good. In retrospect, it is astonishing to reflect that, apart from one essay by Elizabeth Anscombe protesting Oxford's awarding an honorary degree to Harry Truman, on the ground that he had ordered the slaughter of civilians in the Second World War, moral philosophers had virtually nothing to say about either of the world wars or the ways in which they were conducted, or the Nazi Holocaust, or the atrocities perpetrated by the regimes of Stalin and Mao, or any of the other moral horrors of the first two-thirds of the twentieth century.

In the late 1960s and early 1970s, however, moral and political philosophy finally recovered from the long period in which it had seemed not quite respectable for a philosopher to say anything that might really matter. In part this was because there simply had to be an end at some point to the sterile work that most moral philosophers had been doing. It was also in part a result of the demand by students in the 1960s for "relevance" in university classes, which itself arose largely in response to the war in Vietnam and also to the spread of sympathy among the young for the civil rights movement. And there was also the impact of the work that John Rawls was known to be doing on his theory of justice, which culminated in the publication of his magisterial book of that title in 1971. With the publication of that book, it again became respectable for moral and political philosophers to write on matters of substance.

Two developments quickly followed. One was the revival of philosophical writing on practical moral issues that led to the establishment in professional philosophy of a new area of moral philosophy that came to be known as "practical ethics." The other was the reengagement of moral philosophers with substantive issues in normative ethics, such as whether agents' intentions are relevant to the permissibility of their action, whether the reason not to do harm is stronger than the reason to prevent equivalent harm from occurring, and so on. Normative ethics and practical ethics came to be regarded by many,

---

[1] A.J. Ayer, "On the Analysis of Moral Judgements," *Horizon* 20 (1949), reprinted in A.J. Ayer, *Philosophical Essays*, London: Macmillan, 1954, pp. 231–49.

[2] C.D. Broad, "Conscience and Conscientious Action," *Philosophy* 15 (1940), reprinted in C.D. Broad, *Ethics and the History of Philosophy*, New York: Humanities Press, 1952. The quotations in this and the preceding note are cited in Peter Singer's Tanner Lecture, "From Moral Neutrality to Effective Altruism: The Changing Scope and Significance of Moral Philosophy," a PDF of which may be found on the Tanner website at http://tannerlectures .utah.edu/Singer%20manuscript.pdf

in my view correctly, as interdependent, in that work in either area could not be done well independently of work in the other.

In the early 1970s, major philosophers, such as Thomas Nagel, published essays on the morality of war, primarily in the newly created journal *Philosophy and Public Affairs*, which for the whole of that decade was the leading place of publication for work in practical ethics and practically oriented political philosophy. In 1977, in the immediate aftermath of the war in Vietnam, Michael Walzer, another major philosopher, published his highly influential book *Just and Unjust Wars*, which was the most philosophically sophisticated work in Just War theory in more than a century. This was followed, in the 1980s, by discussions among philosophers of the morality of nuclear deterrence, and then, in the 1990s and into the new century, of the morality of the various wars in which the United States became embroiled – in Kuwait and Iraq, Panama, Kosovo, Afghanistan, and again in Iraq – and also of the conflicts in which it refused to become involved when arguably it ought to have been – for example, in Rwanda.

In the course of the debates about nuclear deterrence in the 1980s and about the wars fought by the United States in the ensuing decades, philosophers trained in the rigorous methods of analytic philosophy naturally looked to Just War theory for guidance. Yet when they sought to apply the principles it offered in a careful, scrupulous way, they discovered a range of problems of interpretation that had apparently never been addressed. They found powerful and unanswered objections to virtually all the elements of the theory. And further investigation revealed what seemed to some of them to be inconsistencies and even incoherence in the foundations of the theory. It was these discoveries, rather than the changes in the nature of war itself, that led to the revisionist challenges to traditional Just War theory. Revisionist Just War theory has no doubt gained in credibility from the way its shift of focus from states to individuals has better enabled it to understand the morality of conflicts other than traditional state-against-state conflicts. But this is largely serendipitous.

The past couple of decades have witnessed a renaissance in the effort to understand the ethics of war. This is mere speculation but I suspect that more books and articles have been published on the ethics of war in English during the past ten years than during the whole of the twentieth century. And the quality of this recent writing is unquestionably higher than that of most of the writing that has preceded it. By far the greater part of this work has been done by secular analytic philosophers who have devoted much care to grounding their arguments in the firmest possible foundations and to achieving the greatest possible rigor in argument. The result has been, in my view, a deeper, more sophisticated understanding of the ways in which morality constrains the practice of war than we have ever had before. The chapters in this *Handbook* provide testimony to how far our understanding has advanced in recent decades. They also offer evidence that the work of contemporary Just War theorists has begun to influence the thinking of those concerned with the interpretation and indeed the formulation of the international law of armed conflict. And, finally, they add to the great progress that has been made, and that we can hope will continue to be made, in both understanding and achieving respect for the moral constraints that govern the practice of war.

Introduction

Larry May

The idea of a "just war" has been with us since at least Mesopotamian times. From very early times comes the idea that a war could be unjust, that a ruler could act unjustly or wrongly in initiating war aggressively. And nearly every philosopher since Plato has also written about the conditions that would make a war somehow morally justifiable. Today, interest in war has been renewed among philosophers, political theorists, and international lawyers. The debates about whether there is such a thing as a just war, and what its elements are, have raged throughout the millennia and are as spirited as ever today.

In this *Handbook* we aim to give readers a thorough sense of these debates. To do so, we have invited some of the best-known, as well as some of the younger, participants of these debates to do two things. First we have asked our authors to set out clearly what the issues are, illustrating these issues with real-world examples. And second our authors aim to provide a sense of the most recent debates by arguing for a solution to one or another of the most vexing puzzles of the idea that war and all its obvious horrors could nonetheless be also seen as just in some cases. In addition, the authors provide lively discussion of special topics such as terrorism, targeted killing by unpiloted devices, as well as humanitarian efforts to minimize the effects of war.

The introduction that follows presents an overview of the terrain of these debates. In the first section, a brief summary of some of the oldest of texts on the legality and morality of war is provided. Then the two main categories of the Just War, justice in the initiation of war and justice in the conduct of war are surveyed. Then there is a brief introduction to the way that international lawyers approach our topic as well as how the philosophical debate intersects with the legal debate today. And this introduction ends with a few words about how pacifism relates to the idea of a just war.

I The Just War in Ancient Legal and Moral Thought

We can find an especially interesting perspective on the justness of war in ancient legal texts, especially from Mesopotamia (Iraq) as well as from Anatolia (Turkey) and Egypt. These very old texts speak clearly to the idea that war has always been seen in need of a justification – and that when a war is unjust the rulers who started that war are seen in a bad light. And despite what many may think, the perspective on war that is found in these ancient legal texts can provide clear guidance today, despite the differences between the time of the Mesopotamian ruler Hammurabi, around 1750 BCE, and now. In particular, we will find that the dominant perspective of humanitarianism of many ancient rulers manifests itself in a strong concern for achieving peace, and a peace that involves minimizing oppression. And the emphasis on eliminating or minimizing oppression can give us a model of understanding how wars for national defense or for rescuing those who are oppressed can be justified.

The nearly constant wars in the early history of Mesopotamia and the rest of the ancient Near East are often discussed in terms of one or another city-state seeking to gain advantage over others whenever the opportunity presented itself.[1] But there is an alternative explanation for why so many wars were fought in ancient times – various city-states tried to gain control over enough territory so that pacification could be accomplished, thereby putting an end to the previous threat of invasion. Yet, even so, invasion was a relatively rare circumstance.[2]

The pure desire for increased territory, or for the gain in wealth or resources, is condemned from a very early point in history. We can turn to Hammurabi whose writings take us back to roughly 1750 BCE. Here is how he describes himself in the Epilogue to his "code" of law:

I am Hammurabi, noble king. I have not been careless or negligent toward humankind, granted to my care by the god Enlil, and with whose shepherding the god Marduk charged me. I have sought for them peaceful places, I removed serious difficulties, I spread light over them. With the mighty weapons which the gods Zababa and Ishtar bestowed upon me, with the wisdom of the god Ea allotted to me, with the ability which the god Marduk gave me, I annihilated enemies everywhere, I put an end to wars, I enhanced the well being of the land, I made the people of all settlements lie in safe pastures, I did not tolerate anyone intimidating them. The great gods have chosen me, I am indeed the shepherd who brings peace, whose scepter is just.[3]

Scholars debate whether we should trust Hammurabi's words here, but the point is just that in this very early text Hammurabi believes that he should explain that the reason for the many wars he initiated was to pacify a region, between the Tigris and Euphrates Rivers, which had had very little peace during hundreds of years of war up to his time.

---

[1] See Alexander Gillespie, *The Causes of War*: Vol. I: *3000 BCE to 1000 CE*, Oxford: Hart Publishing, 2013, Part II.

[2] See Benjamin Forester, "Water under the Straw: Peace in Mesopotamia," in *War and Peace in the Ancient World*, ed. Kurt A. Raaflaub, Oxford: Blackwell Publishing, 2007, pp. 66–80.

[3] Hammurabi, *The Laws of Hammurabi* (c. 1750 BCE), in *Law Collections from Mesopotamia and Asia Minor*, trans. and ed. Martha T. Ross, 2nd ed., Atlanta: Scholars Press, 1997, p. 133.

In the middle of the fourteenth century BCE, we have a record of a treaty struck between a Hittite ruler Suppiluliuma I and Aziru of Amurru. This is largely a vassal treaty that Aziru was probably forced to sign. But what is interesting is that Aziru agrees to aid the Hittite ruler in both defensive and offensive wars. And what is important for us is that the treaty to aid each other in offensive wars is couched in defensive terms:

If the King of Hatti [Hittite kingdom] goes against the land of Hurri, or Egypt, or Babylonia, or the land of Ashtata, or the land of Alshi – whatever foreign lands located near your borders are hostile to My Majesty, or whatever friendly lands – [that is, friendly to My Majesty] – located near your borders – the land of Mukish, the land of Kinza, the land of Nuhashshi – turn and become hostile to the King of Hatti – when the King of Hatti goes to attack this enemy, if you, Aziru, do not mobilize wholeheartedly with infantry and chariotry, and do not fight him whole-heartedly, you will have transgressed the oath.[4]

Here we have an exchange of oaths to come to one another's aid in seemingly offensive wars, but where even offensive war alliances were justified by references to "hostile" and threatening forces to be combated, hence giving them a defensive dimension. This wording was repeated in several other treaties of the Hittites and their close neighbors.[5]

In 1285 BCE, after a major battle, Pharaoh Ramses II of Egypt and Hittite King Hattusili III completed an agreement that is often cited as one of the first, if not actually the first, truly "international" treaties for which a record exists. This important document contains a nonaggression pact that is its center-piece. Here the alliance is portrayed as purely defensive – aiding in the defense of each other against both foreign attacks as well as attacks from within each country:

And if someone else, an enemy, comes against Egypt, and Ramses, Beloved of Amon, King of Egypt, your brother, send to Hattusili, King of Hatti, his brother: "Come to my aid against him," then Hattusili, King of Hatti, shall send his infantry and his chariotry, and they will defeat his enemy.[6]

Of special importance is the part of this agreement concerning fugitives, which was a common feature of treaties at this time. And while fugitives, including fugitive slaves, were to be returned, "they shall not punish them for their offenses" or "destroy their households, together with their wives and sons."[7] There is here a clear statement that prisoners are not to be treated inhumanely, and also a separation between those who were warriors and those

---

[4] Gary Beckman, *Hittite Diplomatic Texts*, 2nd ed., Atlanta, Georgia: Scholars Press, 1999, treaty 5, pp. 37–38.
[5] Ibid., see treaties 7 and 9.   [6] Ibid., treaty 15, p. 98.   [7] Ibid., treaty 15, p. 99.

who were civilians ("wives and sons"), with a prohibition on destroying the civilians, similar to provisions for civilian immunity today.

In the Middle Hittite Period, we see even a reference to what today would be called the rules concerning the end of war. The treaty among the Elders of Several Anatolian Communities requires that "after the campaign you shall not violate the wife or daughter of a man, [nor] shall you injure them. After the campaign no one shall steal a man, woman, son, daughter, slave, slave girl, sheep, [horse], mule, ass, silver, gold, bronze, or copper implements."[8] Here we have a strong statement of *jus post bellum*, justice after war ends, and a surprising attention being given to a prohibition on sexual violence.

The two historically oriented contributions to the *Handbook* pick up the story first with Augustine and the medieval idea of a Just War (Maddox, Chapter 1) and then with the early modern ideas (Olsthoorn, Chapter 2). We then move to the contemporary debates starting with the ideas of self-defense, just cause, and last resort as elements of the just initiation of war, and then to the justice of waging war, before examining the connection between these just war categories and similar ways of thinking in international law today.

II Elements of a Justly Initiated War

Over the centuries the one uncontroversial basis for initiating a just war is state self-defense. Self-defense and other possible reasons to go to war are classified as "causes" of war; if these causes are considered legitimate reasons to go to war, then these reasons are called "just causes," the first element in a justly initiated war. Other causes of war include territorial expansion, punishment, conversion, and stopping oppression. Only the last of these causes is considered just, and even this cause is controversial. But self-defense as a cause of war is nearly universally accepted as a just cause to initiate war. This has been true of the work of philosophers and is also true today among international lawyers. Benbaji, in Chapter 3, takes up the idea of self-defense of states in initiating war.

If war is ever to be considered just, one plausible reason is that initiating war is necessary to save people from oppression – especially the prospect of one's own people being conquered and oppressed by a foreign state. This is similar to the claim that if the use of lethal violence is ever justified among individual humans, it is most plausibly justified to prevent the person employing the defensive violence from being killed by an unjust attacker. But as should be clear from this example, a plausible defense of the use of lethal force will require more than the showing that the lethal force was used in defense of self. Steinhoff (Chapter 4) deals with the topic of just cause.

---

[8] Ibid., miscellaneous text 27a, p. 165.

In addition to having a just cause, a justly initiated war must also satisfy a necessity or last resort requirement. It is not sufficient that the lethal violence was used to defend oneself; it must also be true that nonlethal use of force could not have achieved the same defensive effects – the taking of life, even in self-defense, is considered so important that it is not just to do so unless it is the only way that one's own life can be saved. When we apply these intuitions to the case of war, similar although not identical considerations apply. Uniacke (Chapter 5) addresses the idea of last resort.

States are like individual humans in some significant respects in that they have interests and can even be thought to be subject to various harms, including a kind of death – a dismemberment such that the state no longer has any members. But being conquered is not necessarily as bad as being enslaved or killed on the part of an individual human. A new state can be formed on the ashes of an old state, unlike humans who cannot be regenerated. And for this reason the intuitions we have about self-defense of individual humans cannot be perfectly fitted onto the self-defense of states. Nonetheless, initial insights can be said based on the analogy.

There is also the intuitively plausible further condition that the use of force must be proportionate. The idea of proportionality runs throughout the categories of just war, as well as international law. In criminal law, the corresponding idea is that the punishment should fit the crime, an age-old condition we can find since states first distinguished criminal from civil matters. Aristotle actually set out this idea in terms of a mathematical formula in discussing justice in Book V of his *Nicomachean Ethics*. Force used by the state against a citizen of the state must not be excessive in that the punishment is greater than the offense being punished. Davidovic (Chapter 9) deals with proportionality.

Another issue that has been important of late is that most wars today are not the traditional ones between two states that are relatively equal in terms of war-making capacity. Wars are more likely to be civil wars or wars where one or both parties are not states, such as Hezbollah or ISIS. The question arises of whether or not the categories just described can be applied to these asymmetric wars. Lee (Chapter 6) takes on this issue.

III   A Justly Conducted War

For a war to be just, it must not only be initiated justly but it must also be conducted justly. This second set of considerations has to do primarily with tactics and weaponry employed during war rather than with the reasons for which the war was started. There are elements that must be satisfied for a war to be justly waged, most important are that civilians not be directly targeted and that the strategy must be both proportionate and necessary to achieve a legitimate military goal. And there are new types of weaponry that raise a host of relatively new questions for the just war.

We begin by considering how self-defense matters in whether or not a war is justly conducted. In some respects all soldiers who are engaged in war (say, on the traditional battlefield) are placed in situations where they must kill or be killed – where all combatants seem to have a right to kill on grounds of self-defense. This idea has led many to believe that combatants have an equal right to kill and an equal liability to be killed. This view is referred to as the "moral equality of soldiers." Michael Walzer famously defended this idea which was already widely recognized among military and political leaders.[9]

Recently, so-called revisionist Just War theorists have mounted a sustained critique of the moral equality of soldiers. Jeff McMahan is the most prominent of those philosophers who have contended that whether or not the war was justly initiated matters for whether or not the war is justly conducted. Think of an armed bank robber confronted by an armed police officer – both must either kill or be killed. Yet, no one would think that they are in an identical moral position. The fact that one person, the bank robber, has no right to be in a position where he must kill the police officer or be killed by that officer surely matters. Similarly, so the argument goes, when two soldiers confront each other, it matters whether one of the soldiers has no right to be in the position where he must kill or be killed.[10]

One response to this commonsensical point is that war and bank robbery are not closely analogous. The bank robber has done something wrong and the wrongness of his act colors his moral situation and means that he no longer can kill those who have the role to protect society. The soldier on the other hand has not himself done anything wrong merely by stepping onto the battlefield. The soldier is not a wrongdoer whose moral situation has been colored by his wrongful acts since he has done nothing wrong. It is true that if the war is initiated unjustly, then those who prosecute such a war can be seen as complicit – but they are not wrongdoers in the way that the bank robber is.[11] This gives a flavor of how this debate begins. McPherson (Chapter 7) takes up this topic in detail.

The traditional cornerstone of a war that is justly conducted is the idea that soldiers should not directly target civilians. The reason for this is that while war often involves the killing of soldiers by other soldiers, those who are not involved in war should not be killed. There is though an important exception to this principle, often called the "civilian immunity principle": when the death of civilians is an unintended but necessary consequence of a legitimate strategy of war. Such civilian deaths are then described as collateral damage. French (Chapter 8) and Bazargan-Forward (Chapter 10) take up these issues.

---

[9] See Michael Walzer, *Just and Unjust Wars*, New York: Basic Books, 1977.
[10] See Jeff McMahan, *Killing in War*, Oxford: Oxford University Press, 2009.
[11] See Larry May, *War Crimes and Just War*, New York: Cambridge University Press, 2007.

As with the justly initiated war, a justly conducted war must also satisfy necessity and proportionality conditions. The tactic must be necessary to achieve a legitimate military objective. What is meant here is controversial, but nearly everyone agrees that if a lethal tactic is used when it is clear that a nonlethal tactic would accomplish the same objective and without significant risk, then it is not just to employ it. In addition, the tactic must meet a proportionality constraint. What this means is also highly controversial, but most would agree that excessive violence or cruelty cannot be employed. What counts as excessive is where the controversy arises. Davidovic (Chapter 9) examines both of these topics.

Certain weapons also have come into scrutiny on grounds that their use is not just. Most recently controversy has focused on the use of drones – unpiloted planes that fire missiles at specific individual targets. The targeted killings that employ drones and other automatic weaponry raise questions first and foremost about what sort of restraints must be satisfied to employ these weapons. Some have argued that since individuals are targeted because of what they have allegedly done, the killing resembles assassination more than wartime killing. If so, the restraints imposed on law enforcement officers who kill suspected felons might be more appropriate than the restraints on wartime killing where individuals are killed because they are members of a class of soldiers, not because of their wrongful individual acts. Ritter (Chapter 11) examines this debate.

IV   International Law and the Just War

Many of the same categories employed by discussants of the just war are also employed by international lawyers today. And there are very interesting debates about how close moral considerations should be to legal considerations. Some argue that the two sets of questions should be kept radically separate, while others argue that moral considerations should themselves be constrained by the realization that decisions about initiating or waging war must be made by fallible humans who must decide in real time. The chapters in this part of the *Handbook* describe the state of international law and then draw connections to the Just War literature.

The United Nations Charter, along with various interpretive rulings by the International Court of Justice, forms the conditions upon which legally justified war can take place. As in the just war tradition, war initiated for the self-defense of a state that has been attacked is the war that is least controversial. But while the UN Charter recognizes an "inherent" right of self-defense for states, it also tries to put an end to war as it has been known, especially during the two World Wars. The idea is that the UN should decide when lethal forced could be used. International criminal law has also made international legal debates look more like those in moral theory today since there is a focus on individual liability in both domains, rather than the old exclusively state-oriented international legal debates from before the Nuremberg trials. May (Chapter 12) takes up these themes in more detail.

The Geneva and Hague Conventions as well as the Additional Protocols and the Rome Statute of the International Criminal Court have set the law concerning the waging of war. As in traditional just war thinking, the idea that civilians should not be directly attacked is of central importance in the justly fought war in international law. In philosophical debates this is called the "principle of discrimination," and in international law it is the "principle of distinction" – but the idea is roughly the same, namely, that there should be civilian immunity during war. Ohlin (Chapter 13) addresses these related ideas.

Recent debates about proportionality and necessity in international law mirror to a certain extent the debates about these topics in the Just War literature.[12] In Israel's various wars against Palestinians, the idea of proportionate response has been at the forefront. And necessity has also received increasing attention especially since the International Committee for the Red Cross set out a 2009 document that tried to define the realm of necessity in combat. Haque (Chapter 14) addresses proportionality and necessity in international law and the overlap with just war thinking.

Another topic that spans the various categories of the just war and international law is the idea of humanitarianism. Since the nineteenth century, humanitarian aid groups have been recognized as having special protection and immunity during war. Today, in various conflicts hospitals and aid workers have been targeted especially by non-state actors but also by some states such as Syria. There is thus a challenge to the traditional humanitarian concerns that the horrible effects of war be contained. Lanphier (Chapter 15) addresses this issue.

Finally, the recent rise of various Islamic terrorist groups has posed a challenge to the categories of international law and also just war. These groups have often targeted civilians as well as ignored the rules of war having to do with initiating and conducting war justly. Why this has come about and what can be done about it – especially about the challenge that is brought to the international legal realm is the subject of Fyfe's chapter (Chapter 16).

V   A Few Words about Pacifism

The philosophical ideas about a just war arose as a response to pacifism of the early Church Fathers. The problem faced by pacifists can be posed this way: if protecting the innocent is the reason to oppose war, then one must also acknowledge that sometimes protection of the innocent can only be

---

[12] See Michael Newton and Larry May, *Proportionality in International Law*, Oxford: Oxford University Press, 2014; and Jens Ohlin and Larry May, *Necessity in International Law*, Oxford: Oxford University Press, 2016.

accomplished through war. So, if one's pacifism is grounded in protection of the innocent, in principle some wars should be justifiable insofar as those wars are fought to stave off aggression or to stop oppression. For this reason, philosophers since Augustine have espoused the view that there can be just wars, even as they have opposed most wars.

Pacifism comes in many flavors. Absolute unconditional pacifism does not recognize even the possibility that a war could ever be just. This view has never had many adherents, but it does represent the way that most people think of pacifism. Yet, especially today, there are also other forms of pacifism that admit of the possibility of a just war, but not in the current circumstances or in the way that humans interact with each other. It is these conditional or contingent versions of pacifism that have been most important for the just war.[13]

Today, pacifists and just war adherents share some common ground in that, for instance, they often both support some forms of conscientious refusal to serve in war as well as certain forms of civil disobedience also grounded in principled critique of particular wars. Indeed, as the revisionist Just War theorists have denied that all soldiers have a right to kill other enemy soldiers, and since it is often hard to tell whether or not a particular war is justly initiated, many just war adherents have recognized a smaller and smaller set of justly initiated wars. Concerns about pacifism can be seen in several of the chapters.

There is a good question of whether or not the rules of war, understood from the perspective of international law or the just war, can deal with the new war regime where reciprocity and civility are not taken seriously. The so-called new wars would not even be recognized as wars by traditional state-centered perspectives in law and morals. The authors in the *Handbook* are aware that there may need to be new categories or old categories differently understood. War has remained with us even as its form has shifted. Some see war being replaced by police action, while others have renewed the call to take pacifism seriously, perhaps a different kind pacifism from how it has been traditionally understood.

The *Handbook* aims to bring the reader from a beginning-level knowledge of the normative issues concerning war to a point where the reader has enough knowledge for advanced reading in the most recent literature. Our authors have tried to avoid technical discussions that have characterized a lot of the more recent literature in the journals. It is our hope that those who read this *Handbook* will come to grasp how theorists approach such an incredibly non-theoretical topic such as war and in so doing begin to form judgments of their own about current wars and wars to come.

---

[13] See Larry May, *Contingent Pacifism*, Cambridge: Cambridge University Press, 2015.

Part I

Historical Background

1 The Just War Tradition in Late Antiquity and the Middle Ages

John Mark Mattox

Ⅰ Augustine's Pervasive Influence

Any consideration of the just war tradition must be prefaced with the question, "Why should it matter in the first instance whether or not a war is 'just'" – and even more fundamentally, "What exactly does it mean for something to be 'just'"? These and related questions have been asked since the dawn of the Western intellectual tradition. However, by late antiquity, the questions had become particularly pressing: the great military and political empire of the West was collapsing, and with it, an ancient secular understanding of justice defined in strictly rational, human terms. As Christianity emerged as the unifying force in the West, so too came new questions about the nature of justice. Less compelling became the argument that human existence realized its highest expression in the flourishing of the state and more compelling became the argument that human existence was part of a purposeful, divine design, even if those purposes were not well understood. It is at this juncture of Western history that one finds Aurelius Augustinus (AD 354–430) – better known today as Augustine, whose views on justice, the role of the state, the institution of war, and the place of humankind in the universe laid the groundwork for the Western just war tradition.

Augustine was a skilled Roman-trained rhetorician; a prolific writer (who produced more than 110 works over a 30-year period); the Catholic bishop of Hippo in northern Africa; and, by wide acclamation, the first Christian philosopher. Writing from a unique background and vantage point as a keen observer of society both before and during the fall of the Roman Empire, Augustine constitutes an important intellectual bridge between late antiquity and the emerging medieval world. As a Christian cleric, he takes it as his task to defend his flock against unremitting assault by heresies spawned in an era uninformed by the immediate, divine revelations that had characterized the apostolic age. As a philosopher, he situates his arguments against the backdrop of Greek philosophy in the Platonic tradition, particularly as formulated by the Neo-Platonists of Alexandria. As a Roman, he views the empire, even in the twilight of its power, as the divinely

The views expressed in this chapter are those of the author and do not represent the official views of the National Defense University, the Department of Defense, or any other U.S. government entity. For an extended treatment of the subject, see *Saint Augustine and the Theory of Just War*, Bloomsbury-Continuum Series in Philosophy; London: Bloomsbury Publishing, 2006, 2009, by the author.

ordained medium for the spread and safeguarding of the truths of Christianity. By the time of his death, his intellectual contribution to the matter of the just application of violence was such that he could rightly be called the father of Just War theory in the West. Even so, such a title deserves some explanation.

Augustine certainly is not the first person in the West to attach philosophical significance either to justice or to war. Philosophers going back at least as far as Plato discuss war in a moral-philosophical context. Neither can one claim for Augustine the distinction of having been the first person in the West to use the words "just" (or "unjust") and "war" in tandem; that distinction belongs to Aristotle. Augustine is not even the first Christian author to explore just war issues; these receive attention in the writings of the Church Fathers in the centuries preceding Augustine. In what sense, then, is Augustine fairly to be regarded as the father of Just War theory in the West? He is to be thus regarded in the sense that the whole Western Just War tradition that follows from the fifth century AD on, in both its Christian and secular varieties, traces its roots not to Plato or Aristotle, nor even to earlier Church Fathers, but rather to Augustine. It may be that Just War theory has secured a permanent place in Western philosophy in part because a figure of Augustine's stature deemed it of sufficient significance to address it repeatedly. As we shall see, luminaries of the Middle Ages who undertake to elucidate just war principles, to include Gratian, Alexander of Hales, and most prominently Thomas Aquinas, explicitly invoke Augustine in favor of their respective arguments. Thus, it may be said that Augustine is to Just War theory in the West as Christopher Columbus is to the discovery of America: not the first to come in contact with it, but certainly the one whose contact with it, unlike all those who came before him, made a lasting impression upon the entire subsequent development of the Western world. That lasting impression comes as the direct result of the synthesis that Augustine achieves between the Western philosophical tradition – particularly Neo-Platonism – and fifth-century Christianity, which found itself confronted with the practical mandate to reconcile itself to the immediately pressing concerns of the mundane world of emperors and armies.

Intellectual Forebears

In Augustine's statements on just war, one finds echoes of Cicero (106–43 BC – a Roman pagan) and Ambrose (c. AD 340–AD 397 – the Catholic bishop of Milan and a contemporary of the youthful Augustine). Augustine was a great admirer of Cicero, to whom he refers as one "among the most learned and eloquent of all mankind,"[1] whom Augustine quotes extensively in his *magnum opus, The City of God.* Indeed, Augustine is the source for numerous fragments of the Ciceronian corpus, which, absent Augustine, would have

---

[1] Augustine, *City of God* XXII.6, trans. Henry Bettenson, London: Penguin Books, 1984, p. 1030. All references to *City of God* are taken from this translation.

been altogether lost.[2] Moreover, Augustine credits Cicero for introducing him to philosophy via Cicero's now lost work, the *Hortentius*.[3] Augustine's admiration for Cicero as a just war thinker is evidenced by the fact that it is to Augustine that we owe the preservation of Cicero's classic definition of a just war: "a war is never undertaken by the ideal State, except in defence of its honour and safety."[4]

Augustine's estimation of Ambrose is similarly exalted: Ambrose is to Augustine, with respect to Christianity, as Socrates is to Plato, with respect to philosophy. In his *Confessions*, Augustine gives credit to Ambrose as the person who, more than any other mortal, helped him acquire an appreciation of the interiority of the Gospel precepts – a notion that later will figure so prominently in Augustine's own just war thinking specifically and will pervade his theology in general. Augustine muses, "I was pleased to hear that in his sermons to the people Ambrose often repeated the text: 'The written law inflicts death, whereas the spiritual law brings life'[5], as though this were a rule upon which he wished to insist most carefully."[6] Ambrose recognized that the laws of men have both an exterior and an interior aspect, the former being the legal code itself and the latter being the spirit or intent that vitiates the law. In this way, he was able, *inter alia*, to view the taking of life as a contingent good rather than as an intrinsic evil. Ambrose represents an advance beyond Cicero in that Ambrose was faced with the challenge of understanding war in the context of Christian theology and practice and of reconciling the two. Standing both temporally and intellectually at the confluence of the Ciceronian and Ambrosian streams, Augustine becomes the direct heir to this challenge.

II Augustine's World View

Because Augustine considers the Christian scriptures to constitute the touch-stone against which philosophy – including political philosophy – must be assayed, his world view necessarily includes the Christian doctrines of the Creation and the Fall and Redemption of man. These doctrines were largely

---

[2] See, for example, *The Republic* (Ziegler's pagination) 2.32; 2.69a, c; 3.34a, b; 3.36; 3.40b; 4.9a; 4.10; 4.11–12; 4.13b; 5.1–2a; 5.9a; 6.4. In addition to the numerous Ciceronian quotations preserved by Augustine and as an interesting convergence of history, "[t]he incomplete Vatican manuscript" for Cicero's *Republic* is itself a palimpsest of "an eighth-century copy of St Augustine's commentary on the Psalms, written at the monastery of Bobbio in northern Italy." See Jonathan Powell's and Niall Rudd's editorial preface to Niall Rudd's translation of Cicero's *The Republic* and *The Laws*, Oxford: Oxford University Press, 1998, p. xxxii.

[3] See Augustine, *Confessions* XIII. 7, trans. R. S. Pine-Coffin, New York: Penguin Books, 1981, p. 169. All reference to *Confessions* are taken from this translation.

[4] Marcus Tullius Cicero, *De Re Publica* III.xxiii, in Loeb Classical Library: Cicero XVI, *De Re Publica* and *De Legibus*, trans. Clinton Walker Keyes, Cambridge: Harvard University Press, 1928, p. 211.

[5] An allusion to 2 Corinthians 3:6.   [6] Augustine, *Confessions* VI.4, pp. 115–116.

foreign to pagan philosophies[7], which generally viewed history as a cyclical phenomenon. This cyclical view is evident, for example, among the pre-Socratic Greek philosophers, including Anaximander and Empedocles; among later Greeks, including Zeno of Citium, the founder of Stoicism; as well as among the ancient Egyptians. Even though Augustine may not have known of these particular philosophers, the cyclical view of history included in their teachings was well known in the ancient world. In stark contrast, Augustine, widely regarded as the first Christian philosopher, conceives history in strictly linear terms, with a beginning and an end. According to Augustine, the earth was brought into existence *ex nihilo* by a perfectly good and just God, who created man. The earth is not eternal; the earth, as well as time, has both a beginning and an end. Man, on the other hand, was brought into existence to endure eternally. Damnation is the just desert of all men because of the Fall of Adam, who, having been endowed with free will, chose through his disobedience to disrupt the perfectly good order established by God. As the result of Adam's Fall, all human beings are heirs to the effects of Adam's original sin, and all are vessels of pride, avarice, greed, and self-interest. However, for reasons known only to God, He has predestined some fixed number of men for salvation (as a display of His unmerited mercy – a purely gratuitous act altogether independent even of God's foreknowledge of any good deeds those men might do while on earth), while most He has predestined for damnation as a just consequence of the Fall. The onward march of human history, then, constitutes the unfolding of the divine plan that will culminate in one or the other outcome for every member of the human family. Within this grand Augustinian schema, several concepts are foundational for understanding Augustine vis-à-vis just war.

Two Cities By Augustine's account, those elected for salvation and those elected for damnation are thoroughly intermingled, and the distinction arising from their respective destinies creates two classes of persons, to whom Augustine refers collectively and allegorically as "cities" – the City of God and the earthly city. Citizens of the earthly city are the unregenerate progeny of Adam and Eve, who are justifiably damned because of Adam's Fall. These persons, according to Augustine, are aliens to God's love *not* because God refuses to love them but because they refuse to love God, as evidenced by their rebellious disposition inherited from the Fall. In particular, citizens of the earthly city are distinguished by their lust for domination over others – the fundamental motivation that prompts human beings to engage unjustly in war. On the other hand, citizens of the City of God – although likewise subject to the practical effects of Adam's Fall – are, in the language of the New Testament,

---

[7] Note, for example, the great surprise, even astonishment, with which both the Epicureans and the Stoics greet St. Paul's teaching on the Creation, the Redemption (and by implication, the Fall) during his famous discourse on Mars's hill in Athens, as recorded in the Acts of the Apostles 17:15–34.

"strangers and pilgrims"[8] on earth who, because the presence of God – the true Object of their love – is not immediately available for their enjoyment, are very much out of place in the present world. No political state, nor even the institutional church, can be equated with the City of God. Moreover, there is no such thing as "dual citizenship" in the two cities; every member of the human family belongs to one – and only one.

The State Augustine views the state as a divinely ordained institution through which God shapes the ultimate ends of humankind. With its coercive power – its armies and power to command, punish, and even put to death, it constitutes a fit punishment for fallen man. At the same time, it constitutes a sort of palliative remedy for the effects of the Fall in that it maintains such a modicum of peace and order as it is possible for fallen man to enjoy in the present world. Augustine clearly holds that the establishment and success of the Roman Empire, along with its embracing of Christianity as its official religion, was part of the divine plan of the true God. Nevertheless, he also recognizes that Rome's official embrace of Christianity does not automatically transform it or any other political state into the City of God. Indeed, he regards Rome as "a kind of second Babylon"[9] because it lacks true justice.

Justice Augustine clearly points to God's overruling justice as *true* justice from which none are exempt, whether or not elected for salvation. The punishments that flow from that justice "are a means of purification only to those who are disciplined and corrected by them. All other punishments, whether temporal or eternal, are imposed on every person" – whether the person has been elected for salvation or damnation – "in accordance with the treatment he is to receive from God's providence," which is, by definition, "just, albeit inscrutable."[10] "Justice," as it is to be practiced by humans, "is love serving God only, and therefore ruling well all else."[11] His definition is a Christianized version of the Platonic ideal. Not surprisingly, because perfect justice is not to be found in the present world, there can be no truly just states. "Remove justice," Augustine famously asks, "and what are kingdoms but gangs of criminals on a large scale? What are criminal gangs but petty kingdoms?"[12] Although Augustine views Rome as the last bastion against the advances of the pagan barbarians who surely must not be allowed to overrun Christendom, still he admits that Rome lacks true justice. Nevertheless, as he observes the unraveling of the social order in the twilight years of the Roman Empire, Augustine finds himself faced with what for him are the central questions of politics: How do the elect operate successfully – that is to say, justly – in an unjust world, where selfish interests

---

[8] Hebrews 11:13; 1 Peter 2:11.   [9] Augustine, *City of God* XVIII.22, p. 787.

[10] Augustine, *City of God* XXI.14, p. 990.

[11] Augustine, *Of the Morals of the Catholic Church* XV.25, *The Nicene and Post-Nicene Fathers* [hereafter *NPNF*], Grand Rapids: Eerdmans Publishing Company, IV, p. 48.

[12] Augustine, *City of God* IV.4, p. 139.

dominate, where the general welfare is rarely sought, and where good and evil men are inextricably (and, to human eyes, often unidentifiably) intermingled? In particular, what are faithful rulers to do when confronted with the prospect of war, and in what ways are their subjects justified in engaging in war?

III   Just and Unjust War

Augustine understands that the wicked are not particularly concerned about whether or not the wars they fight are just. On the other hand, he understands that the righteous vainly hope to avoid being confronted with wars in this life and that the best they can hope for is the choice to fight just wars rather than unjust ones. This is by no means a perfect solution; but then again, this is not a perfect world. Thus, for Augustine, the idea of a just war is a sort of coping mechanism for those who aspire to citizenship in the City of God. Hence, he urges that "the wise man . . . will wage just [as opposed to unjust] wars. Surely if he remembers that he is a human being, he will lament the fact that he is faced with the necessity of waging just wars" – especially since "it is the injustice of the opposing side that lays on the wise man the duty of waging wars."[13] But exactly what *is* a "just war"? Augustine states: "As a rule just wars are defined as those which avenge injuries, if some nation or state against whom one is waging war has neglected to punish a wrong committed by its citizens, or to return something that was wrongfully taken."[14] In short, whatever else a just war may entail, its most fundamental practical purpose, as far as Augustine is concerned, is to right wrongs. For Augustine, "injuries" refers not only to damages or losses sustained through violation of the customarily observed norms for relationships among nations but also for violations of the moral order. Hence, those undertaking war under the terms of Augustine's definition do not necessarily have to be justified by reason of their having been aggrieved themselves.

One finds in Augustine's words what Russell describes as "the first new definition of the just war since Cicero."[15] In Cicero's view, the justification for war is "limited in its aims to securing redress of grievances and compensation for losses occasioned by crimes of the offending party to the persons, property (*res*) or rights (*iura*) of the aggrieved party."[16] The aim contemplated by Cicero's definition is "a simple return to the *status quo ante bellum*."[17] However, Augustine's definition serves not only as a means for restoring the *status quo ante bellum* but also as an international sort of "penal sanction analogous to the awarding of punitive damages in private law."[18] Augustine's definition

---

[13] Ibid. XIX.7, pp. 861–62.

[14] Augustine, *Questions on the Heptateuch* 6.10, Louis J., *The Early Fathers on War and Military Service*, Wilmington: Michael Glazier, Inc., 1983, p. 135.

[15] Frederick H. Russell, *The Just War in the Middle Ages*, Cambridge: Cambridge University Press, 1975, p. 18.

[16] Ibid., pp. 18–19.   [17] Ibid., p. 19.   [18] Ibid.

contemplates not only material compensation for property unjustly taken or destroyed but also moral compensation – a recognition and admission on the part of the offending state that its actions were morally reprehensible. From the perspective of the twenty-first century, the idea of war as a vehicle for exacting moral compensation may seem foreign indeed. However, as Augustine argues in one of his most famous statements on warfare, the key to understanding war in this way lies in properly identifying what it is that makes war either an evil or praiseworthy institution:

> What is the evil in war? Is it the death of some who will soon die in any case, that others may live in peaceful subjection? . . . The real evils in war are love of violence, revengeful cruelty, fierce and implacable enmity, wild resistance, and the lust of power, and such like; and it is generally to punish these things, when force is required to inflict the punishment, that, in obedience to God or some lawful authority, good men undertake wars, when they find themselves in such a position as regards the conduct of human affairs, that right conduct requires them to act, or to make others act in this way.[19]

As Augustine is aware, not all injuries are such as will admit of restitution. In that case, the aggrieved party must be willing to content itself with a result that falls short of the exacting "a compensation in revenge."[20] For, to take delight in the suffering of those upon whom even just vengeance is visited is itself an injustice, and thus to do so runs counter to the aims for which just wars are fought. But how, exactly, are humans supposed to administer punishment to others as a just recompense for their wrongs while still refraining from delight in their sufferings? According to Augustine, the answer lies in the recognition that "many things must be done in correcting with a certain benevolent severity, even against their own wishes, men whose welfare rather than their wishes it is our duty to consult."[21] Augustine analogizes thus: "In the correction of a son, even with some sternness, there is assuredly no diminution of a father's love; yet, in the correction, that is done which is received with reluctance and pain by one whom it seems necessary to heal by pain."[22] In support of this view, Augustine invokes the authority of the Christian scriptures, which, he says, "have most unambiguously commended this virtue [of benevolent severity] in a magistrate"[23] (although, curiously, he makes this claim without referring to a specific passage). His reference to a magistrate is nevertheless significant, because it clearly suggests that benevolent severity is desirable as a public virtue, and not merely a private one.

With this general insight into Augustine's view of just retribution in place, we can consider its operationalization in the case of war. Traditionally, the philosophical treatment of the just war is divided into two categories: *jus ad bellum* and *jus in bello*. The former describes the necessary (and, by some

---

[19] Augustine, *Reply to Faustus the Manichæan* 22.74, *NPNF* IV, p. 301.
[20] Augustine, *Our Lord's Sermon on the Mount* I.XX.62, *NPNF* VI, p. 27.
[21] Augustine, *Letter* 138.14, *NPNF* I, p. 485.   [22] Ibid.   [23] Ibid.

accounts, sufficient) conditions for justifying engagement in war. The latter describes the necessary conditions for conducting war in a just manner. Augustine's *jus ad bellum* prescripts enjoin that wars can be initiated justly only on the basis of the following:

1. *A just cause*, such as to defend the state from external invasion; to defend the safety or honor of the state, with the realization that their simultaneous defense might be impossible; to avenge injuries; to punish a nation for failure to take corrective action for wrongs (legal or moral) committed by its citizens; to come to the defense of allies; to gain the return of something that was wrongfully taken; or to obey a divine command to go to war (which, in practice, issues from the political head of state acting as God's lieutenant on earth); and in any case, the just cause must be at least more just than the cause of one's enemies;
2. *A rightly intended will*, which has the restoration of peace as its prime objective, takes no delight in the wickedness of potential adversaries, views waging war as a stern necessity, tolerates no action calculated to provoke a war, and does not seek to conquer others merely for conquest's sake or for territorial expansion; and
3. *A declaration of war by a competent authority*, and except in the most unusual of circumstances, in a public manner, and only as a last resort.

Concerning *jus in bello*, Augustine holds that wars, once begun, must be fought in a manner that:

1. *Responds proportionally* to the wrong to be avenged, with violence being constrained within the limits of military necessity;
2. *Discriminates* among proper objects of violence (i.e., combatants) and noncombatants, such as women, children, the elderly, the clergy, and so on; and
3. *Maintains good faith* in its interactions with the enemy, by scrupulously keeping one's word and not prosecuting the war in a treacherous manner.

Jus ad Bellum
Just Cause "A great deal depends," says Augustine, "on the causes for which men undertake wars."[24] In this famous definition, he lists what he considers to be exemplary just causes. For Augustine, a war justly undertaken is, by definition, a defensive war. Augustine appears to justify wars undertaken as punitive actions, because he regards them as defensive actions. (This is so in spite of the fact that, militarily speaking, such a war would be considered offensive.) Since these wars constitute punishments for violations of the moral order, they are, from Augustine's perspective, necessary to preserve moral values.

---

[24] Augustine, *Reply to Faustus the Manichœan* 22.75, *NPNF* IV, p. 301.

Upon cursory examination, Augustine's explanation of what constitutes a just cause might lead one to conclude that Augustine is prepared to allow almost any reason as a just cause for going to war. However, Augustine also identifies circumstances under which he positively disallows the possibility of a cause's being just. For example, Augustine considers the expansionist wars of the Roman Empire to have been anything but just, and he questions whether Rome could have become the expansive empire that it was if not for its engagement in continual warfare and whether the greatness that it obtained really justified its sacrifice of peace.[25] On the other hand, Augustine acknowledges the case in which a war that expands national territory sometimes must be fought to preserve the nation's security. Indeed, he is willing to justify Rome in undertaking wars resulting from "unprovoked attacks by their enemies" to "defend their life and liberty."[26]

Although Augustine holds that "it is the injustice of the opposing side that lays on the wise man the duty of waging wars,"[27] he does not take an explicit stand on the issue of *how* just a cause must be before it warrants going to war over it. Moreover, since both sides in a conflict are likely to claim a just cause, the best that can be hoped is that the side whose cause is *more* just will prevail: "Now when the victory goes to those who were fighting for the juster [sic] cause, can anyone doubt that the victory is a matter for rejoicing and the resulting peace is something to be desired?"[28]

Right Intention Augustine deeply believed that for an act to be justifiable it must proceed from a rightly intended will. Accordingly, a rightly intended war is one that is "waged by the good in order that, by bringing under the yoke the unbridled lusts of men, those vices might be abolished which ought, under a just government, to be either extirpated or suppressed."[29] Hence, a just person would never view even a just war as anything to be desired in and of itself, but only as a stern necessity that is better than a less just alternative. Right intention utterly prevents one from taking delight in any kind of violence. Delight of this kind, evidenced by the "lust for domination," has no other effect than to "vex and exhaust the whole human race."[30] Violence, even when justly undertaken, is not supposed to be a source of enjoyment or amusement. While Augustine concedes that "the wise man ... will wage just wars,"[31] he also points out that if the wise man but reflects upon his own humanity, he surely will "lament the fact that he is faced with the necessity of waging just wars; for if they were not just, he would not have to engage in them, and consequently there would be no wars for a wise man."[32]

The responsibility to administer justice is a grave and onerous burden. As an illustration of the gravity of this duty, Augustine examines the case of the judge

---

[25] Augustine, *City of God* III.10, p. 97.   [26] Ibid., III.10, p. 98.   [27] Ibid., XIX.7, p. 862.
[28] Ibid., XV.4, p. 600.   [29] Augustine, *Letter* 138.14, *NPNF* I, p. 486.
[30] Augustine, *City of God* III.14, p. 104.   [31] Ibid., XIX.7, p. 861.   [32] Ibid., pp. 861–62.

who is called upon to determine the guilt or innocence of one who has been accused of a crime.[33] The judge cannot see into the conscience of the accused, so he cannot know whether whatever was done was done with criminal intent. The judge, therefore, turns to the generally accepted method for ascertaining guilt or innocence in late antiquity, namely torture. However, this merely creates yet another problem, because, whether or not the accused admits to guilt, the judge still cannot know whether the accused actually is guilty. The accused may admit guilt to avoid additional torture with the result that he is executed for a crime that he may not have committed. Conversely, he may resist admitting guilt and die as the result of the torture, which would have otherwise continued until a confession of guilt issued – again for a crime which the accused may or may not have committed. The judge can be exonerated from responsibility for the man's death in the eyes of his fellows by virtue of his judicial capacity. However, ultimate exoneration – in the sight of God – can only come as the judge acts with the right intention: the righteous desire to safeguard justice. Hence, he is left to cry out, in the words of Augustine borrowed from the Psalms,[34] "Deliver me from my necessities!"[35]

Peace, Augustine argues, is the ultimate aim toward which anyone fights in the first instance. However, the peace sought is one whose terms are favorable to the person fighting. Indeed, men do not disturb peace because they dislike peace, "but because they desire the present peace to be exchanged for one that suits their wishes."[36] Hence, it becomes clear that "their desire is not that there should not be peace but that it should be the kind of peace they wish for"[37] – a peace that they then can impose upon those whom they conquer.[38] "Even robbers," Augustine argues, desire to preserve peace among themselves so as "to ensure greater efficiency and security in their assaults on the peace of the rest of mankind."[39] However, peace is not simply the ultimate objective, as a practical matter, toward which everyone, in fact, fights – the just and the unjust; it is also the ultimate objective toward which the righteous *should* fight: "For peace is so great a good that even in relation to the affairs of earth and of our mortal estate no word ever falls more gratefully upon the ear, nothing is desired with greater longing, in fact, nothing greater can be found."[40] Accordingly, both the sovereign and the sovereign's armies must understand the attainment of a just peace to be the true object for which they are called upon to fight: "Peace should be the object of your desire; war should be waged only as a necessity, and waged only that God may by it deliver men from the necessity and preserve them in peace. For peace is not sought in order to the kindling of war, but war is waged in order that peace may be obtained."[41] If peace can be obtained without the sword, all the better. As Augustine exhorts one correspondent:

---

[33] Ibid., XIX.6, pp. 859–61.   [34] Psalms 25:17.   [35] Augustine, *City of God* XIX.6, p. 861.
[36] Ibid.   [37] Ibid.   [38] Ibid., p. 867.   [39] Ibid.   [40] Ibid., XIX.11, p. 866.
[41] Augustine, *Letter* 189.6 *NPNF* I, p. 554.

But it is a higher glory still to stay war itself with a word, than to slay men with the sword, and to procure or maintain peace by peace, not by war. For those who fight, if they are good men, doubtless seek for peace; nevertheless it is through blood. Your mission, however, is to prevent the shedding of blood. Yours, therefore, is the privilege of averting that calamity which others are under the necessity of producing.[42]

Competent Authority Augustine considers the political sovereign to occupy the role of God's lieutenant on earth. One of the prerogatives that God "either orders or permits" the sovereign to exercise is the right to wage war. Moreover, this right belongs exclusively to the sovereign. However, that does not necessarily mean that the sovereign is, himself, just.

The fact that "one weareth purple, is a Magistrate, is Ædile, is Proconsul, is Emperor"[43] provides no guarantee that one so recognized can be counted upon to rule justly, "because even the sons of pestilence sit sometimes in the seat of Moses."[44] Even so, this has no bearing for Augustine upon the fact that citizens of duly constituted governments have a divinely appointed obligation to obey their sovereign, including the sovereign's call to arms. There is one case, however, in which Augustine recognizes an exception, namely, the case in which the sovereign directs his subjects to act in a way that is diametrically opposed to the law of God. As a case in point, Augustine refers to the apostate Emperor Julian who, after Constantine had granted official recognition to Christianity as the religion of the state, sought to reinstitute pagan rites of worship in the Roman Army. Augustine calls Julian "an infidel Emperor, an apostate, a wicked man, an idolater"[45] under whom Roman Christians nonetheless served as soldiers. He notes that whenever Julian commanded these soldiers "to deploy into line, to march against this or that nation, they at once obeyed."[46] However, when Julian directed them to worship idols or to burn incense after the pagan manner of worship, "they preferred God to him"[47] and disobeyed his commands. Augustine commends the actions of these soldiers, stating, "They distinguished their everlasting from their temporal master; and yet they were, for the sake of their everlasting Master, submissive to their temporal master."[48] However, short of this exceptional case, subjects are to render due obedience to the sovereign who orders them to war. Hence, if obedience to God necessitates conscientious disobedience of the sovereign, even Augustine is forced to concede that those who thus disobey will, like Shadrach, Meshach, and Abednego of old, be forced to wait on the justice of God for their redress and vindication.[49]

---

[42] Augustine, *Letter* 229.2, *NPNF* I, p. 582.

[43] Augustine, *Expositions on the Book of Psalms* LII.2, *NPNF* VIII, p. 197.

[44] Ibid. The passage alluded to here is Matthew 23:1–3: "Then spake Jesus to the multitude, and to his disciples, saying, The scribes and the Pharisees sit in Moses' seat: All therefore whatsoever they bid you observe and do; but do not ye after their works: for they say and do not."

[45] Augustine, *Expositions on the Book of Psalms* CXXV.7, *NPNF* VIII, p. 602.

[46] Ibid., p. 603.   [47] Ibid.   [48] Ibid.   [49] See Daniel 3, especially verses 16–18.

Jus in Bello

Proportionality Augustine acknowledges the horrors of war in a way that suggests that he believes that, given the choice, the evil effects of war should be minimized; and to that extent, he advocates observance of the *jus in bello* principle of proportionality. War is horrible enough, even under the best of circumstances, and anyone who is not moved to sorrow upon contemplation of the evils that war entails is a just object of pity as one who has "lost all human feeling."[50] For this reason, Augustine urges soldiers not to induce gratuitous suffering. Even in the special case of a war fought to mete out divine retribution, the aim is not merely to give one's enemies their just deserts but to "lead them back to the advantages of peace."[51]

Augustine may well be the first figure in the just war tradition to offer a version of what is now known as the doctrine of military necessity: that armies can justly take only such violent actions as may be necessary to accomplish a military objective, consistent with the aim of restoring peace and order. Augustine admonishes, "Let necessity, therefore, and not your will, slay the enemy who fights against you."[52] His point is that the doctrine of military necessity specifies the upper bounds of permissible violence – not the lower bounds. As a consequence, he urges that the taking of lives in war ought to be minimized to the greatest extent possible; and by so doing, he gives recognition to the founding principle upon which all future developments in the doctrine of *jus in bello* are based:

For he whose aim is to kill is not careful how he wounds, but he whose aim it is to cure is cautious with his lancet; for the one seeks to destroy what is sound, the other that which is decaying . . . [W]hat is important to attend to but this: who were on the side of truth, and who were on the side of iniquity; who acted from a desire to injure, and who from a desire to correct what was amiss?[53]

Discrimination Augustine concerns himself with three topics relative to discrimination: the special moral status of soldiers, of noncombatants in general, and of the clergy specifically: "The power of a king, the death penalty of the judge, the hoods of the executioner, the weapons of the soldier"[54] have in common the fact that they stand as examples of duties in which Augustine holds that, in certain cases, the taking of human life can find legal and moral justification.

Most fundamentally, Augustine discriminates on the basis of who is and is not authorized to perform violent acts on behalf of a sovereign power. He notes, "in killing the enemy, the soldier is the agent of the law. Thus, he merely fulfills his duty."[55] Moreover, Augustine argues, "If to murder means to kill a man,

[50] Augustine, *City of God* XIX.7, p. 862.   [51] Augustine, *Letter* 189.6, *NPNF* I, p. 554.
[52] Ibid.   [53] Augustine, *Letter* 93.8, *NPNF* I, p. 385.
[54] Augustine, *Letter* 156.6.16, quoted in Swift 1983, p. 112.
[55] Augustine, *On Free Choice of the Will* I.V, trans. Anna S. Benjamin and L. H. Hackstaff, New York: Macmillan Publishing Company, 1964, p. 11.

murder can occur sometimes without sin."[56] He not only exonerates the soldier from moral responsibility for the taking of life but goes so far as to impose upon him the obligation to do so when required:

> For when a soldier kills a man in obedience to the legitimate authority under which he served, he is not chargeable with murder by the laws of his country; in fact he is chargeable with insubordination and mutiny if he refuses ... Thus he is punished if he did it without orders for the same reason that he will be punished if he refuses when ordered.[57]

Thus the soldier is innocent, because his position makes obedience a duty.[58]

Next, Augustine discriminates between combatants and noncombatants. With respect to interactions between the two classes, Augustine unambiguously advocates that a spirit of mercy and forbearance should be displayed toward all those who fall into the power of their enemies: "As violence is used towards him who rebels and resists, so mercy is due to the vanquished or the captive, especially in the case in which future troubling of the peace is not to be feared."[59]

Finally, Augustine gives specific attention to the status of the clergy during war. As the Vandals under Genseric were crossing over the Mediterranean from Spain and overrunning northern Africa, Augustine gave permission to the clergy to "flee from one city to another"[60] and thereby to stay ahead of the invaders, provided that two conditions were met: first, those members of the clergy taking to flight had to be among those "specially sought for by persecutors."[61] Second, their departure could not leave the church without "others who are not specially sought after" who could "remain to supply spiritual food to their fellow-servants, whom they know to be unable otherwise to maintain spiritual life."[62] In the case of a general emergency, however, the clergy were not to flee. Rather, they were to "share in common" with all who were in danger – clergy and laity alike – that which God "appoints them to suffer."[63]

In connection with these instructions given in some of Augustine's darkest hours at the twilight of his life, three observations seem appropriate. First, Augustine establishes beyond dispute that the clergy form a class of noncombatants. Second, Augustine seems to suggest that even the case of what Walzer calls a "supreme emergency,"[64] in which the very existence of the society is threatened – as indeed it was – does not automatically justify women, children, clerics, and men who would otherwise be noncombatants in taking up arms. Third, we might infer, consistent with his other *jus in bello* statements, that his reason for not urging the general civilian populace to fight is precisely because they are not

---

[56] Ibid., I. IV.25, p. 9.   [57] Augustine, *City of God* I.26, p. 37.
[58] Augustine, *On Free Choice of the Will* I.V, p. 11.
[59] Augustine, *Letter* 189.6, *NPNF* I, p. 554.   [60] Augustine, *Letter* 228.2, *NPNF* I, p. 577.
[61] Ibid.   [62] Ibid.   [63] Ibid.
[64] See Michael Walzer, *Just and Unjust Wars*, 2d ed., New York: Harper-Collins Publishers, 1992, chap. 16.

soldiers and cannot therefore be justified in committing violence. If this concern were not the source of his reservation, it is difficult to understand why Augustine did not call at least the able-bodied male portion of the civilian population to arms. Indeed, one is reminded of the mobilization order issued in 1935 by a fellow African, Emperor Haile Selassie, to his subjects, as his nation, threatened with invasion by Mussolini's forces, was faced with a "supreme emergency":

Everyone will now be mobilized and all boys old enough to carry a spear will be sent to Addis Ababa. Married men will take their wives to carry food and cook. Those without wives will take any woman without a husband. Women with small babies need not go. The blind, those who cannot carry a spear, are exempted. Anyone found at home after receipt of this order will be hanged.[65]

Good Faith Augustine enjoins the maintenance of good faith, even with an enemy. Referring to Joshua's divinely approved employment of ruse and ambush in the conquest of Ai[66], Augustine reasons that military deception, as such, is not inherently evil:

This teaches us that such things are legitimate for those who are engaged in a just war. In these matters the only thing a righteous man has to worry about is that the just war is waged by someone who has the right to do so because not all men have that right. Once an individual has undertaken this kind of war, it does not matter at all, as far as justice is concerned, whether he wins victory in open combat or through ruses.[67]

This passage presents some unusually perplexing problems that deserve separate treatment.[68] For the present, however, suffice it to say that once it has been established that the war being fought is a just war, the Christian need not have scruples about the use of stratagems, ruses, or other deceptive tactics in war. On the other hand, Augustine urges, "when faith is pledged, it is to be kept even with the enemy against whom the war is waged."[69] Whenever a nation makes a pledge to another, the pledge is to be regarded as inviolable. Augustine tacitly acknowledges, then, and is understood by his interpreters throughout the Middle Ages[70] to acknowledge, that just warfare may properly involve deliberately deceptive acts – provided that they do not likewise involve breaches of good faith. Cicero certainly held the same opinion. However, Augustine notes a problem that seems to have eluded Cicero, namely, that it is not always possible to maintain good faith with

---

[65] *Mobilization and Strategic Mobility Planning*, Fort Leavenworth: United States Army Command and General Staff College, 1989, pp. 1–5.

[66] Joshua 8.

[67] Augustine, *Questions on the Heptateuch* 6.10, quoted in Swift, 1983, p. 138.

[68] For a detailed discussion of the issues involved, see John Mark Mattox, "The Moral Limits of Military Deception," *Journal of Military Ethics* 1 (2002), no. 1, pp. 4–15.

[69] Augustine, *Letter* 189.6, *NPNF* I, p. 554.

[70] See, for example, Hugo Grotius, *On the Law of War and Peace [De Jure Belli ac Pacis]*, ed. Wei Wilson Chen, Book III, Chapter I:VI; available from www.geocities.com/Athens/Thebes/8098; accessed June 29, 2001.

the enemy and at the same time to maintain the safety of one's own nation or city – both of which Cicero considered to be imperatives.[71] Augustine's treatment of good faith in warfare serves as the *point de depart* for virtually all subsequent discussions on good faith in the Middle Ages.

Augustine's Conception of Peace

According to Augustine, God designed all humans to live together in the "bond of peace."[72] Nevertheless, because the common choice of fallen man is a peace that selfishly serves his own immediate or foreseeable ends, peace becomes, in practice, merely an interlude between ongoing states of war. Augustine delineates three kinds of peace: the ultimate and perfect peace that exists exclusively in the City of God in heaven, the interior peace enjoyed by the pilgrim citizens of the City of God as they sojourn on earth, and the peace that is common to the two cities (i.e., imperfect human attempts to maintain peace that do not, at the same time, impede the realization of divine purposes).[73] For Augustine, the possession of any one of these kinds of peace does not imply the possession of the other two. Moreover, Augustine is abundantly clear that temporal peace is rather an anomalous condition in the totality of human history and that perfect peace is altogether unattainable on earth: "Such is the instability of human affairs that no people has ever been allowed such a degree of tranquility as to remove all dread of hostile attacks on their dwelling in this world. That place, then, which is promised as a dwelling of such peace and security is eternal, and is reserved for eternal beings."[74] While men do not agree on which kind of peace to seek, all agree that peace in some form is the end they desire to achieve. Even in war, all parties desire – and fight to obtain – some kind of peace. Ironically, although peace is the end toward which wars are fought, war seems to be the more enduring, more characteristic of the two states in the human experience. War is the natural (albeit lamentable) state in which fallen man finds himself. The flesh and the spirit of man – although both are good – are in perpetual opposition:

But what in fact, do we achieve, when we desire to be made perfect by the Highest Good? It can, surely, only be a situation where the desires of the flesh do not oppose the spirit, and where there is in us no vice for the spirit to oppose with its desires. Now we cannot achieve this in our present life, for all our wishing. But we can at least, with God's help, see to it that we do not give way to the desires of the flesh which oppose the spirit to be overcome, and that we are not dragged to the perpetration of sin with our own consent.[75]

Augustine concludes that war among men and nations cannot be avoided altogether because it is simply characteristic of the present existence. The contention

---

[71] See, for example, Augustine, *City of God* XXII.6, p. 1032.

[72] Augustine Letter 93.5:18, *NFPF*, p. 388.   [73] Augustine, *City of God* XIX.17, p. 878.

[74] Augustine, *City of God* XVII.13, pp. 743–744.   [75] Augustine, *City of God* XIX.4, p. 854.

that typifies war is merely the social counterpart to the spirit-body tension that typifies every individual person. However, man can, through the general application of divine precepts contained in scripture and through the pursuit of virtue as dictated by reason, manage that tension on both the individual and societal levels in such a way as to obtain a transitory peace. War and peace are two sides of the same Augustinian coin. Owing to the injustice that is inherent in the mortal state, the former is presently unavoidable, and the latter, in its perfect manifestation, is presently unattainable.

In sum, the state is an institution imposed upon fallen man for his temporal benefit, even if the majority of men will not ultimately benefit from it in light of their predestination to damnation. However, if one can successfully set aside Augustine's doctrine of predestination (which poses a major – perhaps insurmountable – obstacle for Augustine's overall project), one finds in his writings an enormously valuable descriptive account of the psychology of fallen man, which can take the reader a very great distance toward understanding social interactions among men and nations.

IV   Augustinian Influence on Just War Thought in the Middle Ages

A thoroughgoing account of both the extent of and the reason for Augustine's authority into the Middle Ages and beyond awaits and requires a future, monumental scholarly undertaking. However, this much is certain: "Augustine's surviving works comprise about four times the words of the surviving works of Cicero, and the extant writings of the first generations of Latin Christian fathers down to Augustine, Jerome, and Cassian," and "those writings alone add up to a corpus larger than all of surviving classical Latin literature."[76] Hence, as O'Donnell rightly observes, Augustine's ecclesiastical "office, his holiness, and his orthodoxy were all factors in claiming his place: but had he not written, had he not written so much, and had his works not survived so consistently … he would never have become the authority figure that he did become. He was the right man in the right place at the right time."[77] Although Augustine influenced the whole of medieval just war discourse either directly or indirectly, several representative figures of the era deserve special mention.

Gratian In the mid-twelfth century, a Camalolese monk known today simply as Gratian published a textbook entitled *Concordia discordantium canonum*, which, as the name implies, sought to assemble and to some degree

---

[76] James J. O'Donnell, "The Authority of Augustine," 1991 St. Augustine Lecture, Villanova University, 13 November 1991, http://faculty.georgetown.edu/jod/augustine/augustine/au gauth.notes.html#1, accessed July 7, 2016.
[77] Ibid.

harmonize various pronouncements of canon law as it had by that time developed. Gratian states that a war is *un*just if it is waged

1. by the wrong kind of person (*persona*, i.e., one who is a cleric and thus not permitted to shed blood);
2. for the wrong object (*res*, e.g., not for the purpose of recovering property or defending the country);
3. for the wrong reason (*causa*, i.e., by choice and not by necessity);
4. on the basis of the wrong motivation (*animus*, e.g., revenge); and
5. by virtue of the wrong authority (*auctoritas*, i.e., a prince has not authorized it).[78]

Although Gratian cites Isadore of Seville as the source of this rubric – the positive formulation of which Decretalists such as Laurentius Hispanus, Johannes Teutonicus, and Raymond de Peñafort will later use to establish the necessary conditions for the just resort to war – it is nonetheless thoroughly Augustinian in character. So is Gratian's explicit answer to the question, "What is a just war?" – namely, one "waged by an edict in order to regain what has been stolen or to repel the attack of enemies."[79] He then quotes Augustine at length to establish each of the following canons found in *causa* 23:

- "It is of no concern to justice whether one fights openly or by ambushes."[80]
- "The sons of Israel were refused innocent passage, and therefore they waged just wars."[81]
- "Vengeance that aims at correction is not to be prohibited."[82]
- "It is no sin to kill a man in the exercise of a public function."[83]
- "Those who made war with God's authority in no way transgressed the command not to kill."[84]
- "The soldier who kills a man in obedience to the powers that be does not commit homicide."[85]

---

[78] See Gregory M. Reichberg, Henrik Syse, and Endre Begby, eds., *The Ethics of War: Classic and Contemporary Readings*, Oxford: Blackwell Publishing Ltd., 2006, pp. 112–113.

[79] Gratian, *Concordia discordantium canonum*, part II, causa 23, Question II, Canon 1, quoted in *The Ethics of War*, eds. Reichberg et al., p. 113. All subsequent references to *Concordia discordantium canonum* are likewise taken from Reichberg et al.

[80] Augustine, *Seven Questions on the Heptateuch*, cited by Gratian in *Concordia discordantium canonum*, part II, causa 23, Question II, Canon 2.

[81] Augustine, *Questions on [the book of] Numbers*, cited by Gratian in *Concordia discordantium canonum*, part II, causa 23, Question II, Canon 3.

[82] Augustine, *against Manicheans*, cited by Gratian in *Concordia discordantium canonum*, part II, causa 23, Question III, Canon 51.

[83] Augustine, writing to Publicola, cited by *Gratian in Concordia discordantium canonum*, part II, causa 23, Question V, Canon 8.

[84] Augustine, *City of God* I, cited by Gratian in *Concordia discordantium canonum*, part II, causa 23, Question V, Canon 9.

[85] Ibid., Canon 13.

- "He is not a murderer who willfully kills those whom the judge orders to be killed."[86]
- "The duties of revenge can be fulfilled in good conscience."[87]
- "He is not iniquitous but humane who prosecutes crime in order to liberate man."[88]
- "Why regal power and legal tortures have been instituted [sic]."[89]
- "Sometimes he who is the cause of death is guiltier than he who inflicted death."[90]
- "He does not sin who kills a criminal by virtue of his functions."[91]

Gratian's summary is likewise thoroughly Augustinian in spirit: "From all this we gather that vengeance is to be inflicted not out of passion for vengeance itself, but out of zeal for justice."[92] In short, Gratian makes Augustine's transformation of Christian charity into a motivation for waging war "the cornerstone of his own and therefore the medieval jurisprudential analysis of warfare."[93]

Alexander of Hales Writing in the middle of the thirteenth century, Alexander of Hales, known as *Doctor irrefragabilis* – the Irrefutable Doctor – states the following:

One can distinguish between a just and an unjust war according to authority (*auctoriatem*), state of mind (*affectum*), intention (*intentionem*), condition (*conditionem*), desert (*meritum*), and cause (*causam*). State of mind and authority should be considered in the person who declares the war; condition and intention in the person who fights the war; desert in the person who is warred upon; and the cause in the person for whom the war is fought.[94]

This summation, like Gratian's, is thoroughly grounded in Augustinian notions, as Alexander himself explicitly acknowledges: "It should be said that for a war to be just requires that the person declaring the war has a just state of mind and a just

---

[86] Augustine, *Questions on Exodus*, cited by Gratian in *Concordia discordantium canonum*, part II, causa 23, Question V, Canon 14.

[87] Augustine, *Questions on Matthew*, cited by Gratian in *Concordia discordantium canonum*, part II, causa 23, Question V, Canon 16.

[88] Augustine, writing to Macedonius, cited by Gratian in *Concordia discordantium canonum*, part II, causa 23, Question V, Canon 17.

[89] Ibid., Canon 18.   [90] Ibid., Canon 19.

[91] Augustine, *On Free Will* book I, cited by Gratian in *Concordia discordantium canonum*, part II, causa 23, Question V, Canon 41.

[92] Gratian in Concordia discordantium canonum, part II, causa 23, Question IV, dictum post canon 54.

[93] Russell, *The Just War in the Middle Ages*, p. 60.

[94] Alexander of Hales, *Summa theologica*, III, n. 466: *Utrum bellare sit licitum*, quoted in *The Ethics of War*, eds. Reichberg et al., p. 158. All subsequent references to Alexander of Hales are likewise taken from Reichberg et al.

authority ... Just authority is ordained according to what Augustine shows in his writing against the Manicheans."[95] "Furthermore," says Alexander,

in the person for whom the war is fought there should be found a just cause, which is the restoration of the good, the suppression of the wicked, and peace for all. Augustine says in *Diverse Observations on the Church*: "The truly peaceful servants of God are those who wage war not for motives of aggrandizement, or cruelty, but with the object of securing peace, of punishing evildoers, and of uplifting the good."[96]

Thomas Aquinas For some, Aquinas, and not Augustine, is the principal source from which just war thinking develops in the Latin West. In point of fact, however, Aquinas merely crystalizes and formalizes earlier Augustinian positions. Whereas Augustine devotes no treatise – much less a formal analysis – to the topic of just war, Aquinas, in his *Summa theologiae* II-II, authored formal analyses on the subjects of peace (Question 29), strife (Question 41), sedition (Question 42), military prudence (Question 50, Answer 3), battlefield courage (Question 123, Answer 5), and most famously on war (Question 40). Indeed, it is not unfair to identify Question 40 as the first truly systematic moral-philosophical treatment of the fundamental issues of the just war tradition in the Latin West. Even so, Aquinas's treatment of the question "Whether it is always sinful to wage war?" is, at its heart, thoroughly Augustinian – and overtly so (even if Aquinas's elaborations on just war issues newly incorporate Aristotelian terms and themes). Aquinas identifies four objections to the proposition that "It would seem that it is always sinful to wage war," and his replies to three of these propositions quote Augustine. Moreover, Aquinas famously states, "In order for a war to be just, three things are required. First, the authority of the prince by whose command the war is to be waged ... Secondly, a just cause is required ... Thirdly ... that those waging war should have a rightful intention"[97]; and on all three of these accounts, Aquinas appeals by direct quote to Augustine. Even the specific selection of the necessary elements of Aquinas's just war definition are taken directly from Augustine.

Augustinian Influence on Later Generations of Just War Theorists

Augustine's basic definition of a just war remains practically unmodified until Roland of Cremona (AD 1178–1259), a contemporary of Aquinas, named the "authority of a prince; maintenance of faith (i.e., the Christian faith); and the

[95] Augustine, *Contra Faustum* XXIII, c. 74, cited in Alexander de Hales, *Summa theological seu sic ab origine dicta* "Summa fratris Alexandri," vol. 4, trans. Robert Andrews, Florence: Quaracchi, 1948, pp. 683–86.

[96] Alexander of Hales, *Summa theologica*, III, n. 466: *Utrum bellare sit licitum*. Although this passage appears in none of Augustine's extant works, it is preserved not only here by Alexander of Hales, but elsewhere by Gratian (*Decretum*, Causa 23, question 1, canon 6) and by Thomas Aquinas.

[97] Thomas Aquinas, *Summa theologiae*, II-II, Question 40, quoted in *The Ethics of War*, eds. Reichberg et. al., pp. 176–78.

righteous consciences of both prince and his warriors"[98] as the basic principles of *jus ad bellum*. However, even here, one detects a distinctively Augustinian flavor. For, although these points are not elemental to Augustine's just war definition per se, all three themes are prominent in the Augustinian corpus.

Over the course of the sixteen centuries that have passed since Augustine's day, secular Western society has reorganized itself on the basis of operating assumptions very different from those used by Augustine. Indeed, by the end of his life, the social context of the West was already undergoing perceptible change. As long as the Roman Empire recognizably endured and was forced to defend itself against "barbarian" (or, more to the point, non-Christian) invaders, the cause of church and state comingled, and Christian arguments justifying war could be brought to bear with more or less success. However, as Europe became "Christianized" and ostensibly Christian kings and princes began to war among themselves, questions of comparative justice – a notion courted only briefly by Augustine – began to assert themselves with greater force. Moreover, concomitant with the effective merger of church and state, the spirit of Augustinian interiority that required a truly right-intended motivation to justify resort to war gave way in many cases to the exteriority of "holy war"–based justifications propounded by ostensibly Christian political leaders and finding their most extraordinary expression in the Crusades.[99]

Ironically, the Peace of Westphalia provided a greater rationale for appeal to Augustinian just war concepts than did many of the medieval justifications claimed to be based on religious principles. Of course, after the Peace of Westphalia, the West felt itself far less obligated than Augustine did to derive just war principles from a world view reflective of divine rather than human will.[100] Nevertheless, even if subsequent attempts to elucidate the theory of just war do not obviously rely on Augustine's most fundamental assumptions, his influence becomes evident as one examines the similarities between Augustine's actual statements on just war and contemporary statements on the same or similar issues. This is true even if earlier or later authors in diverse societies also addressed similar just war themes, and in a more systematic way. In short, the role of Augustine as the father of the theory of just war in the West is frequently underappreciated but cannot be overstated. Indeed, the subsequent development in Just War theory in the West is essentially either a recapitulation of and an outgrowth from or a reaction to Augustinian thought.

---

[98] Russell, *The Just War in the Middle Ages*, p. 219.

[99] Strictly speaking, a "holy war" requires no human justification; it requires only a divine command. Whether or not Augustine would have ascribed divine warrant to the Crusades would be simply a matter of speculation.

[100] See Russell, *The Just War in the Middle Ages*, pp. 16–39.

2 Grotius and the Early Modern Tradition

Johan Olsthoorn

Introduction

This chapter offers an introduction to early modern Just War theory by analysing one of the most important and influential treatises written on the subject: *On the Law of War and Peace* (*LWP*), by the Dutch philosopher and statesman Hugo Grotius (1583–1645).[1] First published in 1625, the book was tremendously popular for more than two centuries. It is infrequently read and taught today. Its massive size – a popular modern edition runs to almost 2000 pages – and its arcane style, full of legal casuistry and obscure references to ancient poets, puts off many a well-intended reader. As does the bewildering range of topics covered in the book: *LWP* contains insightful analyses of property, sovereignty, and the nature of morality but also lengthy discussions of alluvial sediments and archaic burial rituals. Not exactly the kinds of themes one expects to find in a book on war and peace.[2] Sections more directly pertaining to war have equally befuddled modern readers. Oftentimes Grotius seems to permit conduct he elsewhere roundly rejects as unjust. This has allowed commentators to present deeply conflicting interpretations of Grotius. Some interpreters place him in the bellicose humanist tradition of Alberico Gentili (1552–1608) and Thomas Hobbes (1588–1679).[3] Others have argued that the Dutch philosopher is committed to "contingent pacifism": while waging war is morally permissible under certain conditions, these conditions are almost impossible to meet in practice.[4]

As this chapter reveals, *LWP* is in fact a highly systematic and original exploration of four sets of rules governing war: justice, morality, the voluntary law of

---

[1] All in-text references are to *LWP* by [book-chapter-paragraph-subsection]. The title *De Iure Belli ac Pacis* is sometimes translated as *Rights of War and Peace*. While "ius" may indeed mean both "right" and "law," the latter is clearly preferable here: the book examines the totality of rules governing war. Thomas Mautner, "War and peace," *British Journal for the History of Philosophy* 15 (2007) no. 2, pp. 373–74. For an excellent biography of Grotius, see Henk Nellen, *Hugo Grotius: A Lifelong Struggle for Peace in Church and State, 1583–1645*, Leiden: Brill, 2014.

[2] "What has circumcision to do with the laws of war and peace?," wondered Voltaire in *Political Writings*, ed. David Williams, Cambridge: Cambridge University Press, 1994, p. 89.

[3] Richard Tuck, *The Rights of War and Peace: Political Thought and the International Order from Grotius to Kant*, Oxford: Oxford University Press, 1999, pp. 12–13, 108, 228–29.

[4] Larry May, *Aggression and Crimes against Peace*, Cambridge: Cambridge University Press, 2008, pp. 25–34. More generally, see May's *Contingent Pacifism: Revisiting Just War Theory*, Cambridge: Cambridge University Press, 2015.

nations, and divine positive law (as expressed in the Bible). By clearly distinguishing between these four kinds of norms and explaining their interrelations, I hope to offer guidelines for how to read Grotius's *magnum opus*, thus helping make this rich and intellectually rewarding text accessible to modern readers.[5] Doing so also allows me to dispel three common misconceptions: (1) that Grotius's voluntary law of nations somehow "replaces" or "suspends" natural law, (2) that he advances a minimalist conception of morality, and (3) that Grotius is not an original thinker.

One major difference between seventeenth-century and modern Just War theories worth clarifying straight away concerns the realm governed by norms of war and peace. Notwithstanding his epithet "father of international law," Grotius's laws of war and peace are not exclusively international laws. *Jus belli* governs the use of force in *any* dispute where there is no common superior to appeal to (1.1.1).[6] Quarrels in the state of nature and the international arena are necessarily of such a kind. But so are certain conflicts within the state – namely, those in which judicial appeal is unavailable – whether because of the imminence of the threat or because the conflict opposes two sovereign powers (e.g. the people vs. the king) (1.3.2).[7]

Three caveats: first, I should emphasize that the philosophical significance of Grotius today will primarily reside in the rich conceptual and theoretical framework he erects rather than in his normative ethics. Grotius's substantive views are often highly objectionable. For instance, he deems both slavery and political absolutism morally justifiable.[8] Second, I confine myself to *LWP*. Grotius, an extraordinarily prolific author, wrote a number of other treaties on the ethics of war, most published posthumously if at all.[9] The philosophical development across Grotius's works is much vaster, I believe, than is commonly recognized. Discussing other lesser-known texts would needlessly complicate my ambition to expound

---

[5]   Compare the diagram in Onuma Yasuaki, ed., *A Normative Approach to War: Peace, War, and Justice in Hugo Grotius*, Oxford: Clarendon Press, 1993, pp. 342–43.

[6]   It thus includes what is today called "political violence." C.A.J. Coady, *Morality and Political Violence*, Cambridge: Cambridge University Press, 2008, pp. 3–8. Locke agrees with Grotius on this point; indeed, his doctrine of individual rights of resistance can be interpreted as a radicalization of Grotius's Just War theory. Jonathan Scott, "The law of war: Grotius, Sidney, Locke and the political theory of rebellion," *History of Political Thought* 13 (1992) no. 4: 565–85; Deborah Baumgold, "Pacifying politics: resistance, violence, and accountability in seventeenth-century contract theory," in her *Contract Theory in Historical Context: Essays on Grotius, Hobbes, and Locke*, Leiden: Brill, 2010, pp. 27–49.

[7]   Grotius accepts the legal possibility of divided sovereignty (1.3.17; 3.19.10).

[8]   Grotius was a theorist of *natural*, not of *human* rights (a much more recent notion). While both natural and human rights are pre-institutional, only the latter are inalienable.

[9]   E.g. Hugo Grotius, *"Commentarius in Theses XI": An Early Treatise on Sovereignty, the Just War, and the Legitimacy of the Dutch Revolt*, ed. Peter Borschberg, Bern: Peter Lang, 1994; *Commentary on the Law of Prize and Booty*, ed. M.J. van Ittersum, Indianapolis: Liberty Fund, 2006; *Mare Liberum*, ed. Robert Feenstra, Leiden: Brill, 2009. Peter Borschberg, "'De Pace': Ein unveröffentlichtes Fragment von Hugo Grotius über Krieg und Frieden," *Zeitschrift der Savigny-Stiftung für Rechtsgeschichte* 113 (1996) no. 1: 268–92.

the system behind Grotius's mature Just War theory. Third, I regularly contrast Grotius's views with those of other well-known early modern theorists, including Vitoria, Suárez, Gentili, Hobbes, and Locke. But my aim in doing so is largely illustrative. For a detailed treatment of these thinkers, the reader should look elsewhere.

I Natural Law vs. the Law of Nations

Just War theory is a branch of ethics. It studies moral norms and considerations applying to decisions to start war and to conduct within war. *LWP* is widely regarded as a classic statement of Just War theory. And Grotius indeed presents an elaborate and innovative theory of the ethics of war and peace. But he also discusses relevant non-moral norms, including foremost the voluntary law of nations (*jus gentium*). The law of nations consists of customary norms agreed upon either by the whole international community or by a considerable part of it (e.g. by all Christian states). These customary norms change over time (Prol. 31). *LWP* is thus a work in moral philosophy *and* a study of then-extant international law.

We are unaccustomed to seeing moral and legal rules discussed under the same general heading ("law"). Moral philosophers rightly sideline the question of what is existing law as irrelevant for what is morally the case. Legal scholars, in turn, are more interested in what is binding law right now than in what ideally should be law. Grotius, confusingly, dons the hats of ethicist and jurist within the same work.

This seems a call for trouble. Existing laws commonly fall short of moral perfection. Many entrenched international regulations pertaining to war, including the right of states to national self-defence and the normative equality of combatants, are morally questionable.[10] In Grotius's time, international law permitted unrestricted plunder and collective enslavement of innocent peoples. Grotius does not morally approve of such practices. But he does accept that prevailing international norms have some legal effect. His aim in *LWP* is to arrive at an integrative theory of *all* the rules governing war and peace, both moral and legal in nature. This mixed approach has led to confusion about Grotius's "real" position.

Take plunder in war. In 3.6.2.1 we read that "by the Law of Nations, not only he that makes War for a just Cause, but every Man in a solemn War acquires the Property of what he takes from the Enemy, and that without Rule or Measure." (What "solemn wars" are I discuss shortly.) In other words, belligerents fighting an unjust war become rightful owners of plundered goods and conquered territory. One recent commentator claims that Grotius is here codifying "a near-perfect law of 'might makes right.'" "Might vests the right to rule conquered territory and the right to own captured property."[11]

---

[10] David Rodin, *War and Self-Defense*, Oxford: Clarendon Press, 2002; Jeff McMahan, *Killing in War*, Oxford: Clarendon Press, 2009.

[11] Leif Wenar, *Blood Oil: Tyrants, Violence, and the Rules that Run the World*, Oxford: Oxford University Press, 2015, pp. 137, 142.

Worse, Grotius's "pro-plunder rule" extends to people as well. The law of nations authorizes combatants fighting an unjust but properly declared war to enslave their innocent enemies – both individuals and entire peoples (3.7.1.2; 3.8.1.1). Is Grotius here justifying colonialization by unjust conquerors?! Rousseau exclaimed, full of fury, that Grotius's "most persistent mode of reasoning is always to establish right by fact. One could use a more consistent method, but not one more favourable to Tyrants."[12] But as we will see, Grotius did not *morally* condone plunder and conquest by unjust combatants. He merely observed that international law had sanctioned such conduct in his day and age and tried to incorporate that contingent empirical fact into his theory of the general rules of war and peace.

The voluntary law of nations issues three kinds of norms. First, it may prohibit what natural law permits; that is, it may forbid morally optional actions. An example is the ban on using poison in war (3.4.15–16). Second, the law of nations may endow combatants with legally enforceable rights, including ownership of pillaged goods (e.g. 3.4.4; 3.6.2.1). Third, by common agreement states may render permissible what is morally forbidden. Permission here means legal impunity, not moral licence. By "the Law of Nations . . . many Things are said to be of Right and lawful, because they escape Punishment, and partly because Courts of Justice have given them their Authority, tho' they are contrary to the Rules, either of Justice properly so called, or of other Vertues" (3.10.1.1). Many terrible war crimes had been rendered unpunishable in Grotius's time, including plunder, killing just combatants (3.4.3), butchering hostages (3.4.14; 3.20.53), and the "Slaughter of Infants and Women" (3.4.9.1). "Whence it appears how much that Inhumanity was turned into Custom" (3.4.9.2). War crimes do not just happen to go unpunished, for example because of power differentials. Rather, the law of nations endows unjust belligerents with legal rights, "actionable in Courts of Judicature," not to be punished for war crimes (3.10.1.3).

The last two legal effects – authorization of plunder and immunity to criminal prosecution – apply only in what Grotius calls "solemn wars." Solemn wars are formally declared wars between sovereign states. Such wars are called "just" or "lawful" in the sense that by international agreement they assort legal effect; they need not be "just" according to natural law (1.3.4; 3.3.1.1).[13] A formal declaration of war is required to attest that the war is fought by "Consent of both

---

[12] Rousseau, *Social Contract*, 1.2.4.

[13] This distinction between two senses of "just" – morally right vs. with legal effect – is also found in Balthazar Ayala and arguably in Alberico Gentili. Yet neither of them linked these two senses of "just" to the distinction between natural law and the law of nations – a distinction Gentili explicitly rejects: "the law of nations, which is the law of nature." Ayala, *Three Books on the Law of War* [1582], 2 vols., ed. John Westlake, trans. John Pawley Bate, Washington: Carnegie Institution,1912, p. 22; Gentili, *De Jure Belli Libri Tres* [1598], 2 vols., ed. John C. Rolfe, Oxford: Clarendon Press, 1933, pp. 5, 13–14.

Nations, or of their Sovereigns" (3.3.11). The legal effects follow not from *this* act of consenting however, but from prior agreement to the voluntary law of nations. It would be a mistake to think that by declaring their consent to fight belligerents waive their rights to punish war crimes and to compensation for unjustly plundered goods. After all, solemn wars need to be formally declared by only one of the contending parties (e.g. 3.3.5; 3.3.6.2). Moreover, the legal implications of solemn wars extend to the entire international community. Indeed, the point of formal declarations of war is to announce to the international community that the rules peculiar to solemn wars apply. Without it, unjust belligerents would be liable to criminal prosecution, also by third parties. The pro-plunder rule ensures that the international community can continue to trade with belligerent parties as usual (3.4.4).[14]

Solemn wars are akin to what the Swiss philosopher and diplomat Emer de Vattel (1714–1767) would later dub "regular war" (*guerre réglée*).[15] This concept, developed in the early modern period, is indebted to ancient Roman thought. Roman jurists distinguished between war and other violent conflicts, and between lawful enemies and unlawful ones (such as pirates and rebels). A war, properly understood, was a formally declared violent conflict between political communities, regulated by *jus belli*.[16] The regular war paradigm elaborates on these Roman doctrines, adding that the same rules apply to all belligerents, irrespective of the justness of their cause (the "symmetry thesis"). The symmetry thesis seems to hold for Grotius's solemn wars too: all parties are by common custom granted equal licence to kill and plunder.

Grotius's attempt to incorporate both just war and regular war features within the same theory has been criticized as incoherent.[17] "Human Laws," he states, "may enjoin many Things that are no where commanded by the Law of Nature, but

---

[14] Neff's suggestion that a failure to properly denounce war does not make "any practical difference to the belligerents" should therefore be rejected. Stephen C. Neff, *War and the Law of Nations: A General* History, Cambridge: Cambridge University Press, 2005, p. 111.

[15] Vattel, *The Law of Nations*, 3.4 §66.

[16] Frederick H. Russell, *The Just War in the Middle* Ages, Cambridge: Cambridge University Press, 1975, pp. 4–8, 49–54. On the idea of regular wars, see Peter Haggenmacher, "Just war and regular war in sixteenth-century Spanish doctrine," *International Review of the Red Cross* 32 (1992) no. 290: 434–45; Neff, *War and the Law of Nations*, pp. 95–130; Gregory M. Reichberg, "Just war and regular war: competing paradigms," in *Just and Unjust Warriors: The Moral and Legal Status of Soldiers*, eds. David Rodin and Henry Shue, Oxford: Oxford University Press, 2008, pp. 193–213; Pablo Kalmanovitz, "Early modern sources of the regular war tradition," in *The Oxford Handbook of Ethics of War*, eds. Seth Lazar and Helen Frowe, Oxford: Oxford University Press, forthcoming.

[17] Kalmanovitz, "Early modern sources": "Grotius did not integrate systematically these elements into a cohesive legal theory. In particular, he did not solve the question of how the positive law of nations and the natural law could fit together within a single system of law." Also Tanaka Tadashi, "*Temperamenta* (moderation)," in *A Normative Approach to War*, ed. Yasuaki, pp. 291, 303–4.

can enforce nothing that is contrary to it" (2.3.6). But by granting legal impunity to war crimes the law of nations seems to be "sanctioning ... injustice, often great injustice, in the conduct of war and elsewhere."[18] Grotius's dualist theory is more coherent, I contend, than usually claimed. Moreover, it has some philosophical appeal: Grotius can avoid a major objection raised against Michael Walzer precisely by holding fast to the distinction between just and solemn wars.

Walzer has influentially argued that the symmetry thesis is a *moral* truth. Both just and unjust belligerents would have the same moral rights, obligations, immunities, and liabilities, either because they have consented or have been compelled to fight.[19] Combatants have an "equal right to kill," regardless of what they are fighting for.[20] Soldiers fighting an unjust war therefore do not act wrongly merely by killing their opponents. In support, Walzer advances the "independence thesis": one's *jus ad bellum* status does not affect the obligations and privileges one has in war.[21] The symmetry thesis has recently come under heavy fire. The main set of objections, developed by Jeff McMahan, starts from reflections on moral liability. McMahan argues that there is no good reason to think that combatants fighting just wars have somehow waived or forfeited their right not to be killed.[22] Did Norwegians soldiers really make themselves morally liable to be killed by valiantly resisting the unjust invasion by the Nazi army in April 1940? If McMahan is right, then unjust aggressors wrong just combatants by killing them. Moreover, since the cause of the former is *ex hypothesi* unjust, they cannot appeal to lesser evil justifications. Extreme duress and the difficulty to determine the justness of their cause may perhaps excuse unjust soldiers, rendering them morally blameless. Even so, the symmetry thesis remains false at the level of justification.[23]

Like Walzer, Grotius claims that belligerents in solemn wars have, in a sense, an equal right to kill. But for Grotius, this equal footing implies no moral equality.[24] Grotius rejects the independence thesis. *Ad bellum* status does determine which

---

[18]   Steven Forde, "Hugo Grotius on ethics and war," *American Political Science Review* 92 (1998) no. 3, p. 644.

[19]   Michael Walzer, *Just and Unjust Wars: A Moral Argument with Historical Illustrations*, 5th edn, New York: Basic Books, 2015, p. 37.

[20]   Walzer, *Just and Unjust Wars*, p. 41.   [21]   Walzer, *Just and Unjust Wars*, p. 21.

[22]   Jeff McMahan, "The sources and status of just war principles," *Journal of Military Ethics* 6 (2007) no. 2, pp. 97–101; McMahan, "The morality of war and the law of war," in *Just and Unjust Warriors*, eds. Rodin and Shue, pp. 24–27; McMahan, *Killing in War*, pp. 51–60. Cf. Thomas Hurka, "Liability and just cause," *Ethics & International Affairs* 21 (2007) no. 2, pp. 210–16.

[23]   David Rodin, "The moral inequality of soldiers: why *jus in bello* asymmetry is half right," in *Just and Unjust Warriors*, eds. Rodin and Shue, p. 51.

[24]   Even Gentili, who unconditionally granted the same legal rights and duties to just and unjust combatants alike, did not endorse the *moral* equality of combatants. Unjust belligerents remain subject to moral disapproval and the pangs of conscience; moreover, "[t]here is also Hell." Gentili, *De Jure Belli*, p. 33. For general discussion, see Gregory M. Reichberg, "The moral equality of combatants – a doctrine in classical just war theory?" *Journal of Military Ethics* 12 (2013) no. 2: 181–94.

moral rights and duties combatants have: "if the Cause of the War be unjust, tho' it be undertaken in a solemn Manner, yet all the Acts of Hostility done in it are unjust in themselves" (3.10.3; also 2.1.1.3). The law of nations does not morally exculpate wrongdoers. The permissions it gives are "incomplete" ones: "only an Impunity with Men, and a Right to do a Thing, so that no Man shall molest and hinder us" (1.1.17; also 2.5.28; 3.4.5.2).[25] The suggestion that "the law of nations has simply overthrown the notion of just war" is inaccurate.[26] Natural law has not been "suspended" or "overridden" by international law. Plundering and slaying the innocent continue to be moral wrongs of the highest order. Though freed from prosecution in human courts, unjust belligerents remain accountable to God. Atonement for their sins is needed to obtain salvation. Genuine repentance "absolutely requires" full restitution of plundered goods and compensation of damage done (3.10.3; also 3.19.11.2). Third parties who honestly come to own pillaged goods are morally obliged to return these goods to their erstwhile owners (3.10.6.1; 3.16.1.1). Failure to restore unjustly plundered goods does not, however, constitute a new just cause for war. After all, unjustly dispossessed owners have lost their legal claims to the pillaged goods. In short, the law of nations provides belligerents with legally enforceable rights of impunity and ownership without in any way morally justifying war crimes.[27]

Equally questionable is the suggestion that Grotius develops a middle position between pessimistic realism and excessive idealism in international affairs "by combining natural law with the more flexible institution of positive law, rooted in human volition."[28] Grotius does not introduce the concept of a solemn war to provide an alternative set of rules that combatants can more realistically be expected to adhere to. To let plunder go unpunished is not to render plundering morally permissible. It is a virtue of Grotius's dualist account that the question of which rule combatants ought to follow in case the precepts of morality and the law of nations conflict does not arise: belligerents remain morally obliged to abide by natural law at all times – even by those prescriptions whose violation international law has rendered unpunishable.

---

[25] A "complete" permission is "a Right to do something with an intire Liberty in all Respects" (1.1.17). On Grotian permissions, see Tanaka, "*Temperamenta*"; Brian Tierney, *Liberty and Law: The Idea of Permissive Natural Law, 1100–1800*, Washington: Catholic University of America Press, 2014, pp. 215–47.

[26] Forde, "Hugo Grotius," p. 644.

[27] Grotius does not use the modern language of "moral" vs. "legal" rights and duties. Instead, he speaks of "internal" vs. "external" rights and justice – that which binds in conscience vs. that which has effect only in human courts. E.g. 3.16.1; 3.16.5; 3.20.53. Tanaka, "*Temperamenta*," pp. 280, 294–304. Thus, while international law endows masters with a legally enforceable "external" right over unjustly enslaved individuals, the latter are not morally obliged to obey their captors and may escape if they can (3.7.6).

[28] Forde, "Hugo Grotius," p. 639. Also Joan D. Tooke, *The Just War in Aquinas and Grotius*, London: S.P.C.K., 1965, p. 230; Neff, *War and the Law of Nations*, pp. 101, 139.

Is Grotius's dualist theory internally coherent? I have argued that the law of nations does not enjoin injustice; it merely institutionalizes impunity (within constraints). But isn't that a way of sanctioning injustice? In some sense, yes. The law of nations normatively validates a pattern of holdings that has been unjustly brought about. Grotius's dualist theory is coherent only if the act of normative validation by the international community is itself permitted by natural law. Institutionalizing impunity is itself wrong. It can hence be morally permissible only as a lesser evil. Grotius indeed claims that peace is better served by abstaining from *post-bellum* international arbitration. Nations have agreed to licence murder of just combatants in part because of epistemic hurdles in establishing which belligerent party is in the right. These hurdles make settling guilt often controversial, inviting further conflict (3.4.4).[29] The same lesser evil justification applies to the pro-plunder rule. By sanctioning seizure, a potential cause for war is eliminated: belligerents have lost the right to be compensated for seized property, the denial of which would have justified reigniting war.

Recent philosophers have followed Grotius in keeping sharply and explicitly distinct the moral and legal dimensions of war. McMahan has offered similar pragmatic reasons for upholding for the present the war convention of granting combatants equal legal status – despite it being morally false that all combatants have a like right to kill.[30] Grotius's version of such a dualist theory nonetheless strikes me as hard to defend. Whether peace requires non-prosecution of plunder and war crimes is an empirical claim. Perhaps it was true in Grotius's time; it no longer is now. And even had it been, we may not value peace so highly as to let war crimes go unpunished. Moreover, Grotius undermines the lesser evil justification for institutionalizing impunity by allowing non-moral reasons to inform *jus gentium*. The law of nations is instituted "for the Interest of Nations" (e.g. Prol. 18; 3.3.12), including their commercial interests, and sometimes even for the benefit of kings alone (3.4.15.1). Condoning plunder for economic reasons is surely morally wrong. Grotius vehemently rejected any attempts to reduce morality to considerations of self-interest, however well understood. But the law of nations – instituted by the international community – *does* spring purely from considerations of expediency.[31]

The distinction between just and solemn/regular wars had far-reaching implications for a controversial question in Grotius's time. Can war be just on both sides? Like the Spanish jurist Balthazar Ayala (1548–1584), Grotius concedes the possibility of bilateral justice as long as "just" refers not to the cause

---

[29] A point also emphasized by Vattel, *The Law of Nations*, 3.12 §188.

[30] McMahan, "The morality of war," pp. 27–33, 36 (Grotius is mentioned at p. 34); "Sources and status"; *Killing in War*, pp. 104–10. For critical discussion of McMahan's views, see Jeremy Waldron, "Deep morality and the laws of war," in *The Oxford Handbook of Ethics of War*, eds. Lazar and Frowe.

[31] A further weakness of Grotius's theory is that no attempt is made to justify the voluntary laws of nations to individual soldiers.

of war but "to the Effects it produces" (i.e. its legal implications).[32] Solemn wars are always just on both sides in this sense. "In the same Manner as a wrong Sentence, and an unjust Possession have some Effects of Right" (2.23.13.5).

The philosophically more interesting question is whether both sides in a conflict can be *morally* justified in fighting. Except for cases of "invincible ignorance," early modern thinkers generally considered this impossible. At most one of the contending parties can be "truly" or "objectively" right. But who that is, is typically hard to discover. Both sides, it was commonly conceded, can be *epistemically* justified in believing in the rightness of their cause, rendering their use of force morally blameless.[33] Epistemic justification does not, however, imply moral justification. It merely excuses an otherwise wrong action.[34] Grotius agrees that "inevitable Ignorance" can in principle render both parties "free from Injustice or any other Fault" (2.23.13.3). But given the high stakes involved in war, the level of epistemic justification required for moral blamelessness is exceptionally high (2.23.13.4).

Grotius's declared view is that both sides cannot have truly just grounds for war (2.26.6.2).[35] But his theory does implicitly provide a way for bilateral justice to occur in war. Natural law endows individuals with a last resort right to kill innocent persons posing an imminent threat to their survival. Think of a driver whose car, because of a technical malfunction, is out of control and coming right at you. Grotius believes that you may kill the driver, her innocence notwithstanding: "Because this Right [of self-defence] does not properly arise from the other's Crime, but from that Prerogative with which Nature has invested me, of defending myself" (3.1.2.1; also 2.1.3). Since the opposing driver is not morally liable to be killed, she may kill you in self-defence, too.[36] By disentangling the right to kill in self-defence from the threat's moral liability to be killed, Grotius thus opens up the possibility of rare and tragic circumstances in which two innocent parties may justly kill each other in self-defence.

Hobbes would later exploit a similar self-defence–based argument for the possibility of bilateral justice to dramatic effect. According to the English

---

[32] Ayala, *Three Books*, pp. 22–23. On Ayala's doctrine of war, see Peter Haggenmacher, *Grotius et la Doctrine de la Guerre Juste*, Paris: Presses Universitaires de France, 1983, pp. 138–39, 298–300.

[33] E.g. Francisco Suárez, "A work on the three theological virtues: faith, hope and charity," in *Selections from Three Works*, 2 vols., eds. Gwladis L. Williams, Ammi Brown, and John Waldron, Oxford: At the Clarendon Press, 1944, p. 816; Francisco de Vitoria, *Political Writings*, eds. Anthony Pagden and Jeremy Lawrance, Cambridge: Cambridge University Press, 1991, pp. 282, 312–13. On Vitoria on bilateral justice, see Haggenmacher, *Grotius*, pp. 209–12; Daniel Schwartz, "Late scholastic just war theory," in *The Oxford Handbook of Ethics of War*, eds. Lazar and Frowe. The protestant Gentili greatly enlarged the scope of the epistemic argument for bilateral justice by emphasizing humanity's fallen nature. He also added that the laws of war, being general in nature, do not refuse clearly unjust belligerents the full rights of war. *De Jure Belli*, pp. 31–33.

[34] McMahan, *Killing in War*, p. 111.   [35] Haggenmacher, *Grotius*, pp. 561–63.

[36] Cf. McMahan, *Killing in War*, pp. 39–42.

philosopher, the individual right of self-defence entails a right to everything in conditions of war. For everything can be sincerely judged as conducive to survival. Besides, human natural equality entails that each individual has the moral authority to make these judgements herself.[37] In Hobbes's view, *in every war* "one man *rightly* attacks and the other *rightly* resists" – where "right" signifies "objectively right."[38] Grotius is far from countenancing such radical implications. Unlike Hobbes, the Dutchman insists that the natural right of self-defence, though normatively fundamental, can be exercised only as a last resort. The relation between Grotius and Hobbes is worth dwelling on further because of the prominence in the literature of a Hobbist reading of Grotius.

II Justice

"Grotius endorsed for a state the most far-reaching set of rights to make war which were available in the contemporary repertoire," writes Richard Tuck, making him a "most improbable figure to be the tutelary deity of the Peace Palace at The Hague."[39] Tuck presents his revisionist reading of Grotius in a study of early modern justifications for expansionist foreign policy. He identifies two schools of thought in the early modern just war tradition. Scholastic theologians such as Francisco de Vitoria (1483?–1546), Francisco Suárez (1548–1617), and Luis de Molina (1535–1600), developed restrained Just War theories in a Thomist mould. Humanist jurists like Andrea Alciato (1492–1550), Pierino Belli (1502–1575), and Alberico Gentili were much more apologetic about political violence and closer to reason-of-state theorists such as Machiavelli. These jurists managed to include considerations of expediency within a just war framework through an expansive conception of self-defence. With respect to rights of war, Tuck traces a straight link from Gentili to Hobbes, with Grotius as the key transitional figure.[40] Indeed, he argues that the modern natural law tradition, which Grotius putatively initiated, was characterized by the attempt to derive a set of universally acceptable moral norms from the natural right of self-preservation.[41]

---

[37] Hobbes, *Leviathan*, 14.4, 28.2. On the various grounds of Hobbes's right to everything, see Johan Olsthoorn, "Why justice and injustice have no place outside the Hobbesian State," *European Journal of Political Theory* 14 (2015) no. 1, pp. 22–25, 29–30.

[38] Hobbes, *De Cive*, 1.12.   [39] Tuck, *Rights of War*, pp. 95, 108.   [40] Ibid., pp. 108, 228.

[41] Grotius presumably developed his minimalist natural law theory to counter a form of moral scepticism revived by Charron and Montaigne. See Tuck's "Grotius, Carneades and Hobbes," *Grotiana* 4 (1983) no. 1: 43–62; "The 'modern' theory of natural law," in *The Languages of Political Theory in Early-Modern Europe*, ed. Anthony Pagden, Cambridge: Cambridge University Press, 1987, pp. 99–120; *Philosophy and Government, 1572–1651*, Cambridge: Cambridge University Press, 1993, pp. xv–xvi, 173–76, 196–99, 347–48; *Rights of War*, pp. 5–6; "Introduction," in Hugo Grotius, *The Rights of War and Peace*, 3 vols., Indianapolis: Liberty Fund, 2005, pp. xviii–xxvii. For rebuttals to Tuck's interpretation, see Robert Shaver, "Grotius on scepticism and self-interest," *Archiv für Geschichte der Philosophie* 78 (1996) no. 1: 27–47; Thomas Mautner, "Grotius and the skeptics," *Journal of the History of Ideas* 66 (2005) no. 4: 577–601.

This section quarrels with Tuck's bellicose and Hobbist reading of Grotius. The Dutch philosopher gives the right of self-preservation much less theoretical prominence than either Gentili or Hobbes. This is evinced by their diverging views on the permissibility of preventive war and breaking faith, on bilateral justice, and on just causes of war. Tuck is right to stress the pugnacious implications of Grotius's endorsement of an individual natural right to punish. Moreover, as the next section shows, Grotius departs from the scholastics by maintaining that any rights-violation justifies war: questions of proportionality are placed outside *jus ad bellum*. However, neither doctrine brings Grotius any closer to Gentili or Hobbes.

Common to both the reason-of-state and the humanist jurisprudence traditions in which Tuck locates Grotius is the permissibility of pre-emptive strikes out of just fear.[42] To grasp Grotius's views on anticipatory violence, we should distinguish *pre-emptive* from *preventive* attacks/wars. Pre-emptive attacks can be defined as first strikes on an imminent and direct threat; preventive ones as first strikes on a distant threat.[43] "Distant" is best understood probabilistically rather than temporally – as *probable* threats.[44]

Gentili insisted that waging non-punitive wars is justified only in case of necessity.[45] But what counts as necessity? The Italian humanist conceded that his criteria for "necessity," like Machiavelli's, are rather undemanding.[46] Killing in self-defence is lawful even if other life-saving options are available.[47] And preventive wars fought out of just fear count as "necessary" and "defensive" as well.[48] (A fear is just if you have reason to think that a greater evil may befall you.) "No one ought to expose himself to danger. No one ought to wait to be struck, unless he is a fool."[49] It is often lawful, Gentili concluded, "to injure others to avoid an injury to yourself."[50]

The justification of first strikes against any "probable and possible" attack makes Gentili's theory truly groundbreaking – and unambiguously a theory of preventive war.[51] Gentili roundly rejected the scholastic commonplace that war

---

[42] Tuck, *Rights of War*, p. 11.

[43] David Luban, "Preventive war," *Philosophy and Public Affairs* 32 (2004) no. 3, p. 213. For general discussion, see Henry Shue and David Rodin, eds., *Preemption: Military Action and Moral Justification*, Oxford: Oxford University Press, 2007.

[44] Luban, "Preventive war," p. 230. I leave undiscussed the pertinent question of what is being threatened (one's life, a state's territorial integrity, basic interests, etc.).

[45] Gentili, *De Jure Belli*, p. 20.

[46] Ibid., pp. 58, 60. Quoting Livy, Machiavelli proclaimed: "necessary wars are just wars" in *The Prince* [1532], eds. Quentin Skinner and Russell Price, Cambridge: Cambridge University Press, 1988, p. 88.

[47] Gentili, *De Jure Belli*, pp. 58–59.   [48] Ibid., 61.   [49] Ibid., 62.   [50] Ibid., 73.

[51] Ibid., 66. Gregory M. Reichberg calls Gentili "one of the first authors in the Christian West openly to endorse the idea of preventive war" in "Preventive war in classical just war theory," *Journal of the History of International Law* 9 (2007) no. 1, p. 15. Although otherwise critical of Tuck's depiction of Gentili, Kingsbury and Straumann admit: "While Gentili thus cannot be situated in any simple way in a 'humanist' camp, his views, especially on preemptive

may only be waged in response to wrongdoing. Vitoria, for instance, had maintained that "the sole and only just cause for waging war is when harm [*injuria*] has been inflicted," adding that "all the doctors" agreed on this.[52] Hobbes's one-time employer Francis Bacon (1561–1626) sided with Gentili. Bacon dismissed "the opinion of some of the schoolmen . . . that a war cannot justly be made but upon a precedent injury or provocation. For there is no question but a just fear of an imminent danger, though there be no blow given, is a lawful cause of war."[53] Preventive wars waged out of just fear, he insisted, are really defensive.[54] Hobbes extended the right of anticipatory strikes to its logical limit:

There is no way for any man to secure himselfe, so reasonable, as Anticipation; that is, by force, or wiles, to master the persons of all men he can, so long, till he see no other power great enough to endanger him: And this is no more than his own conservation requireth, and is generally allowed.[55]

Grotius, however, vehemently rejects Gentili's doctrine of preventive war: "to pretend to have a Right to injure another, merely from a Possibility that he may injure me, is repugnant to all the Justice in the World" (2.1.17).[56] Fear of one's neighbour's strength, however reasonable, is not a just cause for war (2.2.13.4; 2.22.5.1). "There is no other *reasonable* Cause of making War," Grotius insists, "but an *Injury* received" (2.1.1.4). The right of self-defence justifies only pre-emptive attacks, and only in case of "present" and "inevitable" danger to one's life (2.1.3; 2.1.5). Even within war, necessity generates only limited rights. Belligerents may lawfully take from the enemy and from civilians whatever resources are necessary to procure self-defence (3.13.1.1; 3.18.2.2). But as with any right of necessity, combatants are obliged to

---

warfare and the bilateral justice of war, were original and strained the framework of traditional just-war doctrine." Benedict Kingsbury and Benjamin Straumann, "Introduction," in idem eds., *Alberico Gentili: The Wars of the Romans*, trans. David Lupher, Oxford: Oxford University Press, 2011, p. xxiii. Cf. Benedict Kingsbury and Benjamin Straumann, "Introduction," in idem eds., *The Roman Foundations of the Law of Nations: Alberico Gentili and the Justice of Empire*, Oxford: Oxford University Press, 2010, pp. 3, 9–15.

[52] Vitoria, *Political Writings*, 303. Also e.g. Aquinas, ST II-II q.40-a.1. For helpful discussion, see Jonathan Barnes, "The just war," in *The Cambridge History of Later Medieval Philosophy*, eds. Norman Kretzman, Anthony Kenny, and Jan Pinborg, Cambridge: Cambridge University Press, 1982, pp. 777–82.

[53] Francis Bacon, "Of empire," in *The Essays or Counsels, Civil and Moral*, ed. Brian Vickers, Oxford: Oxford University Press, 1999, p. 44.

[54] Francis Bacon, *Considerations Touching a Warre with Spaine*, London: Imprinted, 1629, p. 15.

[55] Hobbes, *Leviathan*, 13.4.

[56] Grotius refers to Gentili in the marginalia. Tuck does not discuss Grotius's views on preventive war. For discussion, see Reichberg, "Preventive war," pp. 19–25 and more generally, Peter Haggenmacher, "Grotius and Gentili: a reassessment of Thomas E. Holland's Inaugural Lecture," in *Hugo Grotius and International Relations*, eds. Hedley Bull, Benedict Kingsbury, and Adam Roberts, Oxford: Clarendon Press, 1990, pp. 133–76.

compensate the lawful owner afterwards – necessity does not itself create moral ownership rights (2.2.9; 3.12.1.1).[57]

One problematic implication of permitting preventive strikes – against possible threats – is that it abets bilateral justice. Since the attacked party has by definition not committed any crime yet, it retains its right to resist. Indeed, the permissibility of anticipatory strikes underlies Hobbes's notorious doctrine of "a right of every man to every thing, whereby one man invadeth with right, and another with right resisteth."[58] Extending the right of self-defence to unjust aggressors further increases occurrences of bilateral justice. Gentili permitted an unjust aggressor the right to defensive force, as she "is not obliged to suffer such a death."[59] Hobbes is even more explicit. Defending one's life, "the Guilty man may as well do, as the Innocent."[60] Even duly convicted criminals may resist the punishment due to them.[61] Grotius, by contrast, gainsays unjust aggressors a right of self-defence, "no more than a Criminal can plead a Right of defending himself against the publick Officers of Justice" (2.1.18.1). Delinquents, Grotius contends, have a duty to submit themselves to lawful punishment (2.5.32; 2.20.2.3). Only if an unjust aggressor's offer of satisfactory compensation is refused, then "he may in Conscience defend himself" (2.1.18.2). Those who do not or cannot offer sufficient compensation are consequently not allowed to defend themselves from justified retaliation.

Grotius's strict views on the impermissibility of breaking faith likewise set him apart from Machiavelli, Hobbes, and Gentili. According to Machiavelli, "A prudent ruler cannot keep his word, nor should he, when such fidelity would damage him, and when the reasons that made him promise are no longer relevant."[62] Hobbes declared covenants in conditions of war void "upon any reasonable suspition."[63] Gentili regarded breaking promises out of fear "unbecoming." But he did insist that every promise includes a tacit rider annulling the agreement whenever its fulfilment becomes "contrary to natural reason," for example, because circumstances have changed.[64] Grotius, by contrast, stresses that natural law requires that promises be kept, including those made to open enemies in situations of duress (2.11.7; 3.19.4). Even tacit promises retain their full validity within war (3.1.18). And where Hobbes called "fraud" a cardinal virtue in war,[65] Grotius judges lying in either word or action almost always impermissible.

---

[57] The law of nations may grant legal titles to goods thus taken to belligerents, as well as post-war legal impunity.

[58] Hobbes, *Elements of Law*, 14.11.   [59] Gentili, *De Jure Belli*, p. 126, also p. 59.

[60] Hobbes, *Leviathan*, 21.17.   [61] Ibid., 14.29.   [62] Machiavelli, *The Prince*, pp. 61–62.

[63] Hobbes, *Leviathan*, 14.18.

[64] Gentili, *De Jure Belli*, pp. 363, 365 and more generally, pp. 186–94, 360–66, 426. Suárez agreed with Gentili on this point: "On charity," pp. 852–53. On Suárez's Just War theory, see Gregory M. Reichberg, "Suárez on just war," in *Interpreting Suárez: Critical Essays*, ed. Daniel Schwartz, Cambridge: Cambridge University Press, 2012, pp. 184–204.

[65] Hobbes, *Leviathan*, 13.13.

For it violates the general right, implied by the social function of language, of each to be communicated to truthfully (3.1.11).

Grotius even defended the claim, extraordinary at the time, that promises made with pirates, rebels, and tyrants are morally binding (2.13.15; 3.19.2; 3.19.13.1). Following Cicero, these people were usually seen as placed outside of human society altogether.[66] The rules of war, including the duty to keep promises, were not considered to apply to interactions with them:

> If an agreement is made with pirates in return for your life, and you do not pay the price, there is no deceit, not even if you swore to do so and did not. For a pirate is not counted as an enemy proper, but is the common foe of all. There ought to be no faith with him.[67]

Grotius is adamant that natural law continues to govern interaction with pirates – "their being Enemies, does not make them cease to be Men" (3.19.1.2). The law of nations has, however, rendered breaches of faith with pirates unpunishable (3.4.18.6; 3.19.5).[68] This example reveals a practical implication of Grotius's sharp distinction between natural law, applying in virtue of human nature, and the law of nations, instituted by international consent.

Other proof Tuck musters for his revisionist reading of Grotius is more compelling. Tuck rightly highlights the originality of Grotius's endorsement of a "strong version of an international right to punish."[69] This right chimes badly with the widespread reading of Grotius as a proponent of the Westphalian international order. The idea of punitive wars itself was by no means new. Indeed, war was traditionally seen as an essentially punitive exercise. The sixteenth-century Spanish scholastics gradually shifted to a defensive war paradigm.[70] Citing a well-known Roman law maxim, Vitoria argued that every individual may wage defensive war, to resist force with force.[71] Yet he denied that individuals have the right "to avenge and punish injuries" already committed. Only states may wage punitive wars. The right to punish, Gentili explained, presupposes jurisdiction over the criminal: "To punish a guilty person whom you have no right to punish is equivalent to chastizing an innocent person."[72] Human natural equality means

---

[66] E.g. Gentili, *De Jure Belli*, p. 124.

[67] Cicero, *On Duties*, 3.107. Ayala, *Three Books*, pp. 59–61, 64; and Gentili, *De Jure Belli*, pp. 22–26, 143–44 followed Cicero's views on pirates, as did Locke, *Second Treatise*, §176.

[68] Perhaps Grotius had the recent Dutch Revolt in mind when insisting that treaties made with rebels are valid (3.19.6). Gentili had denied their validity in *De Jure Belli*, pp. 23–25. Ayala, writing for the Spanish throne during the Dutch rebellion, had done the same in *Three Books*, pp. 60, 64.

[69] Tuck, *Rights of War*, p. 108.

[70] Pärtel Piirimäe, "Alberico Gentili's doctrine of defensive war and its impact on seventeenth-century normative views," in *The Roman Foundations of the Law of Nations*, eds. Kingsbury and Straumann, pp. 191–92.

[71] Vitoria, *Political Writings*, p. 297, citing Digest 1.1.3.

[72] Gentili, *De Jure Belli*, p. 41. Also Vitoria, *Political Writings*, pp. 273–75.

that no one is subject to another by nature. Punishment therefore presupposes political authority. It follows that a state may only punish injustices within its jurisdiction, done to itself or to its citizens. The opposite view, Suárez exclaimed, "is entirely false, and throws into confusion all the orderly distinctions of jurisdiction".[73]

Grotius broke sharply with tradition by denying that the right to punish presupposes political authority over the wrongdoer. He challenged those who "assert, that the Power of punishing is properly an Effect of Civil Jurisdiction; whereas our Opinion is, that it proceeds from the Law of Nature" (2.20.40.4). By nature, every individual may punish through war all those who transgress natural law, provided the punishment is undertaken for "the good of the Publick" (2.20.9). States may likewise punish severe wrongdoings "which do not peculiarly concern them," committed by persons beyond their jurisdiction – and not just violations of international law but also of natural law (2.20.40.1). Grotius's innovative decoupling of the right to punish from political authority greatly increased the rights of wars available to individuals and states. While thus anticipating Locke's "very strange Doctrine," it does not align him with either Gentili or Hobbes.[74] Neither of the latter recognized a natural right to punish – indeed, for Hobbes, the very idea is incoherent.[75] To understand the full implications of Grotius's novelty, we should examine which kinds of wrongdoings justify punishment and war generally.

III Wrongdoing

Grotius, we have seen, criticized in *LWP* Gentili's lax stand on just causes of war. The Dutch philosopher stuck to the orthodox view, expounded by the Spanish theologians, that force is permitted only in response to injuries (wrongdoings). This scholastic criterion for just war was informed by a principle of liability and confined by a norm of *ad bellum* proportionality. As Vitoria writes, "for the just war a just cause is required; namely, that those who are attacked have deserved attack by some culpable action ... If the barbarians have done no wrong, there is no just cause for war; this is the opinion shared by all the doctors."[76] Doing wrong makes one liable to attack. But for war to be justified, the gravity of the wrong must also be proportionate to the evils inflicted

---

[73] Suárez, "On charity," p. 818. Also Vitoria, *Political Writings*, p. 300.

[74] Locke, *Second Treatise*, §9. Grotius's and Locke's arguments for this right differ, however. Locke argues that the law of nature would be "in vain, if there were no body that in the State of Nature, had a *Power to Execute* that Law" (§7). Since the separate right to avenge injuries done to you already gives some teeth to natural law (§§10–11), the additional right to punish is at most needed for further deterrence (§8). Grotius contends that punishment by third parties is naturally permissible because and insofar as it upholds human society (1.2.1.3). Cf. Richard Tuck, *Natural Rights Theories: Their Origin and Development*, Cambridge: Cambridge University Press, 1979, p. 63; Tuck, *Philosophy and Government*, p. 177; Tuck, *Rights of War*, p. 82.

[75] Hobbes, *Leviathan*, 28.1–2.

[76] Vitoria, *Political Writings*, p. 270, quoting Aquinas, ST II-II q.40-a.1.

by war. "Not every or any injury gives sufficient grounds for waging war," Vitoria averred. Given the horrible nature of war, only crimes meriting "cruel punishments" justify combat.[77] Suárez concurred: a "just and sufficient reason for war is the infliction of a grave injustice which cannot be avenged or repaired in any other way."[78] Grotius, I contend, broke with tradition by altogether excluding considerations of proportionality from *jus ad bellum*. He could plausibly do so by eliminating a whole set of wrongdoings as just causes of war and by subsuming *ad bellum* proportionality under charity instead (Section IV).

"Now, as many *Sources* as there are of *judicial* Actions, so many *Causes* may there be of *War*," Grotius writes. "For where the Methods of Justice cease, War begins" (2.1.2.1). To be sure, use of force is permitted only when conflict cannot be settled peacefully (i.e. by judicial arbitration). But that should not blind us to the pugnaciousness of Grotius's doctrine: any wrong that generates a legal claim, however trivial, constitutes a possible *casus belli*. Grotius diminishes its bellicose effects by systematically distinguishing between two kinds of rights: "perfect" and "imperfect" (1.1.4).[79] In general, to form a just cause for war, the injurious action must violate a perfect right.

Perfect rights pick out everything that individuals can properly call "their own." "Own" is here understood in an expansive sense. Besides property, it includes life, limbs, and reputation; authority over ourselves ("liberty") and others; as well as whatever others strictly owe us (credit) (1.1.5). We may also have perfect rights to enjoy things in common (2.2.1). Some perfect rights we have by nature (1.2.1.3; 2.17.2.1). Others we have by positive law or through someone else's crime (e.g. rights to compensation). Only perfect rights generate actionable claims: we may go to court and ultimately even to war for it. Their violation justifies taking coercive measures against the wrongdoer – to recover or seek reparation for what has been unjustly taken away.

An imperfect right, by contrast, is really "an Aptitude or Merit, which doth not contain in it a Right strictly so called, but gives Occasion to it" (2.20.2.2). "Aptitude" denotes that a person is worthy to obtain a perfect right. Imperfect rights pertain to virtues other than justice – for example, to charity, liberality, and mercy (1.1.8.1). Characteristic of these virtues is that they are unenforceable: they entail no "Right to any other over us" (2.11.3). Suppose that Hugo merits amnesty. In Grotius's vocabulary: Hugo has an imperfect right to receive amnesty. The imperfect right expresses that it is morally fitting to give Hugo reprieve; he deserves it. While the world would be morally better for him receiving amnesty, Hugo cannot *claim* amnesty as his due. Merely having an imperfect right does not give you the distinct moral authority to demand whatever you are worthy to receive. Imperfect rights are thus unenforceable in court and in the extra-judicial

---

[77] Vitoria, *Political Writings*, p. 304.   [78] Suárez, "On charity," p. 816.

[79] The nomenclature was actually introduced by Grotius's commentators. Grotius himself used "faculty"/"right properly and strictly taken" vs. "aptitude"/"right improperly taken". Mautner, "War and peace," p. 369. I will talk about "perfect/imperfect rights" for convenience's sake.

process of war (2.22.16; 2.25.3.4). Moreover, failure to properly respect such rights is not unjust, properly speaking (2.12.9.2); does not warrant punishment (2.20.20.1); and damage done by their violation does not need to be repaid (2.17.3.1; 2.17.9).

Grotius forges a strict conceptual link between perfect rights and justice: "the very Nature of Injustice consists in nothing, else, but in the Violation of another's Rights" (Prol. 45). Hobbes would later equate "injury" with "injustice."[80] Grotius did not: "We here call any Fault or Trespass, whether of Commission or Omission, that is contrary to a Man's Duty … an Injury" (2.17.1). Injuries are thus not the same as injustices/rights violations. Rather, injury is a violation of any moral duty. This qualification may seem unimportant. After all, Grotius is frequently read as not recognizing any moral duties other than justice. As one recent commentator writes, "nor, in Grotius's theory, are there positive duties of charity, which oblige us to assist others in distress."[81] But this reading is mistaken. "There are many Duties," Grotius writes, "not of strict Justice but of Charity, which are not only very commendable … but which cannot be dispensed with without a Crime" (2.25.3.3).[82] Violations of duties of charity thus qualify as injuries as well. Why don't such crimes justify war?

To understand this, we should distinguish between three just causes for war: "*Defence*, the *Recovery* of what's our own, and *Punishment*" (2.1.2.2). Each of these causes entitles individuals to use force. The right to use force in self-defence "arises directly and immediately from the Care of our Preservation, which *Nature* recommends to every one, and not from the Injustice or Crime of the *Aggressor*" (2.1.3).[83] Grotius distinguishes the right to punish from the right of recovery ("repair"). Punitive wars are waged not to seek reparations or to recover what was unjustly taken away from us but to punish wrongdoers (2.20.1). As we have seen, the right to punish can belong to anyone, including to third parties. The right of recovery belongs to the injured person alone. Recovery presupposes perfect rights. Individuals may forcibly seek compensation only if they have wrongfully suffered damage to an object, tangible or intangible, to which they have a perfect right: it must be their property.[84] Now from what "is improperly called a Right … arises no

---

[80] Hobbes, *Elements of Law*, 16.4: "Justice and injustice, when they be attributed to actions, signify the same thing with no injury, and injury." Also *De Cive*, 3.3; *Leviathan*, 14.7.

[81] John Salter, "Hugo Grotius: property and consent," *Political Theory* 29 (2001) no. 4, p. 551. Also Stephen Buckle, *Natural Law and the Theory of Property: Grotius to Hume*, Oxford: Clarendon Press, 1991, pp. 31–32.

[82] Also e.g. 2.22.10.1; 2.24.2.3; 3.1.4.2; 3.21.24.2. Grotius explicitly distinguishes between obligations which give others a right over us and obligations which don't (2.7.4.1; 2.11.3; 2.14.6.1).

[83] Defence does not require that the injury is already committed – we may take coercive measures whenever what we "own" is immediately threatened by wrongdoing. The other two just causes for war presuppose that the injury has taken place (2.1.2.1).

[84] Book III adds a further qualification. Injuries are foreseeable and intended moral faults. Rights violations that were unintended but could have been foreseen make one liable to

true Property, and consequently no Obligation to make Restitution; because a Man cannot call that his own, which he is only capable of, or fit for" (2.17.3.1). Duties of charity (and mercy, etc.) do not give prospective beneficiaries a right against the duty-holders: "For it happens in many Cases, that we may lay ourselves under an Obligation, and at the same Time give no Right to any other over us, as appears in the Duties of Charity and Gratitude" (2.11.3). Failures to perform duties of charity, although wrong, do not therefore warrant recovery. While not a matter of tort law, can such wrongs be a matter of criminal law?[85] Do they ever warrant punishment?

No, claims Grotius. On what grounds? Some commentators assert that only violations of perfect rights are punishable: "Not every moral fault is punishable, but only those that do injury, which violate the rights of others."[86] This suggestion must be rejected. It conflates injury with injustice. Injuries which only "indirectly and consequentially" hurt others – such as suicide, bestiality, and atheism – *are* punishable (2.20.44.2). By definition, such "indirect crimes" do not violate anyone's rights. They are rather crimes against human society as such. Atheism, for instance, must be punished "in the name of human society, to which they do violence without a defensible reason" (2.20.46.4). (Unafraid of God's wrath and hence supposedly incapable of virtue, atheists would undermine the preconditions for peaceful society.[87]) The reason violations of duties of charity and the like are unpunishable is somewhat *ad hoc*: these virtues are deemed inherently non-compulsory. "Nor are Actions to be punished, that are done in Opposition to Virtues, which by their very Nature are averse from all Compulsion, such as Mercy, Liberality and Gratitude" (2.20.20.1). Thus, "a rich Man who is indeed by the Laws of Charity and Compassion obliged to relieve the Poor, but yet cannot be compelled to do it" (2.25.3.4).

Book II of *LWP* is largely devoted to outlining which kinds of perfect rights humans may have in order to enumerate potential just causes of war. Two *casus belli* deserve further discussion. A main tenet of the Westphalian "legalist paradigm" of just war, ably set out by Walzer, is that "nothing but aggression can justify war." Aggression, in turn, is defined as "any use of force or imminent threat of force by one state against the political sovereignty or territorial integrity of another."[88] Only wars fought in self-defence or to uphold international law are justifiable. Offensive wars are permissible, if at all, for humanitarian reasons alone. Walzer associates the legalist position with the

---

reparation but not to punishment. Unintended and unforeseeable faults neither merit punishment, nor require reparation (3.11.3–4). Tanaka, "*Temperamenta*," p. 282.

[85] Benjamin Straumann, *Roman Law in the State of Nature: The Classical Foundations of Hugo Grotius' Natural Law*, trans. Belinda Cooper, Cambridge: Cambridge University Press, 2015, p. 213.

[86] Andrew Blom, "Owing punishment: Grotius on right and merit," *Grotiana* 36 (2015), p. 25.

[87] Bracketing atheism, mere differences in religion are no just causes for war (2.20.47–50). To be punishable, a crime must undermine the possibility of human society, and religious differences do not do so.

[88] Walzer, *Just and Unjust Wars*, p. 62.

Spanish theologians, quoting their doctrine that war is justified only in response to wrongdoing (injuries).[89] Yet in truth, neither Grotius nor his predecessors quite fit this paradigm. Not every wrong justifying war is an instance of aggression thus defined. Some such wrongs do not threaten the injured state's territorial integrity or even involve the use of military force at all. Examples include refusals to grant free passage or to allow free trade (2.2.13). Even denying (male) foreigners the right to marry (female) citizens was deemed a lawful cause of war (2.2.21.1).[90]

The second notable just cause of war is extreme need. Cécile Fabre has recently argued that military aggression is not the only form of wrongdoing capable of justifying defensive war. She maintains, provocatively, that dereliction of duties of global distributive justice may be a just cause of war: the severely deprived have a *prima facie* right to wage war against the affluent insofar as the latter are causally responsible for their plight by failing to fulfil duties of distributive justice.[91] Fabre duly cites Grotius on this point.[92] Grotius indeed attributes to individuals a perfect right of necessity. This right justifies using resources owned by others without their consent in case of dire need. The institution of private property, Grotius explains, was instituted with this exception (2.2.6.4; 2.6.5). The right of necessity renders "subsistence wars" lawful: the destitute may ultimately wage war against property holders who withhold the use of their goods from them.

Force can be used only in response to wrongdoing. War may not be started merely to obtain an advantage, whether military, political, or economic (2.22.6) – regardless of whether the benefit propounds to the aggressor or to her victim. The last clause may sound redundant. How can it ever be in one's interest to be on the receiving end of a war? George W. Bush, august deliverer of democracy, thought he knew. Aristotle offered a rival explanation. His doctrine of natural slavery may well be the most objectionable idea ever advanced in the just war tradition, far worse than Bush-era justifications of torture.[93] Aristotle's doctrine is premised on the claim that certain human beings lack the capacity for autonomous practical deliberation. These individuals – "natural slaves" – are mentally incapable of judging what is good for them.[94] Natural slaves may be justly conquered and

---

[89] Ibid.

[90] Also e.g. Vitoria, *Political Writings*, pp. 278–84; Suárez, "On charity," pp. 803–4, 817; Gentili, *De Jure Belli*, p. 79. For general discussion of this class of *casus belli*, see Georg Cavallar, *The Rights of Strangers: Theories of International Hospitality, the Global Community, and Political Justice since Vitoria*, Aldershot: Ashgate, 2002, esp. pp. 107–12, 156–62.

[91] Cécile Fabre, *Cosmopolitan War*, Oxford: Oxford University Press, 2012, pp. 97–129 and "Rights, justice and war: a reply," *Law and Philosophy* 33 (2014) no. 3: 416–25. Also David Luban, "Just war and human rights," *Philosophy and Public Affairs* 9 (1980) no. 2, pp. 174–78.

[92] Fabre, *Cosmopolitan War*, pp. 103–5.

[93] E.g. Alan Dershowitz, *Why Terrorism Works: Understanding the Threat, Responding to the Challenge*, New Haven: Yale University Press, 2002, pp. 131–63.

[94] Malcolm Heath, "Aristotle on natural slavery," *Phronesis* 53 (2008) no. 3: 243–70.

enslaved since it is *in their interest* to be governed. As Aristotle writes in a harrowing passage: "The art of war is a natural art of acquisition, for the art of acquisition includes hunting, an art which we ought to practice against wild beasts, and against men who, though intended by nature to be governed, will not submit; for war of such a kind is naturally just."[95]

Grotius considered slavery morally permissible. Humans are born free by nature but may become slaves either "by Vertue of some Agreement, or in Consequence of some Crime" (3.7.1.1; also 2.22.11).[96] Like Locke, the Dutch jurist holds that those who have forfeited their right to live (e.g. because of unjust aggression) may be lawfully enslaved as a lesser punishment (3.14.1–2).[97] Rousseau rightly mocked this idea: "Grotius and others derive from war another origin of the alleged right of slavery. As the victor has the right to kill the vanquished, according to them, the latter can buy back his life at the cost of his freedom – a convention all the more legitimate in that it is profitable for both of them."[98] Unlike Locke, Grotius deems it "lawful for any Man to engage himself as a Slave to whom he pleases" (1.3.8.1). The Dutchman even accepts the legal validity of agreements by individuals and entire peoples of unconditional submission – "the most ignoble and scandalous kind of Subjection" (2.5.27). One argument he musters in support is the Aristotelian idea that some humans are better off being governed: "Besides, as *Aristotle* said, some Men are naturally slaves, that is, suited for Slavery. And some Nations also are of such a Temper, that they know better how to obey than to command" (1.3.8.1).

However, Grotius sharply denies that natural slaves may therefore be justly conquered. The fact that it is fitting or suitable for a people to be governed does not establish a right to forcefully subject them:

It is unjust likewise to bring under Subjection by Force of Arms, such as we may fancy are fit for nothing else, or (as the Philosophers sometimes stile them) are Slaves by Nature; for I must not compel a Man even to what is advantageous to him. For the Choice of what is profitable or not profitable, where People enjoy their Senses and their Reason, is to be left to themselves, unless some other Person has gained any Right over them. (2.22.12)

This anti-paternalistic principle does not rule out humanitarian intervention. Vitoria permitted humanitarian intervention "in defence of the innocent against tyranny," even if the oppressed "refuse to accept the

---

[95] Aristotle, *Politics*, 1256^{b}22-26.

[96] By the law of nations, offspring of slaves are born into slavery "for ever" (3.7.2). But by the law of nature, children of slaves are born free. Their parents may place their progeny into slavery only if this is necessary to "find them Victuals and other Necessaries of Life" (2.5.29). Slave owners have no right to kill their slaves, although "the Laws of some Nations" grant legal impunity (2.5.28).

[97] Locke, *Second Treatise*, §23.   [98] Rousseau, *Social Contract*, 1.4.7.

Spaniards as their liberators in the matter."[99] Grotius further bolsters rights of humanitarian intervention by allowing the international community to wage *punitive* wars against tyrants gravely oppressing and terrorizing their subjects (2.25.8.4).

Grotius's rejection of paternalism as a justification for war contrasts favourably with the views of his contemporaries.[100] According to Vitoria, charity requires bringing people so dim-witted as to be "unsuited" to properly take care of their own affairs into political subjection "for their own benefit."[101] His fellow theologian Suárez likewise maintained that *if* there are humans "so wretched as to live in general more like wild beasts than like men" – practicing cannibalism, going naked, and living in a state of nature – then "they may be brought into subjection by war, not with the purpose of destroying them, but rather that they may be organized in human fashion, and justly governed."[102] Both Vitoria and Suárez doubted whether natural slaves really exist. But unlike Grotius they did not in principle reject paternalistic justifications for *jus ad bellum*.[103] This may well be because for the scholastics charity, not justice, was the primary regulative norm in war.

IV Charity and the Christian Gospel

A remarkable feature of scholastic Just War theory is that it generally discussed "war" under the heading of charity (*caritas*). Charity was understood rather differently then as now. It primarily captured the love for God and, secondarily, the love and benevolence due to our fellow humans (for "belonging to" God).[104] The biblical duty to love your neighbour as yourself thus determined when, how,

[99] Vitoria, *Political Writings*, pp. 287–88. Cf. Theodor Meron, "Common rights of mankind in Gentili, Grotius and Suarez," *The American Journal of International Law* 85 (1991) no. 1: 110–16.

[100] Edward Keene highlights several ideas of Grotius capable of justifying extra-European colonialism and imperialism, without mentioning his principled rejection of the just war doctrine of natural slavery. Keene, *Beyond the Anarchical Society: Grotius, Colonialism and Order in World Politics*, Cambridge: Cambridge University Press, 2002. On medieval and early modern debates on natural slavery, see Anthony Pagden, *The Fall of Natural Man: The American Indian and the Origins of Comparative Ethnology*, Cambridge: Cambridge University Press, 1986, pp. 27–56; Tuck, *Rights of War*, pp. 40–47, 65–72.

[101] Vitoria, *Political Writings*, pp. 290–91. Elsewhere, in what may seem a dismissal of Aristotelian natural slavery, Vitoria actually only rejects as unjustified any claim to political authority based on superior intelligence (251). Grotius agrees with Vitoria that "People totally void of Reason" may be justly conquered – not because of paternalistic reasons, however, but because madmen can have neither property rights nor sovereignty (2.22.10.1). Cf. Vitoria, *Political Writings*, pp. 249–50.

[102] Suárez, "On charity," pp. 825–26.

[103] Neither did John Stuart Mill (1806–1873). The arch liberal deemed military intervention against "barbarous nations" justifiable since "it is likely to be for their benefit that they should be conquered and held in subjection by foreigners." J.S. Mill, "A few words on non-intervention," in his *Collected Works, Vol. XXI: Essays on Equality, Law, and Education*, ed. John M. Robson, Toronto: University of Toronto Press, 1984, p. 118.

[104] Aquinas, ST II-II q.23-a.1, 5, q.25-a.1.

and to what end military force may be used. Grotius departed from this model. The previous section highlighted the general connections between the right to use force and wrongdoing. Justice – regulating the domain of perfect rights – exclusively determines when humans are entitled to wage war. This section reveals that charity nonetheless plays an important role in Grotius's Just War theory, both *in bello* and *ad bellum*. Even if we have a just cause to wage war, Grotius claims, love for humanity makes it often "much more commendable to abate somewhat of our Right, than rigorously pursue it" (2.24.1). Sometimes charity even requires us to forgo our rights. Yet other humans may never compel us to do so: after all, it is still our right. Duties of charity are consequently internalized. What we owe *to* one another is determined wholly by justice.

Justice deals exclusively with perfect rights. It commands individuals to abstain from taking what is another's and to give each their due. Charity is a more stringent moral norm, ordering us to give away what is ours – that is, what we have a perfect right to – and to not press our rights to the fullest out of benevolence. Charity actually consists of not one set of precepts but two. Charity may be "considered in itself" (as falling under natural law) "or as it is what the sacred Rule of the Gospel requires at our Hands" (2.24.2.3; also 3.18.4).[105] As a natural virtue, charitable actions always promote societal welfare. After all, charity asks us to forgo what is ours for the good of others. There is no upper limit to what charity counsels us to do. The more lovingly, the better. While acts of charity are always morally good and praiseworthy, their omission is not always a sin. Acts of charity are often supererogatory (beyond the call of duty): "if one follows it, he does something commendable, and yet, without being guilty of any moral wrong, he may not follow it, or may even act quite otherwise" (1.2.1.3). Charitable acts are not prescribed by natural law whenever they can be omitted without sin. For natural law is by definition obligatory: "Counsels, and such other Precepts, which, however honest and reasonable they be, lay us under no Obligation, come not under this Notion of Law, or Right" (1.1.9; also 1.1.10.3; 2.14.6.1).

Natural law obliges us to act charitably whenever human life and society require it. "Circumstances too may sometimes fall out so, that it may not only be laudable, but an Obligation in us to forbear claiming our Right, on account of that Charity which we owe to all Men, even tho' our Enemies" (2.24.2.3). In those situations, paradoxically, charity orders us to refrain from exercising our perfect rights: "Every Thing that is conformable to Right properly so called, is not always absolutely lawful; for sometimes our Charity to our Neighbour will not suffer us to use this rigorous Right" (3.1.4.2). Take the general right of self-defence against unlawful aggression. Notwithstanding this right, natural law strictly prohibits killing tyrants who attack you unjustly even in self-defence.

---

[105] James Turner Johnson overlooks the twofold sense of charity. This impairs his contentions about Grotius's putative naturalization of charity. Johnson, *Just War Tradition and the Restraint of War: A Moral and Historical Inquiry*, Princeton: Princeton University Press, 1981, pp. 178–79; Johnson, "Grotius' use of history and charity in the modern transformation of the just war idea," *Grotiana* 4 (1983): 21–34.

Whenever "the *Aggressor*'s Life may be serviceable to *many*, it would be *criminal* to take it from him … by the very Law of *Nature*" (2.1.9.1). For "to prefer the Advantage of many Persons to my own single Interest, is what *Charity* often advises, sometimes commands" (2.1.9.3; also 2.25.3.3). (This example attests, by the way, that for Grotius – if not for Gentili and Hobbes – self-preservation does not always take precedence over societal welfare.)

The rules of charity found in the Gospel – obliging Christians alone – are more demanding still. The Biblical duty to love our neighbour as ourselves goes beyond what "the meer Law of Nature in itself requires" (Prol. 51). Christian charity prescribes actions which are in themselves morally optional: "The Christian Religion commands, that we should lay down our Lives one for another; but who will pretend to say, that we are obliged to this by the Law of Nature"? (1.2.6.2)[106] Indeed, "many Things which are permitted by the Law of Nature" are "forbidden by the divine Law … the most perfect of all Laws" (2.20.10.1). For instance, natural law permits us to unintentionally but foreseeably kill innocent bystanders in self-defence, but the Gospel prohibits this categorically (2.1.4). And Christians should not only forgo avenging injuries in exceptional circumstances, they generally ought to turn the other cheek (1.2.8.2; 2.24.1).

Grotius subsumes considerations of *ad bellum* proportionality under charity. Individuals are in principle entitled to use force to avenge any wrongfully suffered harm. Yet charity – both for the offender and for innocent bystanders – forbids the forceful pursuit of rights whenever the evils war is likely to cause outweigh the benefits to human society resulting from avenging or punishing wrongdoing (including deterrence and restoration of law and order) (3.1.4.2). The Dutch philosopher further departs from scholastic Just War theory by denying that having a right intention is a necessary condition of *jus ad bellum*.[107] Grotius distinguishes between the motivations belligerents have for waging war and the reasons justifying use of force. Only the latter are relevant for just causes. Starting a war for the wrong kinds of reasons (e.g. for glory or profit) is sinful, but it does not render the war unjust by itself (2.22.17.2). For fighting with bad intentions is a violation of charity, not of justice.

It is frequently claimed that Grotius defends a moral theory with minimal binding content.[108] This reading arguably reveals more about the interpreters' attitude to morality than about Grotius himself. *LWP* contains many lengthy discussions about what charity and other moral norms recommend and command of belligerents. Commentators do not always take these norms seriously since they are unenforceable in court and war. In fact, the distinction between what we are

---

[106] Also 2.1.10.1; 2.20.10 and, more generally, Prol. 51, 1.1.17, 2.12.20.3.

[107] Cf. e.g. Aquinas, ST II-II q.40-a.1.

[108] E.g. Forde, "Hugo Grotius," p. 640; Tuck, *Natural Rights Theories*, pp. 72–75 and *Philosophy and Government*, pp. 174–76, 197–200; Knud Haakonssen, "Hugo Grotius and the history of political thought," *Political Theory* 13 (1985) no. 2, 241–43. A richer view of Grotius's ethics is developed by Tobias Schaffner, "The eudaemonist ethics of Hugo Grotius (1583–1645): pre-modern moral philosophy for the twenty-first century?" *Jurisprudence* 7 (2016) no. 3: 478–522.

authorized to do against others and what we morally ought to do is absolutely pivotal to Grotius's moral theory.[109] Indeed, Grotius's greatest contribution to Just War theory may be his systematic differentiation between the "political" question of authority and liability to coercion from the "moral" question of what is the best thing to do all things considered. This differentiation makes it coherent to claim that the Syrian people have a right to revolt against their tyrannical oppressor *and* a moral duty not to exercise this right in order to avoid disastrous civil war. Moreover, Grotius realized that unjust aggressors, having made themselves liable to be killed, have no rights of defence whatsoever – even if it is morally better for people to abstain from pressing their right to resist to the fullest.

Summing up, charity is a stricter moral norm *than* justice, not a stricter form *of* justice. Obligations of charity are not owed to other humans. Consequently, a failure to fulfil duties of charity, although morally wrong, does not justify war. J.S. Mill has pointed out that *any* moral duty is enforceable – if not by force, then by moral blame and censure. Since *LWP* is a treatise about war and peace, Grotius conceptualizes enforceability quite differently. We should not be misled into thinking that charity and other moral virtues therefore have no normative weight or theoretical significance.

Conclusion

"Many have before this designed to reduce [the laws of war and peace] into a System; but none has accomplished it" (Prol. 31). Whether Grotius has succeeded in this ambition is subject of debate. In Hedley Bull's verdict, "if not the most original treatise written on the law of nations up to that time [*LWP*] was certainly the most *systematic*."[110] Carl Schmitt, on the other hand, maintained that "Grotius had a strong, general pathos for justice, but no juridical or scientific awareness of the problem."[111] This chapter has tried to show that Grotius's Just War theory is both more systematic and considerably more original than is generally acknowledged. To fully grasp Grotius's complex theory, we must be attentive to a series of subtle distinctions, cast in a conceptual framework in part foreign to us. By systematically distinguishing the four norms that together make up *jus belli* – the voluntary law of nations, justice, morality, and the Gospel – and by explaining their interrelations, I hope to have clarified the basic structure of Grotius's Just War theory. A theory that, nearly four centuries after initial publication, remains of philosophical interest.

---

[109] For an alternative analysis of moral accountability in Grotius, see Stephen Darwall, "Grotius at the creation of modern moral philosophy," *Archiv für Geschichte der Philosophie* 94 (2012) no. 3: 296–325.

[110] Hedley Bull, "The importance of Grotius in the study of international relations," in *Hugo Grotius and International Relations*, eds. Bull, Kingsbury, and Roberts, p. 74.

[111] Carl Schmitt, *The Nomos of the Earth in the International Law of the Jus Publicum Europaeum*, trans. G.L. Ulmen, New York: Telos Press Publishing, 2003, p. 135.

Part II

Initiating a Just War

3 State Defense

Yitzhak Benbaji

Introduction

Traditional Just War theory is based on a simple principle. Military aggression against a state that is recognized as a member in the society of states (or, nowadays, as a member in the United Nations) is a crime of aggression (or a crime against peace). States possess an inherent right to wage a defensive war, whose aim is averting aggressive threats, thereby defending their sovereignty and territorial integrity. They possess this right in virtue of their international legitimacy. Moreover, national defense is the only just cause for war that individual states are entitled to without the authorization of the UN Security Council.[1]

As it is usually interpreted, the right to national defense is an element in a complex right, composed of (1) a right of states to exercise political power by making, enforcing, and applying laws over a particular territory and (2) an immunity-right from interference with their rule over that entire area, by attempts at regime change, annexation, colonization, or secession; the right to national defense is a remedial right that the immunity-right entails.[2]

Founders of international law infer the rights of states in general, and the right to national defense in particular, from an analogy between states and individuals, arguing, in effect, that the moral standing of the two is equally fundamental and self-evident:

Just as by force of natural liberty it must be allowed to every man that he abide by his own judgement in acting ... as long as he does nothing which is contrary to your right, so likewise by force of the natural liberty of nations it must be

This research was supported by The Israeli Research Foundation, grant number 304/15.

[1] Michael Walzer, *Just and Unjust Wars: A Moral Argument with Historical Illustrations*, New York: Basic Books, 1977, and Michael Walzer, "The Moral Standing of States: A Response to Four Critics," *Philosophy & Public Affairs* 9 (1980), pp. 209–29. John Rawls, *The Law of Peoples*, Cambridge, MA: Harvard University Press, 1999, especially p. 37. For a detailed account of the legal aspects of the crime of aggression, see Larry May, *Aggression and Crimes against Peace*, Cambridge: Cambridge University Press, 2008. For a lucid introduction of the traditional view, see the editors' introduction in *The Morality of Defensive War*, eds. Cécile Fabre and Seth Lazar, Oxford: Oxford University Press, 2014.

[2] I am relying on Anna Stilz, "Territorial Rights and National Defense," in *The Morality of Defensive War*, eds. Fabre and Lazar, p. 204.

allowed to any one of them to abide by its own judgement in the exercise of sovereignty.[3]

Drawing on this tradition, contemporary international law asserts, "the use of force is prohibited as a choice of conduct toward another state, just as domestically the criminal law forbids individuals from violence toward one another. A monopoly on legal use of force rests with the supranational organization, the UN, not individual states, just as domestically the government controls the legitimate use of force." Accordingly, Article 51 to the UN Charter "copies the domestic system's rule of self-defense in cases in which the government cannot bring its power to bear to prevent illegal violence."[4]

Unlike founders of international law, most contemporary moral theories attach to states instrumental value rather than intrinsic value. That is, they suggest that the "domestic analogy" between states and individuals should be conceived as a heuristics that lacks any deeper moral significance.[5]

Instrumentalist theories of the moral standing of states are divided between strictly individualist and collectivist theories. Individualists believe that individuals are the sole locus of moral concern. Accordingly, states have a right against external intervention as far as they secure the rights of individuals to life, bodily integrity, health, safety, and so on.[6] Under some versions of individualism, states should also secure the political autonomy of individuals by protecting the communal integrity of the civic nation to which individuals belong, and by which they identify themselves. Collectivists claim to identify values to which individualists are blind. For example, a version of Kantian statism attaches value to maintaining existing just state institutions, even if the alternative is a different set of institutions that are no less just. Communitarians and nationalists claim that a good state protects valuable things, such as the way of life of a national community, its collective agency, or its concrete conception of justice and the solidarity that allows it.

A theory of the moral standing of states would require an answer to a further crucial question: What are the measures that legitimate states are allowed to take to protect their (derivative) moral rights to political independence and territorial integrity? Are they allowed to kill to avert a violation of their rights, and if so, why and in what conditions?

---

[3] Christian Wolff, *Jus Gentium Methodo Scientifica Pertractatum* (1749), trans. Joseph H. Drake, Oxford: Clarendon Press, 1934, para. 9 quoted in Charles Beitz, "The Moral Standing of States Revisited," in *Reading Walzer*, eds. Yitzhak Benbaji and Naomi Sussmann, London: Routledge, p. 64.

[4] John Yoo, "Using Force," *University of Chicago Law Review* 71 (2004), p. 738.

[5] See Walzer, *Just and Unjust Wars*, p. 61.

[6] See Charles R. Beitz, "Nonintervention and Communal Integrity," *Philosophy and Public Affairs* 9 (1980): 385–91; David Luban, "The Romance of the Nation-State," *Philosophy and Public Affairs* 9 (1980): 392–97; David Rodin, *War and Self-Defence*, Oxford: Clarendon Press, 2002.

Individualists tend to adopt a reductionist answer to this question. Acts of killing or maiming in war are subject to the same principles that govern killing in self- or other-defense in domestic circumstances; war is an aggregation of individual acts performed by individual actors that should be subject to the constraints of interpersonal morality.[7] The morality of defensive war "is continuous with the morality of individual self-defense ... justified warfare just is the collective of individual rights of self- and other-defense in a coordinated manner against a common threat."[8] In particular, "just causes for war are limited to the prevention or correction of wrongs that are serious enough to make the perpetrators liable to be killed or maimed."[9] Thus, "the difference between war and other forms of conflict is a difference only of degree and thus the moral principles that govern killing in lesser forms of conflict govern killing in war as well" and "a state of war makes no difference other than to make the application of the relevant principles more complicated and difficult."[10]

An individualist partial defense of the UN Charter would assert that as far as legitimate states are the vehicle through which human rights are secured, once the borders of such states are crossed by military force, "safety is gone." "There is no certainty this side of the border, any more than there is safety ... once a criminal has entered the house." States that violate the territorial integrity of another state are not "under the ties of Common Law of Reason."[11]

It follows, however, that reductive individualism has to deny from a legitimate state a right to wage wars whose aim is averting *purely* political aggression. In cases of purely political aggression, it is merely the territorial integrity and sovereignty of a legitimate state that is threatened. As a result, the aggressor offends the political liberty of individuals, but not their lives, health, bodily integrity, or personal liberty. In other, more difficult cases, the aggressor's success would bring about a regime change that would not imply any significant change in the human or political rights of individuals.

At first glance, reductive individualism entails that defenders should surrender if the aggressor cannot be repelled without intentionally or unintentionally killing people who have not culpably contributed to the threat against

---

[7] See especially McMahan, "The Ethics of Killing in War," *Ethics*, 114 (2004): 693–732; McMahan, "The Basis of Moral Liability to Defensive Killing," *Philosophical Issues* 15 (2005): 386–405; McMahan, *Killing in War*, Oxford: Oxford University Press, 2009.

[8] McMahan, "The Ethics of Killing in War," p. 717. Cf. Jeff McMahan, "War as Self-Defense," *Ethics & International Affairs*, 18 (2004): 75–80.

[9] Jeff McMahan, "Just Cause for War," *Ethics and International Affairs* 19 (2005): 1–21 at p. 11 and p. 14 ff.

[10] McMahan, *Killing in War*, p. 156. See also Helen Frowe, *Defensive Killing*, Oxford: Oxford University Press, 2014, p. 123.

[11] Walzer, *Just and Unjust Wars*, p. 57. See also Luban "Just Wars and Human Rights," *Philosophy and Public Affairs*, 9 (1980) no. 2, p. 177, and Charles R. Beitz, *Political Theory in International Relations*, Princeton: Princeton University Press, 1979, pp. 175-76, all quoted in Rodin, *War and Self-Defense*, p. 186.

which defenders fight. The good effect of these killings, that is, protecting the political liberty of individuals, or preventing an unjustified regime change, does not outweigh its bad effects, namely, the death of many innocent people. I call this implication of reductive individualism "the proportionality challenge."[12]

In light of the radically revisionist version of the *jus ad bellum* code, to which reductive individualism seems to be committed, some writers abandon this conception of the moral standing of states and appeal to collective values to validate a more traditional Just War theory.

I argue that this literature misses a deeper challenge that the UN Charter regime faces. As I read it, the Charter confers a right against purely political aggression, and a remedial right to national defense, even on thoroughly dysfunctional and corrupt states that, under any theory that will be reviewed here, have no moral standing. With the important exception of humanitarian intervention and wars against brutally oppressive (and yet non-murderous) states, use of force is an illegitimate means for promoting political or distributive justice under international law. Aggression is defined as unprovoked military invasion into the territory of another state (or as an imminent threat to do so) whatever the moral status of the state in question might be. The deeper challenge that the UN regime faces is therefore "the just cause challenge," rather than the proportionality challenge. Surprisingly, national defense is a right that even dysfunctional or corrupt states possess; they possess this right even though they have no intrinsic or instrumental value.

In addressing the just cause challenge, I argue that the UN Charter treats the use of force as a crime of means.[13] The Charter prohibits any use of force, including bloodless invasion, as the means for promoting any political goal such as secession, annexation, or regime change. Even a state whose regime should be changed by external coercion (through, say, political and economic pressure that involves collaterally harming innocents) has a right to keep its regime from being changed by military force. Similarly, a state whose borders ought to be redrawn by external coercion has a right that its territorial integrity not be violated by military invasion.

I argue in this chapter that, so understood, the regime that the Charter embeds is morally justified. In rare cases, international actors might have a *pre-contractual* liberty-right to use force to implement political or distributive justice. They nevertheless should undertake a duty not to do so even in these cases. Article 51 of the UN Charter, which allows defensive wars, is an essential element of this regime; a permission to go to defensive wars is the most effective way to enforce the duty not to change the status quo by military force.

---

[12] For a careful analysis of the proportionality challenge, see Seth Lazar, "National Defense, Self-Defense, and the Problem of Political Aggression," in *The Morality of Defensive War*, eds. Fabre and Lazar. I borrow the term "purely political aggression" from Lazar.

[13] Arthur Ripstein explores this idea in great depth in his "Beyond the Harm Principle," *Philosophy and Public Affairs* 34 (2006): 215–45, and elsewhere.

I proceed as follows. Section I presents the proportionality challenge and the way it was addressed by individualists. Following other critics of reductive individualism, I argue that as a morality of killing in war, reductive individualism is inconsistent with the *jus ad bellum* code that the Charter embeds. In Section II, I sketch the non-individualist responses to the proportionality challenge. Ultimately, they fail to address it as well. Section III presents the case of the 1982 war in Lebanon that Israel initiated; I then offer a hypothetical (inspired by this case) to show that even a dysfunctional state that has no moral standing (according to all theories sketched in the first two sections) has a right against aggression and a right to national defense. Section IV sketches a contractarian theory of the right to national defense that addresses both the just cause challenge and the proportionality challenge.

I Reductive Individualism and the Proportionality Challenge

A purely political aggression is not merely a hypothetical that philosophers invented: nations have sometimes been bloodlessly annexed and incorporated into a larger nation, by force. The U.S. annexation of Hawaii at the end of the nineteenth century is a case in point. Done for purely economic reasons, the American aggression was obviously wrong. The invasion was bloodless, since the queen of Hawaii had decided to surrender to prevent bloodshed.[14]

Did Hawaii have a right to use lethal force in defending its sovereignty? A negative answer suggests itself: Hawaii became part of the Union, and its subjects became equal members in the American constituency. The process was illegitimate and involved rights violation. But, on the face of it, this is not a reason to kill innocents.

The Hawaii case raises more general questions: Can a defensive war which involves intentionally killing unjust combatants and collaterally killing unjust noncombatants be proportionate, even if it is fought against a threat that is purely political? Is it permissible to kill to avert aggressions whose aim is merely expansionist?[15]

In discussing these questions, Cécile Fabre offers several helpful observations. First, killing to avert purely political aggression is proportionate if the individuals' prospects for a minimally decent life radically diminish in case the aggressor

---

[14] For a short overview of this case (including the queen's statement), see www.hawaii-nati on.orgsoa.html, and for a philosophical analysis of it (on which I am relying) see Anna Stilz, "Authority, Self-Determination, and Community in Cosmopolitan War," *Law and Philosophy* 33 (2014) no. 3: 309–35.

[15] For a negative answer to this question, see Richard Norman, *Ethics, Killing and War*, New York: Cambridge University Press, 1995, p. 133; Rodin, *War and Self-Defense*, pp. 133–38; Rodin "The Myth of National Defense"; and Seth Lazar, "National Defense, Self-Defense, and the Problem of Political Aggression"; the last two are in *The Morality of Defensive War*, eds. Fabre and Lazar.

achieves her aims.[16] But in and of itself, this observation cannot explain all considered judgments. The law and commonsense morality assert that states are permitted to use lethal force in self-defense in a wider range of cases.

Fabre further argues that killing in addressing a purely political aggression might be proportionate in other circumstances: suppose unjust combatants pose a lethal threat to defenders but only if defenders resist the threat that the aggressor poses to their interests in political autonomy. In these cases, victims resisting the nonlethal threat posed to them will foreseeably cause aggressors to pose an imminent threat to their lives. Fabre maintains that intentionally killing in self-defense in such cases might be proportionate. Although the initial threat was only to victims' lesser interests (their interest in political freedom or in maintaining certain state institutions), the relevant proportionality calculation at the time where defensive lethal force is exercised is with the threat to life. The fact that the lethal threat was created by defenders' resistance rather than by the initial threat to the defenders' political rights should not matter.

Fabre's claim can be strengthened: suppose a mugger demands your money and you cannot prevent the robbery except by killing him; lethal defense would be disproportionate unless a more modest response (such as, say, beating him) would bring the mugger to kill you. In that case you do face a (conditional) unjustified threat to your life. And, lethal self-defense seems proportionate.[17] If a defender would later use lethal force in response to the lethal threat from the mugger, "why can't she proceed immediately to the lethal defense?"[18]

Seth Lazar's response to this argument offers an example that suggests that the mugger case is far from being intuitive: suppose the "aggressor" is about to insult a defender in a way that does not threaten a serious interest of hers. The defender knows that if she tries to prevent the aggressor from insulting her by using force against him, he will try to kill her. Needless to say, it is disproportionate for the defender to use lethal force before the insulter has had the chance to do so: "Lethal force is not a proportionate means to stop someone insulting you," and it cannot be rendered proportionate by the fact that if you attempt to use force, the insulter will try to defend himself by resorting to lethal force.[19]

Another attempt to address the proportionality challenge posed by the case of bloodless invasion observes that reductive proportionality calculation might appeal to the advantages that individuals gain from impersonal and collective goods.[20] Suppose I value my democratic, free, and just state because it secures

[16] Cécile Fabre, *Cosmopolitan War*, Oxford: Oxford University Press, 2012, chap. 2, see in particular, p. 69.

[17] For a nuanced re-articulation of this view which I do not address here, see Cécile Fabre, "Cosmopolitanism and Wars of Self-Defense," in *The Morality of Defensive War*, eds. Fabre and Lazar pp. 103–13.

[18] Lazar, "National Defense, Self-Defense, and the Problem of Political Aggression," p. 30.

[19] Ibid., p. 27. I somewhat modified Lazar's case.   [20] Ibid., pp. 32–33.

my well-being in a dignified way. I do not value any other state, even those that have the same features, merely because I am unrelated to these states in the way I am related to my own. Among other things, demolishing the state that I am attached to is hard to justify because of these relational facts. But might using lethal force in its defense be proportionate because of my, and my conationals', special relation to it?

As both Seth Lazar and Jeremy Davis observe, if the proportionality of national defense depends on the aggregate advantages that individuals gain from it, a state's all-things-considered justification to use force in defending its sovereignty and territorial integrity would depend on the numbers of individuals who are attached to it and value it. If this were so, it would follow that the value of big states adds up to more than that of small states, since many individuals are attached to highly populated states, while only few are attached to small states. Therefore, the big state has more total value than the small one, and using lethal force in its defense is more likely to be proportionate. But this result is both counterintuitive and inconsistent with international law. As Davis observes, all else being equal, the sovereignty of Australia (with a population of about 23 million) is not more or less defensible than that of New Zealand (with a population of about 4.5 million).[21]

Finally, and most importantly, David Luban is right in urging us to acknowledge that reductive individualism is inconsistent with the UN Charter, for a more fundamental reason. A true commitment to individualist morality implies a radically revisionist conception of just cause for war. If states possess merely a derivative right to national defense, "we should be able to define [just cause] directly in terms of human rights, without the needless detour of talk about states . . . the rights of states are derived from the rights of humans, and are thus in a sense one kind of human rights."[22]

II A Kantian Response to the Proportionality Challenge

This section and the next one present non-reductionist justifications to the "inherent right" to national defense that Article 51 confers on states. Those theories assert that a purely political aggression against a legitimate state is wrong because it threatens to demolish an entity whose value cannot be cashed out by reductive individualism. To distinguish between the collective (or impersonal) values that good states allegedly supply, I use Fabre's articulation of the distinction between a state, a regime, and a political community. A *legitimate state* is "the set of institutions and the individuals who occupy roles within those institutions, which together govern over a given territory in a legitimate way," while a *legitimate regime* "is a subset of these institutions

---

[21] Jeremy Davis, "Toward a Non-Reductionist National Defense" (unpublished ms.).
[22] David Luban, "Just War and Human Rights," p. 166.

which are tasked with enacting and enforcing the laws of the state." *Political community* is a group of individuals linked by a set of shared political values and ideals who inhabit a given territory and are represented by a state.[23] The views sketched in this and the following sections attach value to the legitimacy of sufficiently just states; the culture and history of the people(s) whom states represent; and the agency, self-determination, and autonomy of the political society/societies to which legitimate states belong.

On the Kantian/statist view that Anna Stilz developed recently, a state has a right to its sovereignty and territorial integrity if three conditions are met.[24] First, the individuals represented by that state have a right claim to occupy a particular territory over which the state rules. Second, the state imposes a legitimate legal system on the territory by enacting and enforcing personal and property law there.

To understand the third condition, we should first note that individuals are under duty to enter a well-ordered political society (or a rightful condition) that only legitimate states can form; they cannot live together in a condition of justice in "the state of nature." States can acquire jurisdiction over a territory simply by imposing a sufficiently just scheme of law, a system whose reasonable addressees should have accepted to realize their political freedom. Yet – this is the third condition – a state has a right against regime change, annexation, colonization, or secession only if its citizenry has willingly established a relationship of political cooperation through the political framework this state established.[25]

Consider a state – call it Well-Ordered – that meets the Kantian criteria. Imagine that its sovereignty and territorial integrity are threatened by a state that fails the Kantian test. In that case, demolishing the rightful condition of the political community of Well-Ordered might be so bad that preventing it by killing innocents is a lesser evil. Indeed, killing innocents while defending the political framework that Well-Ordered maintains might be proportionate even if most of Well-Ordered's citizens can find another decent political home. It is the just institutions of Well-Ordered, and the rightful condition that these institutions form, that should be protected. Hence, justice and political autonomy might be a just cause for war.[26]

Notwithstanding this result, the Kantian view is inconsistent with the UN regime.[27] First, the proportionality challenge is not fully resolved since it is hard to compare the value of a rightful condition (that a legitimate state establishes and maintains) to the value of the lives of the innocents who

---

[23] Fabre, *Cosmopolitan Wars*, p. 15.

[24] Stilz, "Territorial Rights and National Defense."

[25] For the detailed account, see Anna Stilz, "Nations, States, and Territory," *Ethics* 121 (2011): 572–601.

[26] Stilz, "Territorial Rights and National Defense," p. 225.

[27] Stilz acknowledges that her view does not ground our pre-theoretical intuitions.

would be killed in maintaining it. It is hard to determine how many innocent people it would be proportionate to kill in protecting Well-Ordered and its territorial integrity.

Second, Stilz's Kantian view still faces the just cause challenge. If a just state such as Well-Ordered can bloodlessly invade an unjust state (which I will call Divided) – a state whose citizens do not fulfill their natural duty to form a legitimate political framework – then it is permissible for Well-Ordered to annex Divided's territory, and to accommodate its population. Note that this is true even if Divided is not murderous, even if, that is, Divided respects basic human rights. Indeed, we can suppose that Divided fails the Kantian test of legitimacy because it does not generate a well-ordered regime of property rights, or because it has not enough enforcement power to implement it. Annexing Divided seems permissible, under the Kantian view, but impermissible under the *jus ad bellum* embedded in the UN Charter.

Worse, the Kantian view does not protect democracies from a forced regime change. Consider a hypothetical war between two democracies.[28] Suppose that Canadians are bothered by the extraordinary role played by private money in the U.S. political system. Canadians realize that those who most profit from the U.S. system support the politicians that preserve it and in doing so secure an effective veto over policy innovations. Canada concludes that not only does respect for democracy not stand in the way of invasion, but, moreover, the invasion will institute a comprehensive, transparent, publicly funded democracy, which is a much better form of democracy.

Finally, as Stilz concedes, her Kantian view denies the right to kill and maim in defense of one's interest in a *willing* compliance with one's just institutions. The very identity of one's national home is not a reason for intentional or collateral killing. *A fortiori*, maintaining a relatively unjust regime does not constitute a reason to go to war that involves killing if the alternative is a better regime, regarding welfare, political, and human rights fulfillment.[29]

III   The Communitarian Responses to the Proportionality Challenge

In light of the results of reductive individualism and the Kantian conception of the moral standing of states, communitarians and nationalists advance a different interpretation of the right to sovereignty, territorial integrity, and national defense. On the communitarian view, while the law confers these rights on states, morally speaking, their prime holders are the political communities to which states "belong." The core idea was articulated by Michael Walzer: the right to political independence depends "upon the reality of the

---

[28] I borrow this example from Christopher Kutz, "Democracy, Defense, and the Threat of Intervention," in *The Morality of Defensive War*, eds. Fabre and Lazar, p. 234.

[29] Stilz, "Territorial Rights and National Defense," p. 228.

common life it protects and the extent to which the sacrifices required by that protection are willingly accepted and thought worthwhile."[30]

Margaret Moore reads this idea as follows: political communities have a claim for self-determination since they realize justice in their own way.[31] Their right to self-determination is justified by the solidarity and the feelings of co-membership, co-participation, and commitment to a common political project, which enable members of this community to practice their conception of justice. Christopher Kutz reads it somewhat differently. He believes that a defensible community manifests a collective agency that depends on (but is not constituted by) the ties of identity, culture, and sympathy. Group agency has a distinctive intrinsic value: "deplorable as our policy ... is, it is all the same *our* policy ... and that policy deserves respect and non-intervention."[32]

Following Walzer, Kutz infers that undemocratic or unjust states might well have a weighty claim to self-determination because self-determination and political freedom are not equivalent terms: "The first is the more inclusive idea; it describes not only a particular institutional arrangement but also the process by which a community arrives at that arrangement – or does not." A state is self-determining even "if its citizens struggle and fail to establish free institutions."[33] Moreover, whether the state and the political community are normatively integrated is a matter for the members of the community to judge, not for outsiders. Kutz insists that a nondemocratic state might manifest collective action through its overall structure of organization: his agentic view "locates value at the level of the active community ... the political community formed by that agency has moral standing in its own right – a standing that generates the right of communal ... self-defense.[34] Hence, non-liberal states lose the right of national defense only in cases of gross abuse.

Moore draws from the communitarian idea a similar conclusion: since political communities (not states) bear a right to national defense, then, although "Saddam's government was illegitimate, it didn't mean that invasion was permissible, because the right is held by the people ... even if Somalia is a failed state, in the sense that its authority does not extend across its geographical domain and it has no functioning government, this does not mean that the people lose the right to defend themselves as a people capable of exercising self-government."[35]

This similarity notwithstanding, the Moore and the Kutz interpretations lead to different practical verdicts: Moore believes that intervention against an

---

[30] Walzer, *Just and Unjust Wars*, p. 54.
[31] Margaret Moore, "Collective Self-Determination, Institutions of Justice, and Wars of National Defense" *The Morality of Defensive War*, eds. Fabre and Lazar, pp. 193–94.
[32] Kutz, "Democracy, Defense, and the Threat of Intervention," pp. 234–35.
[33] Walzer, "The Moral Standing of States," p. 211.
[34] Kutz, "Democracy, Defence, and the Threat of Intervention," p. 244.
[35] Moore, "Collective Self-Determination, Institutions of Justice, and Wars of National Defense," p. 193.

illegitimate government or a failed state on behalf of an oppressed political community is perfectly permissible, especially if the community asks for an intervention or consents to it. Walzer and Kutz seem to believe that this intervention compromises the ideal of group agency and therefore of self-determination: "a democracy is something that can, structurally, be developed from the inside out."[36] Other things being equal, intervention is less desirable than revolution or self-improvement.

This analysis of the right to self-determination suggests a simple interpretation of the territorial right that states possess. Maintaining and practicing a common way of life require some geographical space. If a state protects its citizens' common life, then it has a weighty claim to self-determination in a territory to which their national ethos relates them. Presumably, this is because over time, nations "mix" their culture with the land they have historically inhabited, shaping its physical appearance and infrastructure. The value they added gives them a special claim to reside in the territory and exercise jurisdiction over it.[37] Therefore, the boundaries that mark off a people's territory, and the state that defends these boundaries for the sake of the common life that individuals develop within it, have a "presumptive value."[38]

The communitarian justification of territorial rights is less conservative than it might seem.[39] Citing Hobbes, Walzer argues that an invasion to an empty land, or to a land that is not sufficiently inhabited, should not be considered aggression "as far as the lives of the original natives are not threatened." Moreover, there might be cases in which the original natives ought to move over to make room for the invaders: "Hobbes is right to set aside any consideration of territorial integrity-as-ownership and to focus instead on life."[40]

Finally, the communitarian analysis of the right to self-determination suggests a simple interpretation of the defensive right that states possess. Kutz believes that the value of group agency might clarify the justice of national defense: "violence is justified when it is essential to the formation of a

---

[36] Kutz, "Democracy, Defense, and the Threat of Intervention," p. 244.

[37] David Miller, *National Responsibility and Global Justice*, Oxford: Oxford University Press, 2007, p. 217; and Miller, "Territorial Rights: Concept and Justification," *Political Studies* 60 (2012): 252–68, at p. 264.

[38] Walzer, *Just and Unjust Wars*, pp. 56–57. Responding to a communitarian interpretation of the right to self-determination, statists argue that nations are not discrete, delineable cultural wholes, coextensive with geographically bounded population groups (Stilz, "Territorial Rights and National Defense," p. 205).

[39] As Stilz reads it, Walzer's view entails that if a group of settlers drives out inhabitants of a certain territory and sets up a perfect state in it, the settlers would have a territorial right over the territory. But I think she misunderstands Walzer: in the passage she quotes, Walzer tries to distinguish between titles that a *state* has over a territory and its territorial right, arguing that formal titles of states are less important than the relation between living cultural groups and the territory they demand.

[40] Walzer, *Just and Unjust Wars*, p. 57. See also Luban, "Just Wars and Human Rights," p. 177; and Beitz, *Political Theory in International Relations*, pp. 175–76.

collective democratic agent – a people defining a politics in their own name."[41] This seems right: a collective-agency–based right to self-determination yields a broader range of self-defensive rights than a purely moralized theory of war (which rests on individual interests and individual measures of culpability and liability). Moore believes that a rule permitting national defense has a lesser evil justification. If we are not permitted to fight back against purely political aggression, then all peoples are at risk of having their collective self-determination undermined and will live in an institutional order characterized by relations of domination and subordination.[42]

And yet, ultimately, these responses to the proportionality challenge leave it unaddressed: first, just as it is difficult to measure the value of a concrete rightful condition that a legitimate state constitutes and compare it to the value of lives of innocents, so it is hard to compare the value of innocent lives to the value of an ongoing way of life (Walzer), to the value of collective agency (Kutz), or to the value of solidarity and the concrete conception of justice that solidarity maintains (Moore). Averting the purely political aggression by killing has not been shown to be a lesser evil.

Furthermore, like reductive individualism, communitarian theories fail to address the just cause challenge, and therefore they are all inconsistent with the Charter's conception of just cause. The Charter allows states to protect their internationally recognized borders by deadly force however poorly – and unjustly – they have been drawn; *pace* Walzer (and Hobbes), a defensive war is legal (and seems to be moral as well) even if the territorial integrity of a state has nothing to do with the value of group agency, the way of life of a community, and the solidarity that enables individuals to practice a shared conception of justice.

Similarly, states are entitled to use force to prevent aggression against their political independence even when purely political aggression would bring about a better political framework. Imagine cases where, thanks to the intervention in the internal affairs of a dysfunctional state, this state better supports the cultures of the political communities living in it; or suppose the external military intervention enhances the capacity of a political society to exercise group agency; or suppose that thanks to the intervention, solidarity in this society is enhanced, and it does better in elaborating its own conception of justice. Even then, the use of force is legally prohibited.

If my reading of the UN regime is correct, then whatever the values that underlie the moral standing of states (i.e., the value that grounds their moral right to their sovereignty and territorial integrity), the legal right of states against aggression and their legal right to national defense are independent

---

[41] Kutz, "Democracy, Defense, and the Threat of Intervention," p. 243.

[42] Moore, "Collective Self-Determination, Institutions of Justice, and Wars of National Defense," p. 198.

of these values. Implementing political justice by force through violating the sovereignty or territorial integrity of a dysfunctional or clearly unjust state is illegal, even if it is legally permissible to demolish this state, reshape its regime, or redraw its borders *by other coercive means*. It is legally impermissible to use force but permissible to use soft-power measures, such as economic and diplomatic sanctions, even if these measures would be as harmful to innocents.

To show that this legislation might be morally justified, the next section describes an imaginary non-defensive war that Well-Ordered initiates against Divided – a dysfunctional, corrupt state, whose political society is thoroughly and irrecoverably sectarian. There is a very good reason to coercively reshape Divided's regime and force its political society to reorganize itself through, say, secession or annexation. The theories reviewed so far have no resources to explain why international actors should not use force in doing this. In Section V, I offer a contractarian justification for this prohibition.

IV   A Historic Example Followed by a Hypothetical

Before elaborating the Well-Ordered/Divided hypothetical, let me present a real war that inspires it: I am referring to the war that Israel initiated against certain political groups that were based in Lebanon in the early eighties. I refer to this war as "the 1982 Lebanon War" or as we call it in Israel "the first Lebanon War." Some generals and politicians on the Israeli side believed (or pretended to believe) that the Lebanon war was a clash between a well-ordered society represented by a legitimate state and a divided society represented by a dysfunctional state. Israel was constantly threatened by the instability of a deeply sectarian society that could not rule its territory by law and had no effective monopoly on the use of force within it. Lebanon, they inferred, had no right against military invasion.[43] I am not entitled to examine this factual analysis; I argue, however, that even had it been accurate, the first Lebanon war would have been illegal and unjust, and that Lebanon had the right to defend itself by lethal force.

The Lebanon War began on June 6, 1982, when the Israeli Defense Force invaded southern Lebanon. The "official" cause of the invasion, as Prime Minister Menachem Begin put it to the Israeli parliament, was to eliminate the threat that the Palestine Liberation Organization (PLO) posed to the Israeli north. Begin himself conceded later that the threat that the PLO posed was not imminent – that the war had been a preventive rather than a preemptive war.

For weeks, most members of the Israeli government, most parliament members, and the majority of the Israeli public were led to believe that the aims of

---

[43] For the factual claims I make on the first Lebanon war, I am relying on Ze'ev Schiff and Ehud Ya'ari, *Israel's Lebanon War*, New York: Simon & Schuster, 1984.

the war were limited: conquering 40 kilometers in southern Lebanon to distance Israel's north from the scope of PLO rockets. Yet, it soon became clear that
the secretary of defense, Ariel Sharon, and a group of generals who followed
him, had a hidden agenda: they aimed to force a regime change in Lebanon and
to undermine the Syrian influence in it. They hoped that under the new regime,
Lebanon would be much less hostile to Israel and much less supportive of the
PLO.

Could a war whose aim is a regime change in Lebanon be just? A positive
answer that supporters of the war might offer can be based on the following
factual analysis (whose validity is not assessed here). The Lebanese society
was deeply divided between Maronite Christians, Sunni Muslims, Shia
Muslims, and a large Druze community. Each group dominated a certain
territory. The Lebanese Constitution was pro-Western and relatedly, favored
a leading position for the Christians. It underrepresented the large Muslim
population; therefore, an opposition of pan-Arabist and secular left-wing
groups to the pro-Western government became more and more powerful.

Lebanon was in the midst of a bloody civil war, which it had no chance of
ending by unification: the military groups that fought each other represented
the communities to which their leaders belonged, and openly identified with
them. The two main alliances were the Lebanese Front, consisting of nationalist
Maronite Christians, and the Lebanese National Movement, which consisted of
pro-Palestinian leftists. Each side was supported by two more stable and more
powerful countries. In 1976, Syrian troops moved into Lebanon under the guise
of the Palestine Liberation Army to bring the PLO back under Syrian influence
and to prevent the disintegration of Lebanon. Israel (and the United States) had
supported the Maronite Christians for many years. *De facto* Lebanon had no
political autonomy.

Based on this factual analysis, supporters of a coerced regime change insist
that Lebanese state institutions had no moral standing. Since Lebanon's political instability and weakness were dangerous for Israel, Israel had a right to use
force to implement a regime change that would make Lebanon less hostile.
Israel initiated a war during which its support of the Maronite Christians, led by
Bashir Gemayel, became open and official. And, after a siege on Beirut that
caused the PLO leader Yasser Arafat to leave Lebanon for Tunisia, Gemayel was
elected president. Three weeks later he was assassinated, and soon thereafter, a
horrific massacre in a Palestinian refugees camp (known as the Sabra and
Shatila massacre) occurred.

I argue that, even had the factual analysis been accurate – even if there were
a weighty moral reason to force a regime change in Lebanon or to annex some
of its territory – a war whose aim is doing so is morally impermissible:
international law justifiably prohibits using force in implementing political
justice and/or justice in the distribution of territories. Indeed, with the exception of humanitarian intervention or an intervention in the internal affairs of a

brutal state (such as North Korea or Saddam's Iraq), a contract (that states ought to enter) would rule out unprovoked use of force, *independently of its aims*.

To clarify this claim, let me apply it to a hypothetical that abstracts from the muddy reality. Suppose that the main aspects of the simplistic story that was told about Lebanon are true of Divided. The political community to which Divided belongs is divided into four powerful ethnic groups, and other weakened minorities; members of each powerful group have different ethnic origins, societal cultures, and religions. The hostility between the groups is an essential element of their history and the historical memories and the self-identification of their members. The four sects do not form a group agent, and, given the animosity and mistrust between their members, they cannot become a group agent. Furthermore, the weakness of the civil society in Divided makes it extremely vulnerable to external forces.

After a long and bloody civil war, an unstable, paralyzing compromise between the four big groups was achieved: each group controls a proper subset of the state institutions. Divided is corrupt first and foremost because the public interest has no action-guiding role in the institutional decision making of its leaders. The main goal of role holders in these institutions is gaining more political power for themselves within their groups, and gaining more political clout for the group to which they belong. As a result, mistrust, bribery, and other types of corruption become prevalent.

It seems that according to all theories that I have sketched earlier, Divided has no moral right to territorial integrity or to political independence. The institutional arrangement that Divided enforces is illegitimate. Since bribery is the only way to do things there, Divided does not establish a regime of property rights by which individuals can realize their political freedom. Divide's civil society is too polarized, and the suspicion and distrust between the groups are thorough; no shared civil culture can be created by these groups. Since group agency depends upon the ties of identity, culture, and sympathy, Divided has no chance of becoming the national home of a group agent.

The other hero of our story is Well-Ordered. Its regime is sufficiently just and therefore legitimate, by the Kantian criteria. Well-Ordered is the national home of a civil society whose members share a stable and solid societal culture; hence, its moral standing is indisputable under the Walzerian view. Well-Ordered requires some of Divided's territory for security reasons: Divided is unstable, and hostile groups within it permanently pose immature threats to its neighbors. Well-Ordered can now conquer the territory by using force. This would violate the sovereignty and territorial integrity of Divided; still, since Well-Ordered is so much stronger than Divided, the invasion is expected to be bloodless. Being members of the weakened groups in Divided, inhabitants of the conquered territory are underrepresented by its regime; the occupation would not worsen their condition, nor would it compromise the fulfillment of their political rights.

International law does not condemn changing the status quo in Divided by coercive measures. Well-Ordered might try to impose economic sanctions. It might campaign for secession, using propaganda to convince the residents of the territory that it would like to annex to struggle for secession; Well-Ordered might openly or secretly support one of the groups in Divided, if this might further its security. Yet, Well-Ordered ought not to change the status quo by using force.

Compare the way the Charter treats the use of force to the way it is handled within domestic societies. I grow sunflowers in my yard, and you put up a garage in yours, thereby depriving me of light. My sunflowers die. You harm me but do not wrong me. You do wrong me if you bring about the same outcome by violating my sovereignty: you ruin my sunflowers by trespassing in my yard or by using force against me.[44] Likewise, you might permissibly harm me by opening a competing business that lures away my customers, but you ought not to bring about the same outcome by stealing a patent and selling it in the free market, even if both actions are equally harmful to me.[45] The Kantian explanation appeals to autonomy: no person is in charge of another; people are free to act in pursuing their own goals as far as they do not violate each other's autonomy, as it is defined by the rightful condition within which they live.

Similarly, I suggest that the Charter regulates the means that a state might use in pursuing ends, rather than the ends being pursued. Use of force is an inappropriate means for promoting the good, even if it involves no bloodshed and, consequently, has no bad effects. This legal regime seems to accord with our considered moral judgments: even those who believe that international law should allow humanitarian intervention against a brutal, oppressive (even if not murderous) regime concede that in less extreme cases, where a state is merely corrupt, dysfunctional, irrecoverably divided, and so on, bloodless military intervention whose aim is annexation or a regime change is morally impermissible. And yet, Kantian sovereignty-based explanations cannot be applied to the Divided/Well-Ordered war: it would be better if Divided ceased to exist, and another state founded in its stead; it would be better if its borders were to be redrawn. Divided has *no* right claim to prevent actors from taking coercive measures to demolish its regime and/or redraw its borders. The point of international law is different: these outcomes should not be brought about by use of force, even if they cannot be brought about by nonmilitary coercion.

We now come to the question: Why shouldn't Well-Ordered bloodlessly use proportionate force to redraw better borders in Divided?

---

[44] Arthur Ripstein, *Force and Freedom*, Cambridge: Cambridge University Press, 2009, p. 78.
[45] Ibid., p. 22.

V   The UN Charter and the Value of Unjust Peace

I argue in this section that even a dysfunctional state such as Divided might have a contractual right claim preventing international actors from using force against it: if certain conditions (to be presented shortly) are met, the right against aggression and the remedial right to use force in addressing it are two essential elements in a mutually beneficial and fair contractual regime that international persons should enter.[46]

The contract that the UN Charter embeds is mutually beneficial in circumstances where peace (even an unjust peace) tends to be better in terms of welfare and justice than wars whose aim is implementing justice. Under those circumstances, wars are expected to be counterproductive since resolving the conflicts between the warring parties by peaceful bargaining is typically *ex ante* better than fighting, to all parties involved in them. The UN contract aims to maintain peace by outlawing non-defensive wars (viz., first use of force) and by allowing states to prevent violations of their contractual claim by force against the aggressors. Indeed, the right to national defense is the most effective way to enforce the duties that the contract imposes, and, therefore, the right to wage defensive wars is the most efficient way to preserve peace.

Moreover, in the circumstance I describe, the contract that the Charter embeds is fair, despite the fact that it does rarely maintain unjust distribution of political power, territories, resources, and welfare. In these rare cases, negotiations, economic pressure, and diplomatic efforts are fruitless and useless, while violence might change the unjust status quo without being disproportionate. I argue that, nevertheless, the UN Charter prohibition on wars whose aim is implementing justice might be fair, if, in general, it is hard to obtain the information required to render pre-contractually just wars permissible. Since at least some states are naturally biased toward erring on the side of aggression, a fair contract would deny all states a right to wage all non-defensive wars, even wars that, absent the contract, would be permissible. By explicitly consenting to such a contract, decent states are able to keep those biases in check.

In the remainder of this section, I sketch out a model under which states and other international actors (such as non-state organizations that represent stateless nations) should enter a contract that prohibits all non-defensive wars. Under this model, decently partial states will accept it since they are prudent and modestly self-interested; they will undertake the contractual duty not to implement pre-contractual justice by force to advance their own self-interest.

---

[46] This section draws heavily on Yitzhak Benbaji, "Distributive Justice, Human Rights, and Territorial Integrity: A Contractarian Account of the Crime of Aggression" in *The Morality of Defensive Wars*, eds. Fabre and Lazar.

The model makes a series of realistic assumptions. The first concerns the interests of partial states: in the great majority of conflicts between states and between states and non-state actors, peaceful negotiations better advance the interests of all the parties. More formally, regarding most conflicts C between two partial/decent states, there is at least one peaceful resolution of C that is *ex ante* Pareto superior to a war whose aim is to resolve it.

Consider a conflict between two states, Weak and Strong, over resources whose value is 10,000 to both sides. Suppose that the probability that Weak will win the war is 0.3, while the probability of Strong's victory is 0.7. Suppose that the cost of the war for Weak is 2000. Then, Weak's expected benefit from the war is 1000. Therefore, any compromise or peaceful resolution of the conflict under which Weak accepts more than 1000 is *ex ante* better for Weak than going to war. Suppose further that the cost of the war for Strong is 3000. Hence, the expected benefit of its war against Weak is 4000. Therefore, any compromise under which Weak gets more than 1000 and Strong gets more than 4000 is *ex-ante* preferable to both parties than the costly war. Following James Fearon, I say that any agreement that commands Weak more than 1000 and Strong more than 4000 belongs to the "bargaining range" of the conflict. The Charter assumes that in our world, most conflicts between states resemble the one I have just illustrated.[47]

Fearon shows that despite the fact that peace is better than war to both parties, rationally led states might resolve it by going to (Pareto inferior) war. States in conflict (are known to each other to) have an incentive to present themselves as more powerful than they actually are, and to present their use of force as less costly to them than it would actually be. The obvious reason is that a successful bluff might secure a party a better deal: if Weak is able to convince Strong that its chance of winning is 0.4, Strong would offer a compromise under which Weak gets more than 2000. Thus, in many conflicts, both parties have a good reason to suspect that the other party is bluffing. Consequently, despite the fact that peace is better than war to both parties, they might nevertheless fight.

The model assumes that undertaking a duty not to use force in the future might help states avoid Pareto inferior wars. But it also assumes that a contract that commands pacifism and a complete disarmament is unstable; such a contract would not advance the interests of the parties. States need armies to address indecent actors and to deter decent actors from becoming indecent. Moreover, since decent states are partial, they would like to be able to use force in defense of (what they conceive to be) their rights. Hence, they prefer a disarmed world to a world in which most states have armies, and yet, each state would nevertheless like everyone *else* to be committed to pacifism and

---

[47] James Fearon, "Rationalist Explanations for War," *International Organization* 49 (1995): 379–414.

disarmament, while it alone retains its pre-contractual right to go to pre-contractually just wars. This would enable it to enforce what it takes to be its rights. In the absence of a universally recognized authority to ensure that all parties respect their commitment, a pacifistic contract that commands a disarmed world is unworkable.

Hence, the model assumes that in a decentralized world, a contract under which states undertake a duty not to use force is possible if (and only if) they enforce their contractual right by self-help. A valid contract would allow defensive wars against states that violated their contractual duty (viz., against states that went to wars that they believe to be pre-contractually just wars). A remedial right to use force in averting threats posed by wars that the contract prohibits is an essential element of the contract that the UN Charter embeds. Thus, under the contract, states have a right to eliminate an imminent threat to their territorial integrity, whether or not this threat is pre-contractually just.

As the model has been construed so far, the Charter might maintain peace by solidifying political injustice: Well-Ordered should not invade Divided, even if the invasion would be bloodless and the consequences of the invasion are better than the status quo in every respect (i.e., in terms of welfare, rights fulfillment, and justice). Another realistic assumption that the model makes explains why the contract is fair despite the possibility that it prohibits a proportionate war that eliminates unjust political arrangements and/or unjust differences in the distribution of territories. The assumption reads as follows: while, by entering the contract, states create a mechanism that prevents few wars that could have changed the status quo for the better, usually, even these wars should not be fought for reasons of normative uncertainty.

I offer two illustrations of the normative uncertainties that surround pre-contractually just wars. First, a war supported by standard lesser evil considerations (i.e., its good effects, as measured by standard consequentialism, outweigh its bad effects) might be overall impermissible merely because of the means by which the good effects have been achieved. Consequences are not all that matter. Yet, there is no clear-cut line between cases where the deontological principles render an action that promotes the good impermissible and cases where lesser evil considerations prevail.

Second, let's turn to distributive wars whose aim is a fairer distribution of resources and territories. The injustice of the global distribution of resources is clear enough: many people live in starvation or on its fringes, while others have plenty; we can know that almost any theory of distributive justice would render this situation as unfair. But this piece of knowledge does not entail any decisive verdict about the morality of wars whose aim is implementing distributive justice. An argument for the justice of such a war should identify an agent who is responsible for the wrongness of the distribution or at least an agent whose duty it is to eliminate this wrong. This knowledge is hard to obtain.

The Charter assumes that most wars would be unjustified under normative and factual uncertainties even if, actually, the cause of these wars is just (in the fact relative sense), the violence exercised there is necessary for achieving the cause, and the size of the harm to innocents is tiny. States should usually avoid these wars because of the normative uncertainty with respect to pre-contractual justice as well as the factual uncertainty with respect to how bloody the invasion will be. These uncertainties, on the one hand, and a generalization as to the huge moral cost that the great majority of wars involve on the other, entail that states should avoid most pre-contractually just wars.

Under the model described here, rationally self-interested, decent states/non-state actors would sign a contract that prohibits the use of force to promote their narrow self-interest. And, the system that emerges from this exchange of rights would also be better in terms of justice: thanks to it, states would not fight wars they should not fight for reasons of normative uncertainty.

The other side of this coin is the right liberty to national defense that the UN Charter legislates. To enforce the prohibition against pre-contractually just wars, the Charter allows states to use force in averting illegal threats to their territorial integrity and sovereignty. Violations of territorial integrity are the most visible link in the chains of events that lead to the Pareto inferior wars the Charter aims to prevent. Defining aggression as an unprovoked violation of territorial integrity (or, more precisely, as an imminent threat to do so) and determining it as the only just cause for war is the simplest and most effective way to enforce the terms of the Charter. It is therefore the most effective way to prevent wars that international actors ought not to fight.

Divided has a right claim not to be demolished by force as well as a right claim that its borders will not be redrawn by war, despite the fact that it has no right to political independence, and no right to territorial integrity. Those rights claims are conferred on it by a contract whose aim is to prevent all wars whose initiators attempt to implement pre-contractual justice in the distribution of territories, political power, and resources. The remedial right to self-help is the means taken by the society of states to ensure that international actors will advance justice in a peaceful way: bargaining; negotiations; and, in less happy circumstances, more coercive measures such as sanctions and diplomatic pressure. The right to self-defense is conferred on all states to maintain peace, which is one of the basic values that the Charter aims to implement.

Conclusion

The first purpose of the United Nations is

to maintain international peace and security, and to that end: to take effective collective measures for the prevention and removal of threats to the peace, and for the suppression of acts of aggression or other breaches of the peace, and to bring about by peaceful means, and in conformity with the principles of justice and international law, adjustment or settlement of international disputes or situations which might lead to a breach of the peace.

A second purpose is "to develop friendly relations among nations based on respect for the principle of equal rights and self-determination of peoples."

In many cases, the right of legitimate states against aggression and their right to national defense have to do with the second purpose of the UN: legitimate states have a right to their sovereignty, and the peoples they represent have a right to self-determination. Legitimate states rule in a way that enhances the autonomy of their subjects and supports the culture, way of life, and agency of the groups that they represent. Supposedly, the right of states to use force against an unjust aggressor is grounded also in the values of political autonomy, collective way of life, and collective agency.

However, I have argued that the ultimate grounds of the right to national defense have to do with the value of peace, as it is articulated in the first purpose of the Charter. The UN Charter is built on the assumption that global political and distributive justice should be implemented by peaceful means, not by war. The right to national defense is designed to deter just states from using force in resolving their disputes with unjust states or non-state actors.

4 Just Cause and the Continuous Application of *Jus ad Bellum*

Uwe Steinhoff

What one is ultimately interested in with regard to "just cause" is whether a *specific* war, actual or potential, is justified – for example, the concrete historical 2003 Iraqi war against the invading Coalition forces, or a war one is contemplating in response to some concrete aggression. I call this "the applied question." Answering this question requires knowing the empirical facts on the ground, but answering it with reference to any concrete historical or potential war is beyond the scope of the present chapter. However, an answer to the applied question regarding a specific war requires a prior answer to some more general questions, both descriptive and normative. It is these questions that are the subject of this chapter: What *kind of thing* is a "just cause" for war (an aim, an injury, or wrong suffered or something different altogether)? I call this "the formal question." Then there is what I call the "the general substantive question." Depending on the answer to the formal question, the general substantive question can be formulated as follows: Which causes are just? or as Under what conditions is there a just cause? A final question, which has recently elicited increased interest, is what I call "the question of timing": Does the just cause criterion only apply to the *initiation* of a war or also to the *continuation* of a war; that is, can a war that had a just cause at the beginning lose it at some point in its course (and vice versa)?

In the following I argue, regarding the formal question, that a just cause is a state of affairs. Moreover, the criterion of just cause is not independent of proportionality and other valid *jus ad bellum* criteria. One cannot know whether there is a just cause without knowing whether the other (valid) criteria (apart from "right intention") are satisfied. The advantage of this account is that it is applicable to all wars, even to wars in which nobody will be killed or when the enemy has not committed a rights violation but can be justifiably warred against anyway. This account also avoids the inefficiency of having proportionality considerations come up at two points: in a separate criterion of just cause and in the criterion of proportionality proper. As regards the general substantive question, I argue that all kinds of aims can, in principle, be legitimately pursued by means of war, even aims that might sound dubious

I thank Nicholas Parkin and the editors of this volume for useful written comments on earlier drafts of this chapter.

at first, such as vengeance or the search for glory. Thus, the pursuit of such aims does not make the war disproportionate or deprive it of just cause. As regards the question of timing, I argue that the criteria of *jus ad bellum* apply throughout the war, not only at the point of its initiation. While starting a war at t^1 might be justified, continuing it at time t^2 might be unjustified (and vice versa), and this insight does not require an addition to *jus ad bellum* but is already contained in it.

I   The Formal Question: What Kind of Thing Is a "Just Cause" for War?

The term "just cause" is used in different ways in just war theory and political discourse. In one sense, a just cause refers to what causes the war, to what *gives occasion* to it. As the sixteenth-century just war theorist Francisco de Vitoria states: "There is a single and only just cause for commencing a war, namely, a wrong received."[1] In law, for example, a so-called cause of action is a fact or set of facts sufficient to justify a right to sue to obtain money, property, or the enforcement of a right against another party. Clearly, a rights violation, or the fact that it has occurred, would give one a cause of action to sue for compensation or for the enforcement of the right. It is conceivable, therefore, that a rights violation can also provide a cause of action in other contexts: a rights violation might give one a justification to seriously consider the use of force, including military force. Whether one may then actually use force, however, might still be dependent on further conditions, in particular on whether the use of force would be proportionate and necessary.

In another sense of just cause, however, the term refers to a *goal or aim one is fighting for*. For instance, for Frances Kamm the term refers to "a limited set of goals, called a just cause, that would justify starting a war."[2] Thus in the first sense "just cause" refers to a rights violation (or at least an immoral act); in the second sense of the term it refers to the aim of defending against, rectifying, or punishing said rights violation.

Both uses of the term "just cause" are problematic. The problem with conceiving of just cause as an aim is that something can only be an aim if, in fact, somebody is aiming at it. However, if innocent people are threatened with total annihilation by a genocidal aggressor, it seems to make perfect sense to say that the attacked people have a just cause to resort to a war of self-defence even if they are all pacifists, do not aim at defending themselves (nor does anybody else) and in fact do not resort to war but allow the enemy to slaughter them. To say that under these circumstances they do not have a just cause is just to

---

[1] Francisco de Vitoria, *De Indis et de Iure Belli, Relectiones*, ed. Ernest Nys, New York and London: Oceana Publications and Wildy & Sons, 1964, Second Relectio, § 13, available at http://en.wikisource.org/wiki/De_Indis_De_Jure_Belli/Part_3.

[2] Frances Kamm, *Ethics for Enemies*, Oxford: Oxford University Press, 2011, p. 119.

confuse the criterion of just cause with the different one of right intention. In other words, there can be a just cause without anybody fighting for or intending to militarily achieve a certain just goal.[3]

In addition, Kamm's claim that a certain "limited set of goals" can "justify starting a war" is rather odd for a deontologist such as Kamm: after all, a defining element of deontology is the view that the ends (by themselves) do not justify the means. This is, of course, also the position taken by traditional just war theory, which insists on the satisfaction of criteria such as proportionality, last resort, and so on.

This leads us back to the first rendering of just cause: why should we not just conceive of just cause as a rights violation – or as the fact that a rights violation has occurred – and simultaneously accept that for the justification of a war more is needed than a mere rights violation?

There are two problems with this proposal. First, it seems implausible to say that every rights violation, even the mildest, is a just cause for war. If blogger A from state B insults innocent writer C from state D as an "untalented little pig," we would hardly consider this a just cause for war (nor would B's refusal to punish A be such a cause) – otherwise just cause could hardly still exercise a restraining function on the pursuit of war and would be misplaced in just war theory (which does purport to restrain war). Second, it is not conceptually impossible to have legitimate wars without any prior rights violation: there could be consensual wars, for example, or wars where two parties fight over scarce resources that both need to survive. Instead of saying that both parties are unjustified, it is arguably also possible to say that both parties have a necessity justification (and one should at least not exclude this possibility by definitional fiat). It should also be noted that the rights violation is supposed to be one that has been committed by the party one is warring against. However, there could in principle be situations where a third party credibly threatens to commit some catastrophic crime unless A wages some restrained war against innocent B. In this case, again, there can be a necessity or lesser evil justification to engage in a war.[4]

Thus, both senses of just cause discussed so far have serious shortcomings. Two alternative understandings of just cause, however, could avoid the shortcomings just mentioned (it remains to be seen whether they both avoid other shortcomings). The one defended here is to conceive of just cause as a criterion

---

[3] This also affects Steven P. Lee's account, according to which a "just cause is a *justifying reason*, that is, a reason for an action, such as going to war, that morally justifies (or helps to justify) it. A state goes to war for a reason or reasons, which may be just or unjust." See Lee, *Ethics and War: An Introduction*, Cambridge: Cambridge University Press, 2012, p. 73.

[4] For a related example, see Jeff McMahan, "Just Cause for War," *Ethics and International Affairs* 19 (2005): 1–21, at pp. 15–16. McMahan, however, denies that such wars have a just cause. Yet he has no plausible argument for this denial. See on this Uwe Steinhoff, "Just Cause and 'Right Intention'," *Journal of Military Ethics* 13 (2014) no. 1: 32–48, esp. at p. 37.

that is not independent of (all the) other just war criteria. On my account, proportionality is a sub-criterion of just cause; furthermore, last resort and prospects of success are sub-criteria of proportionality: whether a war is proportionate also depends on what other means are available and how likely they are to achieve the positive results the war is supposed to bring about. Thus one can only determine whether there is a just cause by considering these other criteria.[5]

This account is not so different from traditional accounts. For example, the sixteenth- and early seventeenth-century just war theorist Francisco Suárez explains that "not every cause [is] sufficient to justify war, *but only those causes which are serious and commensurate with the losses that the war would occasion. For it would be contrary to reason to inflict very grave harm because of a slight injustice.*"[6] Thus in Suárez's account the presence of a just cause for war is not independent of proportionality considerations; on the contrary, only by taking proportionality into account can one establish whether or not there is a just cause for war. Luis de Molina, around the same time, takes the same position, talking of "a just cause *in comparison to the damages that will be inflicted* by the war."[7] He further clarifies that "there is a just cause for war if we take possession of that which belongs to us or is owed to us, *provided that we cannot obtain it in any other way than by the means of war,*"[8] thus connecting just cause also with the criterion of last resort: if there are less harmful means to get what others owe you, there is no just cause for war in the first place.

The second alternative, in contrast, is to claim that a just cause for war is an aim of a certain, particularly weighty kind. That is, authors taking this route conceive of the criterion of just cause as some kind of list of acceptable aims that a war is to achieve, for example: defending the nation against an aggressor, stopping a genocide, toppling a tyrant, and so on. (Some authors, alternatively, consider a just cause as being a list of rights violations that a war is supposed to avert, for example: aggressive invasion, genocide, tyranny, etc. However, this approach cannot overcome the second problem mentioned earlier.) These authors regard just cause as independent of proportionality (and

---

[5] I do not regard last resort and prospects of success as *necessary* conditions for the justification of a war, though; still, they need to be taken into account. I do not need to go into this any further for present purposes, but see Uwe Steinhoff, *On the Ethics of War and Terrorism,* Oxford: Oxford University Press, 2007, pp. 23–25 and 28–30, where I further discuss these two criteria and their relation to proportionality.

[6] Francisco Suárez, *Selections from Three Works of Francisco Suarez,* Vol. 2, Oxford: Clarendon Press; London: Humphrey Milford, 1944, p. 816, my emphasis. Compare also Melchor Cano, "Questio XL 'De Bello'" (Prima Quaestio, Sexta Conclusio), in Heinz-Gerhard Justenhoven and Joachim Stüben, eds., *Kann Krieg erlaubt sein? Eine Quellensammlung zur politischen Ethik der Spanischen Spätscholastik,* Stuttgart: Kohlhammer, 2006, p. 151.

[7] Molina, "Questio XL 'De Bello'" (Articulus Primus, Disputatio Segunda, 50), ibid., p. 271, my emphasis.

[8] Ibid. (23), p. 247, my emphasis.

last resort and prospects of success). They think that only particularly important aims can be a just cause for war, and that there can be a just cause for war without the war being just or justified (even if the condition of right intention is satisfied): the war might still be disproportionate or not a last resort, for instance. Since war normally involves the killing of persons, these authors seem to think a just cause must be an aim (or rights violation) that can in principle justify killing people to achieve the aim or stop, mitigate, or punish the rights violation.

I reject this approach for three reasons. The first reason is that war does not *necessarily* involve the killing of people,[9] and thus such non-lethal wars can be justified even if the aims pursued in them cannot justify the killing of people. The second reason not to conceive of a just cause as an aim of a certain kind, in particular, an aim that can in principle justify killing (or at least maiming) people is that such a conception has the embarrassing consequence of making just causes shoot up like mushrooms and in the most unlikely places. The aim of avoiding the killing of innocent people through enemy force is certainly an aim that can in principle justify killing the killers in self- or other-defence. Yet in virtually all[10] modern wars, including those that allegedly have a just cause and are justified, innocent bystanders are "collaterally" killed even by the justified side. Thus if Noble Defender State invades Evil Genocidal State to stop the latter's ongoing genocide of some ethnic group and in the process kills only *one* innocent bystander collaterally, then every state, on the account criticized here, suddenly has a just cause of war against Noble Defender State, even Evil Genocidal State. This seems absurd.

The third reason for rejecting this approach is that it is impossible to give a list of all aims that "could in principle" justify a war without in the end relying on some more general criteria. In other words, while one can indeed give some examples, in the end one has to say (or imply) things such as the following: "Just causes are those aims the pursuit of which by means of war can in principle, that is, under conditions that are at least possible, satisfy the criteria of proportionality, last resort, and so on." However, this has the consequence that we end up using the criterion of proportionality (and other criteria) twice: first to establish whether there are in principle conditions under which measures involving the killing of people are proportionate and necessary means to retaliate against a foreign power's insulting one's own king, and subsequently to establish whether this is so *in the concrete case*. What, one might wonder, is the purpose of this procedure, given that it seems to be somewhat superfluous and uneconomical? After all, the result of the second application of the criteria

---

[9] This might appear to be a weird claim, but I have shown elsewhere that it is not. See "What Is War – And Can a Lone Individual Wage One?" *International Journal of Applied Philosophy* 23 (2009) vol. 1: 133–50, at pp.141–42; and "Just Cause and 'Right Intention'," pp. 34–35.

[10] Not necessarily in absolutely all wars.

is decisive, not the result of the first one, and the second application by no means presupposes the first one.

The previous three objections, incidentally, do not just apply to the view that a just cause is an aim of a certain, particularly weighty kind, but also to the view that a just cause is a rights violation of a certain, particularly severe kind.[11] It is instructive, and also further confirms my assessment of the two approaches, that Jeff McMahan, who has provided the most elaborate defence of the importance of weight or severity in this context in the past,[12] has recently felt compelled to abandon this position precisely, it seems, in the light of the first and the third objections just mentioned.[13] (As already noted, however, both his old and his new account succumb to the second objection.) To wit, in the past McMahan claimed that "the just causes for war are limited to *the prevention or correction of wrongs that are serious enough to make the perpetrators liable to be killed or maimed.*"[14] Now, in contrast, McMahan claims that

there is a just cause for war when those whom it is necessary to attack or kill as a means of achieving a war's aim or aims satisfy the agent-based conditions of liability to be attacked or killed, and thus will be actually and not merely potentially liable to be attacked or killed if the circumstance-based conditions of necessity [and] proportionality are satisfied as well.[15]

As formulated, this is difficult to understand. So let us explain. There are three noteworthy changes in comparison to McMahan's earlier account. First, just cause is now no longer an *aim*. I am not entirely sure whether McMahan actually realizes this shift since he does not explicitly note it, although it would certainly have been noteworthy. In any case, I will set this issue aside. More important for present purposes is that he is, second, merely talking of attack now, and attacks, of course, need neither kill nor maim – they could be comparatively mild. The third change is the introduction of the odd category of "potential liability."[16] What is that? We first have to know what liability is. McMahan explains that "part of what it means to say that a person is *liable* to attack is that he would not be *wronged* by being attacked."[17] (The other part,

---

[11] This latter view, unlike the former, also succumbs to the previously mentioned problem that it simply stipulates that only rights violations can be just causes – but there is no reason to accept such a stipulation. I overlooked this actually rather obvious additional problem in Steinhoff, "Just Cause and 'Right Intention'."

[12] McMahan, "Just Cause for War."

[13] Jeff McMahan, "Proportionality and Just Cause: A Comment on Kamm," *Journal of Moral Philosophy* 11 (2014): 428–53.

[14] McMahan, "Just Cause for War," p. 11.

[15] McMahan, "Proportionality and Just Cause," p. 434.

[16] He had already talked of "potential liability" in Jeff McMahan, *Killing in War*, Oxford: Clarendon Press, 2009, pp. 19–20 but made no further use of the concept there.

[17] Ibid., p. 8.

which need not concern us here, is that on his concept of liability people can only become liable to attack by forfeiting rights through their own responsible action.[18]) People are "*potentially* liable to be attacked" if they are "morally responsible to a sufficient degree for a threat of sufficiently serious harm to make them liable to be attacked or killed *if*, but only if, the circumstance-based conditions of liability are also satisfied."[19] The two "agent-based conditions of liability" are precisely "posing a threat of unjustified harm" and being "morally responsible for doing so"[20]; the circumstance-based conditions are, as we already saw, necessity and proportionality. Given, however, that on McMahan's account necessity and proportionality are "internal to liability,"[21] which means that one cannot be liable to just any harm, but only to proportionate and necessary harm, his talk about "potential liability" is confused. To repeat, McMahan says that people are "*potentially* liable to be attacked" if they are "liable to be attacked or killed *if*, but only if, the circumstance-based conditions of liability are also satisfied," that is, if, but only if, the attack is necessary and proportionate. However, since people can, on his account, only be liable to necessary and proportionate attack (not to an unnecessary and disproportionate one), he is in effect saying that people are potentially liable to necessary and proportionate attack if and only if they are morally responsible to a sufficient degree for a threat of sufficiently serious harm to make them liable *to proportionate and necessary attack* if, but only if, *the attack is necessary and proportionate*. The italicized parts of this sentence show that this is a mere tautology: in other words, "potential liability" and liability are exactly the same thing in McMahan's account, although he has not noticed this. Given McMahan's own framework, one cannot be potentially liable without being liable, and vice versa – which is also confirmed by the fact that according to McMahan "the criterion of liability to attack in war is moral responsibility for an objectively unjustified threat of harm,"[22] that is, one is not only "potentially" liable but liable to proportionate and necessary force if one fulfils the "agent-based conditions of liability."

If, however, one insists on rejecting the tautological reading of McMahan's potential liability formula, then the only alternative that might suggest itself is that McMahan wants to say that people are potentially liable to necessary and proportionate attack if and only if they are morally responsible to a sufficient degree for a threat of sufficiently serious harm to make them liable to proportionate and necessary attack if, but only if, they are actually subjected to a proportionate and necessary attack. This would mean that as long as they are not actually subjected to necessary and proportionate attack, they are also

[18] Ibid., pp. 7–37; see also Jeff McMahan, "Individual Liability in War: A Response to Fabre, Leveringhaus and Tadros," *Utilitas* 24 (2012) vol. 2: 279–99, at p. 296.
[19] McMahan, "Proportionality and Just Cause," pp. 433–34.   [20] Ibid., p. 433.   [21] Ibid.
[22] McMahan, *Killing in War*, p. 35.

not liable to proportionate attack. This, however, not only contradicts what McMahan says about the criterion of liability; it is, in addition, also like saying that a sugar cube is only then solu*ble* (that is, *able* to be dissolved) in water if it is actually put into water. Such a stance shows a lack of understanding of what solubility or, in the case at hand, liability means. It simply makes no sense. For the reasons given, therefore, both McMahan's old and his new (or not so new) account of just cause must be rejected.[23]

A noteworthy additional reason to reject McMahan's new account in particular is its underlying motivation. McMahan claims that the appeal to potential liability "secures the independence of the requirement of just cause from the *ad bellum* necessity and proportionality conditions, so that there can be a just cause for war even if war would be unnecessary or disproportionate."[24] We already saw that this is incorrect since potential liability either is liability or else makes no sense. Even if it were correct, however, it is entirely unclear (McMahan certainly does not provide an explanation) why this alleged independence should be an advantage.

Some might argue that a separate criterion of just cause, incoherent or not, offers an additional protection against precipitate recourse to war. If one already knows that certain acts, *lèse-majesté* for example (as we want to assume), cannot even in principle justify killing people to avert, rectify, or punish such acts, then this is to be welcomed, after all. Such knowledge prevents people from "getting bad ideas" in the first place.

But if such acts cannot justify killing in principle they cannot justify it in the concrete case either. Conversely, however, there are things that are unable to justify killing a person in the concrete case at hand – but can do so "in principle." If on the basis of this one then assumes that one does have a just cause for war, this only invites "bad ideas" instead of avoiding them.

These remarks might be somewhat abstract, so let me offer an example from the sphere of personal self-defence (which is to be understood as including other-defence). In many jurisdictions (and morally as well, in my view), the danger of losing an arm at the hands of an unjustified attacker can justify killing the attacker. It justifies it, for example, if the arm cannot be saved from the attacker by any other means than killing him. The aim of defending one's arm against an unjustified attacker could thus be a just cause for self-defence. However, if in the concrete case the arm can be saved as effectively and efficiently, that is, without additional costs and risks for the defender, by

---

[23] An additional reason for rejecting McMahan's definitions of "just cause" and also of "just combatants" and "unjust combatants" is that they make his thesis of the "moral inequality of combatants" true by stipulative definition (and irrelevant for practice). See Uwe Steinhoff, "Rights, Liability, and the Moral Equality of Combatants," *The Journal of Ethics* 13 (2012): 339–66, section 4.1. McMahan has never addressed this issue, let alone overcome it.

[24] McMahan, "Proportionality and Just Cause," p. 434.

merely knocking the attacker down, then killing the attacker would be excessive and hence unjustified in this case.

Thus, while according to accounts that make just cause independent of proportionality (which comprises last resort), there would be a just cause for killing in this case, on the account defended here there is *no* just cause for killing in this case. It would appear that the latter account is to be preferred if one would like to avoid misunderstandings that could have grave consequences. After all, the more or less subtle point that one has a just cause for war (or killing) but is nonetheless unjustified in resorting to war (or killing) will hardly be one that can be successfully communicated to all politicians, military brass, soldiers, and citizens.

With regard to just cause one also has to make a distinction that, unfortunately, is never made in the literature – which often leads to considerable confusion. To wit, one has to distinguish the question *whether an agent* (e.g. a private person or a state) has a just cause for war from the question *whether a particular war* (which can be actual or potential) has a just cause. Let us again use the self-defence example. If in a concrete case a potential defender can save her arm from an unjustified attack only by knocking down the attacker, then the potential defender has a just cause for using force against the attacker. If, however, the force or violence she actually uses far exceeds what is necessary under the circumstances – if, for example, she kills him although simply knocking him down would have been as easy, safe, and efficient – then there is no just cause for this use of force. This distinction relates to (but does not coincide with) Elizabeth Anscombe's correct (and almost completely ignored) observation that waging *a* war can be morally justified under certain circumstances while *the* war that is actually waged under said circumstances is impermissible. For instance, she was of the opinion that the British were justified in waging *a* war against the Nazis but that the war they actually waged was nevertheless unjustified as it was disproportionate, guided by illicit intentions, and violated the principle of discrimination between the guilty and the innocent.[25]

Thus, I propose the following characterizations regarding just cause:

An agent has a just cause for waging war (alternatively we could say: there is a just cause for waging a war) if there is an injustice, an emergency, or an agreement to wage war between the potential parties to the war,[26] such that under the given

---

[25] Gertrude Elizabeth Margaret Anscombe, "The Justice of the Present War Examined," in *The Collected Philosophical Papers*, ed. idem, Vol. 3: *Ethics, Religion and Politics*, Oxford: Blackwell, 1981, pp. 72–81, esp. at p. 73. Note that Anscombe's observation does not "relativize" the crimes of the Nazis. A murderer is a murderer even if the measures used against him happen to be unjustified.

[26] The idea of a (justified) consensual war will seem absurd to many people. However, see Steinhoff, *On the Ethics of War and Terrorism*, pp. 23–25. Eberle criticizes my view but has little to offer beyond dogmatic stipulation. See Christopher J. Eberle, *Justice and the Just War*

(e.g.geographic, strategic, military-technological) circumstances the military rectification or punishment of the injustice or the defence against it, the military response to the emergency, or the military realization of the agreement, is not necessarily disproportionate; that is, under the given circumstances *a* proportionate war is possible.

A particular war has a just cause if there is an injustice, an emergency, or an agreement to wage war between the potential parties to the war, such that under the given circumstances the military rectification or punishment of the injustice or the defence against it *through this particular war*, or the military response to the emergency or the military realization of the agreement through this particular war, is not disproportionate (or would not be disproportionate, in the case of a potential war).[27]

It is thus possible for an agent (i.e. a person, a state, or some other collective) to have a just cause for war without the (kind of) war the agent is actually waging or contemplating having a just cause. Moreover, the account defended here has the attractive feature that it both continues a venerable tradition and need not be supplemented with additional theories (of *jus ad vim*, for example[28]) that deal separately with non-lethal force and separately with force that answers to things other than rights violations. In short, it is both simpler and more comprehensive than alternative accounts – two features that make this theory more useful in its practical application.

We are now in a position to answer the question asked at the beginning of this section, namely: What kind of thing is a just cause? In the light of the previous discussion, the proposals that a just cause is an aim or some kind of injury or wrong or something that is necessarily connected to "liability" or "potential liability" must be rejected. Instead, as implied by the characterization of a just cause I have given, a just cause is a set of circumstances or conditions. A just cause is a certain state of affairs.[29]

Tradition: Human Worth, Moral Formation, and Armed Conflict, New York and London: Routledge, 2016, pp. 84–85, esp. n. 39. He promises his readers to offer "a full-scale critique" of my "dubious claim" on another occasion. I will postpone my criticism of his own dubious claims until then.

[27] In Steinhoff, "Just Cause and 'Right Intention'," I had forgotten to include emergencies in my final formulation of the conditions of a just cause, although of course the importance of emergencies (which give rise to necessity justifications) was and is part of my criticism of accounts which claim that just cause is necessarily connected to wrongs or injuries.

[28] See Daniel Brunstetter and Megan Braun, "From *Jus ad Bellum* to *Jus ad Vim*: Recalibrating Our Understanding of the Moral Use of Force," *Ethics and International Affairs* 27 (2013) vol. 1: 87–106. These two authors overlook the fact that we can also "recalibrate" (to use their term) our understanding of the moral use of force as I did here, by recalibrating *jus ad bellum* instead of coming up with an additional theory of *jus ad vim*.

[29] Some paragraphs of this section draw on material from Steinhoff, "Just Cause and 'Right Intention'."

II The General Substantive Question: "Which Causes Are Just?" or "Under What Conditions Is There a Just Cause?"

As far as my own account of a just cause is concerned, I have already answered this latter question with the two highlighted characterizations at the end of the previous section. Of course, this answer raises additional questions, in particular the question as to when, exactly, a war is or is not proportionate. A precise answer to this latter question, however, is beyond the scope of this chapter. Nevertheless, some general things can be said, which will also help further clarify how the account of just cause defended here works in practice.

We can approach the issue by considering the distinctions that accounts which conceive of a just cause as an aim tend to make. The general aims regularly appearing in the literature are a defence against ongoing or imminent attacks, prevention of some non-imminent future attacks or threatened evils, rectification (of some injustice, e.g. unjust seizure of property or territory), and punishment. Punishment is the most protean concept here since punishment can have different sub-aims, in particular special deterrence (the punished agent is deterred from further punishable acts), general deterrence (the punishment of the agent also deters other agents), and retribution (making the punished agent suffer is considered as good in itself or as something that is good insofar as it satisfies the unjustly harmed victims' desire for revenge[30]). Moreover, some authors claim that punishment can, via deterrence, be a means of defence.[31] Yet it should be noted that *defence*, properly speaking, can only be directed against ongoing or imminent attacks, not against future threats.[32] This is not a mere quibble about words; rather, the self-defence justification (applicable only to ongoing and imminent attacks) and the justifying emergency

---

[30] There are many different characterizations of what "retribution" and the philosophical view called "retributivism" amount to. For an overview, see Alec Walen, "Retributive Justice", *The Stanford Encyclopedia of Philosophy* (Summer 2015 Edition), ed. Edward N. Zalta, http://plato.stanford.edu/archives/sum2015/entries/justice-retributive/. For a critical discussion of retribution as a good insofar as it satisfies the victim's desire for revenge, see David Boonin, *The Problem of Punishment*, Cambridge: Cambridge University Press, 2008, pp. 152–54 and 269–75. I find Boonin's criticism of this "revenge-based retributivism" entirely unconvincing but need not go into this here.

[31] Kenneth W. Kemp, "Punishment as Just Cause for War," *Public Affairs Quarterly* 10 (1996) vol.4: 335–53; Jeff McMahan, "Aggression and Punishment," in Larry May, ed. *War: Essays in Political Philosophy*, Cambridge: Cambridge University Press, 2008, pp. 67–84; David Luban, "War as Punishment," *Philosophy and Public Affairs* 39 (2012) vol. 4: 299–330; Nigel Biggar, *In Defence of War*, Oxford: Oxford University Press, 2013, p. 161; Victor Tadros, "Punitive War," in *How We Fight: Ethics in War*, eds. Helen Frowe and Gerald Lang, Oxford: Oxford University Press, 2014, pp. 18–37, at pp. 19–20.

[32] Kimberley Kessler Ferzan, "Defending Imminence: From Battered Women to Iraq," *Arizona Law Review* 46 (2004): 213–62; Shawn Kaplan, "Punitive Warfare, Counterterrorism, and *Jus ad Bellum*," in *Routledge Handbook of Ethics and War: Just War Theory in the Twenty-First Century*, eds. Fritz Allhof, Nicholas G. Evans, and Adam Henschke, New York and London: Routledge, 2013, pp. 236–49, at pp. 236–38.

justification (applicable also to future threats) are governed by different justificatory requirements and thus yield different results.[33]

Be that as it may, it would appear that at least some defensive, preventive, rectificatory, and deterrent wars can be justified – and hence have a just cause – if the stakes are high enough. In fact, if the stakes are high enough, there is very little that cannot be justified.[34] On the other hand, however, one can make the stakes part of the characterization of certain wars and certain war aims, thus arriving at more specific aims. For instance, David Rodin claims that one cannot, for reasons of proportionality, justifiably pursue by means of war the aim of defending one's nation against what he calls a "bloodless invasion"[35] or "political aggression," namely against an aggression that "is primarily directed towards obtaining a political or material advantage for the attackers."[36] He comes to this assessment on the basis of his premise that lethal self-defence is only permissible against threats to "vital rights" (such as the rights not to be killed or raped) but not, for example, in defence of mere property, territory, or the right to vote.[37] If he were right (and if one accepted Rodin's implicit further premise, which I do not, that wars will necessarily involve killing people), then these kinds of wars could not have a just cause provided a just cause is tied to proportionality (as it is in the account defended here). Yet Rodin's account is based on a gross misinterpretation of the proportionality requirement of self-defence. On more plausible interpretations of the proportionality requirement, wars of national self-defence against political aggression can be justified and have a just cause, which indeed is the traditional view of the matter. Since I have argued this point at length elsewhere,[38] I will not pursue it further here.

In any case, short of stipulatively inserting the violation of certain valid just war criteria into the very definition of certain war aims, all kinds of aims can be legitimately pursued by means of war, even aims that might sound dubious at first, such as the search for glory. If, for instance, Christine kills Betty (who is about to murder Alfred) in order to enjoy the glory of the intrepid defender (but not to save Alfred's life), then her act is still justified. What matters is that Christine knew that Betty was about to kill Alfred and that Christine's measures were a necessary and proportionate means to stop her from doing so.[39] Her aims, in contrast, do not matter. This is a further reason why conceiving of a

---

[33] See Uwe Steinhoff, "Self-Defense and Imminence," ms. available at http://papers.ssrn.com/sol3/papers.cfm?abstract_id=2653669.

[34] Uwe Steinhoff, *On the Ethics of Torture*, Albany: State University of New York Press, 2013, pp. 150–53.

[35] David Rodin, *War and Self-Defense*, Oxford: Oxford University Press, 2002, pp. 127–38.

[36] David Rodin, "The Myth of National Self-Defence," in *The Morality of Defensive War*, eds. Cécile Fabre and Seth Lazar, Oxford: Oxford University Press, 2014, pp. 69–89, at p. 81.

[37] Rodin, *War and Self-Defense*, pp. 43–48, 127–38.

[38] Uwe Steinhoff, "Rodin on Self-Defense and the 'Myth' of National Self-Defense: A Refutation," *Philosophia* 41 (2013): 1017–36.

[39] See Steinhoff, "Just Cause and 'Right Intention'," section II.

just cause as an aim either will hardly serve to restrict war or will only serve to incorrectly restrict it, prohibiting it where it should be allowed. The account defended here avoids such mistakes.

Finally, if retribution is actually a good in itself insofar as it makes guilty people suffer what they deserve and also good because the victims of the guilty draw satisfaction from retribution (and why should that not be a good?), then the fact that a war is also retributive counts *for* its proportionality, not against it. Accordingly, on my account, which tightly connects just cause to proportionality, retribution can contribute to a war's having a just cause.

III The Question of Timing: Does the "Just Cause" Criterion Only Apply to the Initiation of a War or Also to Its Continuation?

Some authors have recently argued that "moral considerations regarding whether and how to end a war are distinct from *jus ad bellum*."[40] All three authors mentioned in the footnote deem it necessary to complement *jus ad bellum* with what they call *jus ex bello, jus terminatio,* or the ethics of "war exit," respectively. And all three think that this complementation is a significant innovation.

It would indeed be an innovation, yet an entirely superfluous one. The three authors simply misunderstand *jus ad bellum*: it does not only refer to the initiation of war, as they suggest, but also to its continuation.[41] In fact, this should be glaringly obvious: after all, it is clearly also the case for the analogous examples of the self-defence justification and the necessity justification. I know of no jurisdiction on the planet that would, for instance, distinguish between the criteria governing the initiation of self-defence and those governing its termination. The reason is that, again, it is simply obvious that the criteria have to be applied "diachronically," as Schulzke would say. To wit, that you have at a time t^1 a self-defence justification to beat Paul does not mean that you also have a justification to continue beating him at t^2. For self-defence to be justified there has to be an imminent or ongoing attack, and the defensive measures have to be necessary – it is not sufficient that they once were

---

[40] Darrel Moellendorf, "Jus ex Bello," *The Journal of Political Philosophy* 16 (2008) vol. 2: 123–36; Moellendorf, "Two Doctrines of *Jus ex Bello*," *Ethics* 125 (2015) vol. 3: 653–73; David Rodin, "Two Emerging Issues of Jus Post Bellum: War Termination and the Liability of Soldiers for Crimes of Aggression," in *Jus Post Bellum: Towards a Law of Transition from Conflict to Peace* , eds. Carsten Stahn and Jann Kleffner, The Hague: T.M.C. Asser, 2008, pp. 53–77; Rodin, "The War Trap: Dilemmas of *Jus Terminatio*," *Ethics* 125 (2015) vol. 3: 674–95; Cécile Fabre, "War Exit," *Ethics* 125 (2015) vol. 3: 631–52.

[41] Steinhoff, *On the Ethics of War and Terrorism*, p. 2; Marcus Schulzke, "The Contingent Morality of War: Establishing a Diachronic Model of *Jus Ad Bellum*," *Critical Review of International Social and Political Philosophy* 18 (2015) vol. 3: 264–84; Eberle, *Justice and the Just War Tradition*, pp. 105–7.

necessary and that once there was an attack. Every lawyer, every judge, and every citizen knows that: if you beat Paul because he tries to slit your throat, you will have a self-defence justification for beating him if this is necessary to stop him, but this does not provide you with a justification to continue beating him if he already lies unconscious on the ground – it is not necessary anymore and there is not even an ongoing or imminent attack. Realizing this and operationalizing this insight most certainly does not require an "ethics of defence exit" to complement self-defence statutes; rather, the existing law and morality of self-defence already cover this because it is universally understood that they must be applied diachronically. The same is true for the existing just war criteria in the case of war.

Yet Rodin claims that "in fact *jus terminatio* poses distinctive moral problems that cannot be resolved by simply applying *ad bellum* conditions continuously over the course of a conflict."[42] Why not? Because, says Rodin, of "new emergent costs, like the risk of defeat." He thinks that before you fight you only risk, let's say, the enemy seizing your territory or killing your people, but once you start to fight you also risk being defeated (in the sense of losing a fight – you cannot lose a fight if you have not fought at all). And Rodin asks: "How did the defender acquire a permission to inflict additional harms [in trying to avoid defeat] over and above the initial [before one started fighting] proportionality assessment ... simply by entering into a state of war? This looks entirely mysterious."[43] However, first, Rodin's argument rests on a wrong premise: he makes it appear as though in the initial proportionality consideration, the risk of defeat must not be considered. But that is like saying that a doctor who considers operating on a patient must not consider the risk of botching the operation before she starts but only once she has started it. Such a suggestion, however, is inane. Moreover, even if one granted Rodin that assumption, there would still be no mystery involved. To wit, if at time t^1 someone faces a threat against which the use of some force would be proportionate and at time t^2 he faces more threats or a bigger or more comprehensive one, then, all else being equal, the use of more force would be proportionate. That is not mysterious but logical. To give an example: You stand in front of your apartment with an apple in your hand and someone tries to steal the apple from you. It would, let's assume, be proportionate to push him away (but not to knock him down). Instead of pushing him away, you take a step back into your apartment. A person's dwelling, however, is afforded special protection by law and morality. If now the thief still comes after you to get the apple, you would be permitted to use more force in defence against a more severe threat – the threat not only of losing the apple but now also of the violation of your apartment. While Rodin might find it "mysterious" why you are allowed to use more force "simply by entering" your apartment, nobody else will.

---

[42] Rodin, "The War Trap," p. 677.   [43] Ibid., p. 678.

Rodin also adduces what he calls "a fanciful case"[44] to argue against doing proportionality assessments in war (and elsewhere, it seems) on a purely "forward-looking basis" (which considers harms or wrongs done during the war as sunk costs that need not now be further considered).[45] Note, however, that I am arguing here for applying *ad bellum* conditions continuously over the course of a conflict, but such continuous application is quite compatible with also looking backwards. Rodin seems to equate the continuity account with forward-looking accounts, but that is a mistake. The forward-looking account is only one version of the continuity account. However, since it is indeed a version of the continuity account, it is instructive to see why Rodin's argument against it fails.

Rodin considers a case where one dangles another person out of the window for the mere fun of it and without the person's consent, and then realizes that it is wrong but is unable to lift the person back into the room without help. Rodin claims that both continuing to dangle the person and stopping doing so (by letting go) are wrong. Accordingly, he thinks that both the continuation and the discontinuation of a war can be wrong. Thus, he sees a dilemma here.[46] But there simply is no dilemma since continuing to dangle the person as part of an attempt to rescue her is not wrong.[47] Rodin claims, however, that this is "clearly false."[48] He states that if

dangling for less than ten minutes and dangling for ten minutes or longer are separate offences, then I will clearly be morally and legally liable for the more serious offence, even though I only dangled you for five minutes prior to the epiphany. The continued dangling after the epiphany contributes to my culpability, despite the fact that I am morally required to do it.[49]

This is clearly false. Part of an offence, and element of the crime, is *mens rea*, the guilty mind, but once I dangle the person with the intent to rescue her, I have no guilty mind anymore. (Rodin claims that "no one can benefit morally from his own wrongdoing, and removing or mitigating my culpability for harmful action that would otherwise be wrong would be a benefit to me."[50] Yet both law and morality, quite reasonably, do allow people to benefit from not having a guilty mind, and this is the only benefit that is accorded here.) Incidentally, if *mens rea* were not an element of the crime, then you would also be culpable and committing an offence if you had grabbed a person who fell out of the window by no fault of yours, trying to save her. But that, of course, is absurd. In Rodin's case, I would, however, be *civilly* liable (I would have to pay adequate compensation) for the continued dangling, for this is a consequence of my initial wrongdoing and I am responsible for it. But that in no way implies

---

[44] Ibid., p. 687.   [45] Ibid., p. 689.   [46] Ibid., p. 687.
[47] See also Moellendorf, "Two Doctrines of *Jus ex Bello*," p. 659.
[48] Rodin, "The War Trap," p. 687.   [49] Ibid.   [50] Ibid., p. 688.

that the rescue dangling after my moral epiphany is criminal or culpable. Thus the dilemma that Rodin unnecessarily wants to construe can easily be avoided by simply applying the appropriate moral and legal categories.

Moellendorf, like Rodin, also argues against the "forward-looking conception of proportionality"[51] and thus against one version of the continuity account. He considers an argument provided by McMahan in support of the forward-looking account. McMahan considers a case where a runaway trolley will kill five innocent people unless the trolley is diverted onto another track where it would kill only one innocent person.[52] Assuming that even killing two – but not three – innocent people as a side effect of saving the five is proportionate, a bystander would be justified in diverting the trolley. Yet when the bystander pulls the switch, there is an unforeseen malfunction that fails to affect the trolley but accidentally kills two other innocent persons. The bystander quickly repairs the switch and thus can still divert the trolley. Is it still permissible for him to do so? It is if one regards the previous accidental killing of the two bystanders as "sunken costs" that need not be considered in the decision now; it is not, however, if the two previously killed persons enter into the new proportionality consideration, for then the saving of the five would have the total cost of killing three, and that would, *ex exemplo*, be disproportionate. McMahan thinks that it would be counter-intuitive to take the latter position and to declare that now the bystander has to let the five innocent people die instead of being permitted to divert the trolley to the track with only one innocent person. I agree with him.

Moellendorf does not. He thinks that the forward-looking account faces two problems, namely that it "seems inconsistent with the concept of proportionality, which requires that there is in principle some limit to the costs that can be imposed in the pursuit of the just cause" and that it "would evacuate proportionality of much of its important critical force, for it renders incomprehensible the claim that a war is disproportionate because of its cumulative costs."[53] Both claims are mistaken. First, there obviously is a clear limit set by the continuity account in the given example: *ex hypothesi* the proportionality requirement would make it disproportionate for the bystander to divert the trolley if he foresees that at least three people will then be killed. Of course, Moellendorf's point is that one could kill two people again and again if each time the (miraculously still unforeseen) malfunction occurs (killing two people) and it appears that one could still save the five by diverting the trolley to the one. Yet that does not in the least change the fact that at each time there is a clear proportionality constraint. Moreover, Moellendorf's second point is wrong too. There is a limit also to the cumulative costs. While it might be proportionate to

---

[51] Moellendorf, "Two Doctrines of *Jus ex Bello*," p. 663.

[52] Jeff McMahan, "Proportionality and Time," *Ethics* 125 (2015) vol. 3: 696–719, at pp. 703–4. He provides another good and rather convincing example, see ibid., p. 708.

[53] Moellendorf, "Two Doctrines of *Jus ex Bello*," p. 663.

save the five at the cost of killing two people as a side effect, saving the five at the cost of slowly torturing one person to death (or of having her, as a side effect, transported into an automated torture machine that will do the same) might well be disproportionate. If so, then there is no limit on how many people can be "cumulatively" killed in the endless reiteration of the attempt to save the five, but there is a limit on how many people can be cumulatively tortured (namely none), and thus the continuous account also sets a proportionality limit for the cumulative case.

Finally, if Moellendorf's account of proportionality were correct, it would also have to apply, for the same reasons, to proportionality in self-defence. Suppose it were proportionate to defend your wallet against a thief by knocking him down, but anything beyond this were disproportionate. You are walking through a tough neighbourhood. A robber tries to take your wallet, and in pursuit of the just cause of keeping it you knock him down. After 100 metres more you come across another robber (or perhaps even the same one: he tries again) who tries to take your wallet. On Moellendorf's "budget" account you have to let him because you already exhausted what he calls your "proportionality budget"[54] with the first robber. In other words, you cannot defend your wallet anymore now. This is entirely counter-intuitive if not downright absurd, however, and most certainly not an account of proportionality that any jurisdiction on this planet subscribes to. Accordingly, there is also no reason to subscribe to such an account in the case of war.[55] To wit, if a genocidal enemy attempts to kill the entire population of one million people in a certain territory, then Moellendorf's account implies that there is some proportionality budget so that, for instance, collaterally killing 1000 innocent civilians in the course of the whole defensive war against this genocide attempt would be proportionate while killing 1001 would not. This further implies that after already having collaterally killed 970 innocent civilians without having averted the genocide, one would now have to let the genocide simply take its course if one could only avert it by collaterally killing 31 additional civilians. Again, this seems to be absurd (at least barring absolutist convictions).

Finally, it should perhaps be noted that the continuous application of *jus ad bellum* does not undermine the distinction between *jus ad bellum* and *jus in bello*. This distinction does not concern timing (nor does it concern any declarations of war or of peace), but the level of agency and decision making. To wit, imagine a people can only save themselves from being malevolently slaughtered by an enemy group if they engage in organized collective self-defence. Their *jus ad bellum* question is: "May we, as a collective, wage war?" Assume they know that if they do, a few of their soldiers will violate *jus in bello*

---

[54] Ibid., p. 661–62, italics removed.
[55] If one *knows* that one will be attacked again and again and perhaps that each defence would produce slight collateral damage, then this could go into the proportionality consideration. However, this would of course be forward looking.

restrictions, for example, kill some wounded enemy soldiers who are already *hors de combat*. This fact and knowledge would not necessarily undermine the justifiability of the war as a whole, as a collective action, since the war could still be justifiable as the lesser evil even if some individual acts of the soldiers are unjustifiable. To use an analogy: if a person can only save herself from being killed by a culpable aggressor if she asks someone for help who she knows will use slightly excessive force, then she is nevertheless justified in doing so (an attempted murderer being exposed to somewhat excessive force is a lesser evil than his succeeding in his murder attempt), even though her helper is not justified in using excessive force. She is justified since she has no alternative means than asking the helper and the helper's acts are not under her control. The helper, on the other hand, is not justified in using unnecessary force since his own acts obviously are under his control. In the same vein, a collective can be justified in resorting to war (and thus in enlisting its soldiers' help) even if it is known that some of the soldiers will, against the collective's wishes, use excessive force.

We can thus conclude that the objections against the continuous application of *jus ad bellum*, including just cause and proportionality, are spurious. The criteria of *jus ad bellum* apply throughout the war, not only at the point of its initiation. While starting a war at t^1 might be justified, continuing it at time t^2 might be unjustified (and vice versa), and this insight neither requires an addition to *jus ad bellum* (it is already contained in it) nor does it undermine the distinction between *jus ad bellum* and *jus in bello*.

5 The Condition of Last Resort

Suzanne Uniacke

Just War theory specifies that recourse to war must be a last resort. This specification accords with a more general aim to limit the occurrence of war by articulating demanding conditions under which war can be morally legitimate. Although it has critics among contemporary Western philosophers, the condition of last resort is widely accepted as a basic element of Just War theory. It is not itself an issue of dispute between historical as opposed to contemporary Just War theorists, or between traditional as opposed to revisionist Just War theorists.[1] The defensibility of "last resort" as a necessary condition of legitimate recourse to war will depend on how the condition is best interpreted and on its moral rationale.

I Last Resort: Interpretation, Rationale, Acceptability

Three philosophical questions about the condition of last resort rise at the most basic level: How should we interpret this condition? What is its moral rationale? Should we accept last resort as a necessary condition of legitimate recourse to war? These questions are interrelated. For instance, a defensible interpretation of last resort as a condition of *jus ad bellum* is shaped by what we take the moral rationale of this condition to be. In the other direction, the moral considerations that ground the requirement that recourse to war be a last resort have a significant bearing on how we should interpret this condition. An account of what last resort requires and implies, both in theory and in practice, is directly relevant to whether this condition ought to be accepted as necessary to legitimate recourse to war. The answers to these philosophical questions are highly significant to whether a condition of last resort should be adopted in policy or incorporated as part of international law. They are also relevant to how this condition is to be applied in practice.

In this chapter I address these three philosophical questions. Before doing so it is important to acknowledge that the interpretation and the rationale and justification of last resort as a condition of *jus ad bellum* depend on what we

---

[1] These differences within Just War theory are outlined in Seth Lazar, "War," *The Stanford Encyclopedia of Philosophy* (Summer 2016 Edition), ed. Edward N. Zalta, http://plato.stanford.edu/archives/sum2016/entries/war/.

take war to be: according to Just War theory recourse to war must be a last resort because of what war is and does.

The Significance of War

I regard war as armed conflict that can include the use of conventional or non-conventional weapons. Moreover, armed conflict that amounts to war achieves a certain scale, as opposed to being, for example, a skirmish or series of small-scale conflicts that do not escalate into war. The duration of armed conflict that amounts to war can be relatively short, as was the 1967 Arab-Israeli Six-Day War, or it can be conducted over years, as were World Wars I and II. War is sometimes characterised in terms of military conflict. A key role of the military or armed forces of a state is the prosecution of war. However, combatants who fight a war need not be military personnel or under military command nor need war be fought by or between states. My discussion does not assume that adversaries in a war are always sovereign states or that those who fight wars are always military personnel. There are tribal wars and civil wars, and there can be guerrilla warfare, for instance.[2]

Nonetheless, traditional Just War theory requires, as an additional condition, that war is declared by a legitimate authority. Since war is of its nature an activity conducted by collectives (such as states) and by individual actors as part of a collective (e.g. an army), I take the "legitimate authority" condition of *jus ad bellum* to require that a decision to wage war is made by an actor who has the normative standing to commit the relevant group to engaging in armed conflict that amounts to war and for the purpose for which the war is to be fought.[3] It is with reference to such wars that I apply the condition of last resort in this chapter. This does not imply that a requirement of last resort cannot or ought not be among the conditions of legitimate recourse to other types of war or armed conflict or violence.

In characterising war as essentially involving armed conflict, it is appropriate to note familiar terms such as "trade war" and more recently "cyber war" that refer to various types of non-armed conflict. However, it is because the phenomenon of war in its central sense is armed conflict on a large scale that for Just War theory, it must be pursued only as a last resort. This point about the nature of war will be relevant to my later discussion of the moral rationale of the condition of last resort and to whether we ought to accept this condition as necessary to legitimate recourse to war. Before we come to those issues, we must address the question of what last resort implies and requires in the just war context.

---

[2] Here I invoke the everyday senses of "armed conflict" and "war," as distinct from how these terms are defined in international law.

[3] This interpretation is neutral between those traditional Just War theorists who maintain that only states can wage legitimate wars and those revisionist Just War theorists who question this.

II   Last Resort as a "Necessity" Condition

The *jus ad bellum* condition of last resort requires that recourse to war is necessary in the circumstances.[4] I take the rationale of this condition to be grounded in a general moral requirement not to cause needless harm. (I take this up in the next section.) For our present discussion, it is important to clarify the sense in which recourse to war must be necessary for it to be legitimate. The term "necessary" in this context is both instrumental and elliptical: the condition of last resort requires that recourse to war is an effective means of achieving a particular aim and also that recourse to war is indispensable in the circumstances if that aim is to be achieved.

Whether recourse to war can be effective in achieving a particular aim will partly depend on what we take that aim to be. In this chapter and for the sake of argument, I take the aim in focus to be the *just cause* for which the war is fought. I note, however, that traditional Just War theory also requires that legitimate warfare goes beyond achieving a more immediate just cause, such as national defence against external attack, and aims to secure a lasting peace. With respect to the pursuit of some just causes, a requirement that legitimate war must also aim to secure a lasting peace is arguably morally too demanding. Nonetheless, those who accept this longer-term imperative as necessary to legitimate war must recognise that recourse to war that can achieve a more limited just cause could be ineffective in securing a lasting peace, and in some cases war might even undermine it. For example, on the assumption that a war of humanitarian intervention by one state to prevent persecution of an ethnic minority within another state could constitute a just cause, such a war might succeed in this aim but in the process also destroy the invaded state's political order and infrastructure and unleash the forces of a prolonged, devastating civil war.

The Structure of Necessity

The structure of the *jus ad bellum* condition of last resort is analogous to the "necessity" condition of permissible personal self-defence which requires that harmful force that is used against an unjust threat is necessary in the circumstances. In the case of personal self-defence, we can distinguish two steps of this condition. First, the use of self-defensive force must be necessary in the circumstances to prevent the infliction of unjust harm, as opposed to the use of other available means of self-protection such as calling the police or leaving

---

[4]   Those who interpret "last resort" in this way include Jeff McMahan, "Just War," in *A Companion to Contemporary Political Philosophy*, vol. 2, eds. Robert Goodin et al., Chichester, UK: Wiley-Blackwell, 2012, p. 673; and Seth Lazar, "War," op cit.; Henry Shue, "Last Resort and Proportionality," in *The Oxford Handbook of Ethics of War*, eds. Seth Lazar and Helen Frowe, Oxford Handbooks Online, 2016.

the scene. Second, where use of self-defensive force is necessary, the degree of force used must also be necessary. The use of lethal force, for instance, is permissible only if less harmful force would be ineffective in fending off the threat.

Not all wars are defensive wars, and my discussion of the condition of last resort leaves open the question of whether wars that are waged for reasons other than (national) defence can meet the *jus ad bellum* condition of just cause. (Historically, Saint Augustine thought that punitive wars could be just.[5] Contemporary Just War theorists debate the legitimacy of wars of humanitarian intervention.[6]) The conditions of just war differ from those of personal self-defence in several other respects.[7] These differences do not detract from my point that the structure of the *jus ad bellum* condition of last resort is like that of the self-defence "necessity" condition in requiring that both the *type* and the *degree* of force used are necessary: recourse to war must be necessary in the circumstances if the just cause is to be achieved.

The critical issues in relation to whether recourse to war is necessary are, first, whether recourse to war *can* achieve the just cause and, second, whether recourse to war is *indispensable* if the just cause is to be achieved.

War as a Means

Clearly recourse to war cannot be necessary as a means of achieving any aim, however legitimate the aim itself might be, if recourse to war cannot in fact achieve that aim. This point recognises that the relevant sense of 'necessity' in this context is that of instrumentalist justification, and that one cannot justify recourse to an activity, *y*, as a means of achieving an aim, *x*, if *y* cannot in fact achieve *x*. Nonetheless, fulfilment of the condition of last resort is consistent with there being a low probability that recourse to war will achieve the just cause for which the war is fought.

Whether war can achieve a particular just cause is largely an empirical matter that for the purpose of satisfying the *jus ad bellum* condition of last resort must be subject to judgement at the time that a decision to wage war is taken. War is typically a complex activity that develops over time, sometimes in unpredictable ways. Obviously, a judgement about what recourse to war could achieve in relation to a just cause needs to involve assessments of relative fighting capacities, including a comparative estimation of weaponry, infra-

---

[5] Saint Augustine, *The City of God*, trans. John Healey, ed. R.V.G. Tasker, London: J.M. Dent & Sons, 1945, Book 1, chapter XX.

[6] See e.g. C.A.J. Coady, "The Ethics of Armed Humanitarian Intervention," *Peaceworks* 45, United States Institute of Peace, 2002.

[7] Legitimate personal self-defence against unjust attack does not require a reasonable prospect of success or the securing of a lasting peace, for instance.

structure, personnel, resources and tactics. Such a judgement will also need to anticipate the types of collective action that are essential to fighting a war, and this necessarily includes predictions of the actions of others. For instance, *A* might regard an aim as achievable by recourse to war against *B* only if *A* does not suffer significant civil unrest, or only if *C* comes to *A*'s assistance, or only if *D* does not join the conflict on *B*'s side. Factors such as existing treaties can add weight to judgements of the latter type, but third parties can default on such agreements and they can join in a common cause for other principled or pragmatic reasons. The many contingencies that might need to be considered in judging whether recourse to war could achieve a particular aim could also include the possibility that the war will escalate in other directions. Some such possibilities can be reasonably anticipated; others cannot be. For example, in invading Poland in 1939, Hitler might reasonably have anticipated that Britain would then declare war on Germany in accordance with the Anglo-Polish Agreement. However, in declaring war on Germany in 1939 in the face of the Nazi-Soviet Pact, Britain could not reasonably have predicted Hitler's decision to invade the Soviet Union in 1941, a decision that greatly influenced the course of the war.

Within a just war framework, predications about what recourse to war can achieve will also need to consider legitimate ways of fighting. Within traditional Just War theory, *A*'s judgement about what war against *B* can achieve must assume that *A* will act within the *jus in bello* conditions of non-combatant immunity and proportionality and the constraints imposed by international law. (Revisionist Just War theorists adopt various positions on who are (il)legitimate targets in war.) *A* must also consider how (un)likely it is that an adversary will comply with *jus in bello* norms. (Can it be anticipated that *B* would target innocent people, or embed its weapons in heavily populated civilian areas, or use prohibited weapons, for instance?) An expectation about whether an adversary will fight "clean" or "dirty" can have significant implications for *A*'s judgement about what recourse to war could achieve.

In deliberating about what recourse to war could achieve, various complex sequences or developments of events need to present themselves as possibilities about which judgements need to be made and compared. Authorities making an overall judgement on this also need to know what range of considerations they are required to take into account and how various considerations are to be compared against one another, and at what point the judgement itself should be made. For instance, a remote possible development should be a factor in such deliberation if, were it to eventuate, its effects on the course of the war would be significant. But how much weight should be placed on a remote possibility in relation to other more immediate factors at the time of decision? How much time should be allowed to elapse in the decision process for clarification on some issues or for other, possibly relevant factors to come to light? The effects that prolonging the decision might have on relative fighting capacities, or on the source of the conflict itself, also need to be considered.

In practice the *jus ad bellum* condition of last resort is based on a predictive judgement from the perspective of an actor in a particular set of circumstances. A belief about what recourse to war can achieve that is made on reasonable grounds, that properly considers all relevant factors, and that is formed at the most appropriate time, might nonetheless turn out to be false. This can be the result of factors that are unknown or unforeseeable when the judgement is made. The fact that recourse to war does not as it happens achieve a just cause for which the war is fought is insufficient to show that it could not have done so when the decision for recourse to war was taken. Nonetheless, when as the result of unknown or unforeseen factors, an aim is or becomes unachievable, we could allow that in this case recourse to war does not actually fulfil the condition of last resort, even though it was reasonable for the relevant authority to believe otherwise at the time the decision was taken. (In retrospect and from a more informed perspective we sometimes similarly regard an instrumentally motivated course of action that hits unpredictable, insurmountable obstacles or that unexpectedly goes significantly off course.) However, a predictive judgement that is made on reasonable grounds is the most that this first aspect of the last resort condition can realistically require in practice. What this first step clearly disallows is recourse to a war that the relevant authority can predict, on all the available evidence properly considered at the time of decision, will be futile in achieving a just cause for which the war would be fought

Just War theory requires, additionally, that recourse to war has a reasonable prospect of success in achieving a just cause. In coming to a view about what last resort requires and implies in the just war context, it is important not to conflate this condition with the distinguishable condition of a reasonable prospect of success. War can be necessary *if* a just cause is to be achieved even when the prospect of success is very low.[8] Nor does the condition of there being a reasonable prospect of success together with the *jus ad bellum* requirement that war be a proportionate response in relation to a just cause make the condition of last resort redundant.[9] A war that has a reasonable prospect of achieving a just cause, and that would be a proportionate response in relation to the significance of that just cause, can nonetheless be *unnecessary* where other means are available to achieve the same outcome.

---

[8] These two conditions are distinguished in Suzanne Uniacke, "Self-Defence, Just War, and a Reasonable Prospect of Success," in *How We Fight*, eds. Helen Frowe and Gerald Lang, Oxford: Oxford University Press, 2014, pp. 63–66. Fulfillment of a "reasonable prospect of success" condition is also consistent with failure to achieve the just cause.

[9] *Contra* Eamon Aloyo, "Just War Theory and the Last of Last Resort," *Ethics and International Affairs*, 29 (2015) vol. 2, p. 194.

War as an Indispensable Means

This brings us to the second critical issue in explicating the sense of "necessity" relevant to the condition of last resort, namely, the requirement that recourse to war be indispensable if the just cause is to be achieved. Here again a comparison with the necessity condition of permissible personal self-defence is helpful. This condition means that I cannot, for example, legitimately use lethal force against an attacker if I am able effectively to protect myself by, say, leaving the scene or pushing the attacker to the ground. Similarly, the *jus ad bellum* condition of last resort requires consideration of possible alternatives to recourse to war as means of achieving the just cause. What the last resort condition requires in relation to those alternatives is open to discussion, however. Just as recourse to war must be capable of achieving a just cause for which the war is fought, so too a course of action that can be regarded as a genuine alternative to war must be realistic as a means of achieving a just cause. We can say that a realistic alternative to war must meet a threshold above its being merely empirically possible that it could achieve the just cause. However, this sets the bar very low in relation to what other courses of action need seriously to be considered as alternatives to recourse to war.

A straightforward account of what the *jus ad bellum* last resort condition requires in practice would be that pursuit of any alternative course of action that could realistically achieve the just cause must take precedence over recourse to war. This would be so even if attempting to achieve the just cause by, for example, diplomacy, peaceful negotiation or imposition of trade sanctions would be far less likely to succeed than would recourse to war.[10] On this straightforward view, recourse to war can be legitimate only after any such alternatives have been tried without success.[11]

In responding to this straightforward interpretation of what the condition requires, we notice that the term "last resort" is itself ambiguous between interpretations that would carry different practical requirements for the legitimacy of a decision to wage war. To characterise a particular action, x, as being a last resort implies that x is an unfavourable option, indeed (usually) the least favourable or worst case option. However, last resort sometimes additionally refers to a (temporally) final course of action, the only remaining, unwanted, course of action when all else has been tried without success. So, when we say that the *jus ad bellum* condition of last resort means that recourse to war must be indispensable in achieving a just cause for which the war is fought, does this always require in practice that all alternative means of achieving that aim have

---

[10] John W. Lango, "Before Military Force, Nonviolent Action: An Application of the Generalized Just War Principle of Last Resort," *Public Affairs Quarterly*, 23 (2009) vo. 2, p. 119.

[11] Bruno Coppieters et al., "Last Resort," in *Moral Constraints on War*, eds. Bruno Coppieters and Nick Foton, Lanham, MD, and Plymouth: Lexington Books, 2008, 2nd edn, p. 139.

been exhausted? Can the term "last resort" in this context imply that recourse to war is the least favourable option and, if so, in what respect(s)?

In asking these particular questions I do not underestimate what can be required to establish that recourse to war is indispensable if a just cause is to be achieved. The condition of last resort can require not only the careful consideration but also the practical exhaustion of reasonable alternatives to war, such as attempted peaceful negotiation and compromise. Moreover, in addressing the question of whether the condition of last resort always requires the testing and failure of other means, we obviously need to acknowledge cases in which there are in fact no available alternative means of achieving the just cause. (This might happen when, for example, a group under attack has no means of self-protection other than to fight back.) Rather, the critical questions I have posed about what the condition of last resort requires and implies in relation to the indispensability of war arise from cases in which there *are* alternatives to war that represent inherently less harmful means and that might (still) achieve the just cause, but where pursuing these alternatives would involve significant risks or costs compared with recourse to war.

To explain how this might be so, again a simplified example based on what the necessity condition requires in a case of personal self-defence will help illustrate the point. If at time *t*, *A* is about to be attacked by *B*, *A* might be able to use harmful force to fend off *B*'s attack. At this time *A* could also be in a position to try to avoid *B*'s attack by non-violent means. *A* might, for instance, be able to mount a last-ditch attempt to reason or plead with *B*, or *A* might be able to take cover or try to run away. But at time *t*, any of these alternatives to *A*'s using harmful force in self-defence against *B* might be unlikely to succeed and expose *A* to a significantly greater risk of harm from *B* or impede *A*'s capacity or opportunity effectively to resist *B*'s attack by forceful means should these attempts fail. *A* might then be in a significantly worse position in relation to fending off *B*'s attack than were *A* to have used self-defensive force on *B* at time *t*. In judging *A*'s use of defensive force on *B* at time *t* as necessary in these circumstances, we regard the risks or costs to *A* of pursuing alternative means of trying to avoid *B*'s threat as unreasonable to expect *A* to assume.

A possible response to the question of whether the *jus ad bellum* condition of last resort always requires the absence or exhaustion of alternatives to war would be to accept a close analogy with the necessity condition of self-defence in this respect. On this interpretation, just as fulfilment of the self-defence requirement of necessary force can legitimately invoke unreasonable risks or costs of attempting some non-violent means of avoiding threatened unjust harm, so too the *jus ad bellum* condition of last resort can legitimately invoke a comparison of alternative means of achieving the just cause that takes unreasonable risks or costs into account. To regard a risk or cost as *unreasonable* is itself an evaluative judgement of course, and this is something about which there might be disagreement in some circumstances. All the same, I assume that the least controversial basis on which the risks or costs associated with pursuing alternatives to war might be deemed unreasonable are those that are evident in the self-defence example outlined in the previous paragraph. As applied to war, these would be circumstances in which alternative means of achieving the just cause are unlikely to succeed and pursing them would significantly increase the danger or compromise A's capability or opportunity to achieve the just cause by recourse to war should these alternatives fail. On this interpretation of last resort, there can come a point at which recourse to war could be necessary given the significant risks or costs associated with pursuing available inherently less harmful means, where these alternatives to recourse to war have not all been tried or exhausted.

The previous interpretation of what last resort requires can be expressed as the following disjunction: the condition of last resort can be met if realistic alternatives to war have been tried without success or if alternatives that could achieve the just cause would incur unreasonable risk or cost compared with recourse to war. This interpretation contrasts with the straightforward one suggested earlier that would accept only the first half of the disjunction in regarding recourse to war as legitimate only when all of the available alternatives have been tried and have failed. Implicit in the straightforward, much stricter interpretation of last resort is the view that the risks or costs associated with pursuing alternatives to war are never unreasonable; on this interpretation, war is so terrible that the risks or costs associated with exhausting all of the alternatives must be borne rather than resort to war.

Both of these interpretations of what the condition of last resort requires might be thought problematic. The straightforward, stricter interpretation seems morally unreasonable since it is committed to pursuing alternative means that have a low chance of succeeding and that could significantly increase the danger or compromise the capacity or opportunity to achieve the just cause by recourse to war should these alternatives fail. On the other hand, the disjunctive interpretation would imply that compared with available alternative means that are inherently less harmful, recourse to war is not always the last resort in the sense of being the least favourable, the worst case option.

The disjunctive interpretation can easily counter this last query however, when we recognise that any justification of an inherently harmful course of action, x, that invokes x's necessity as a means of achieving y will imply that available alternative means of achieving y are *worse* than x. The respect in which alternative courses of action are worse than x can differ. Consider, for example, A's claim that it is necessary for her to destroy B's property to save a child's life. As part of an instrumentalist justification of destroying B's property, A's claim implies that the type and the degree of harm that A causes (in destroying B's property) are not excessive in the circumstances. The claim that the type and degree of harm that A causes are not excessive might be established in distinguishable ways. One way would be where alternative, inherently less harmful means of attempting to save the child's life are worse than destroying B's property because *as means* they are insufficiently reliable; for example, A could try merely damaging as opposed to outright destroying B's property, but this would make it much less likely that A could save the child's life. Another way is where alternative effective means of saving the child's life would be worse because they risk greater harm; for example, A could have a choice between saving the child's life by destroying B's property or by alternative means that would save B's property but expose A to the risk of being seriously injured or killed. Tellingly, in neither of these ways in which it could be necessary for A to destroy B's property to save the child's life is A's destroying B's property a last resort in the sense of its being the least favourable option, morally speaking. Stephen P. Lee notes, "assuming that it is the most [inherently] harmful means, war is always the *least to be preferred means* of achieving results in international relations. But war might not be *the option least to be preferred*, if another resort would actually cause more harm."[12] Here we need to recognise, more strongly, that where the necessity of recourse to war is a component of its moral justification, recourse to war *cannot* be the least preferable option morally speaking.

Certainly, the *jus ad bellum* condition of last resort represents a very strong presumption against recourse to war as a means of pursuing a just cause. Reasonably interpreted, this condition also constitutes a strict moral constraint on recourse to war: a war that will cause needless harm in pursuit of a just cause is illegitimate. But this constraint is not akin to a formula that will always yield a definitive answer in its practical application. There can and there will be cases in which the condition of last resort is arguably but not convincingly met. The sense in which recourse to war must be a last resort, and the considerations relevant to determining this, will be shaped by what we take the moral rationale of this condition to be. I now turn more directly to this question.

III   The Moral Rationale of Last Resort

The *jus ad bellum* condition that specifies that recourse to war can be legitimate only as a last resort arises within a normative context in which the proposed war has a just cause. Without a morally legitimate cause for recourse to war, the condition of last resort is otiose. As a component of an instrumentalist justification for waging war, the condition of last resort invokes a more general, widely accepted moral directive to avoid causing unnecessary harm in the achievement of a legitimate aim. Harm that is caused needlessly in pursuit of a legitimate aim is not simply regrettable but wrongful. Recourse to war will be

---

[12]   Stephen P. Lee, *Ethics and War: An Introduction*, Cambridge: Cambridge University Press, 2012, p. 93 (my emphases).

needless if it cannot achieve the just cause or if, as a means of achieving the just cause, it involves excessive harm.

Avoiding Needless Harm

In the previous section, in addressing the sense in which recourse to war must be a last resort, I made the point that as a component of moral justification, the condition of last resort cannot imply that war is the least favourable existing option, morally speaking. An option that is a last resort is unwanted, something to be accepted very reluctantly; and as an inherently very harmful activity, war is always undesirable in itself. War typically involves large-scale loss of life; it injures or otherwise harms many people; it damages property and environment and societal infrastructure (including food production and distribution, essential services, education, employment); and it causes significant and widespread disruption of what for most people are aspects of a worthwhile life, such as security and family and other relationships. Even when war has ended, its harmful effects can and usually do persist, sometimes well into the future. Various types of highly limited wars and the use of precisely targeted weaponry can aim to minimise war's inherent and associated harms, and they can succeed in doing this to some extent. However, there is no avoiding the fact that war's very purpose is to advance a cause by inherently harmful means. To be sure, some of the harms that war inflicts are incidental (collateral), as opposed to being strictly intended (part of a war's purpose). But they are inherently bad and foreseeable all the same.

The *jus ad bellum* condition of last resort implies more than recognition of war's inherent badness, however. As a condition of legitimate recourse to war, it represents a strong presumption against recourse to war *as a means* of achieving a just cause. As discussed in the previous section, if the condition of last resort were to require that, irrespective of their associated risks or costs, all other available means of achieving a just cause have been exhausted before recourse to war can be legitimate, then the condition of last resort seems unreasonable. More tellingly, compliance with this condition, thus interpreted, would in some circumstances undermine a moral requirement to minimise harm.

For these reasons, the most defensible interpretation of last resort as a condition of *jus ad bellum* is that recourse to war can be legitimate only if it clearly represents the least harmful available option for achieving a just cause, all things considered.[13] A more literal interpretation of last resort in this context would maintain that this condition (also) implies that recourse to war is always the most harmful means of pursuing a just cause. Some explications

---

[13] As Shue, "Last Resort and Proportionality," p. 4, puts it, "warfare is the effective means that accomplishes the end [aim] with the least evil."

of the condition explicitly adopt this more literal interpretation;[14] some critical discussions implicitly accept it in questioning whether some alternatives to war, such as prolonged trade embargoes or economic boycotts, are always in fact less harmful means compared with a relatively short-term and well-directed armed conflict. However, we should reject this more literal interpretation. As Henry Shue says, the claim that other means of pursuing an aim will cause less evil than recourse to war is largely an empirical generalisation that must be investigated in each case. To this end he questions, for example, whether the sanctions regime against Iraq between 1991 and 2003 actually produced less evil than some highly limited military actions might have done.[15]

Shue's use of the term "evil" in this context also alerts us to the fact that any comparison of the *harms* of war against those of other means of pursing a just cause must also explicitly advert to and include the *wrongs* (rights violations and injustices) that would be perpetrated by the different courses of action under consideration. It is widely accepted, for instance, that innocent people who are killed or otherwise harmed in war are wronged (their rights are infringed), even in circumstances where such wrongs might be incidental, unavoidable and justified. But whether other harms that are an inevitable part of most wars, such as the deaths and injuries suffered by combatants, are also wrongs is disputed.[16] This issue can be relevant to comparing the morally significant negative effects of alternative courses of action.

An assessment of an alternative to recourse to war must also consider whether a proposed alternative is *inherently* evil as opposed to (merely) harmful. For instance, Shue maintains that the protracted sanctions regime against Iraq between 1991 and 2003 caused extensive *wrongful* harm to Iraqi civilians, including many children. Any sanctions regime is coercive: it is intended to bring about a result by pressure caused by the imposition of hardship. If such a regime aims to coerce an outcome by means of causing wrongful harm, that is, by making innocent people the targets of the hardship, then as an alternative to recourse to war it could be less harmful (in terms, say, of total lives lost) but nonetheless more evil. This is not simply because a sanctions regime of this nature could cause more injustices in pursuit of an end, but because by targeting innocent people, by harming them as a means of coercing others, it would constitute an unjust means.[17] Within Just War theory, alternatives to

---

[14] Aloyo, "Just War Theory and the Last of Last Resort."

[15] Shue, "Last Resort and Proportionality."

[16] The moral status of combatants in relation to the rights and wrongs of the conflict represents one point of difference between traditional as opposed to revisionist Just War theorists.

[17] Lee claims in *Ethics and War*, p. 93, that sanctions should be regarded as a use of force and incorporated under last resort. However, some types of sanctions are inherently unjust. Whether highly selectively targeted sanctions can circumvent this objection will depend on whether the intended victims are morally liable to be targeted in this way.

recourse to war must not only be realistic (effective), they must also constitute morally permissible means.

Necessary and Proportionate Harm

In exploring the moral rationale of the condition of last resort, it is important not to confuse this condition with the *jus ad bellum* requirement that recourse to war be a proportionate response.[18] Conflation of these two conditions can be encouraged by the characterisation of judgements about the risks or costs of pursuing alternatives to war as "considerations of proportionality." However, the distinguishable *jus ad bellum* condition of proportionality arises in practice only if recourse to war is necessary.[19] As a condition of necessity, last resort prohibits recourse to war if this would cause needless harm in pursuit of a just cause. (Here it is relevant to consider alternative means.) Recourse to war that is (instrumentally) necessary in pursuit of a just cause can, nonetheless, be disproportionate in relation to the aim that it is intended to achieve. If, for instance, *A* would need to resort to war to reclaim territory that was wrongfully annexed by *B*, war can represent the *least harmful option* in which *A* can re-acquire that territory. It is a further question whether resort to war would be a *proportionate* response, given the aim (re-acquisition of territory) to which recourse to war would be an indispensable means. (The answer to this further question might be no.) The *jus ad bellum* condition of proportionality requires a judgement of comparative value between the harms of war on the one hand and the just cause to be achieved on the other. In relation to proportionality, we must ask: Is the aim to be achieved by war sufficiently weighty to warrant the harm that war will cause?

The *jus ad bellum* condition of proportionality implies that a legitimate grievance might have to be accommodated or endured, rather than recourse to war as an indispensable means of rectification. Circumstances in which recourse to war is indispensable if a just cause is to be achieved, but where peaceful negotiations can achieve a lesser but nonetheless morally accep-table outcome, raise the question of whether war would be a proportionate response. If war is indispensable to achieving a just cause in circumstances where less harmful means could achieve a different but equally good or better outcome, recourse to war should founder on the condition of proportionality.

---

[18] Those who tend to merge these two conditions include Thomas Hurka, "Proportionality and Necessity," in *War: Essays in Political Philosophy*, ed. Larry May, New York: Cambridge University Press, 2008, and Aloyo, "Just War Theory and the Last of Last Resort," p. 196.

[19] See also Shue, "Last Resort and Proportionality."

IV   Last Resort as a Necessary Condition of Just War

If we accept that recourse to war can be justified, what reason could there be for rejecting last resort as a condition of legitimate recourse to war? In this section, I address two distinguishable lines of scepticism about last resort as a necessary condition of *just ad bellum*. Although neither of these lines is persuasive, each serves to underscore the nature of the condition of last resort and its moral rationale.

A first line of scepticism about last resort is empirically based in that it accepts a moral requirement to minimise harm in pursuing a just cause, but it questions whether recourse to war is always the most harmful means of achieving an aim for which a war can be fought, and hence whether war is, among the available options, the least preferable. Scepticism of this type can be met by interpreting the condition of last resort as follows: recourse to war is legitimate only if war is the least harmful option for achieving a just cause. This recognises the inherent harmfulness of war and the need for recourse to war to be indispensable if it is to be justified as a means of achieving a legitimate aim.[20]

All the same, we might think there is something more significant implied by the term "last resort." In the foregoing discussion, I rejected a literalist interpretation of last resort on two grounds. First, an option that is morally justified as the least harmful way of achieving a legitimate aim cannot be the least preferable option, morally speaking. Second, last resort need not imply in this context that all other options have been tried and have failed; indeed, such an interpretation would be inconsistent in some circumstances with fulfilling a moral requirement to minimise harm. Nonetheless, the condition of last resort is very demanding in practice. It serves not only to emphasise that war is always an unwanted option; it also requires that anyone who proposes resort to war must make a sufficiently compelling case for this option as the least harmful way of achieving the just cause. Potential belligerents must take stock and carefully consider and often exhaust inherently less harmful alternatives to war. Taken seriously, the last resort condition can make a significant moral difference and constitute a very strong practical constraint on recourse to war.[21]

A second line of scepticism about last resort as a necessary condition of *jus ad bellum* could be philosophically based. Here I distinguish two possible positions. The first would maintain that recourse to war against unjust aggression could be legitimate as an effective means of defence without any further

---

[20] On this basis, Aloyo's rejection of a last resort condition, "Just War Theory and the Last of Last Resort," pp. 187–201, is unconvincing.

[21] Coppieters et al., *Moral Constraints on War*, pp. 142–47, credit the practical steps that needed to be followed to establish last resort with a crucial "crisis management" role during the Cuban Missile Crisis of 1962.

requirement that war is also indispensable as the least harmful available means of defence. This position rejects the claim that use of excessive force against unjust aggression is unjust.

I merely note here that this first position goes against both sides of a recent philosophical debate about whether, in the case of personal self-defence, an unjust aggressor's liability to suffer defensive harm is limited by a necessity condition. Both sides of this dispute hold, for different reasons, that an unjust aggressor is wronged by use of excessive force.[22] But even were we to accept the (implausible) claim that in a case of personal self-defence, an aggressor who could successfully be fended off by being pushed to the ground would not be wronged in any way by being, say, shot in the heart, this claim cannot simply be extended to unnecessary recourse to war against unjust aggression. Defensive war typically endangers and harms very many people who are not themselves unjust aggressors. The victims of defensive war include combatants fighting for a just cause as well as many people on both sides who will be unjustly directly or indirectly injured or killed. The nature and the scale of the harm and injustice that war causes to all of those who are affected needs to be justified as indispensable if a just cause is to be achieved.

A second philosophically based rejection of last resort might deny that legitimate war even needs to be effective as a means of achieving a just cause. I think any plausibility such a position might be taken to have is likely to be due to its confusion with the appropriate question of what can count as a proportionate just cause in relation to recourse to war. For instance, Daniel Statman argues that in a case of personal self-defence, force that cannot succeed in defending a victim against a threat of rape could nonetheless succeed in defending the victim's honour. It is then a further question whether defence of one's honour is a legitimate aim that is sufficiently weighty to warrant killing someone, for instance. And it is a further question still whether this line of reasoning can plausibly be extended to recourse to war in response to injustice.[23] The salient point here, however, is that this line of reasoning does not maintain that recourse to a war that will be ineffective in achieving any legitimate aim of war could be permissible. Rather, it raises the question of the end(s) to which war might legitimately be waged; defence of honour or re-acquisition of wrongfully annexed territory, for example, might be insufficient to warrant a war that would cause great loss of life and massive disruption.

---

[22] For some classical Just War theorists, a right of defence against unjust aggression is limited *only* by necessity. See e.g. Hugo Grotius, *The Rights of War and Peace*, an abridged translation by William Whewell, Cambridge University Press, 1853, pp. 61–68. Recent discussions of necessity and liability to defensive force include Jeff McMahan, *Killing in War*, Oxford: Oxford University Press, 2009, p. 9; Jonathan Quong and Joanna Firth, "Necessity, Moral Liability and Defensive Harm," *Law and Philosophy*, 31 (2012): 673–701; Helen Frowe, *Defensive Killing*, Oxford: Oxford University Press, 2014, chap. 4.

[23] Daniel Statman, "On the Success Condition for Legitimate Self-Defense," *Ethics* 118 (2008) no. 4: 659–86. See also Frowe, *Defensive Killing*, pp. 116–18.

Conclusion

This chapter has explicated the condition of last resort as a requirement of necessity. This instrumentalist interpretation grounds the condition in a more general moral constraint against causing needless harm, including unjust harm. The moral rationale of the condition of last resort will shape what this condition implies and requires both in theory and in practice. As a condition under which recourse to war can be legitimate, last resort cannot reasonably be interpreted in ways that would mean that recourse to war could never be permissible. Furthermore, an interpretation of last resort that implies that (legitimate) war must be the least favourable option, morally speaking, is indefensible. Whether in a particular case recourse to war is the least favourable means of pursuing a just cause will require careful consideration of whether war is, from the available options, the most harmful means. The most defensible interpretation of last resort as a condition of *jus ad bellum* is that recourse to war is legitimate only if no realistic alternative, less harmful means can achieve a just cause for which the war is fought.

The condition of last resort represents a very strong constraint against recourse to war. Indeed, it is a strict condition in that it prohibits recourse to war that on all the available evidence, properly considered, will be futile as a means of achieving a just cause for which the war would be fought; in practice, the condition can also require the pursuit of realistic inherently less harmful options even to the brink of war.

The condition of last resort is most often taken to apply to the legitimacy of recourse to war. However, wars take place and develop over time and a necessity condition is also applicable to the legitimacy of continuation of a war. A war that was commenced as a last resort might cease to be so if, for example, an adversary's capabilities or responses far exceed expectations or if genuine peace negotiations become realistic. Considerations that are relevant to the need to continue a war that is underway can of course differ from those that were relevant to the need to embark on that war in the first place. Nonetheless, it follows from the interpretation of the condition of last resort developed in this chapter that the indispensability of recourse to war cannot be justified retrospectively solely with reference to what that war has actually achieved.

6 The Moral Problems of Asymmetric War

Steven P. Lee

Asymmetric war (also called unequal combat) is a military conflict where the military capabilities of one of the belligerents far exceed those of the other. (When the belligerents are more evenly matched, their conflict is, in contrast, a conventional war.) Different sorts of asymmetry may exist between belligerents, but the subject here is the asymmetry of military capabilities or *capability asymmetry*, which is how the term *asymmetric war* is most commonly understood.

Asymmetric warfare becomes a moral problem when one of the belligerents, as a result of the asymmetric character of the conflict, adopts morally problematic tactics. For example, the weaker side, in an effort to "level the playing field," may adopt alternative tactics that violate the moral rules of war: "Military imbalances carry incentives for the weaker party to ameliorate its inferiority by disregarding existing rules on the conduct of hostilities."[1] For example, in an asymmetric war, the weaker side may deliberately attack or endanger civilians or combatants in ways that violate the moral rules.

The structure of the moral problem for the weaker side, however, is not simply that by adopting alternative tactics it may violate the moral rules, but also that there may be a presumptive moral case for its doing so. It may be that only by adopting rule-violating tactics can it have a reasonable chance of success. Fairness in this sense, having a reasonable chance of success in a war, is an important moral value.

So, Just War theory may pose a problem for asymmetric warfare, in the sense that the theory may not only prohibit occasional actions within such a war; it may prohibit this form of warfare altogether. But, beyond this, asymmetric warfare may pose a problem for Just War theory, in the sense that the fact of asymmetric warfare (and the need for it) may show the inadequacy of the theory. If Just War theory cannot accommodate asymmetric warfare, if it cannot provide a framework in which such warfare can be morally explained, this may be as much a problem for the theory as the theory is for that form of warfare. This raises the question whether Just War theory is adequate for

---

[1] International Committee of the Red Cross, "International Humanitarian Law and the Challenges of Contemporary Armed Conflict," *International Review of the Red Cross* 89 (September 2007) no. 867, p. 733.

contemporary war, or whether contemporary war stands as a serious counter-example to Just War theory, an argument that the theory needs to be significantly revised or abandoned.

In Section I, I discuss the nature of capability asymmetry, and in Section II, I consider asymmetry and the justice of war. The subject of Section III is asymmetry and justice in fighting war. A moral dilemma arises from this discussion, and I consider in Section IV whether this dilemma is resolvable. In Section V, I consider terrorism, and in the final section, I examine an extreme case of capability asymmetry and its implications for the moral dilemma.

I Capability Asymmetry

Capability asymmetry exists in a war when one side has a significant military superiority over the other in resources, trained personnel, and/or technology. The most common case of asymmetric war is one where the strong belligerent is a state and the weak belligerent is an organized group of non-state actors, and I focus my discussion on this sort of case (though the discussion should also apply to cases where both sides are states). I will use "insurgents" as a general term to refer to members of an organized group of non-state actors (members of an insurgency) fighting against a state. An asymmetric conflict may be within a state; that is, it may be a domestic civil or secessionist struggle, where the insurgents are fighting the central government of their state. Or it may in addition involve an outside party, as when a foreign state intervenes, usually to help the state defeat an insurgency, though sometimes to help the insurgents defeat the state (in which case the conflict may lose its asymmetric character). It is important to note that an asymmetric war, as the term is commonly used, has (at least) two belligerents, so that it is for our purposes two (or more) wars, one fought by the strong side and one fought by the weak side. Only in making this distinction can we talk about a war as just or unjust, or as fought justly or unjustly.

The key feature of asymmetric warfare is that the weak side adopts a different strategy or a different paradigm of warfare to circumvent or counter the strengths of its opponent and to create some advantages for itself. Were the weak side to use the same strategy or paradigm of warfare as the strong side, its weakness would lead almost inevitably to its defeat. So when capabilities are a serious mismatch, the prudent thing for the weak side to do is not to play to the opponent's strengths but to adopt a strategy that provides it with some advantage of its own. The idea that opponents in an asymmetric conflict may use a different strategy is illustrated by an anecdote from the aftermath of the Vietnam War, a reported exchange between a U.S. officer Colonel Harry Summers and a North Vietnamese officer Colonel Tu. Summers: "You know you never defeated us on the battlefield." Tu: "That may be so, but it is also irrelevant."[2] The conventional paradigm is about winning battles, while the insurgent paradigm may be about something else, such as wearing down the opponent, because winning battles is generally not something the weak side can do.

The principal form for the alternative strategy or paradigm adopted by an insurgency is *guerrilla warfare*. The basic idea of guerrilla warfare is to avoid falling victim to the military strength of the stronger opponent by evading direct confrontation with its military forces. Guerrilla warfare, according to Ivan Arreguin-Toft, is defined as follows:

The organization of a portion of society for the purpose of imposing costs on an adversary using armed forces trained to avoid direct confrontation. These costs include the loss of soldiers, supplies, infrastructure, peace of mind, and most important, time … [I]ts goal is to destroy not the capacity but the will of the attacker.[3]

The guerrilla struggle is often a play for the time needed to weaken the will of the opponent. The weak side is incapable of destroying the military capabilities of the opponent. It seeks rather to wear the strong side down. Its struggle is meant to affect the will of the strong side to continue to fight, as the Vietnamese won the Vietnam War by weakening the American will to continue. Insurgents seek "to wear down the opposition by lots of small-scale operations."[4] The guerrillas have an easier time wearing down the opponent's will when the strong side is an intervener, for then the insurgents usually have much more at stake than the intervener, as was the case in the Vietnam War. Willingness to fight and to continue to fight a war is a function of how much a belligerent perceives to be at stake.

In our own time, the focus is on the struggle between states and international terrorism. International terrorism is distinct from guerrilla warfare, and I discuss this contrast later. But in a guerrilla campaign, terrorism is a tactic sometimes employed by the weak side. Terrorism may be defined as deliberate attacks on civilian targets to create terror in the civilian population and thereby achieve some military or political objective.[5] Terrorism, of course, has always played a role in warfare, though it is more often practiced by the strong side than by insurgencies. We should at this point keep the question open whether guerrilla fighters must practice terrorism. Terrorism, like guerrilla tactics more

---

[2] Widely cited. See, for example, www.slate.com/articles/news_and_politics/war_stories/2007/08/irrelevant_exuberance.html, accessed June 10, 2016.

[3] Ivan Arreguin-Toft, "How the Weak Win Wars: A Theory of Asymmetric Conflict," *International Security* 26 (Summer 2001) no. 1: 93–128, at p. 103.

[4] A.P.V. Rogers, "Unequal Combat and the Law of War," *Yearbook of International Humanitarian Law* 7 (2004): 3–34, at p. 4.

[5] Steven P. Lee, *Ethics and War: An Introduction*, Cambridge: Cambridge University Press, 2012, pp. 234–35.

generally, is meant to work on the opponent's will, but through the creation of terror in civilian populations, rather than through the imposition of a series of military loses, as with guerrilla tactics more generally.

Terrorism violates one of the most important moral rules of war, the rule against deliberate attacks on civilians and civilian targets, known as the *principle of discrimination*. In Just War theory, this principle is part of *jus in bello*, which concerns the morality of how a war is fought. A number of other moral rules are part of *jus in bello* as well, but discrimination is the most important of these. In contrast, *jus ad bellum* is the part of Just War theory that concerns the morality of going to war. It is also characterized by a series of rules or criteria, adherence to which is required for a war to be just.

II Asymmetric War and Just War

Consider first asymmetric war and *jus ad bellum*. Is an insurgency able to fight a just war, that is, one that satisfies the criteria of *jus ad bellum*? There is a second, related question: Is an insurgency able to fight a war at all, understanding war in the morally relevant sense of that term? (A military conflict is a war in the morally relevant sense when it is appropriate or possible to apply the moral categories of Just War theory to it.) In war, the typical belligerents are states, and it is to some commentators an open question whether a non-state entity such as an insurgency can be a belligerent at all. A non-state entity may fight against the military forces of a state, but does this fighting constitute a war in the morally relevant sense?

In general, the *ad bellum* criteria apply straightforwardly to asymmetric war, as they do to conventional wars. But one of the criteria plays a special role in the case of asymmetric war, namely, the criterion of *legitimate authority*.[6] To answer the two questions just raised, I focus on this criterion. To be just, a war must be declared by a legitimate authority. Because an insurgency is not run by a state, some argue that its leadership is not an authority that is legitimate. Only a state has a legal structure that can impart legitimacy to its leaders.

But consider the argument for legitimate authority offered by Thomas Aquinas, one of the founders of Just War theory. Aquinas argued that only someone without an earthly superior can declare war, can be a legitimate authority, because someone with an earthly superior can appeal to that superior for redress of grievances that might otherwise be grounds for war.[7] Because there is no global authority, so no earthly superior for states, the leaders of states must have available to them the option of war to settle serious disputes with other states, while lesser authorities do not have this option since they can

---

[6] The other five criteria are just cause, rightful intention, proportionality, last resort, and reasonable chance of success.

[7] Thomas Aquinas, *Summa Theologica*, trans. Fathers of the English Dominican Province, vol. 9, London: Burns, Oates & Washbourne, 1916, p. 501.

appeal to the leaders of their states, their earthly superiors, to respond to grievances. But this seems to assume that lesser authorities can expect that their earthly superiors will give them a hearing regarding their grievances. In the case of potential insurgent groups, however, this may not be the case, as the rulers of their states may ignore their grievances. So seen, Aquinas's point is not so much about leaders of states, but about leaders of any group, state, or sub-state without an effective political mechanism to have their grievances heard. When this is true of sub-state groups, Aquinas's argument should apply to them as well, and the insurgency may, to that extent, be regarded as satisfying the legitimate authority criterion.

To satisfy the legitimate authority criterion, an insurgency must exhibit other features as well. Consider the language of Protocol II of the Geneva Conventions concerning "non-international armed conflicts," which are conflicts within a state. The Protocol applies to conflicts "between [a state's] armed forces and dissident armed forces or other organized armed groups which, under responsible command, exercise such control over a part of its territory as to enable them to carry out sustained and concerted military operations and to implement this Protocol."[8]

The factors referred to here are also part of the idea of legitimate authority. So, to satisfy that criterion, an insurgency must be an organization with a leadership with "responsible command," that is, clear lines of authority to exercise control over its military efforts. This is essential because its combatants must be accountable for their behavior in regard to the rules of war (the groups must be able to "implement the Protocol"). In addition, the insurgency must "exercise such control over a part of its territory." This would ensure that the insurgency represents a significant portion of the population of a territory, under the assumption that effective territorial control indicates the support of a large portion of the population within that territory.[9] An insurgency must represent a large number of individuals who strongly support its efforts to seek redress for its grievances.

Given this discussion of legitimate authority, we can address the second question of whether an insurgency can be considered a war in the morally relevant sense. If only a state has the legitimate authority necessary to initiate a war, the answer would be no. If an insurgency has no legitimate authority, so no moral right to initiate a war, whatever fighting it does cannot count as a war in the morally relevant sense. But because an insurgency can have legitimate authority, it can have a moral right to initiate a war, so that its military struggle can be a war in a morally relevant sense.

---

[8] Adam Roberts and Richard Guelff, *Documents on the Laws of War*, third ed., Oxford: Oxford University Press, 2000, p. 484.

[9] Michael Walzer, *Just and Unjust Wars*, New York: Basic Books, 1977, pp. 184–85.

Let me briefly mention one other of the *ad bellum* criteria, namely, *just cause*, in some ways the most important of the criteria. In a conflict, normally one side has a just cause and the other does not. Insurgencies can readily satisfy this criterion. For a war to be just, the group fighting the war must have a just cause for its struggle. Many states are repressive, often directing their repression especially against specific groups in society, for example, ethnic minorities. If the repression is severe, which it often is, then the fact of that repression would, other things being equal, constitute a just cause for war. In an asymmetric conflict, it cannot be assumed that the strong side always is the one with a just cause. On the contrary, the opposite is more likely the case.

In our world, lacking a true global authority, war is the final arbiter of serious disputes between states and sub-state groups. Our world is one in which, as Aquinas would say, states, and sometimes sub-state groups, have no effective earthly superior from whom to seek redress of grievances that would constitute a just cause for war. Under this condition, each group must be entitled, assuming that it satisfies other *ad bellum* criteria, to take up arms to press for redress. But implicit in this entitlement, it must be possible for a group taking up arms with a just cause to succeed in its struggle. An entitlement to fight must include a possibility of victory, without which the entitlement is meaningless. This point may be expressed by saying that a military force, even when it is an insurgency, must have a *reasonable chance of success.*[10] It need not, of course, be guaranteed success in its resort to arms, but insurgencies must in general have some non-negligible chance for success. Rodin argues that "if (as just war theory assumes) war is a morally appropriate remedy to redress certain kinds of injustice, then fairness ought to dictate that it be a remedy open to the weak as well as the strong."[11] This is for him a principle of fairness.

But an insurgency generally does not have a reasonable chance of success by fighting the strong belligerent using the standard paradigm of war, which would require that it face the opponent in direct and open combat. The insurgency must be able to use an alternative paradigm that gives it a reasonable chance of success. A principle to this effect (a fairness principle) may be formulated as follows:

C1: In asymmetric war, the weak belligerent with grievances that it believes constitute a just cause for war must have the option (assuming it satisfies other *ad bellum* criteria) of taking up arms on terms that provide it with a reasonable chance of success.

---

[10] Reasonable chance of success is one of the six *ad bellum* criteria. What I claim is that fairness requires that, in general, insurgencies have a reasonable chance of success, not that every insurgency must have such a chance.

[11] David Rodin, "Ethics of Asymmetric War," in *The Ethics of War: Shared Problems in Different Traditions*, eds. Richard Sorabji and David Rodin, Aldershot, UK: Ashgate, 2006, p. 159.

Of course, an insurgency's (or any belligerent's) belief that it has a just cause does not guarantee that it does. It may be mistaken. Most belligerents believe they have a just cause, even though at most one side in a conflict has a just cause, so belligerents are often mistaken in their belief. But war must be an option for all belligerents (who can satisfy, or believe they can satisfy, the *ad bellum* criteria), just as filing a tort suit in domestic law should be an option for all individuals. The tort system should be available to all who believe they have been done an injustice. Of course, the tort system determines where justice lies (in a legal sense, though not in a moral sense), and war does not do this (in either sense). There is no guarantee that the just side will win its war. Still, the opportunity must be available. C1 says that if the only way in which the weak side can have a chance to defeat the strong side is to adopt alternative tactics, such as guerrilla warfare, fairness requires that it be allowed to do so. C1 asserts that, in the words of Jacoby Carter: "A defensible set of rules must make it possible for either party to win."[12] Walzer observes: "It is a central principle of just war theory that the self-defense of a people or a country cannot be make morally impossible."[13]

III   Asymmetric War and Fighting Justly

The basic moral problem raised by asymmetric warfare is that C1 may be at odds with the fact that the alternative paradigms of warfare it permits insurgencies to adopt may violate the rules of *jus in bello*. Normally a just war can be fought justly with some prospects for a successful conclusion, though it is in fact frequently fought unjustly, for the sake of expediency.[14] The moral problem is that in the case of asymmetric warfare, this link may be broken. It may be that in general insurgencies fighting a just war cannot fight it justly (in accord with the *in bello* rules) with a reasonable chance of success. Weak belligerents must be allowed to adopt alternative strategies that may be at odds with *in bello* rules because this is "the only kind of military recourse available that would not lead directly to a suicidal defeat."[15] C1 allows insurgencies to do so. But the alternative strategies may put them at odds with *in bello* rules.

---

[12] Jacoby Adeshei Carter, "Just/New War Theory: Non-State Actors in Asymmetric Conflicts," *Philosophy in the Contemporary World* 16 (Fall 2009) no. 2: 1–11, at p. 7.

[13] Michael Walzer, "Responsibility and Proportionality in State and Nonstate Wars," *Parameters* (Spring 2009): 40–52, at p. 48.

[14] Whether the contrary holds, that is, whether an unjust war can be fought justly, is a matter of some dispute. According to one traditional view of Just War theory, the answer is yes, that *jus ad bellum* and *jus in bello* are independent in this respect. According to a recent, revisionist view, the two parts of Just War theory are linked, in that an unjust war cannot be fought justly.

[15] Rodin, "Ethics of Asymmetric War," p. 155.

This is the moral problem: the strategies that a weak belligerent may need to adopt to give it a reasonable chance of success may violate the *in bello* rules. The problem arises when C1 is juxtaposed with this claim:

C2: In asymmetric war, the weak belligerent does not, in general, have a reasonable chance of success unless it adopts strategies that violate *in bello* rules.

If C1 and C2 are both true, a systemic moral dilemma results. The weak side is justified in using strategies that are unjust. It is both just (justified) and unjust (not justified) for the weak side to use such strategies. The conflict between C1 and C2 is a systemic dilemma because it applies to most members of a whole class of belligerents, namely, the weak side in an asymmetric war. Any structure of moral rules is likely to give rise to occasional moral dilemmas, such as that raised by Socrates in response to Cephalus in Book 1 of the *Republic*. But a structure of moral rules that gives rise to a systemic dilemma is to that extent deficient. We might say that a systemic dilemma represents a counterexample to a structure of rules that gives rise to it. This is the risk this dilemma poses to Just War theory.

Should the dilemma stand, there may be need to question the adequacy of Just War theory in regard to its ability to comprehend a form of warfare characteristic of our age. To consider this dilemma further, we must investigate whether C2 is true.

IV   Can the Moral Dilemma Be Resolved?

Is C2 true? Consider first the ways in which the weak side in asymmetric wars has tended to violate *in bello* rules. There is a long history of the weak side in asymmetric wars breaking the rules of war to seek to overcome the advantages of the strong side. What form has that violation usually taken? Many of the rules of war tend to support the standard paradigm of war and the modes of combatant interaction it involves, especially, direct confrontation between opposing forces. Because the weak side adopts a paradigm that avoids direct confrontation, it tends to violate rules that assume or seek to ensure that direct confrontation is the standard mode of interaction. Indirect confrontation, the mode of interaction sought by the weak side, includes tactics involving deception, surprise attack, ambush, placement of booby traps, and so forth. Traditionally there have been moral rules against such tactics, consistent with the assumption that the norm of interaction is the direct confrontation of forces. That is, rules limit or prohibit attacks on combatants that are not direct confrontations. The weak side has most often violated these rules. For example, it used to be part of the rules of war that sentries were not to be attacked, but this rule is no longer recognized.[16] Such a

---

[16] Article 69 of the Lieber Code, promulgated by the Union in the American Civil War, states that "Outposts, sentinels, or pickets are not to be fired upon, except to drive them in, or when a positive order, special or general, has been issued to that effect."

rule would clearly benefit the strong side, and so it was ignored by the weak side and as a result over time abandoned.

Consider the behavior of the Continental Army in the American Revolution. One of its tactics was the use of natural cover to pick off the British Redcoats in formation. Another is illustrated by Washington's attack on the Hessian mercenaries on Christmas Eve in his famous crossing of the Delaware. It would not be surprising if the British saw these sorts of attacks as violations of the rules of war. But Washington's view would probably have been that such tactics were adopted out of necessity to ensure that the weak side had a reasonable chance of success.[17] In any case, the rules changed over time accordingly, and attacks from natural cover and surprise attacks came to be regarded as permissible. These are, of course, the primary tactics of guerrilla forces.

It is helpful to think of these changes in the rules of war in terms of Walzer's distinction between different sorts of questions that can be asked regarding the morality of killing in war. There are who-questions, on the one hand, and when-questions, on the other.[18] Many moral rules of war provide answers to one or the other of these questions. Some *in bello* rules concern *whom* combatants may attack and others concern *when* they may be attacked. The answer to the who-questions, which has been fairly constant throughout the history of just war thinking, is that only combatants may be attacked, a combatant being one who is directly engaged in the fighting. Those not directly engaged in the fighting, civilians, may not be (intentionally) attacked. This answer has, as Walzer notes, a special moral import, as it is "closely connected with universal notions of right and wrong." The answer represents the principle of discrimination, and it is a universal moral rule.

In contrast, the answers to the when-questions have varied over time. Specifically, the answers about when combatants may be attacked and the rules based on them have tended to grow more lenient over time, allowing attacks in a wider range of circumstances. Stricter rules tend to favor the strong side, and the weak side has pushed against these rules by violating them in its effort to achieve its own advantage in competition with its much stronger opponent. Arrangements with stricter rules about attacking combatants, Walzer notes, "have never been stable, because they give a systematic advantage to the army that is larger and better equipped." The instability leads over time to the abandonment of some of the rules: "It is the weaker side that persistently

Available at http://avalon.law.yale.edu/19th_century/lieber.asp, accessed June 24, 2016. Walzer refers to the case of sentries in *Just and Unjust Wars*, p. 143.

[17] But Malcolm Gladwell, quoting author William Polk, points out that after the initial stages of the war, Washington reverted to the standard paradigm, seeking to create "a British-type army," as a result of which he was "defeated time after time and almost lost the war." Gladwell, *David and Goliath*, Boston: Back Bay Books, 2013, p. 32.

[18] Walzer, *Just and Unjust Wars*, pp. 41–43. He also discusses how-questions, which go along with when-questions.

refuses to fix any limits on the vulnerability of enemy soldiers (the extreme form of this refusal is guerrilla war), pleading military necessity."[19] Lenient rules give greater sway to guerrilla tactics. In our own era, the rules allow combatants to be attacked almost anywhere and anytime (unless they are surrendering or *hors de combat*). So, insurgents have tended to violate conventional rules, the answers to the when-questions, leading over time to many of those rules being abandoned. But the universal moral rules, the answers to the who-questions, most importantly the principle of discrimination, have remained constant.

C2 can be revised to take account of the distinction between conventional and universal *in bello* rules:

C2*: In asymmetric war, the weak belligerent does not, in general, have a reasonable chance of success unless it adopts tactics that violate *in bello* rules, both conventional and universal.

The purpose of this revision is to make clear what form C2 would have to take to generate the systemic dilemma. The idea is that it is the systematic violation of the universal moral rules, rather than conventional rules, that is of special moral significance. If insurgents violated only conventional rules, then C2 would not sufficiently counterpose C1 so as to create the dilemma.

I argue that C2* is false because insurgents need not in general violate the universal moral rules to have a reasonable chance of success. If so, the last clause in C2* is false, and so the entire claim. The tendency cited earlier for insurgents to violate conventional rather than universal *in bello* rules at least suggests that C2* is false in this way. But insurgents have sometimes violated universal *in bello* rules, particularly the principle of discrimination. They have practiced terrorism. Moreover, they may need to do so, given contemporary military realities, to have a reasonable chance of success, in which case C2* would be true. So, the question needs more careful examination. Because our focus is on the principle of discrimination, the question is whether insurgents must violate this principle and practice terrorism to have a reasonable chance of success.

Insurgents have indeed violated the principle of discrimination because they have at times intentionally attacked civilians or put them at serious risk. In what ways have they done this? (1) Insurgents may directly attack civilians seeking military advantage; that is, they may practice terrorism. As mentioned earlier, terrorism is practiced in an effort to affect the will of the opponent through creating terror in the civilian population, leading the population to pressure the leadership to withdraw from the war or to make concessions to the insurgents.[20] Insurgents might also practice terrorism to create general confusion, which they believe might benefit them. (2) Insurgents may attack civilians

---

[19] Walzer, *Just and Unjust Wars*, p. 143.

[20] In contrast, attacks by insurgents on military targets, while also meant to work on the will of the opponent, seek to achieve this end through imposing cumulative military losses. This line of causality may also involve the opponent's population and its effect on the leadership, but

intentionally to provoke the strong side to heavy-handed retaliation against civilians in response, hoping that such a response to their provocation would increase insurgent support among the population.

There is a third way. (3) Insurgents often put civilians at serious risk of being attacked by the strong side. Guerrilla warfare by its nature puts civilians at risk of such attacks because the insurgents' methods of indirect confrontation require that they intermingle with the civilian population. Guerrillas live among civilians, use civilians as informants, and often store weapons in and launch attacks from civilian areas and assets. In an extreme form of this sort of case, insurgents may masquerade as civilians in order to attack enemy combatants. These activities, according to Rodin, "subvert *jus in bello* . . . by making it difficult for the enemy to both fight effectively and to respect the principle of [discrimination]."[21] Because of the guerrilla tactics, the strong side is more likely to attack civilians, and the insurgents would be at least indirectly responsible for such attacks.

First consider (1) and (2). I argue that to have a reasonable chance of success, insurgents do not in general need to attack civilians directly. Such behaviors may be expedient, but they are not generally necessary. The case for this claim depends on the way in which guerrillas win, which is to wear down and overcome the will of the strong side, and how this contrasts with the way in which the strong side wins. An insurgent victory, as we have seen, requires that the guerrillas deliver a long series of military "pinpricks," which eventually wears the strong side down, overcoming its will to continue. So long as the insurgents have a base among the local population (in the absence of which they would not satisfy the *ad bellum* criterion of legitimate authority and so not be waging a war in the morally relevant sense[22]), they can continue imposing their pinpricks until the will of the strong side is overcome. This requires time, and they can play for time without attacking civilians. As Douglas McCready notes: "Asymmetric warfare [by the weak side] does not necessarily violate accepted international norms. It is directed far more at the enemy's mental framework and will than is conventional war."[23] Insurgents may believe that they can achieve their goal more quickly or increase the likelihood of its achievement by engaging in the behaviors represented by (1) and (2), but C1 promises neither quick victory nor an increased likelihood of success beyond a reasonable chance. All the argument need show is that eschewing the behaviors represented in (1) and (2) generally provides insurgents with a reasonable

---

through the population's concern about military casualties ("body bags"), not through their being terrorized.

[21] Rodin, "Ethics of Asymmetric War," p. 158.

[22] If the insurgents fail the legitimate authority criterion, they are not fighting a war; the proper response to them falls under the paradigm of policing rather than war.

[23] Douglas McCready, "Now More than Ever: Territorial Asymmetric Warfare, and the Just War Tradition," *Political Theology* 7 (2006) no. 4: 461–74, at p. 470.

chance of success. This shows that practicing terrorism is not something that is generally necessary for insurgents.

A different argument is required in the case of (3). It cannot be doubted that guerrilla warfare, by its nature, creates risks of attacks by the strong side on civilian supporters of the guerrillas. But much of the responsibility for these risks must lie with the strong side, which actually does the attacking. With its greater resources, the strong side has the ability to minimize risks to enemy civilians, even if this is more costly. At the same time, some of the responsibility for these risks must lie with the insurgents, at least to the extent that the risks are inherent in guerrilla warfare. But the insurgents can minimize these risks, consistent with having a reasonable chance of success. In addition, because the insurgents may foresee these risks but do not directly intend them, they may not run afoul of the principle of discrimination nor, if the risks are minimized, the principle of proportionality under the requirements of the doctrine of double effect.[24]

One way to think about the behaviors of the insurgents who create these civilian risks is to think of them as a form of force protection. The strong side is generally able to protect its forces when they are not engaged in fighting by being able to house them at secure bases. The ability of the insurgents to return to their homes when they are not fighting, homes made secure to the extent to which the strong side respects the principle of discrimination, provides an analogous form of force protection. In the spirit of C1, we may say that this is something to which each side is entitled.

The extreme form of (3), which involves insurgents attacking their opponents while masquerading as civilians, is deeply problematic from a moral perspective. Such behavior, for example, feigning civilian status to facilitate an attack, is *perfidy*, a recognized war crime. Perfidy is distinguished from ruse, which is attacking the opponent with forms of trickery other than perfidy. An example of ruse that is not perfidy is setting up a booby trap. In international humanitarian law (IHL), the part of international law covering war, ruse is permissible but perfidy is not. Perfidy would clearly increase greatly the risks to civilians, as one's opponents would not be able to trust the civilian status of any apparent civilian and so be much more inclined to attack civilians. A great portion of guerrilla tactics involve ruse, but my claim regarding (3) is that they need not involve perfidy. Insurgency requires ruse, but it can have a reasonable chance of success without perfidy.

This general picture of the permissible limits of guerrilla activity is largely endorsed by IHL. IHL is not identical with *jus in bello*, but the two overlap extensively. Much of IHL is based on the Geneva Conventions of 1949, and two

---

[24] The doctrine of double effect is the idea that harm to civilians does not run afoul of the principle of discrimination unless the harm is intended. Civilian harm that is not intentioned must satisfy only the weaker principle of proportionality.

additions to the Geneva Conventions (Protocols 1 and 2) adopted in 1977.[25] These Protocols, referred to earlier, expand the understanding of IHL in a way that better accommodates the concerns of the weak side in asymmetric warfare: "In order to promote the protection of the civilian population," the Protocols require that a combatant distinguish himself from civilians by carrying "his arms openly ... during each military engagement" and when "engaged in a military deployment preceding the launching of an attack." Acts in accord with this prescription "shall not be considered as perfidious."[26] Elsewhere the Protocols require that insurgents, when in combat, wear uniforms or insignia designating them as combatants. Presumably the authors of the Protocols considered their prescriptions consistent with the principle of discrimination as this principle is embodied in other provisions of IHL. Moreover, it is consistent with the discussion of (3): insurgents are permitted in a limited way to expose civilians to increased risk of attack by the strong side, so long as they do not perfidiously masquerade as civilians while engaged in military action.

This then is the main argument. The systemic moral dilemma represented by the tension between C1 and C2* is resolved by the showing that C2* is false. To that extent, asymmetric warfare does not challenge the comprehensiveness of Just War theory. When *in bello* rule violations occur in asymmetric war, such violations generally cannot be justified by an appeal to military necessity. In general, insurgents can fight within the moral rules, at least those that are universal rather than merely conventional, with a reasonable chance of success.

I should note, however, as the reader has surely noted, that many of the claims advanced earlier have significant adverbial modifications, such as "generally," "in general," and "tends to," that weaken their force This is consistent with my purpose to show that there is no systemic moral problem with the ability of Just War theory to comprehend asymmetric war. The characteristics of asymmetric war vary considerably in detail, and it could be that my general claims about the falsity of C2* do not apply in all cases. Regarding some particular cases of asymmetric war, there may be genuine moral dilemmas. But this situation is no different from the case with everyday moral reasoning. The fact that the rules of everyday moral reasoning are generally consistent does not preclude the fact that genuine moral dilemmas arise in practice in particular cases.

V International Terrorism

Earlier, I made a distinction between guerrilla war and international terrorism, and I need to fill this out. The focus so far has been on the guerrilla war paradigm as the standard way in which asymmetric war is fought by the

---

[25] For a discussion of the genesis of the Protocols, see Roberts and Guelff, *Documents*, pp. 410–22, 481–83.
[26] In Article 44 of Protocol 1, Roberts and Guelff, *Documents*, p. 445.

weak side, and, indeed, this paradigm is still much practiced today by insurgencies fighting in many parts of the world. But many commentators today use the term "asymmetric war" to refer to the conflict between states and global terrorist networks, a type of conflict that has emerged only in the past two decades. The strong side in this conflict is engaged in a self-described "global war on terror" (GWOT). Speaking of this conflict, David Wippman reports: "The end of the Cold War and the rise of international terrorism have again transformed the nature of armed conflict in ways that have led some commentators to suggest a reconsideration of humanitarian law."[27] This suggests the need to apply an analysis of asymmetric warfare to a new paradigm, the "terrorist paradigm," which pits organized groups promoting terrorist acts at the international level against the many states that are subject to these attacks. Does the rise of international terrorism represent a form of asymmetric warfare different from guerrilla warfare, one that calls into question the adequacy of IHL and the Just War theory? If so, it would serve as a counterexample to the conclusion that asymmetric war does not pose a systemic moral dilemma.

The difference between these two paradigms is that the guerrilla paradigm refers to methods employed by unified sub-state groups fighting against a state from ground held within the territory of that state, while the terrorist paradigm refers to methods employed by groups and individuals only loosely connected and without a fixed base of operation. But does the terrorist paradigm represent a paradigm of warfare at all? In criticism of the view that it does, critics argue, as Wippman reports, that a "move to a new war paradigm obscures important differences between armed conflicts covered by the laws of war (and terrorist acts committed in the course of those conflicts) and terrorist acts committed independently of an armed conflict."[28] There is, as he suggests, a distinction between terrorism perpetrated in the context of a guerrilla conflict, to which the laws of war and Just War theory do apply, and terrorism committed under the terrorist paradigm, outside of a guerrilla conflict, to which they may not apply. They apply in the case of guerrilla war, as I have argued, because the weak side generally has a reasonable chance of success while adhering to the principle of discrimination. So, in the case of a guerrilla war, the principle of discrimination applies, and terrorist acts committed as part of guerrilla war stand morally and legally condemned. But if international terrorism represents a different paradigm of asymmetric warfare, one to which terrorism is inherent, then there are doubts that the earlier argument applies to it. If international terrorists are fighting a war in which they must have a reasonable chance of success, as C1 requires, then C2* is true and the systemic dilemma reemerges. But does C1 apply to the terrorist paradigm?

---

[27] David Wippman, "Introduction: Do New Wars call for New Laws?," in *New Wars, New Laws?*, eds. David Wippman and Matthew Evangelista, Ardsley, NY: Transnational Publishers, 2005, pp. 1–30, at p. 3.

[28] Wippman, *New Wars, New Laws?*, p. 4.

Consider a 2016 newspaper report on the call by a spokesman of the Islamic State for terrorist violence in the West:

We have heard from some of you that you are unable to do your work because of your inability to reach military targets and because you are too embarrassed to target what is called civilian targets. So know that in the heart of the lands of the Crusaders ... there is no presence of what we call innocents.[29]

This statement acknowledges and seeks to dispel the concern some supporters in the West have about attacking civilians by denying the distinction between combatants and civilians.[30] This is a response to the inability of Islamic State insurgents to attack military targets, which are too well protected. In practical terms, only civilian or "soft" targets may be available. But another way to make the case for attacking civilians would be to recall that according to C1, the weak side in an asymmetric war must have a reasonable chance of success, even if this requires that *in bello* rules of war (including universal rules) must be breached. The conclusion that C2* is false shows that this is not the case under the guerrilla war paradigm, but C2* is clearly true under the terrorist paradigm. This argument can be put in the context of our earlier discussion of how the weak side over time has brought about changes in the conventional rules of war. In that move away from the stricter rules, rules that tended to favor the strong, a natural limit, so to speak, was reached with the current conventional rules that allow combatants to be attacked almost anytime and anywhere. These are the rules operative in guerrilla war. Any further change in the rules in that direction would breach that natural limit and endorse attacks on civilians. This breach is the change that the terrorist paradigm seems to demand.

But this outcome can be avoided by showing that C1 does not in fact apply to the terrorist paradigm, because the terrorists' conflict is not a war in the morally relevant sense. If it is not, then there is, in this case, no dilemmatic conflict between C1 and C2*. The struggle involving international terrorism, like any struggle, has two sides, the struggle as prosecuted by the terrorists and the struggle as prosecuted by the target states (the GWOT). Neither of these is a war in the morally relevant sense. The argument is commonly made that the GWOT is not strictly speaking a war. For example, speaking of the GWOT, the International Committee of the Red Cross (ICRC) states: "One needs to examine, in the light of IHL, whether it is merely a rhetorical device or whether it refers to a global armed conflict in the legal sense. On the basis of an analysis of the

---

[29] Rukmini Callimachi "ISIS Remains Silent on Encrypted App," *New York Times*, June 12, 2016, www.nytimes.com/live/orlando-nightclub-shooting-live-updates/comment-on-a-terrorism, accessed July 25, 2016.

[30] It is interesting that qualms about this distinction are sufficiently prevalent among the Islamic State's supporters that the organization feels the need to counter them, suggesting the depth to which this distinction goes in our ordinary moral view of war.

available facts, the ICRC does not share the view that a global war is being waged." But the ICRC also addresses the conflict fought by the terrorists, rejecting the claim that all of the actions of the terrorists "can be attributed to one and same party to an armed conflict as understood under IHL."[31] Thus, it should not be considered a war in the morally relevant sense.

The points made by the ICRC are matters of international law, but they dovetail with the moral concerns presented in our discussion of C1. There we saw that the holding of territory is a requirement for the leadership of an insurgency to have legitimate authority. The grounds for this are that the grievances that the insurgency believes provide a just cause for war must be shared by a large number of individuals, and the control of territory is a stand-in for this. In the absence of holding of territory as a proxy for popular support, whatever violence the insurgents perpetrate cannot be considered part of a war in the morally relevant sense, and so would not fall under Just War theory.[32] The ICRC argument implies that this is also the case for IHL. But the ICRC points out that "the IHL is certainly not the only legal regime that can be used to deal with various forms of such violence."[33] An alternative is domestic legal regimes or international criminal law, both subject to the regime of international human rights law. As many have argued, international terrorism is criminal activity and should be treated as such. The GWOT is a merely rhetorical device. One of the goals of al Qaeda's terrorism was reportedly the removal of U.S. troops from Saudi Arabia. Its struggle might have fallen under Just War theory and IHL if, instead of engaging in acts of international terrorism, it had established a guerrilla struggle in Saudi Arabia against the U.S. troop presence and the Saudi regime.

VI Extreme Asymmetry

There is one last potential counterexample to the argument of this chapter. Extreme asymmetry is a form of asymmetric warfare in which the technological advantages of the strong side are so great as to allow that side to reduce the risk to its own combatants to zero or nearly so, while the combatants on the weak side remain at risk. The combatants of the strong side are, in one way or another, made immune to attack. Part of any belligerent's wartime efforts is to protect its own forces as much as possible.[34] In asymmetric war, the strong side

---

[31] International Committee of the Red Cross, "International Humanitarian Law," pp. 724, 725.

[32] The Islamic State may be distinctive in this regard because it does at the moment hold territory. As a state, it is fighting a local conventional war, though doing so immorally with terrorist attacks, but as the head of a terrorist network, it is fighting under the terrorist paradigm far from its region.

[33] International Committee of the Red Cross, "International Humanitarian Law," p. 721.

[34] Part of the reason for this is that, in many cases, it makes war an easier sell in terms of domestic politics by eliminating or greatly reducing the number of returning body bags.

tends to make use of the advantages it has for force protection. When the technological advantages are great enough, the force protection may be nearly complete, a situation referred to as "radical force protection." This sort of extreme asymmetry is what Paul Kahn has labeled "riskless war,"[35] which is, of course, riskless only for the combatants of the strong side. Extreme asymmetry or riskless war is a potential product of advancing technology, for example, long-range weapons fired accurately from a distance, such as cruise missiles or attack platforms, such as drones, that fly close to their targets but are remotely controlled, often from thousands of miles away. Combatants have for a long time been able to attack opponents from a safe distance, but technology has increased the distance, making more combatants safer. The moral problem raised by extreme asymmetry has been referred to as the "asymmetry objection."[36] This is a moral objection to the use of advanced military technology for force protection in an asymmetric context.

One can imagine that technology could in the future make extreme asymmetry a reality. We have already had one example of extreme asymmetry, namely, the 1999 Kosovo War, a war fought by NATO against Serbia over the Serbian ethnic cleansing of the inhabitants of its province of Kosovo. NATO fought the war entirely from the air, flying more than 35,000 sorties against Serbia before it capitulated. No NATO combatants were lost. But many features of the Kosovo War make it a special case in this regard.

It is, of course, an empirical issue the extent to which the capacity for riskless war will be achieved in years to come. One could argue that in most wars there will always be a need for "boots on the ground," for example, as spotters or to secure territory, which would preclude the war from being riskless.[37] But there are reportedly in development ground combat vehicles remotely controlled (like drones) or even autonomous, which would move us further toward extreme asymmetry. In any case, this prospect raises the asymmetry objection. Note that this concern applies only in a situation of asymmetry; a conflict that was riskless for both sides would be a different matter.

What is the asymmetry objection, and why is extreme asymmetry a moral concern? Paul Kahn offers an argument for this, one that may be understood as based on the following principle: "In war, combatants on each side attack and kill combatants on the other side. The moral justification for this is the mutuality or reciprocity of risk it entails, a mutuality that is destroyed by one side's being immune from risk."[38] In the absence of reciprocal risk, there is no

---

[35] Paul Kahn, "The Paradox of Riskless War," *Philosophy and Public Affairs Quarterly* 22 (summer 2002) no. 3: 2–8.

[36] Jai Galliott, "Uninhabited Aerial Vehicles and the Asymmetry Objection: A Response to Strawser," *Journal of Military Ethics* 11 (March 2012) no. 1: 58–66.

[37] Marcus Schulzke, "The Morality of Remote Warfare: Against the Asymmetry Objection to Remote Weaponry," *Political Studies* 64 (2016) no. 1: 90–105, at p. 92.

[38] Kahn, "Riskless War."

justification for killing in war. This principle assumes what is called the *moral equality of combatants*, which is a traditional way of understanding Just War theory, according to which the *in bello* rules apply equality to all combatants, whether they fight on the just or the unjust side. It holds that combatants cannot be held morally responsible for the justice of the cause for which they fight, only for their adherence to the *in bello* rules. This implies a kind of symmetrical self-defense, where combatants are permitted to harm their opponents because their opponents are harming them. This is what justifies killing in war, according to Kahn, and the moral objection to extreme asymmetry is that it negates this justification.

Kahn's argument, along with the moral equality of combatants, depends on what is in some ways a peculiar understanding of liability to attack on the grounds of self-defense. In individual cases of self-defense, such liability is commonly understood in terms of moral responsibility. The attacker's moral responsibility for putting the defender at risk of harm makes the attacker liable to attack and justifies the defender's using force against the attacker. But the justification works in only one direction. This way of understanding self-defense is asymmetrical. A recent line of interpretation of Just War theory, referred to as revisionism, rejects the moral equality of combatants and argues that the asymmetrical notion of self-defense should be applied in war as well, so that, in general, the combatants fighting for the unjust side are liable to attack, but the combatants fighting for the just side are not.[39] Bradley Strawser uses the revisionist approach to criticize the type of argument Kahn offers. In short, there is nothing wrong with extreme asymmetry so long as the strong side is fighting a just war.[40]

But even if Strawser's criticism of Kahn's argument were successful, it would not settle the matter. For the conclusion of Kahn's argument can be based on C1 rather than on Kahn's principle. His conclusion, that riskless war is morally unacceptable, can also be reached through applying C1 because the strong side's fighting a riskless war denies the weak side a reasonable chance of success.

Just War theory has endured many changes in warfare through its long history. It has largely remained relevant and applicable to the different forms that warfare has taken. More specifically, what has endured has been the fact that war can generally be conducted with a reasonable chance of success consistent with a commitment to the principle of discrimination. The changes in warfare have led the merely conventional *in bello* rules to change, but the

---

[39] The main proponent of revisionism is Jeff McMahan. See his *Killing in War*, New York: Oxford University Press, 2009.

[40] Bradley Strawser, "Moral Predators: The Duty to Employ Uninhabited Aerial Vehicles," *Journal of Military Ethics* 9 (2010) no. 4: 342–68, at pp. 355–57. One problem with Strawser's criticism of Kahn is that it would have little practical import or relevance, given that nearly every belligerent believes that its war has a just cause.

universal rules have remained as part of the theory. The argument of this chapter has been that not even asymmetric war alters this fact. Despite appearances, asymmetric war does not generate a systemic moral dilemma in the theory. But the brief discussion of extreme asymmetry suggests that if the developing technology of war creates a full-blown capacity for riskless war, asymmetric warfare may finally have moved beyond Just War theory.

Part III

Conducting a Just War

7 Individual Self-Defense in War

Lionel K. McPherson

The boxing champion and social activist Muhammad Ali famously said of his refusal to participate in the U.S. war in Vietnam, "I ain't got no quarrel with them Viet Cong." Ali was expressing more than a merely personal reason to resist being drafted into the army: like Martin Luther King Jr. and Malcolm X, he connected the Vietnam War with American racial injustice at home and Western militarism directed at peoples of color abroad.[1] Our focus here is limited to the moral problem of fighting in unjust wars. I work with fairly uncontroversial examples.

The proposition that citizen-soldiers should not participate in an unjust war is controversial. Just War theory sets forth moral limits on why and how wars are fought. Traditionalist accounts maintain that combatants are permitted to fight for their country, right or wrong. International law and practice support this view. In effect, citizen-soldiers on the side of an unjust war are free to kill combatants on the other side. The explanation is that combatants as such have an equal right to fight in individual self-defense. Revisionist accounts maintain that this traditionalist "battlefield equality" doctrine is morally unacceptable.[2]

As a revisionist I propose that international law, at a minimum, ought to affirm the right of every person to refuse to participate in wars there is good reason to believe are unjust. More broadly, the notion that war frees combatants to kill on behalf of their country, regardless of the justice of the cause, is an artifact of a bygone time of autocratic nations and "might makes right" in international relations. Traditionalists claim that rejecting the battlefield equality doctrine would be dangerously impractical. This prevalent sensibility distorts in theory and action the morality of individual self-defense in war.

---

[1] See, e.g., Martin Luther King Jr., "Racism and the World House," in *"In a Single Garment of Destiny": A Global Vision of Justice*, ed. and intro. Lewis V. Baldwin, fore. Charlayne Hunter-Gault, Boston: Beacon Press, 2012, pp. 49–50; and Malcolm X, "The Homecoming Rally of the OAAU," in *By Any Means Necessary*, ed. George Breitman, New York: Pathfinder Press, 1970, pp. 134–37.

[2] See, e.g., Jeff McMahan, "Arguments for the Moral Equality of Combatants," in *Killing in War*, New York: Oxford University Press, 2009.

I The Problem of Unjust Aggression

Muhammad Ali's basic point cannot be dismissed as personal opinion or political disagreement. He rejected possible deployment to Vietnam since nothing there posed an unprovoked, substantial threat to the United States. Vietnam was a distant "proxy" in the Cold War between the United States and the Soviet Union. The notorious Gulf of Tonkin Resolution in 1964 had authorized President Lyndon B. Johnson to use armed force in Southeast Asia. Ernest Gruening, one of two U.S. senators to vote against the resolution, summed up the case against deeper military involvement there: "That means sending our American boys into combat in a war in which we have no business, into which we have been misguidedly drawn, which is steadily being escalated."[3]

Combatants for an unjust war (i.e., unjust combatants) are agents of aggression: their role is to attack another people's combatants who must then fight to defend themselves and their people against that unjust aggression. (By "unjust war" I mean a war of unjust cause, not a war fought using unjust means.) If unjust combatants are successful enough, they enable their people to prevail in their unjust war – which is at least morally paradoxical.[4] But moral paradox is at the heart of the idea that mass killing can be a civilized endeavor. The Just War theory tradition began as an effort to articulate a morality of resort to war (*jus ad bellum*) and conduct in war (*jus in bello*). Traditionalist accounts tacitly assume that political leaders can be expected to use their statecraft and intelligence information to act with integrity and wisdom about whether to go to war. This is the substantive rationale for vesting them with the moral, not simply political and legal, authority to commit their country and its citizen-soldiers to war.

Consider U.S. Secretary of State Colin Powell's sketchy presentation to the United Nations in the run-up to the Iraq War in 2003. Powell leveraged his high reputation to reassure Americans and blunt international skepticism about whether the United States had just cause for the pending war on the basis of Iraq's alleged possession of chemical and biological "weapons of mass destruction." No such weapons were found; he later acknowledged that the United States had lacked real evidence. The United States did not have just cause for war even if Iraq under dictator Saddam Hussein had been in possession of chemical and biological weapons: their possession would not have been tantamount to an imminent threat of aggression. What might be in the interest of the right, good, or valuable (e.g., regime change) can fall well short of just cause.

---

[3] See John Nichols, "Remembering the Folly of 'Blank-Check' War and 'Escalation Unlimited,'" *Nation*, August 7, 2014, www.thenation.com/article/remembering-folly-blank-check-war-and-escalation-unlimited, accessed September 22, 2016.

[4] See Lionel K. McPherson, "Is Terrorism Distinctively Wrong?" *Ethics* 117 (2007), p. 499.

We know that political leaders are susceptible to hubris, shortsighted expediency, and the will to power, mixed with negligence and ignorance. So we should not assume that they are more inclined, and with better judgment, than attentive ordinary citizens to morally assess their country's case for war. Plausible just cause often can be discerned in open societies as a result of freedom of information and freedom to express political dissent – if war as a morally urgent "last resort" is taken seriously in the public culture. Last resort is a *jus ad bellum* requirement and roughly holds that a war can be just only when no other means of thwarting an imminent, unjust threat or seeking redress of just grievances are feasible.

Rather than risk (or endorse) the intentional killing of combatants and unintentional killing of civilians among people his country should not have been at war with in the first place, Ali chose to suffer the weighty legal and professional consequences of his refusal to be drafted into the U.S. Army.[5] Presumably, he thought it was morally impermissible, if not absurd, to become an American soldier in Vietnam, then claim individual "self-defense" as a basis for killing Vietnamese "enemies" he encountered in the jungle there. If this type of moral sensibility is mistaken, the reasons are far from obvious; and if it is not mistaken, the conventional moral wisdom about individual self-defense in war needs revision.

II Conscience and Self-Defense

Traditionalist Just War theory has no room for Muhammad Ali's perspective. Michael Walzer, whose account has been the most influential, dismisses selective conscientious objection (i.e., moral refusal to participate in a war of dubious cause) by countering an unlikely view: "Catholic writers have long argued that [individuals] ought not to volunteer, ought not to serve at all, if they know the war to be unjust. But the knowledge required by Catholic doctrine is hard to come by."[6] He would treat informed judgments about just cause as irrelevant anyway. The background debate between contemporary traditionalists and revisionists is whether citizen-soldiers can rightfully be obliged by their state to fight regardless of the justice of the cause.[7]

The U.S. Conference of Catholic Bishops clarified during the Vietnam War that the role of conscience in Catholic doctrine does not require knowledge that a war is unjust:

---

[5] An estimated 200,000–400,000 civilians were killed in Vietnam; see Chris Hedges, *What Every Person Should Know about War*, New York: Free Press, 2003.

[6] Michael Walzer, *Just and Unjust Wars: A Moral Argument with Historical Illustrations*, 3rd ed., New York: Basic Books, 1977, p. 39.

[7] For a balanced overview of this debate, see Helen Frowe, "The Moral Status of Combatants," in *The Ethics of War and Peace: An Introduction*, 2nd ed., London: Routledge, 2016.

The theory of the just war, beginning with St. Augustine and later developed by Catholic theologians such as St. Thomas Aquinas and Francis Suarez, required that certain conditions be met ... [T]he person who is sincerely trying to form his conscience must judge whether or not the end achieved by a particular war or all-out war is proportionate, in any degree, to the devastation wrought by that war. On the basis of this judgment, he would justify either participation in or abstention from war.[8]

Serious doubt is the standard. The issue of selective conscientious objection is about the morality of individual self-defense in war with respect to *jus ad bellum*, not about freedom of conscience in the abstract. This issue proves awkward for traditionalists since they hold that unjust cause presents no moral dilemma for combatants.

A nonsectarian question prompts Catholic doctrine: How could a person be morally permitted to participate in a killing endeavor he reasonably believes constitutes a grievous injustice that would give him no basic moral claim to fight in self-defense? The question represents more than a general conflict between law and moral conscience; killing is at stake. Traditionalist Just War theory carries a heavy burden of argument. We generally recognize a strong moral presumption against killing persons when there is serious doubt about whether the end is just. When the end is not just, the persons killed are wronged regardless of who is to blame.

The context of war is morally distinctive, traditionalists insist. They have largely skirted addressing head on how it could not be unjust for combatants to enable unjust aggression under the cover of appeal to individual self-defense. Traditionalists emphasize the fog and stress of war, the distorting effects of propaganda, legal and sometimes physical coercion (aka "duress"), the structure of political authority, and the collective political will of a people.[9] None of this directly points toward how the context of war could defy the basic moral logic of interpersonal self-defense. In short, the puzzle is how agents of aggression, especially for a manifestly unjust war, could have a moral claim to fight and kill.

Case law in the United States embodies what I have referred to as the basic moral logic of interpersonal self-defense. The moral sensibilities underlying the legal reasoning are straightforward:

It has long been accepted that one cannot support a claim of self-defense by a self-generated necessity to kill. The right of homicidal self-defense is granted only to those free from fault in the difficulty ... [O]ne who is the aggressor in a conflict

---

[8] "Statement on the Catholic Conscientious Objector," U.S. Conference of Catholic Bishops, October 15, 1969, www.usccb.org/issues-and-action/human-life-and-dignity/war-and-peace/statement-on-the-catholic-conscientious-objector-division-of-world-justice-and-peace-1969–10-15.cfm, accessed September 22, 2016.

[9] See, e.g., Walzer, *Just and Unjust Wars*, pp. 28–29.

culminating in death cannot invoke the necessities of self-preservation ... This body of doctrine traces its origin to the fundamental principle that a killing in self-defense is excusable only as a matter of genuine necessity ...

"Before a person can avail himself of the plea of self-defense against the charge of homicide, he must do everything in his power, consistent with his safety, to avoid the danger and avoid the necessity of taking life. If one has reason to believe that he will be attacked ... he must avoid the attack if it is possible to do so, and the right of self-defense does not arise until he has done everything in his power to prevent its necessity."[10]

Exceptions to this legal principle are possible: (1) when the initial aggressor uses non-deadly force to begin the encounter and the assailed person responds using deadly force and (2) when the initial aggressor withdraws from the encounter and clearly indicates to the assailed person that he has done so.[11] The second exception could apply to individual self-defense in war, for instance, when unjust combatants "wave the white flag" to surrender.

No one denies that political leaders bear the greatest share of moral responsibility for committing to war the political entity and the people under their political authority. Yet when trying to rationalize a special moral logic of individual self-defense in war, traditionalists often focus attention on moral responsibility for an unjust war – as if this lends support to the notion that citizen-soldiers are not merely excused for joining a killing endeavor that is unjust but are morally permitted to join it, provided they fight within the established rules (e.g., limiting intentional attacks to enemy combatants). Rebuttal of this notion is the central challenge posed by revisionist Just War theory.[12] Since revisionists such as Jeff McMahan have been criticized for abstracting from realities of war, I apply the revisionist challenge by working with historical examples, fictionalized and real.

The World War II film *Saving Private Ryan* includes a scene of hand-to-hand combat between an American soldier and a German soldier in a village in German-occupied France after the Allied invasion of Normandy. The American loses the upper hand and has his own knife slowly pushed into his chest by the German, who encourages the American to stop resisting and die more peacefully. While the German soldier does nothing against the *in bello* rules, revisionists would ask by what moral license he could be there, in France, fighting and killing for Nazi Germany. Had he and his comrades

---

[10] United States v. Peterson, 483 F.2d 1222 (D.C. Cir. 1973), at 1231.

[11] See, e.g., Stepp v. Commonwealth, 608 S.W.2d 371 (Ky. 1980).

[12] For a succinct summary of the debate between revisionists and traditionalists over the relation between *jus ad bellum* and *jus in bello*, see Jeff McMahan, "The Ethics of Killing in War," *Ethics* 114 (2004), pp. 693–94. See also Michael Walzer, "Response to McMahan's Paper," *Philosophia* 34 (2006), pp. 43–45.

succeeded overall, their efforts would have yielded the disaster of Germany winning the war.

World War II France under German occupation is one of Walzer's "historical illustrations." Let's stipulate for simplicity of argument, contrary to historical fact, that this occupation did not enable the deportation of tens of thousands of Jews in France to Nazi extermination camps. As a "reflection of the moral realities of military defeat," Walzer asserts, "resistance is legitimate, and the punishment of resistance is legitimate." Otherwise, he asks, "If citizens of a defeated state still have [an uncontested] right to fight, what is the meaning of surrender?"[13] He does not entertain the possibility of surrender as a provisional arrangement reached under coercion – with no transformation of the basic moral logic of interpersonal self-defense, and without an occupied people conceding broader justice claims. In effect, unjust combatants would be entitled to fight to enforce an occupation, for whatever current reasons of state. Any eventual armed resistance would instigate the resumption of war hostilities, triggering distinctive "moral realities." So German soldiers would be morally permitted to fight in individual self-defense against French Resistance and Allied fighters while trying to maintain Nazi Germany's control of France.

Walzer invokes a kind of subjectivism that would render "political judgments" morally irrelevant to combatants' decision making about whether they fight and for what purposes (within formal *in bello* limits).[14] This subjectivism is rejected by, among others, "refuseniks" of the Israel Defense Forces (IDF):

We … have been on reserve duty in the Occupied Territories, and were issued commands and directives that had nothing to do with the security of our country, and that had the sole purpose of perpetuating our control over the Palestinian people … The missions of occupation and oppression do not serve [the] purpose [of Israel's defense] – and we shall take no part in them.[15]

The justice of this occupation is not under debate for us here. The point is that traditionalist Just War theory would have combatants ignore any qualms about just cause. The principles of *jus ad bellum* and *jus in bello* are supposed to be "logically independent."[16] To reiterate, and as Walzer's World War II illustration shows, this traditionalist posture does not rest on concern about combatants' lack of information needed for reasonable *ad bellum* judgments.

From a revisionist perspective, a special moral logic of individual self-defense for unjust combatants is morally implausible. The German soldier in *Saving Private Ryan* surely had a moral prerogative not to fight for Nazi Germany, particularly outside the boundaries of Germany proper. This is a

---

[13] Walzer, *Just and Unjust Wars*, p. 178.
[14] See, e.g., Walzer, *Just and Unjust Wars*, pp. 200–01.
[15] "Combatant's Letter," Courage to Refuse, www.seruv.org.il/english/combatants_letter.asp, accessed September 22, 2016.
[16] Walzer, *Just and Unjust Wars*, p. 21.

reflection of the basic moral logic of interpersonal self-defense, which might excuse but does not morally permit fighting and killing in the service of unjust ends. What McMahan calls "the deep morality of war" would remain unchanged (in contrast to Walzer's "adaptation of [ordinary] morality to the circumstances of war").[17] Nonetheless, the Nazi German state would have tried to coerce the soldier to fight, probably by threatening him with execution. He did nothing that many other persons as citizen-soldiers would not also be prepared to do – whether fighting under the political authority of one's country (as compared to fighting for a fascist, genocidal political entity that is one's country) or fighting to stay alive in a struggle to the death. Doing something that many other persons would also be prepared to do is not equivalent, however, to doing nothing morally objectionable.

Revisionists caution about the moral perils of killing for a dubious cause. The idea that the German soldier was in moral error by fighting for Nazi Germany is compatible with the idea that he might have been individually blameless or marginally blameworthy for killing enemy combatants in the service of a manifestly unjust war. He would have a moral excuse in the sense that his unjust actions might not warrant punishment or blame for the gross injustice he substantially helped perpetrate.[18] (We can distinguish moral error and moral blame.) But he should not have fought, which there was reason for him to believe. Since traditionalists go as far as to claim that unjust combatants do nothing morally wrong when killing enemy combatants (and, collaterally, civilians) within the *in bello* rules, their view is vulnerable to the rejoinder that prospective combatants for an unjust war have moral reason at least to try to refuse to fight or at least have a moral prerogative not to fight. Recognizing this actionable moral role for conscience threatens a central element of traditionalist Just War theory.

III   Revisionist Limits of Duress

Critics of ceding a place for individual moral conscience at the level of *jus ad bellum* raise the political stakes. Selective conscientious objection has been alleged to represent, for example, "an explicit rejection of civilian control of the military." The suggestion is that if citizens have a moral prerogative to refuse to fight even for their country's manifestly unjust wars, "rule of law" would be undermined, especially to the detriment of a collective political will expressed through democratic proceduralism.[19] On a charitable interpretation, the

---

[17]   See, e.g., McMahan, "Ethics of Killing in War," p. 730; and Walzer, "Response to McMahan," p. 45.

[18]   Set aside the complication that the German soldier of the film scene was a member of the Nazi Party's Waffen-SS paramilitary, which was declared a criminal organization at the Nuremberg trials.

[19]   Charles J. Dunlap Jr., response to Jeff McMahan's "The Moral Responsibility of Volunteer Soldiers," *Boston Review*, November 6, 2013, www.bostonreview.net/forum/moral-wounds /charles-j-dunlap-jr-moral-wounds-dunlap, accessed September 22, 2016.

argument would be not that rule of law trumps basic morality but that morality in social practice generally relies on social order that rule of law provides.

By contrast, I would argue, esteem for law is merited by the fundamental aims of justice a particular body of law concretely serves. Rule of law is morally compromised when it would promote gross injustice, if not within some domestic constituency. Traditionalist Just War theory appears to fall back to the position that citizen-soldiers are morally permitted, whether or not morally required, to fight in their country's unjust wars. We are to infer that there must be a morally neutral right of individual self-defense in war. Positive arguments for this view are hard to pin down.

Combatants have an equal right to fight and kill, according to traditionalist Just War theory. There is confusion about whether this is mainly a legal or a moral doctrine. Deliberately or not, Walzer elides the distinction. He describes combatants as "moral equals": "The enemy soldier, though his [country's] war may well be criminal, is nevertheless as blameless as oneself [as a solider on the other side]. [T]he war itself isn't a relation between persons but between political entities and their human instruments." Still, combatants are supposed to bear moral responsibility for how they fight since "military conduct is governed by rules."[20] No real explanation is forthcoming about how instruments at the level of *jus ad bellum* become morally responsible agents at the level of *jus in bello*.[21] A metaphorical story is that "the individual [combatant] is the king" at the *in bello* level – and thus can discern right from wrong "on the battlefield" and bear moral responsibility for his actions there, even when given orders that conflict with *in bello* rules.[22]

Walzer also invites a more legalistic interpretation of the normative status of combatants: "[Soldiers] gain war rights as combatants, but they can now be attacked and killed at will by their enemies. Simply by fighting . . . they have lost their title to life and liberty, and they have lost it even though, unlike aggressor states, they have committed no crime [by fighting]." This is supposed to be the result of "the war convention," which "stipulates [the] battlefield equality" of combatants since they are designated agents of war violence. Combatants as such are deemed non-innocent, namely, in "a term of art" nonmoral sense that distinguishes them from civilians who, with no direct involvement in war violence, are "innocent" in that "they have done nothing, and are doing nothing, that entails the loss of their rights."[23] The fact that combatants on one side kill in the service of a just war would be practically and morally irrelevant. Persons who retain their right to life would have to decline to defend themselves and others against unjust combatants. This catch-22 depends entirely on the initiative of aggressor states and their agents of aggression.

---

[20] Walzer, *Just and Unjust Wars*, p. 36.

[21] For this "two-level objection" regarding the moral agency of combatants, see Lionel K. McPherson, "Innocence and Responsibility in War," *Canadian Journal of Philosophy* 34 (2004), pp. 496–97.

[22] Walzer, *Just and Unjust Wars*, p. 39.   [23] Ibid., pp. 136–37, 146.

What morally authoritative power might a "war convention" have?[24] Walzer does not elaborate: he stops at describing a war convention that is "the set of articulated norms, customs, professional codes, legal precepts, religious and philosophical principles, and reciprocal arrangements that shape our judgments of military conduct."[25] This convention would include what is known in public international law as "the law of war," which recognizes the battlefield legal equality of combatants. But Walzer leaves unaddressed whether and how some of the conventional judgments could be morally mistaken. As Brian Orend acknowledges, moral complacency about war conventionalism is not close to good enough with respect to civilian casualties: "I fail to grasp how it can be morally justified to foreseeably kill innocent civilians in order to hit a target which only serves the final end of an aggressive war."[26] The moral problem is critical in practice since collateral civilian casualties are an almost inevitable by-product of modern warfare.[27] Orend does not pursue the broader revisionist challenge about how it could be morally permissible to kill combatants who are defending (within the *in bello* rules) their country and themselves against an aggressor state's unjust combatants.

I proceed as if the "battlefield equality" doctrine represents "the moral equality of combatants." The moral, not the legal, is our domain of inquiry. The view that combatants as such have reciprocal moral license to kill in individual self-defense needs more than the circular reinforcement of judgments that would grant combatants that license. Traditionalists claim that ascribing moral equality to combatants is backed by common sense. Their version of common sense roughly goes as follows. Ordinary combatants (they are not mercenaries or war criminals) are legally bound to serve. If they did not fight when thrust onto the battlefield, they would be allowing themselves to be killed or captured, which is absurd in warfare: a reasonable personal aim is for them to stay alive while doing their national duty by fighting. It is permissible, then, for them to try to protect themselves and their comrades by fighting enemy combatants.

More specifically, the traditionalist story goes, ordinary combatants are in the same practical, legal, and moral situation: their countries have designated them to fight and risk their lives. Even when they have volunteered to join the military, they have not joined on the condition of fighting in particular wars but fight, per the dictates of their country's political leaders, in whichever wars as "a legal obligation and a patriotic duty," regardless of whether their country has just cause.[28] This also extends to high-ranking officers – including, for

[24]   On the moral instability of a war convention, see Lionel K. McPherson, "The Limits of the War Convention," *Philosophy & Social Criticism* 31 (2005).

[25]   Walzer, *Just and Unjust Wars*, p. 44.

[26]   Brian Orend, *The Morality of War*, 2nd ed., Peterborough: Broadview Press, 2013, p. 124.

[27]   For a revisionist account that takes this problem to be central, see David Rodin, "Terrorism without Intention," *Ethics* 114 (2004).

[28]   Walzer, *Just and Unjust Wars*, p. 28.

instance, Field Marshal Erwin Rommel, who supported "Hitler's aim to make Germany great again," fought for Nazi Germany, and earned his legendary reputation commanding a German mission in World War II to help protect Italy's North African colonies (before moving on to Normandy).[29] Rommel, no less than all other combatants who fight within the *in bello* rules, would have had reciprocal moral license to kill and organize killing enemy combatants in battle anywhere. Walzer cites him as an example of the solider as "a servant" and "a loyal and obedient subject and citizen," who was only doing "the king's business" in fighting in a manifestly unjust war.[30] As a matter of historical fact, this example undermines the instrumentalization of combatants at the *ad bellum* level. Like other high-ranking military officers for Nazi Germany, Rommel did exercise moral agency and judgment relevant to *jus ad bellum*: their sought positions depended on pledging personal, unconditional allegiance to Hitler (not to the constitution of Germany) and supporting the political goals (not necessarily Nazi ideology in full) of the regime.

In the world outside of theory, no firewall exists between political and military judgments.[31] Nor is there reason to imagine that rank-and-file combatants lose moral agency regarding *jus ad bellum* but regain it regarding *jus in bello*: moral agency, tied as it is to the exercise of rational self-control, does not switch off and on that way, which is not to deny that distinctive pressures on moral judgment apply at the different levels. By positing a bifurcation of the moral agency of combatants, traditionalist Just War theory appears to generate its special moral logic that is insensitive to just cause and thereby yields an equal permission for combatants to fight and kill. This might explain why traditionalists sidestep the issue of selective conscientious objection: dissenters such as Muhammad Ali and IDF refuseniks are an embarrassment to the contention that citizen-soldiers are "human instruments" unsuited to make reasonable moral choices about whether to fight. Selective conscientious objection represents rejection of the belief that political leaders, at least for a country under legitimate political authority, have the moral authority to demand that citizens fight in any war (within formal *in bello* limits) the leaders see fit to wage.

A morally consistent position would be that ordinary combatants, when following superior orders, bear moral responsibility neither for whether nor how they fight. After the Nuremberg trials following World War II, however,

---

[29] Charles Messenger, *Rommel: Leadership Lessons from the Desert Fox*, fore. Wesley K. Clark, after. Klaus Naumann, New York: Palgrave Macmillan, 2009, p. 29. The "Rommel myth" of an apolitical, chivalrous commander has come under heightened scrutiny.

[30] Walzer, *Just and Unjust Wars*, p. 39.

[31] On military officers suggesting that "unqualified allegiance to the commander in chief needs to be rethought," see Michael C. Desch, "Bush and the Generals," *Foreign Affairs*, May/June 2007, www.foreignaffairs.com/articles/united-states/2007-05-01/bush-and-the-generals, accessed September 22, 2016.

"superior orders" have been legally rejected as a full defense against *in bello* violations, namely, when the orders are clearly unlawful. Specifically, Principle IV of the Nuremberg principles reads, "The fact that a person acted pursuant to order of his Government or of a superior does not relieve him from responsibility under international law, provided a moral choice was in fact possible to him."[32] If combatants who follow superior orders were absolved of all moral responsibility, there could be no moral problem of individual self-defense for unjust combatants: combatants as such would be akin to attack dogs, which have no moral agency. The notion that citizen-soldiers warrant the status of brute fighting tools is too crude. On this, traditionalists and revisionists agree.

IV   A Special Moral Logic of Self-Defense?

We have not yet pinned down a positive argument for a special moral logic of individual self-defense that supports the doctrine of battlefield equality. An argument directly from domestic legal "obligation" and patriotic "duty" is a non sequitur. Expectations on citizen-soldiers resulting from domestic law and patriotism are subject to purely domestic contingencies – for instance, a strong public ethos against questioning whether there is just cause for a war already begun. It is mysterious how domestic law might morally permit persons to engage in conduct that otherwise would be grossly unjust. It is also mysterious why proper patriotism might be expressed through a moral permission to unquestioningly kill. Love for one's country can be expressed by refusing to participate in unjust violence done in its name, honoring the country's (aspirational) commitment to moral decency that makes the country worthy of its citizens' love. More importantly, being legally compelled to fight declared enemies of the state is not equivalent to being morally permitted to kill them.

A "collectivist" defense of battlefield equality tries to bypass purely domestic contingencies. The nature of the state as a political entity would ground a special moral logic of individual self-defense in war. Walzer suggests something like this, recall, when describing war as a relation "between political entities." What he means is unclear since his war convention also would legally and morally govern person-to-person relations, combatant and noncombatant. Christopher Kutz is more instructive: "When individuals' wills are linked together in politics, this affects the normative valence of what they do individually as part of that politics, even to the point of rendering impunible what would otherwise be criminal." This only speaks to the legal domain. Indeed, Kutz acknowledges, "The privilege to kill as part of a collective is not a moral permission," for "a soldier who kills as part of an unjust war morally wrongs

---

[32] "Principles of International Law recognized in the Charter of the Nürnberg Tribunal and in the Judgment of the Tribunal, with commentaries," in *Yearbook of the International Law Commission, 1950*, vol. II, United Nations, New York: United Nations, 1957, p. 375.

those he kills."[33] His view actually undermines a special moral logic of individual self-defense for unjust combatants. The prevalent view that only political leaders bear substantial moral responsibility for contributing to an unjust war does not sit comfortably with the ideal of political leaders as representatives of a collective political will.

A "communitarian" version of the collectivist defense of battlefield equality ups the ante. The collective political will of a people plus the structure of political authority would disable any individual citizen-soldier's moral choice about whether to fight. According to Walzer, "rights of states rest on the consent of their members," especially to protect against "external encroachment." Moreover, he claims, "The moral standing of any particular state depends upon the reality of the common life it protects and the extent to which the sacrifices required by that protection are willingly accepted and thought worthwhile."[34] These stakes are so high that political leaders would reserve the exclusive legal right and moral responsibility to decide whether to commit their country and its citizen-soldiers to war for the just cause of collective self-defense against aggression. The looming worry is that too many citizens might refuse to participate in just wars in their country's interest, a scenario that seems to lack historical precedent. But when Walzer claims that "personal choice ... for essentially private reasons" about whether to fight "effectively disappears," he means this in a certain normative sense.[35] Any moral reservations citizen-soldiers might have would be irrelevant: unjust cause would not be a legitimate basis for individuals to refuse to fight.

Traditionalist Just War theory of a communitarian orientation therefore seems bound to the view that citizens are not only morally permitted but also can be morally required to fight for their country, right or wrong. Revisionists would have prospective combatants for an unjust war place individual moral conscience ahead of domestic legal obligation. Walzer suggests that citizens instead should let themselves be used for fighting when political leaders have committed the country to war: this would be a shared burden of citizenship, and selective conscientious objectors would not be doing their part. Given that members of every self-respecting political community would find themselves in roughly the same political, legal, and moral condition, all such communities are supposed to have a reasonable interest in accepting that citizen-soldiers are permitted to defend themselves in war. Some traditionalists go further by implying that countries legitimately might require their citizen to fight and kill.

We can now see how, upon further review, traditionalist Just War theory generates its special moral logic of individual self-defense in war. The argument is not really that citizen-soldiers somehow have no moral agency at the

---

[33] Christopher Kutz, "The Difference Uniforms Make: Collective Violence in Criminal Law and War," *Philosophy and Public Affairs* 33 (2005), pp. 156, 173. For a balanced summary of the debate over a collectivist approach to war, see Frowe, *Ethics of War and Peace*, pp. 33–36.

[34] Walzer, *Just and Unjust Wars*, p. 54.   [35] Ibid., p. 28.

level of *jus ad bellum*: rather, the argument is that, at this level, they are not morally required to exercise individual moral conscience. They would have moral license, indifferent to just cause, to fight for their country and kill, in individual self-defense, declared enemy combatants; the basic moral logic of interpersonal self-defense would not apply. This purported moral reality of war would follow from the nature of endorsing membership in a particular domestic political community among others, each of which have quasi-autonomous moral standing that imposes hard limits on what citizens across these communities owe to one another.

In the final analysis, traditionalists return to their version of common sense. The story begins in medias res: war has already started, with soldiers from both sides already engaged on the battlefield. Whether soldiers got there as conscripts or volunteers and which country has just cause are supposed to be practically and morally irrelevant from the perspective of individual soldiers in battle. This approach would preempt moral challenge when traditionalists rhetorically ask, "What can we expect soldiers to do when they're being shot at?" Questions of this sort, revisionists contend, may prompt a sympathetic understanding of the circumstances that nevertheless does not support moral license for unjust combatants to fight and kill. To reiterate, revisionists argue that unjust combatants have moral reason at least to try to refuse to fight.

The in medias res approach to rationalizing battlefield equality is on display in Henry Shue's criticism of McMahan's revisionist account. Shue seems to occupy an intermediate position that in effect tilts traditionalist:

Unjust wars ought not to be pursued, and no one ought to participate in them on the unjust side … Once one has decided that one is fighting on the just side of a war, however, the preceding is very little help … Appreciating that one's beliefs may be mistaken may well encourage restraint … What it will not do is lead one to act as if they are mistaken, while one still believes in them. What one would not decide is not to attack anyone on the other side … McMahan's recommendation … is next to useless as an action-guiding principle for the conduct of war.[36]

Of course, combatants who fail to realize they are fighting in an unjust war will be unable to act on a belief they do not have. What mainly has been in dispute is whether citizen-soldiers have moral license to kill in a war of unjust cause, especially when there is good reason to believe the war is unjust.

A revisionist "action-guiding principle" for unjust combatants already engaged in battle would indeed be impractical. This type of problem is not unique to the context of war. For example, death row officials might learn of credible evidence, after a prisoner's legal and executive appeals have been

---

[36] Henry Shue, "Do We Need a 'Morality of War'?" in *Just and Unjust Warriors: The Moral and Legal Status of Soldiers*, eds. David Rodin and Henry Shue, New York: Oxford University Press, 2008, pp. 107–8. For an overview of McMahan's "deep morality of war" versus Shue's "morally best laws of war," see Frowe, *Ethics of War and Peace*, pp. 41–48.

exhausted, that the person they are about to execute on behalf of the state is probably innocent. Some death penalty opponents emphasize the nontrivial moral risk of executing the innocent, especially when a justice system is plagued by injustice, as a critical reason not to participate in deciding or administering death penalty cases.[37] In a similar spirit, revisionists emphasize that citizen-soldiers ought to be morally wary in the first place about letting themselves be used for fighting, especially when their country has a history of waging wars of dubious cause, since unjust combatants have no moral license to kill.

I propose this applied revisionist principle: combatants who come to realize they are probably participating in an unjust war should stop participating as soon as feasible, say, when they return to base and can refuse to continue fighting without immediately jeopardizing their own lives or those of their comrades. Such a principle grants, at least for the sake of argument, the practical concern that ordinary unjust combatants have a moral allowance to defend their own lives when engaged in a battle, that is, prior to realizing they are probably killing in the service of an unjust cause. At the same time, the principle highlights that unjust combatants not already engaged in battle or not in combat roles have no individual self-defense rationale for directly enabling their country's unjust war and its killing of combatants defending themselves (and their civilian population) against unjust aggression. "I fought on behalf of my country" is never a morally sufficient basis, in itself, to kill or directly enable killing.

Thus revisionists argue that ordinary combatants are morally obliged not to fight in an unjust war. This does not entail that unjust combatants warrant blame or punishment for fighting – except in the limited sense of public recognition that they typically have no moral claim to fight and kill. But unjust combatants would be in moral error. They could have only a moral excuse for killing persons who are defending themselves, using just means, against unjust aggression. Some revisionists would impose concrete moral sanctions on unjust combatants. McMahan proposes that "international law [might] find a way to put soldiers on notice that the war in which they have been commanded to fight, or in which they are at present fighting, is an illegal war and that they can be held legally accountable for participating in it."[38]

A more feasible and constructive alternative than punishing or blaming ordinary combatants, I would argue, is to focus on raising greater awareness about the seriousness of the collective and individual moral perils of participating in unjust wars. Toward this end, international law could recognize,

---

[37] See, e.g., Hugo Adam Bedau and Michael L. Radelet, "Miscarriages of Justice in Potentially Capital Cases," *Stanford Law Review* 40 (1987).

[38] McMahan, *Killing in War*, p. 192. See also, e.g., McMahan, "The Moral Responsibility of Volunteer Soldiers," *Boston Review*, November 6, 2013, www.bostonreview.net/forum/jeff -mcmahan-moral-responsibility-volunteer-soldiers, accessed September 22, 2016.

included by the human right to "freedom of conscience," a right to selective conscientious objection.[39] The United Nations currently adopts the legalistic convention of "a derivative right," as if basic human rights are not grounded in a basic morality.[40] However, the fundamental human rights issue is not morally complicated: how can a state, or any other entity, demand that a person kill another human being, for any reason? There is virtually nothing more basic for freedom of conscience to protect than a right not to kill.

V   A Human Right to Selective Conscientious Objection

The Just War theory tradition has had a tendency to exaggerate about subjective constraints on moral choice for combatants on the battlefield. This contention is borne out, for example, by historical evidence on "firing rates":

In World War II, 80 to 85 percent of riflemen did not fire their weapons at an exposed enemy, even to save their lives and the lives of their friends. In previous wars nonfiring rates were similar. In Vietnam the nonfiring rate was close to 5 percent ... Psychological conditioning was applied en masse to a body of soldiers, who, in previous wars, were shown to be unwilling or unable to engage in killing activities.[41]

Apparently, many citizen-soldiers thrust onto the battlefield were not naturally disposed to kill, even in self-defense, even when they believed they were fighting in a just war. The purported moral reality reflected in the battlefield equality doctrine seems partly an artifact of militarist ideology that is amplified by states devising sophisticated methods to prime their soldiers to kill. Human resistance to killing, including in the context of war, is evidently more ingrained in the natural psyche of citizen-soldiers than the feeling that they are, when political leaders demand, morally free and practically almost bound to kill enemy combatants when in battle.

A last-ditch effort to support the view that combatants as such have reciprocal moral license to kill invokes war as "a rule-governed activity" (Walzer) or a context in which "the morally best rules for the circumstances" take an

---

[39] See McPherson, "Innocence and Responsibility in War," pp. 502–3. See also Lionel K. McPherson, response to Jeff McMahan's "The Moral Responsibility of Volunteer Soldiers," *Boston Review*, November 6, 2013, www.bostonreview.net/forum/moral-wounds/lionel-k-mcpherson-moral-wounds-mcpherson, accessed September 22, 2016.

[40] *Conscientious Objection to Military Service*, United Nations Human Rights Office of the High Commissioner, New York: United Nations, 2012, 7. www.ohchr.org/Documents/Publications/ConscientiousObjection_en.pdf, accessed September 22, 2016.

[41] Dave Grossman, *On Killing: The Psychological Cost of Learning to Kill in War and Society*, rev. ed., New York: Back Bay Books, 2009, p. 252. There has been some dispute about the "firing rate" numbers. Grossman responds that "countless ... observations all confirm ... that the vast majority of combatants throughout history ... have found themselves to be unable to kill," xviii.

inevitable "reality of rights-violation into account" (Shue). The law of war status quo would represent the most we realistically could hope for, legally and morally. Otherwise, we are to imagine an ineffectual, chaotic program of "crime and punishment" or a "morally appealing but impossible dream" that is worse than useless.[42] Once this smoke foretelling catastrophic consequences of a revisionist alternative begins to clear, however, there is not much by way of an argument for the doctrine of battlefield equality. Helen Frowe provides a succinct interpretation of the anti-revisionist rationale:

If we want combatants to constrain their killing and maiming, we must do this on the basis of facts [viz., combatant status, not just cause] that they can determine. And, sadly, these facts will not correspond to moral facts about whether a person bears moral responsibility for [fighting in an unjust] war ... But constraining the killing in this way is better than failing to constrain it at all.[43]

Anti-revisionists would give us a Hobson's choice, take it or leave it, range of possibilities.

Let's withdraw, as I have suggested, the prospect of imposing legal punishment for ordinary unjust combatants. Apart from the threat of punishment, anti-revisionists have yet to articulate a substantial connection between the aim of encouraging combatants to constrain their killing and the position that combatants who (within the *in bello* rules) kill in the service of an unjust cause do nothing morally wrong or nothing they could reasonably be expected not to do. War, for all its complexities, is another context in which there are sensible reasons for the divergence of law (e.g., combatants have a reciprocal legal claim to kill) and morality (e.g., unjust combatants do not have moral license to kill) – with law providing allowances that morality would not. That law does not always have the resources or the wisdom to effectively police all domains of moral life is no embarrassment to either law or morality; trying to force their unity distorts both. There is a practical rationale for not criminalizing adultery, for example, which does not compel us to construct a special moral logic by which partners who have sworn fidelity would have default reciprocal moral allowance to be unfaithful to promote their taking protective measures for sexual health. Any such argument would be widely regarded as a Swiftian proposal, despite the reality of infidelity among ordinary human beings.

The dominant Just War theory tradition has been complicit in the normalization of political violence carried out by the state. The context of war does not point to some sui generis moral domain fundamentally at odds with basic interpersonal morality, namely, whereby agents of aggression for aggressor states acquire a special moral claim to kill in individual self-defense persons who would defend themselves and their people against that aggression. Mass

---

[42] Walzer, *Just and Unjust Wars*, p. 41; and Shue, "'Morality of War'?," pp. 110–11.
[43] Frowe, *Ethics of War and Peace*, p. 48.

killing between tribes or nations too often has been seen as an awful, absurd, sometimes necessary, but anyway common enough activity that we must morally accommodate ourselves to, regrettably. In the twenty-first century, the time for such accommodation has long gone, along with the notion of citizens as unquestioning, obedient subjects in relation to their king's, or their state's, authority in a world of quasi-autonomous political entities ultimately out for their own interests.

Killing in the service of unjust ends, in any context, whatever the reasons and the pressures, never has more than a moral excuse. Individuals always retain and should exercise the moral prerogative to do better by trying to refuse to participate in egregious moral wrongdoing. Recognizing a human right to selective conscientious objection would help drive home this moral reality.

8 Distinction and Civilian Immunity

Shannon E. French

The *jus in bello* principle of distinction – also known as the principle of discrimination – is a cornerstone of traditional Just War theory. It requires distinguishing combatants from noncombatants in a conflict and endeavoring to direct hostilities toward the former while preserving to the greatest degree possible the safety and security of the latter. While this principle is easy to grasp in concept as a way to limit the dreadful toll of war, it can be fiendishly difficult to put into practice. This is true both in the sense of the challenge of designing policies, weapons, and rules of engagement that accurately capture the intent behind the principle and when it comes to actually displaying appropriate discrimination in selecting targets in warfare and other military operations. Even with the best of intentions, combatants can fail to preserve civilian immunity, due – to a wide variety of factors. Other belligerents willfully choose to disregard concern for the preservation of civilian life and not only target noncombatants directly but also take active steps to make it even more problematic for others to identify and protect them. We see the grim results of such efforts throughout the history of armed conflict.

The alternative to adopting the principle of distinction is total war: akin to Thomas Hobbes's imagined State of Nature, this is war of "every man against every man," where life is "solitary, poor, nasty, brutish, and short."[1] In total war, no one is immune, as each side endeavors to annihilate the other. It is not surprising that most human societies have sought to avoid this by constructing at least some boundaries to contain the violence of armed conflict to designated groups of fighters, rather than involving all citizens, regardless of age or role.

Military ethicist Stephen Coleman explains the essential logic behind the principle of noncombatant immunity:

At its most basic, the principle of noncombatant immunity claims that the only people who may legitimately be subjected to direct attacks are enemy combatants, and that noncombatants are never legitimate targets for direct attacks. However, the immunity that noncombatants have is only a qualified one, in that although they may have immunity from direct attack, they do not have immunity from harm.

---

[1] Thomas Hobbes, *Leviathan*, Oxford: Clarendon Press, 1909.

Thus, although it is illegitimate to directly target noncombatants, this certainly does not mean that every attack which causes harm to noncombatants is an illegitimate one, for noncombatants may be harmed, even killed, as a result of an attack against a legitimate military target. Equally important, noncombatants only retain their immunity from direct attack as long as they retain their status as noncombatants, so if a noncombatant actively engages in any form of combatant activity, then they will lose their immunity and may be directly targeted.[2]

In other words, while others may (and most likely will) still suffer harm from the effects of the conflict, this principle suggests that the only people who should be intentionally targeted are those directly involved in the fighting. Troops should direct their violence only against other troops, and not against the broader population.

We can imagine this playing out in a reasonably straightforward manner in a conflict that involves two nation-states fielding professional armies against one another. From the perspective of upholding the principles of distinction and noncombatant immunity, the ideal is structured armies meeting to fight on a designated battlefield a fair distance apart from any homes, hospitals, or schools. Historically, some such battles have occurred, but they are few and far between. More commonly, battles are fought near or in highly populated areas. Thus, unless specific steps are taken to protect them, ordinary citizens will be at as much risk (or perhaps more, if they are unarmed) as uniformed troops.

I Justifications and Restrictions for Killing in War

Killing in war is regarded by the just war tradition as a special category of killing. Providing that certain key conditions are met, the intentional taking of another human life in the context of war is considered not to be the same moral act as murder. In fact, the argument that killing noncombatants is unacceptable can be tied directly to the justifications that are offered to defend any form of killing in war.

In the context of war, regular combatants on either side are allowed to retain something akin to the right of self-defense against one another, although that right does not operate exactly the same as it does in the civilian world. They are not (and should not be) regarded as murderers. They fight as representatives of the state in conflicts chosen by the state, and they are generally held immune from prosecution as murderers for the killing they do within the bounds of the recognized restrictions captured as the law of war or the law of armed conflict (LOAC) or international humanitarian law (IHL) and customary international law. This is known as combatant immunity:

---

[2] Stephen Coleman, *Military Ethics: An Introduction with Case Studies*, Oxford: Oxford University Press, 2013, p. 151.

Under the Geneva Conventions, lawful combatants include members of the regular armed forces of a state party to the conflict; militia, volunteer corps and organized resistance movements belonging to a state party to the conflict, which are under responsible command, wear a fixed distinctive sign recognizable at a distance, carry their arms openly and abide by the laws of war; and members of regular armed forces who profess allegiance to a government or an authority not recognized by the detaining power. They are entitled to prisoner of war status upon capture, and are entitled to "combatant immunity" for their lawful pre-capture warlike acts. Combatant immunity is a doctrine rooted in the customary international law of war, and forbids the prosecution of soldiers for their lawful acts committed during the course of armed conflicts against legitimate military targets.[3]

Combatants cannot kill indiscriminately. They "must learn to take only certain lives in certain ways, at certain times, and for certain reasons."[4] As discussed earlier in this volume, the Western just war tradition requires that war be openly declared by a legitimate authority, fought for a just cause (usually limited to defense against acts of aggression such as violations of sovereignty to seize territory), with noble intentions (where the aim is a just peace), and only as a last resort. Wanton slaughter – killing that is disproportionate and indiscriminate – violates both the letter and spirit of these restrictions. Eighteenth-century diplomat, legal scholar, and philosopher Emer de Vattel explains:

The enemy who unjustly attacks me gives me an unquestionable right to repel his attack; and he who takes up arms against me, when I am demanding only what is due to me, becomes himself the real aggressor by his unjust resistance; he is the original author of the war, since he obliges me to use force in order to protect myself from the wrong he wishes to do me either in my person or in my property. If the use of this force be carried so far as to take away his life, he alone is responsible for that unfortunate result; for if I were obligated to submit to the wrong rather than hurt him, the good would soon become the prey of the wicked. Such is the source of the right to kill our enemies in a just war ... But the very argument for the right to kill our enemies points out the limits of that right. As soon as an enemy submits and hands over his arms we are no longer entitled to take away his life.[5]

Going further, de Vattel clarifies that those who are not part of the armed aggression or resistance are therefore immune from attack:

---

[3] Philip McEvoy, "Law at the Operational Level," in *Ethics, Law, and Military Operations*, ed. David Whetham, New York: Palgrave Macmillan, 2011, p. 123.

[4] Shannon E. French, *The Code of the Warrior: Exploring Warrior Values, Past and Present*, 2nd ed., Lantham, MD and New York: Rowman & Littlefield, 2016.

[5] Emer de Vattel, *War in Due Form*, 1758, chap. VIII ("The Law of Nations in Time of War; First, What is it Justifiable and What is it Permissible to Do to the Person of the Enemy in a Just War," sections 139–40).

Women, children, feeble old men, and sick persons, come under the description of enemies; and we have certain rights over them, inasmuch as they belong to the nation with whom we are at war, and as, between nation and nation, all rights and pretensions affect the body of the society, together with all its members. But these are enemies who make no resistance; and consequently we have no right to mal-treat their persons or use any violence against them, much less to take away their lives. This is so plain a maxim of justice and humanity that at present every nation in the least degree civilized, acquiesces in it.[6]

It is important here to note that the source of the immunity by this account is actual resistance – the lack of a real and direct threat posed by the individual to the troops conducting the just war – not any notion of innocence or nonmaterial support for the enemy's position. It is utterly irrelevant whether or not the noncombatant in question is or is not in favor of the aggression that provoked the conflict, just as it does not matter to their combatant status whether troops are voluntary or conscripted. Imagine the unlikely scenario that in the first Gulf War in 1990, a U.S. soldier had encountered an unarmed civilian woman holding a big sign saying, in English, "Way to go, Saddam! Seize Kuwait!" Her fervor for the Iraqi leader's incursion across his neighbor's border would not have made her a legitimate target to be shot by the soldier. It is not her attitude that matters, only the credible threat she does (or does not) present to the soldier.

In addition to tying the legitimacy of killing in war to the right of defense, this focus on threat matters because it reduces some of the subjectivity in the determi-nation of immunity. It expressly disallows, for example, the claim often attributed to terrorist groups that civilians living in democracies can be appropriately targeted because voting and paying taxes make them morally responsible for perceived acts of aggression sanctioned by their government. Moral responsibility is irrelevant.

At the same time, civilian immunity is not absolute. It is contingent on civilians remaining essentially nonthreatening. As soon as they take up arms against combatants (even in the awful case of child soldiers), they become legitimate targets. This is clearly expressed in the Geneva Conventions and in the LOAC manuals of most nations. For example, consider the language of the LOAC manual of the United Kingdom: "Civilians are protected from attack unless and for such time as they take a direct part in hostilities. Taking direct part in hostilities is more narrowly construed than simply making a contribu-tion to the war effort."[7] This means that an individual can transform in the blink of an eye from a protected noncombatant to a combatant (and legitimate target) – for example, if a civilian woman picks up a fallen weapon from the street and begins to fire against approaching troops, she is no longer immune from attack. This is parallel to the situation of the combatant who disarms and

---

[6] Ibid., section 145.

[7] United Kingdom, *The Manual of the Law of Armed Conflict*, Ministry of Defence, July 2004, as amended by Amendment 3, September 2010.

surrenders and is in that moment granted immunity from attack as a prisoner of war. Thus, combatant/noncombatant status is extremely fluid.

By not focusing on judgments of moral responsibility, guilt, or innocence, this threat-based approach fails to provide blanket immunity for moral patients (persons not considered to have moral agency or responsibility such as babies, young children, or adults unable to commit intentional acts due to extreme physical and mental limitations). Tragically, such persons can sometimes be turned into what is termed an "innocent threat" by others who do have moral agency or by terrible circumstances. For example, a young child can be compelled to be a suicide bomber. In such a case, the child is as much a victim as those targeted by the bomb, but he or she is nevertheless a deadly threat. Therefore, the traditional view of Just War theory and international law is that the child in such a case is a legitimate target, under the principle of distinction.

Philosopher Jefferson McMahan and others have argued that there may be an obligation to use nonlethal force to stop an innocent threat. However, McMahan concedes that neutralizing an innocent threat nonlethally may not always be an option:

Suppose now that the morally innocent person who threatens you in an objectively unjustified way poses a lethal threat. And suppose there is no way to divide the threatened harm between the two of you: either he will kill you or you must kill him in self-defense. The commonsense intuition is that you are morally justified in killing him. While his moral innocence may affect the proportionality calculation when the threat he poses is nonlethal, and there are various options for self-defense, in this case it makes no difference at all.[8]

McMahan goes on to challenge this "commonsense view," noting that the existence of an existential threat does not always produce the right of self-defense:

The mere fact that someone threatens your life is insufficient to ground a justification for killing him in self-defense. If, for example, you are morally liable to be killed, you have no right of self-defense. A rampaging murderer who sees that he is about to be killed by a police sniper will be guilty of one more murder if he kills the sniper in self-defense.[9]

The common response to this objection[10] is that there is a fundamental difference between the case of a child suicide bomber and the rampaging murderer. Unlike the child suicide bomber, the murderer is a moral agent and can be held morally accountable for his actions. Philosophers such as Judith Jarvis

---

[8] Jeff McMahan, "Self Defense Against Morally Innocent Threats," in *Criminal Law Conversations*, eds. Paul Robinson, Stephen Garvey, and Kimberly Kessler, New York: Oxford University Press, 2009, p. 386.

[9] Ibid.   [10] McMahan finds this response unpersuasive.

Thompson and Suzanne Uniacke have argued[11] that self-defense is justified by appeal to a person's right not to be killed. By his murderous intent, the rampaging murderer forfeits this right to self-defense[12] against the police sniper.[13]

An innocent threat such as the child suicide bomber, as a moral patient, may not forfeit his or her right to self-defense in this way. Yet he or she may still be considered a legitimate military target, as the child has, tragically, been turned into a deadly weapon. The same is true of child soldiers, despite their moral innocence. There is room for nuance in the rules of engagement (ROEs) that a force employs when confronted with an innocent threat, and there is certainly strong moral reason to encourage that, whenever possible, less-than-lethal measures be used to neutralize the threat that a moral patient poses. In the end, though, it is again threat level and not innocence that is relevant for the purposes of the principle of distinction.

Importantly, this principle does not permit much extension of the concept of "threateningness." While a child suicide bomber or an armed child soldier may be treated as a legitimate military target, a child who could simply grow up to join the enemy forces (a potential future threat) may not be. The purpose of the principle of distinction is to hold the line on noncombatant immunity, to reduce civilian casualties.

Managing Risk to Civilians and Limiting Collateral Damage

Many civilian casualties, of course, are not caused by the direct targeting of noncombatants but are the side effects of attacks on legitimate targets. They are what is often called "collateral damage." Causing civilian deaths in this way is judged differently by the just war tradition from, for example, a terrorist attack that seeks to create noncombatant casualties. This view has its roots in natural law theory. Military ethicist David Whetham cites the work of medieval theologian and philosopher St. Thomas Aquinas to spell out the connection between the natural law doctrine of double effect (DDE) and the permissibility of unintended harm to civilians as the result of legitimate military operations:

Underpinning both discrimination and proportionality is the doctrine of double effect. As Aquinas explains, individuals are not necessarily morally responsible for a foreseeable, yet unintended side effect of an otherwise legitimate action. However, the foreseeable side effects of any military action, even while not directly

---

[11] See for example Judith Jarvis Thomson, "Self-Defense," *Philosophy and Public Affairs* 20 (1991): 283–310 and Suzanne Uniacke "In Defence of Permissible Killing," *Law and Philosophy* 19 (2000): 627–33.

[12] There is a further discussion to be had here about whether such forfeiture ought ever to be permanent, or if the right not to be killed is only ever temporarily suspended under certain conditions.

[13] Thomson, "Self-Defense," p. 300.

intended, must still be proportionate to the expected military utility of the target. Part of this calculation requires that any noncombatant casualties are to be avoided as far as is possible. Because of this, the doctrine of double effect can only justify military activities up to a point. For example, it cannot be used to defend the use of weapons of mass destruction against an area containing a civilian population, as these weapons are so indiscriminate that the resulting casualties cannot be regarded as merely a secondary result. This is reinforced by the principle of proportionality and also the idea of *mala in se*, which recognizes that some methods of war are simply evil in themselves, and cannot be justified under any circumstances.[14]

DDE is considered in greater detail in a subsequent chapter in this volume, but its basic structure is a set of criteria that must be met before an action with foreseeable harmful side effects can be deemed permissible. These criteria, as applied for example as policy guidance to the modern U.S. military, are well summarized by Paul Christopher:

In its military operations, the United States seems to have adopted a modification to the doctrine of double effect so that one may undertake military operations aimed at legitimate objectives or targets, even though the operations will also have foreseeable "bad" consequences. Such operations become permissible when they meet the following necessary criteria: (1) The bad effect is unintended; (2) The bad effect is proportional to the desired military objective; (3) The bad effect is not a direct means to the good effect (e.g. bomb cities to encourage peace talks); and (4) Actions are taken to minimize the foreseeable bad effects, *even if it means accepting an increased risk to combatants.*[15]

The italicized portion of the final provision reflects the influence of the eminent Michael Walzer. Military ethicists have some disagreement concerning how much additional risk combatants should take upon themselves to decrease risk to civilians. In his seminal work, *Just and Unjust Wars*, Walzer took a firm position on this question, asserting that combatants must do more than merely not intentionally target noncombatants:

Simply not to intend the death of civilians is too easy; most often, under battle conditions, the intentions of soldiers are focused narrowly on the enemy. What we look for in such cases is some sign of a positive commitment to save civilian lives. Not merely to apply the proportionality rule and kill no more civilians than is militarily necessary – that rule applies to soldiers as well; no one can be killed for trivial purposes. Civilians have a right to something more. And if saving civilian lives means risking soldier's lives, the risk must be accepted. But there is a limit to

---

[14] David Whetham, "The Just War Tradition: A Pragmatic Compromise," in *Ethics, Law, and Military Operations*, ed. David Whetham, New York: Palgrave Macmillan, 2011, p. 82.

[15] Paul Christopher, *The Ethics of War and Peace*, Upper Saddle River, NJ: Pearson/Prentice Hall, 2004, p. 92. Emphasis added.

the risks that we require. These are, after all, unintended deaths and legitimate military operations, and the absolute rule against attacking civilians does not apply. War necessarily places civilians in danger; that is another aspect of its hellishness. We can only ask soldiers to minimize the dangers they impose.[16]

Not everyone accepts that troops should bear this burden. Asa Kasher, who shaped the code of ethics for the Israeli Defense Force (IDF) in 1994, has controversially argued that the safety of combatants should come before that of enemy civilians (though not before that of civilians in territories under effective control):

In sum, Israel should favor the lives of its own soldiers over the lives of the well-warned neighbors of a terrorist when it is operating in a territory that it does not effectively control, because in such territories it does not bear moral responsibility for properly separating between dangerous individuals and harmless ones, beyond warning them in an effective way. The sick can wave white flags, their relatives can do it too. The person who is afraid his home would be looted does not create by his odd behavior a reason for jeopardizing soldiers' lives. The person who does not know where to go is a myth.[17]

This, however, is a minority view that is not generally embraced by military ethicists.

Most scholars in the field accept Walzer's perspective (if not an even more restrictive one), and the privileging of civilian lives on both sides of a conflict despite increased risk to combatants is largely upheld in international law.

If Walzer is correct that civilians, since they are not a direct part of the hostilities, "have a right that 'due care' be taken"[18] to minimize harm to them, how does this principle play out in practice? What steps must be taken to make it over the bar of "due care"? The starting point is that military operations that will imperil civilians should be kept to a minimum and, when they must occur, should be as precisely targeted as possible to spare civilian lives. In addition, as alluded to in Asa Kasher's comments, it is necessary to take steps to warn civilians before war fighting operations begin in their area. They must also be given adequate opportunity, direction, and safe passage to flee the area in advance of the hostilities.

In *Just Wars: Cicero to Iraq*, Alex Bellamy notes the epistemic challenge of assessing of whether due care has been taken to protect civilian lives:

The idea that it is possible to separate intent and act, particularly when referring to individuals in combat, has often been criticized. Critics argue that there is no

[16] Michael Walzer, *Just and Unjust Wars: A Moral Argument with Historical Illustrations*, New York: Basic Books, 1977, pp. 155–56.

[17] Asa Kasher, "A Moral Evaluation of the Gaza War – Operation Cast Lead," *Journal of the Jerusalem Center for Public Affairs*, 9 (2010) no. 18, p. 6.

[18] Walzer, *Just and Unjust Wars*, p. 156.

practical difference between *intending* the deaths of non-combatants near military targets and merely *foreseeing* it (McKeogh 2002). According to Walzer and the contemporary laws of war, although we can never fully know an actor's intentions, we can ascertain something approximating intentions by focusing on actions. To display an intention not to harm non-combatants, combatants must demonstrate both that they did not deliberately seek to kill non-combatants and that they have taken every reasonable precaution to minimize the likelihood of harming non-combatants (due care).[19]

Philosopher Henry Shue explicates the important role that military necessity and advantage can play in helping draw the lines between acceptable and unacceptable military operations that put civilians at risk:

The simple fact that a military attack must be expected to produce a military advantage makes a difference. This may simply be a further, specific implication of the requirement of military necessity. It means that the attack must have some rational military purpose, and an attack can hardly be necessary if it has no rational purpose. This is an extremely low standard, but in view of the amount of completely senseless destruction that occurs in war, it is far from negligible. Violence that is at least not senseless is one small step forward. An attack must make some sense. It cannot consist simply of killing people and blowing things up for the sake of doing do. The killing and destruction must play some intelligible role in a coherent plan for military success. Mere high body counts as such, for example, do not constitute a military advantage. Attrition as such is not necessarily militarily advantageous, as the First World War and the American intervention in Vietnam demonstrated beyond all dispute. Whatever is done must have some reasonable prospect of actually advancing some sensible conception of military success.[20]

Shue further emphasizes that the military advantage in question must be "concrete and direct."[21] This is in line with the foundational works of the Western just war tradition, which also focus on absolute necessity. For example, Vitoria writes: "It is never right to slay the guiltless, even as an indirect and unintentional result, except when there is no other means of carrying on the operations of a just war."[22] And in Grotius we also find a warning against allowing our natural bias to drive us to take actions that put civilians at risk for only uncertain gains, "The decision in such matters must be left to a prudent judgment, but in such a way that when in doubt we should favor that course . . . which has regard for the interest of another rather than our own."[23]

Outside the bounds of arguments about military necessity, there are some types of locations that are simply deemed illegitimate targets, due to the risk to

---

[19] Alex J. Bellamy, *Just Wars: From Cicero to Iraq*, Cambridge: Polity Press, 2006, p. 125.
[20] Henry Shue, "Civilian Protection and Force Protection," in *Ethics, Law, and Military Operations*, ed. David Whetham, New York: Palgrave MacMillan, 2011, p. 142.
[21] Ibid.   [22] Christopher, *The Ethics of War and Peace*, p. 56.   [23] Ibid., p. 92.

especially defenseless noncombatant populations. Traditionally, these include sites such as schools, hospitals, and places of sanctuary (which may also be protected for reasons to do with the preservation of cultural property, which is a separate issue). For example, Rule 35 of customary international law as compiled by the International Committee of the Red Cross (ICRC) states, "Directing an attack against a zone established to shelter the wounded, the sick, and civilians from the effects of hostilities is prohibited."[24] The argument is that it is unethical to target such sites, regardless of any potential military gain, since they represent gathering places for persons who are not only not active threats (e.g., children, the wounded, the sick, unarmed refugees, and displaced persons) but are also deserving of special humanitarian protection, due to their unique vulnerability (and, in some cases, status as moral patients).

In practical terms, preserving immunity for such sites is dependent upon protective marks not being abused for military advantage. The principle does not depend on this and reciprocity should never be used as grounds for violating the sanctity of the rule. Sadly, however, there is a history of the perfidious use of protective marks being followed by attacks on previously out-of-bounds locations. This is another reason why it is manifestly illegal under international law to, for instance, deceptively label an active hub from which to launch missiles as a hospital, marking it with Red Cross or Red Crescent symbols,[25] or to intentionally co-locate a school or similar safe zone with an arms depot, thus using civilians as human shields for the weapons. Such practices put the application of the principle of distinction at risk, by blurring the lines between threats and non-threats, as does hiding combatants among civilian populations and their refusing to wear uniforms or other distinguishing marks of combatant status.

II Weapons That Threaten Civilian Immunity

Another grave threat to the safety of civilians in wars and conflict zones is indiscriminate weaponry. The issue of collateral damage was discussed earlier, but there is a difference between causing some collateral damage when deploying a weapon targeted with reasonable precision against a legitimate military target and using weapons that, by their very nature, permit no discrimination between combatants and noncombatants. The ICRC identifies a slew of weapons that it believes fall into this category in its explanation of Rule 71, "Weapons That Are by Nature Indiscriminate," in its summary of customary international humanitarian law:

---

[24] ICRC, Customary IHL Database, https://ihl-databases.icrc.org/customary-ihl/eng/docs/v1_c ha_chapter11_rule35, accessed October 2016.

[25] Article 85, paragraph 3, sub-paragraph (f) of Protocol I states that the perfidious use of these emblems is to be regarded as a war crime (Article 85, para. 5).

The following weapons have been cited in practice as being indiscriminate in certain or all contexts: chemical[26], biological[27], and nuclear weapons[28]; anti-personal landmines[29]; mines[30]; poison[31]; explosives discharged from balloons[32]; V-1 and V-2 rockets[33]; cluster bombs[34]; booby-traps[35]; Scud missiles[36]; Katyusha rockets[37]; incendiary weapons[38]; and environmental modification techniques[39]. There is insufficient consensus concerning all of these examples to conclude that, under customary international law, they all violate the rule prohibiting the use of indiscriminate weapons. However, there is agreement that some of them are prohibited.[40]

The concern about such indiscriminate weapons reflects back to the earlier point raised by Alex Bellamy about the principle of distinction requiring some evidence (through actions) of the intention not to harm civilians. Clearly, that intention is not present when weapons are deployed that, by their very nature, make distinction impossible. Nuclear, chemical, and biological weapons (famously referred to in the run-up to the 2003 launch of the Iraq war as "weapons of mass destruction," or WMDs) fit this category especially well because their effects are widespread, imprecise, difficult to direct or control,

---

[26] *ICRC note:* See, e.g., the military manuals of Australia, France, Russia, and the statements of Romania and U.S.; also UN Sub-Commission on Human Rights, etc.

[27] Ibid.

[28] *ICRC note:* See, e.g., the military manual of Switzerland and statements of Australia, Ecuador, Egypt, Iran, Japan, Lesotho, Malaysia, Marshall Islands, Solomon Islands, and Zimbabwe; see also UN Sub-Commission on Human Rights.

[29] *ICRC note:* See, e.g., the military manuals of France, and the reported practice of Peru.

[30] *ICRC note:* See, e.g., the military manuals of Ecuador and U. S., the statement of Australia, reported practice of Jordan and Rwanda; also UN Secretariat, Existing rules of international law on prohibition or restriction of use of specific weapons.

[31] *ICRC note:* See, e.g., the military manuals of Australia, Canada, France, and Russian Federation.

[32] *ICRC note:* See, e.g., the military manuals of Ecuador and United States.

[33] *ICRC note:* See, e.g., the military manuals of Ecuador and United States and the reported practice of Jordan.

[34] *ICRC note:* See, e.g., the statement of Switzerland; also the UN Sub-Commission on Human Rights, Res. 1996/16 and UN Secretariat, Existing rules of international law concerning the prohibition or restriction of use of specific weapons, Survey.

[35] *ICRC note:* See, e.g., the statements of Australia and Russian Federation; see also UN Secretariat, Existing rules of international law concerning the prohibition or restriction of use of specific weapons, Survey.

[36] *ICRC note:* See, e.g., the military manual of Canada, the statements of Israel, United Kingdom and United States and the reported practice of Israel.

[37] *ICRC note:* See, e.g., the reported practice of Israel.

[38] *ICRC note:* See, e.g., the statements of Australia, Russian Federation, Sweden, Switzerland and Turkey; also UN Secretariat, Existing rules of international law concerning the prohibition or restriction of use of specific weapons, Survey.

[39] *ICRC note:* See, e.g., the military manual of the Russian Federation.

[40] ICRC, Customary IHL Database, https://ihl-databases.icrc.org/customary-ihl/eng/docs/v1_c ha_chapter11_rule71, accessed October 2016.

and likely to last long past the end of the conflict in which the weapons were deployed.

The concept of containing the effects of war to the duration of a particular conflict has deep roots in Western culture. The Old Testament of the Bible contains some *jus in bello* guidance among the rules commonly called the Code of Deuteronomy. Most of this guidance, if followed, would produce horrific war crimes (such as the command in Deuteronomy 20:16 to slaughter every living thing in certain kinds of captured cities), but interestingly it also includes an injunction against cutting down fruit-bearing trees (Deuteronomy 20:19) – such an action causes enduring harm that affects people beyond the conflict and goes against the interests of the very people using the tactic.

There are many modern examples of lingering and far-reaching harms (including blowback onto their users) from certain categories of weapons. In the aftermath of dropping nuclear bombs on the Japanese cities of Hiroshima and Nagasaki, the U.S. military sent some of its own troops to the bombed-out cities, not yet fully understanding that the lingering radiation could prove deadly to them, as well.[41] The chemical Agent Orange released by U.S. troops in the Vietnam War poisoned combatants and noncombatants on both sides of the conflict and produced generations of birth defects and other injuries and illnesses.[42]

The distinguished just war tradition scholar James Turner Johnson has grave doubts about the possibility of ever using such tools as nuclear weapons ethically, without violating the principle of distinction. He joins others in qualifying certain weapons as *mala in se*, or evil in themselves. At the same time, he points out that virtually any weapon – even extremely low-tech ones – can be used in ways that violate just war principles:

As to whether the weapons of modern war make it inherently incapable of combatant–non-combatant discrimination, [it is useful to analyze the conflicts in Rwanda-Zaire and the former Yugoslavia] because these have *not* involved such weapons. In these conflicts, the weapons used – from sticks to knives to rifles to artillery fire – became indiscriminate in their effects only because the persons using them, or their commanders, made the conscious choice to use them in this way. That choice and the resulting action are immoral in any and every war in any and every time, past, present, or future. Of course, weapons of mass destruction are rightly rejected as *mala in se*; this is because their inherent purpose is to target

---

[41] U.S. DoD, *Hiroshima and Nagasaki Occupation Forces*, Washington, DC: Defense Nuclear Agency, 1980, and U.S. DoD, *Radiation Dose Reconstruction U.S. Occupation Forces in Hiroshima and Nagasaki, Japan 1945–1946*, Washington, DC: Defense Nuclear Agency, 1981.

[42] A. Schecter, L. C. Dai, L. T. Thuy, H. T. Quynh, D. Q. Minh, H. D. Cau, P. H. Phiet, N. T. Nguyen, J. D. Constable, and R. Baughman. "Agent Orange and the Vietnamese: The Persistence of Elevated Dioxin Levels in Human Tissues," *American Journal of Public Health*, 85 (2005) no. 4: 516–22.

non-combatants. But even clubs, knives, and bullets become weapons of mass destruction when they are used intentionally and directly to kill masses of people. The point of insisting on a distinction between non-combatants and combatants is exactly to avoid this.[43]

There is some question as to whether modern nuclear weapons should continue to be classified as *mala in se* across the board. Johnson's objection to them applies to their use as counter-value weapons (weapons aimed at goods that are valued by one's opponent but do not represent a military threat), against targets such as cities. However, the creation of relatively small-yield tactical nuclear weapons seemed to open up the option of counter-force applications that would target only enemy combatants. Yet, as Lawrence Freedman observes, this was more theory than reality:

In December 1953 the chairman of the Joint Chiefs of Staff observed that "today atomic weapons have virtually achieved a conventional status within our armed forces" ... It soon became clear, however, that nuclear weapons could not be used just as if they were conventional weapons. Their radius of destruction was too large and their aftereffects too pervasive to employ them in such a precise and discriminating fashion. Once the military began exercising with tactical nuclear weapons, the potentially dire consequences for the civilian population became clear.[44] [...] As Bernard Brodie observed, "a people saved by us through our free use of nuclear weapons over their territories would probably be the last that would ever ask us to help them."[45,46]

Tactical nuclear weapons have continued to evolve, but even with significantly lower-yield nuclear weapons there is the danger that radiological fallout cannot be fully contained, as it will be subject to many variables, including weather conditions and ground water accessibility. And, as Freedman further explains, any use of nuclear weapons, however small, may trigger rapid escalation of a conflict, thus putting more civilians at risk.

As technology advances, sophisticated biological or chemical weapons may be designed that are *more* capable, not less, of targeting only combatants. That remains largely speculative at the moment. Meanwhile, already existing or

---

[43] James Turner Johnson, edited excerpt, "Contemporary Just War," in *The Ethics of War: Classic and Contemporary Readings*, eds. Gregory M. Reichberg, Henrik Syse, and Endre Begby, Oxford: Blackwell Publishing, 2006, p. 667.

[44] *Freedman note*: "The most notorious such exercise was Carte Blanche ... in West Germany in 1955. In it tactical nuclear weapons were only "used" by the NATO side. Over two days 355 devices were "exploded," mostly over West Germany territory ... [T]his would have left up to 1.7 million Germans dead and 3.5 million wounded."

[45] Bernard Brodie, "More about Limited War," *World Politics* 10 (1957) no. 1, p. 117.

[46] Lawrence Freedman, "The First Two Generations of Nuclear Strategists," in *Makers of Modern Strategy: From Machiavelli to the Nuclear Age*, ed. Peter Paret, Oxford: Clarendon Press, 1986, pp. 747–48.

emerging autonomous and semi-autonomous weapons systems, from simple landmines to sophisticated robotics, continue to raise red flags about civilian safety. A basic landmine cannot distinguish a soldier from a child traversing a field and can maim and kill long after the conflict ends, if not disposed of properly. A robotic weapon, such as the sentry robots deployed by South Korea in the demilitarized zone (DMZ) between North and South Korea, may depend on a human in the loop to make target and firing decisions.[47] That is less potentially disruptive to the principle of distinction than a system that is truly autonomous and out of human control. On the other hand, Ron Arkin defends the view that autonomous robots might be able to show a higher degree of appropriate target discrimination under combat conditions than a human could. Here are three of the reasons Arkin presents in support of his view, noting that autonomous robots have

1. The ability to act conservatively: i.e., they do not need to protect themselves in cases of low certainty of target identification. Autonomous armed robotic vehicles do not need to have self-preservation as a foremost drive, if at all . . . There is no need for a "shoot first, ask-questions later" approach. 2. [S]ensors better equipped for battlefield observations than humans currently possess . . . 3. Unmanned robotic systems can be designed without emotions that cloud their judgment or result in anger and frustration with ongoing battlefield events. In addition, "Fear and hysteria are always latent in combat, often real, and they press us toward fearful measures and criminal behavior" (Walzer 1977). Autonomous agents need not suffer similarly.[48]

Arkin's conclusions about the potential for autonomous robots to spare more civilian lives stand in sharp contrast to those of Noel Sharkey, who asserts that autonomous robots represent an enhanced threat to noncombat safety:

A computer can compute any given procedure that can be written down in a programming language. We could, for example, give the robot computer an instruction such as, "If civilian, do not shoot." This would be fine if, and only if, there was some way of giving the computer a clear definition of what a civilian is. We certainly cannot get one from the Laws of War that could provide a machine with the necessary information . . . And even if there was a clear computational definition of a civilian, we would still need all of the relevant information to be made available from the sensing apparatus. All that is available to robots are sensors such as cameras, infrared sensors, sonars, lasers, temperature sensors and ladars, etc. These may be able to tell us that something is a human, but they could not tell us much else . . . Humans understand one another in a way that machines

---

[47] Tim Hornyak, "Korean Machine-Gun Robots Start DMZ Duty," C-Net, July 14, 2010, www.cnet.com/news/korean-machine-gun-robots-start-dmz-duty.

[48] Ronald C. Arkin, "The Case for Ethical Autonomy in Unmanned Systems," *Journal of Military Ethics*, 9 (2010) no. 4. 332–41.

cannot and we don't fully understand how. Cues can be very subtle and there is an infinite number of circumstances where lethal force is inappropriate. Just think of children being forced to carry empty rifles or insurgents burying their dead.[49]

Conclusion

While technological progress may produce fresh problems for those tasked to produce rules for the precise application of the principle of distinction, they do not threaten its relevance. Whether killing and destruction are brought about by a fireball launched from a trebuchet or by a laser beam, the same questions arise in determining legitimate targets. As long as armed conflict persists as an ugly aspect of human politics, military ethics will continue to require respect for noncombatant immunity:

Ethics precede, accompany and follow the action. They are at the same time a factor of balance and a condition of evolution. The fruit of past experience, they are indispensable for the action to come. – General de la Motte[50]

[49] Noel Sharkey, "Ground for Discrimination: Autonomous Robot Weapons," *RUSI Defence Systems*, 11 (2008) no. 2: 86–89.
[50] General Benoit Royal, *The Ethical Challenges of the Soldier: The French Experience*, Paris: Economica, 2010, p. 167.

9 Proportionality and Necessity *in Bello*

Jovana Davidovic

Traditionally, in Just War theory and international law proportionality calculations focus on collateral damage or the number of civilians one might unintentionally, but foreseeably, kill in pursuit of some military advantage. This means that proportionality calculations are not affected, in orthodox Just War theory and international law, by the harm some military action might impose on combatants, or by the moral status of the military advantage one is seeking.[1]

Recently, so-called revisionist just war scholars have started moving away from exclusive focus on collateral damage in evaluations of proportionality (wide proportionality) and have started paying attention to harm military actions might impose on combatants (narrow proportionality).[2] This change in focus has been, at least in part, a result of acknowledging that the line between civilians and combatants is not easily drawn. In addition, some revisionist scholars have also started focusing on the incommensurability between the notions of military advantage and human deaths, and the consequences of admitting such incommensurability for traditional proportionality calculations.

In this chapter, I look at both traditional/orthodox and revisionist (in particular, individualist) accounts of *in bello* proportionality and I examine their strengths and weaknesses. I also consider the closely related *in bello* condition

---

[1] One of the most prominent supporters of traditional Just War theory is Michael Walzer, whose book *Just and Unjust Wars* revived the Just War theory in the 1970s. Michael Walzer, *Just and Unjust Wars: A Moral Argument with Historical Illustrations*, New York: Basic Books, 1977.

[2] This includes a large number of scholars some of the individualist persuasion and some more skeptical of the individualist project, but nonetheless revisionist. They include, for example, Jeff McMahan, "On the moral equality of combatants," *Journal of Political Philosophy* 14 (2006) no. 4; McMahan, *Killing in War*, Oxford: Oxford University Press, 2009; Thomas Hurka, "Proportionality in the morality of war," *Philosophy and Public Affairs* 33 (2005) no. 1: 34–66; Seth Lazar, "Debate: Do Associative Duties Really Not Matter?" *Journal of Political Philosophy* 17 (2009) no. 1: 90–101; Saba Bazargan. "Killing Minimally Responsible Threats," *Ethics* 125 (2014) no. 2:114–36; Helen Frowe, *Defensive Killing: An Essay on War and Self-Defence*, Oxford: Oxford University Press, 2014; Victor Tadros, "Duty and Liability," *Utilitas* 24 (2012) no. 1: 259–277; Cécile Fabre, *Cosmopolitan War*, Oxford: Oxford University Press, 2012; Noam Zohar, "Collective war and individualist ethics: against the conscription of 'self-defence,'" *Political Theory* 21 (1993) no. 4: 606–22, 1993; David Rodin, *War and Self-Defense*, New York: Oxford University Press, 2002.

of necessity and briefly explain how it relates to proportionality. The chapter focuses on, what I take to be, the central debate in just war tradition – between (traditional) scholars who take war to be so different from ordinary life that it requires a *sui generis* set of moral rules and (individualist) scholars who think that the moral rules that apply in ordinary circumstances (and in particular in self- and other-defence) ought to underpin the moral principles that govern behaviour in war.

I start the chapter, in Section I, by looking at traditional Just War theory's account of *in bello* proportionality. I quickly address the main worries traditional accounts of proportionality face. In Section II, I examine the individualist revisions of Just War theory and in particular the individualist account of *in bello* proportionality. I lay out the groundwork for thinking that we should approach proportionality in war as continuous with proportionality in ordinary cases of self- and other-defence. That then leads me, also in Section II, to further and in more detail examine the problems that the traditional accounts of *in bello* proportionality face. In Section III, I address some of the common problems that the individualist accounts of *in bello* proportionality face. In Section IV, I compare the traditional and the individualist approaches to proportionality and further assess their strengths and weaknesses by applying them to a particular case. Finally, in Section V, I look at the notion of necessity *in bello* and its relationship to proportionality *in bello*, and I examine some of the main problems traditional accounts of necessity face.

I   Traditional Accounts of *Jus in Bello* Proportionality

Proportionality calculations matter for moral justification of actions in war. Our laws reflect this. However, while we often hear that some state or non-state actor has acted disproportionately in war, it is not always clear what we mean by that. Israel has, for example, on more than one occasion over the past decade been accused of acting disproportionately. Its 2006 war with Hezbollah as well as its 2008/2009 intervention in Gaza have been called disproportionate by just war scholars as well as the officials from the EU and the UN.[3] The Goldstone Report (the UN Report of the Fact-Finding Mission on the Gaza Conflict), for example, addressed a number of worries about Israel's forces acting disproportionately and indiscriminately during the Gaza Strip "Operation Cast Lead." During this year-long military operation between 1387 and 1417 Palestinians lost their lives, many of whom were, according to the Goldstone Report, civilians.[4] During the same period four Israelis lost their lives in Israel, three

---

[3] Human Rights in Palestine and Other Occupied Arab Territories: Report of the United Nations' Fact-Finding Mission on the Gaza Conflict, also known as the Goldstone Report, is available at www2.ohchr.org/english/bodies/hrcouncil/docs/12session/A-HRC-12-48.pdf. From here on out "report" and "Mission."

[4] Goldstone Report, Executive Summary, 17.

were civilians and another nine soldiers died during the operation. This differential in the number of casualties, while alarming, is certainly not sufficient or even strongly indicative of disproportionality. After all, at least traditionally, proportionality assesses individual actions and strategies used in war and evaluates whether the risk to civilians is proportionate to the military advantage sought. Thus, to assess proportionality *in bello*, we traditionally, as the Goldstone Report did, look to particular actions in war. The report, for example, examined the direct and deliberate attacks on police facilities, during which some 240 police officers were killed. Israel argued that these actions were proportionate and that the police officers were legitimate targets. Whether or not such actions were in fact permissible would depend exactly on whether or not those police officers were in fact legitimate targets and whether the direct attacks endangered too many civilians; in other words, it would depend on whether Israel acted discriminately and proportionately. The question of whether some of these police officers were in fact legitimate targets arose because Hamas had recruited some of them. Nonetheless, as the report noted, many police officers were not Hamas recruits, leading the Mission to conclude that "the attacks . . . failed to strike an acceptable balance between the direct military advantage anticipated (i.e. the killing of those policemen who may have been members of Palestinian armed groups) and the loss of civilian life (i.e. the other policemen killed and members of the public who would inevitably have been present or in the vicinity), and therefore violated international humanitarian law."[5] The Mission relied on traditional Just War theory (which permeates international humanitarian law) – arguing that killing enemy combatants is an acceptable military advantage that one might seek and use to justify collateral damage. The Mission relied both on the number of Hamas-recruited police officers and on the number of civilian police officers to estimate whether the attacks on the police were proportionate and thus permissible. But it should be made clear that traditionally these numbers (of Hamas-recruited police officers and civilian police officers) are in evaluations of proportionality *in bello* neither used simply in comparison (the number of recruited police officers vs. civilian officers), nor are they used to compare, for example, the number of civilian lives lost to the number of civilian lives possibly saved by removal of Hamas-recruited police officers. The number of civilian lives saved by removal of Hamas-recruited police officers *might be* a military advantage, but it need not be. Military advantage is, for the purposes of proportionality calculations in traditional Just War theory, understood in relation to how close a particular action or strategy gets us to the goal of military victory, whatever our overall military goal might be.[6] This might, at first, seem surprising.

---

[5] Goldstone Report, Executive Summary, 18.

[6] I return to this example later in the chapter. The attacks on police stations present a particularly interesting case for trying to compare the tools that the traditional Just War theory and individualist Just War theory have to offer.

After all, proportionality is commonly thought of as a lesser evil calculation. A defensive action is proportionate in as much as it is less *harmful* than the action we are trying to avert. The harm we impose must be lesser than the harm we are trying to avert or it must be worth the good we are trying to achieve. *In bello* proportionality is traditionally also a utilitarian question of lesser evil, but the notions of harmfulness operating on the two sides of the proportionality equation need not be, or are not necessarily, the same. On the one side, we are evaluating the harm to civilians, on the other, the harm to our military aim (or the value of the action for our military aim). This disconnect (between the two sides of the "proportionality equation") is not surprising given that in the traditional Just War theory the *in bello* conditions operate independently from the *ad bellum* conditions, and in particular, independently from the justness of the cause for war. Whether or not one's war is just is, traditionally, irrelevant for the question of *in bello* proportionality. All that the traditional proportionality condition requires is that a military strategist or a combatant consider whether some military advantage is important enough to risk killing some number of civilians and what number.[7] Importantly, that advantage must be a military (as opposed to a political) advantage, meaning that it must contribute to military victory and the defeat of the enemy.

So how then might a traditional just war scholar understand military advantage separate from lives saved or reduction in harm to civilians? And how might one justify such understanding of military advantage? Different scholars answer this question in different ways. The simple way to solve the incommensurability problem, as I had mentioned, would be to suggest that we can make sense of what we mean by "military advantage" by filling that notion out with the same considerations we are weighing on the other side of the equation – namely human lives.[8] As we have seen, traditional scholars do not solve the incommensurability problem in this way, because doing so would cross the boundary between *jus ad bellum* and *jus in bello*, a boundary that is the cornerstone of traditional Just War theory. In traditional Just War theory, *jus ad bellum* conditions and *jus in bello* conditions are kept independent from each other because they have different aims – *jus ad bellum* conditions are meant to limit the resort to war, while *jus in bello* conditions are meant to limit the horrors of war independent of the justness of one's cause, independent of whether *jus ad bellum* conditions have been met. But it is not only this conceptual claim that the *jus ad bellum* and *jus in bello* conditions have separate aims that

---

[7] *In bello* proportionality is dependent on the requirement to discriminate *in bello*. The condition of discrimination in war requires that we make a distinction between civilians, who are seen as fully innocent, and combatants, who are considered legitimate targets in virtue of their combatant status.

[8] The focus is on death (rather than harm to property or displacement) because that is the most significant and common harm in war, and because much of the other harms (such as to property) can be "translated" into harm or risk of harm in the form of deaths.

traditionally justifies the claim that proportionality calculations must be done independently of the justness of one's cause for war. It is also commonly said by traditional scholars that *in bello* rules are meant to be action guiding for both combatants and strategists, whom we cannot expect to engage in assessments of the justness of their own and their enemy's cause. In fact, combatants ought to and do always assume that their side is just, as they commonly add. If *in bello* proportionality then must remain independent from the justness of the cause of war, it follows that we cannot require that we evaluate military advantage in terms of lives saved; we cannot require that the civilian lives always be compared to civilian lives. After all some military advantages cannot be easily translated into civilian lives, nor should they be on this view. This is why suggesting that we ought to evaluate military advantage in the light of the number of lives that will be saved is not readily available to traditional just war scholars.

Instead, orthodox scholars more often suggest that a military advantage is weightier or less weighty in relation to how close it will get us to military victory and the defeat of our enemy. This means that different forces with differing military aims might assess proportionality of the putatively same action in different ways. While we are not allowed to bring in the justness of one's cause in asking whether or not the action is proportionate, we are allowed to bring in the military reality of such a cause in evaluating whether something counts as a military advantage. The purposes for which we are trying to defeat the enemy seem to affect whether or not a particular target is militarily advantageous and how many civilians might be killed relative to the value of that aim. If one's aim is, for example, the occupation of a territory, then military victory is more likely going to require a significant depletion of military forces in the country. Given that, if we were attacking a military facility, we would be more likely to assess (and rightly so) a higher number of civilian deaths as proportionate. If on the other hand we were waging a war of humanitarian assistance or intervention, it might be counter-productive for all sorts of reasons to endanger the lives of civilians to destroy the local military facilities; an attack such as that might undermine the ultimate aim of long-term peace. While the orthodox Just War theory separates the justness of the cause for war from the justness and proportionality of our actions in war, the cause for war does affect what we think is proportionate in war, although in ways that do not track justness of the overall war. It would seem that there are good reasons to think that those pursuing an unjust war of aggression might be on this view entitled to endanger more civilians to secure some military facility than those fighting a war of just humanitarian intervention. This seems, to many, to be a problem.

In addition to the worries regarding the way traditional Just War theory understands military advantage, there are also worries regarding the justification of the claim that harm to combatants ought not to count in our proportionality calculations. Since we cannot, according to traditional Just War theory, distinguish, for the purposes of *in bello* proportionality, between combatants who are fighting a just war and those who are not, we must treat them all the same and in particular, we must treat them as legitimate targets. It is perfectly acceptable to attempt to deplete enemy's forces either as a side effect of pursuing some military advantage or because the depletion of enemy's forces is the military advantage one is seeking.

According to traditional Just War theory, the number of enemy combatants that our action will threaten or knowingly kill is irrelevant; in fact, it might even make the aim we are pursuing weightier. This is often explained in orthodox Just War theory and law by the assumption that combatants take upon themselves the risk of being targets. Other times it is explained by the fact that the enemy combatants pose a threat of harm. The second explanation seems less capable of broadly justifying the orthodox claim that the harm to enemy combatants should not factor in our proportionality calculations, because not all enemy combatants pose an immediate threat of harm and some of them might never. The claim that combatants consent in some sense (e.g. by taking on the risk of harm) and thus make themselves legitimate targets is also problematic but seems better suited for justifying the broader claim that any and all enemy combatants are legitimate targets. Most ways of justifying the claim that combatant deaths are "free" in proportionality calculations run into problems. This is partly because the line between civilians and combatants is not easily drawn in a principled way. In fact, the most plausible line that can be drawn between civilians and combatants, namely, the line grounded in liability to harm (e.g. because of moral responsibility for the threat of unjustified harm), does not allow us to hold on to the stark distinction between combatants and civilians that orthodox Just War theory assumes.

I address this and other problems that orthodox Just War theory faces in the next section. I start by examining the discontinuity between the way traditional theorists think of proportionality in war and the way we commonly think of proportionality in ordinary everyday cases of self- and other-defence.

II   Individualist Accounts of Proportionality

Commonly, in ordinary cases of self-defence, proportionality is necessary to argue that a particular defensive action is morally permissible. For an action to be morally permissible, it is necessary, albeit (on most accounts of proportionality) not sufficient, that the action be proportionate both in the narrow and in the wide senses.

An action is proportionate in the wide sense if it does not increase the risk of harm *to bystanders* to a disproportionate amount. If a victim were trying to protect himself from a malicious attacker who was trying to kill him on a crowded bus, it would likely be widely disproportionate to shoot a gun in that crowded bus to prevent the attacker's lethal threat. On the other hand, if the same malicious attacker were trying to throw a bomb out the window in an effort to kill 25 children and the most likely way to stop him was to shoot a gun risking serious harm to a single person standing next to the attacker, it seems proportionate in the wide sense to discharge that gun.

Proportionality in the narrow sense refers to the amount of harm one is allowed to defensively impose *on an attacker* to prevent him from causing harm. If an attacker were trying to break the victim's finger, it would be, arguably, disproportionate to lethally shoot the attacker even if that were the only way to prevent a broken finger. Proportionality in the narrow sense depends on one's liability to harm. To say one is liable to some amount of harm is to say that one can harm an attacker to that extent without violating his rights. Liability to harm is importantly different from desert, although both desert and liability are related to the loss of rights. Being liable to be killed in some particular set of circumstances means that one has lost the right not to be killed in that particular set of circumstances. Liability to harm can be grounded or explained in a number of ways; moral responsibility for the threat of unjustified harm is not the only such explanation.[9] Some scholars think that one can be liable to harm without the corresponding loss of rights. Others think that one can be liable to be killed in one set of circumstance because of wrongdoing in another set of circumstances. I leave all of these complex issues aside for the sake of brevity, and I focus on the notion of liability to harm grounded in the moral responsibility for the threat of unjustified harm.[10]

To justify defensive harming, the harm one is trying to avert needs to be unjustified; after all it would be odd to say that an action is narrowly proportionate in the case when a malicious murderer is threatening to kill a police officer trying to stop the murder. In that case there is a sense in which the action of the murderer might *appear* to be proportionate, but it is not. The action appears proportionate only if one considers the criterion of posing a threat (regardless of the morality of such threats) as sufficient to ground liability to defensive harm. As numerous scholars argue, and in Just War theory Jeff

---

[9]   Scholars, such as Victor Tadros, have argued that moral responsibility is not the appropriate criterion for grounding moral liability to harm, in general, and moral liability to be killed, in particular. I will, for reasons of space, not engage in such debates. Tadros, "Duty and Liability." I agree there is a lot of space beyond moral responsibility that might be sufficient to ground moral liability to harm, including both stricter and less strict grounds (ranging from culpability to claims that innocents can still be liable to harm).

[10]   It is important to note that much of what follows regarding the grounding of individualist theories can be said even if we embrace other accounts of liability. Nevertheless, the problems that individualist theories face (which I discuss in Section III) are commonly answered differently based on varying notions of what it means to be liable to harm and how one becomes liable to harm.

McMahan most prominently, posing a threat is not sufficient to be liable to defensive harm – what is necessary is posing a threat of *unjustified* harm.[11] If narrow proportionality is necessary for moral permissibility or justification of an action, then such proportionality calculations must take into account the moral permissibility of the harm one is trying to avert.

Similar consideration plays a role in assessing wide proportionality. If wide proportionality plays a role in moral justification, then such proportionality must depend on whether or not the harm one is trying to avert by using defensive or responsive harm is morally justified. I use the term "defensive" harm to refer to harm being imposed on someone who *is liable* for some amount of defensive harm (in virtue of being morally responsible for a threat of unjustified harm), and I use the term "responsive" harm to refer to harm being imposed on someone in response to his or her posing a threat, but independent of whether or not that threat is justified. I do not mean to suggest or assume that all defensive harm is proportionate and thus justified. One can engage in defensive harm – that is, harming someone who is potentially liable to be harmed in an effort to avert the threat of unjustified harm, but can engage in imposing such harm disproportionately. I discuss this claim in more detail later.

Individualist just war scholars start from observations such as these and argue that war is not so significantly different from peacetime that we should abandon this common and straightforward understanding of proportionality that operates in ordinary cases. If proportionality in war functions similarly to proportionality in ordinary cases of self- and other-defence, then the morality of one's aims, that is, the justification behind threatening harm, becomes increasingly important. This then leads to the claim that we cannot easily separate *jus ad bellum* from *jus in bello*. For a combatant to engage in a military action that is proportionate, she must be (among other things) trying to avert a threat of *unjustified harm*. That commonly means (albeit not in all cases) that the combatant's war must have a just cause to be able to justify imposing any amount of harm on civilians (so as to be widely proportionate) or enemy combatants (so as to be narrowly proportionate). It also follows from this that just combatants and unjust combatants are not equals; the morality of their aims matters for whether or not they are legitimate targets. A combatant with a just cause can most likely impose significantly greater risk of harm in trying to prevent some military action of the enemy (who lacks a just cause), while almost all unjust combatants will not be morally permitted to engage in almost any harmful actions in war since almost all such actions would be both widely and narrowly disproportionate. After all, an unjust combatant will act in almost all cases in furtherance of an unjust aim, and no amount of harm can be justified in furtherance of unjust aims.

The suggestion that proportionality calculations in ordinary cases and in war do not differ significantly complicates our analysis of what is permissible in

---

[11] McMahan, *Killing in War* and elsewhere.

war. For an action to be proportionate, combatants have to not only assess the morality of their aim and the aim of the enemy combatants, but they also need to assess the enemy's moral responsibility for the relevant threat of harm. I turn to problems that arise for proportionality calculations from individualist theories next, but for now I just want to acknowledge the exceedingly changed landscape that Just War theory occupies once individualist revisions of Just War theory are taken seriously. Both narrow and wide proportionality are affected by acknowledging that they are relative to the justness (as they are in ordinary circumstances) of the harm one is trying to avert.

III Taking Individualist Accounts Seriously: Narrow Proportionality and Minimal Moral Responsibility

As mentioned, proportionality calculations become significantly more complicated in individualist accounts of just war. Most obviously, whereas the narrow proportionality did not need to be assessed at all in the past – all combatants and any number of them were "fair game" in pursuit of some military advantage – individualist accounts of war require that the actions in war be narrowly proportionate. Narrow proportionality requires that we assess the enemy combatant's moral responsibility for the threat of harm as well as the moral justification of that harm. Both of these assessments are clearly difficult. Not only is it hard to evaluate the justness of the enemy's cause (i.e. the justifiability of the aim in pursuit of which the enemy is threatening to impose harm), but it is also difficult to establish the enemy's moral (and sometimes causal) responsibility for the threat of that harm. In ordinary cases of self-defence or even other-defence, such calculations might seem easier, although we should be careful in thinking that the complexity of such calculations emerges simply or even primarily out of war-dependent (unique to war) circumstances. While moral responsibility for the threat of unjustified harm is relatively easily assessed in a case of a crazed murderer who is holding kids hostage, or a gang member who is engaging in a drive-by shooting, there are times when the cases seem more complicated, or they are presented as more complicated. As recent events have brought forth, even everyday cases are not always simple. The number of police shootings of unarmed civilians in the United States, which are then explained by claims of lack of access to relevant information about the liability to harm of those civilians (and their moral responsibility for appearing threatening), is an obvious case of how difficult it is to evaluate proportionality even in peacetime.[12] It is important to note that there are two separate issues here: one is access to relevant information in trying to evaluate proportionality, and the other is what exactly is "relevant

---

[12] It should be noted that in many recent cases nothing required complicated assessment. The victims neither were nor appeared threatening.

information," that is, how exactly do we assess the amount of defensive harm one is liable to and whether we are justified in imposing that harm.[13]

So how exactly then are we to assess narrow proportionality? Whether or not one is acting proportionately in this sense depends on whether the attacker whose threat they are trying to avert is morally responsible for the threat of unjustified harm. It also depends on the extent of their moral responsibility and the extent of the harm one is threatening as well as the responsibility for that extent of the harm. In cases of full culpability for an unjustified threat of harm, one is, in a central range of cases, liable to the same amount of harm as they are threatening to impose (if that amount of harm is necessary to avert the threat). In a case of a fully culpable murderer, one is likely acting narrowly proportionate in killing him if that is the only way to avert the lethal threat he is posing. The assertion that killing the murderer is "the only way to avert the lethal threat" is important. One can be liable to x amount of harm *only if* that amount of harm is *necessary* to avert the unjustified harm; that is, necessity is internal to liability.

Things get significantly more complicated in cases of partial or minimal moral responsibility. One is a minimally responsible threat if she is, for example, acting out of duress or with significant epistemic excuse. These cases (of minimal or partial moral responsibility) are incredibly significant for (individualist) proportionality calculations, since there are good reasons to think that almost all enemy combatants will be such threats. After all, many, if not most, combatants act with extremely limited knowledge both of the overall justness of the war (often for good national security reasons) and limited knowledge of how their particular actions fit in the larger military strategy. Many combatants are drafted and thus act under some level of duress. Nearly all combatants operate under the belief that the military cannot be efficient if soldiers question their superior officers.

So what happens in cases of minimal or limited moral responsibility? If, for example, certain individuals are minimally morally responsible for a lethal threat and the only way to avert the threat is to kill them, it seems odd to suggest that they are liable to be killed; it seems odd to suggest that they are liable to the same amount of harm as a fully culpable murderer. One might for that reason conclude that in cases of minimal or limited moral responsibility for a lethal threat where lethal harm needs to be imposed to avert the threat, we are

---

[13] This point can also be made in terms of the commonly used distinction between fact-relative and evidence-relative analysis. For more on this distinction, see Derek Parfit, *On What Matters*, vol. 1, Oxford: Oxford University Press, 2011, pp. 150–51. An action is fact-relative morally permissible if with access to all relevant information it would be permissible to engage in such an action, and it is evidence-relative morally permissible if given the morally salient information we have on hand it would be morally permissible to engage in it. Clearly there are cases where an action is not fact-relative morally permissible but is evidence-relative permissible and vice versa.

not justified imposing such harm. But this need not be the case. Consider the often discussed case of a minimally responsible driver.[14] This driver usually keeps good care of her car, checks brakes, drives the speed limit, and so on but is nonetheless engaging in a risky activity of driving knowing she could harm someone.[15] Her car goes out of control and threatens to kill an innocent victim. The only way that the victim can stop the car is by blasting it with a blaster and thus killing the minimally responsible driver. To many it seems like it should be the case that the innocent victim is justified in killing the minimally responsible driver even though the extent of harm the victim needs to impose to avert the threat is the same as in the case of a culpable murderer. So what could explain this? What happens in cases when the harm one is apparently/potentially liable to impose is less than what would be necessary to impose to avert the threatened harm?[16]

First, one can deny that the innocent victim is justified in self-defence. As I mentioned, this seems unintuitive. Even if one thinks that the driver and innocent victim are equally justified in engaging in lethal self-defence, it does not follow that the victim is not allowed to engage in lethal self-defence.

Second, one can suggest that the victim is justified in fighting back and that he is allowed to do so because of agent-relative permissions – he has a moral right to prefer his own life over that of others. A number of scholars argue for a position similar to this one, including Jonathan Quong.[17] But even if we accept agent-relative permissions, we need not accept that they are so significant as to play a meaningful role in considerations of lethal harming. More importantly, we still need to explain (given that both sides have agent-relative permissions that apply to them), or explain away, the intuition that the victim gets to engage in lethal self-defence or that a bystander can engage in other-defence of the victim.

Third, to justify why the victim can engage in lethal self-defence, some scholars point out that there is a relative differential in moral responsibility for the threat and thus liability between the victim and the driver. They argue that when we consider what we may do to another in these sorts of

---

[14] This example is discussed in dozens of articles; see Jeff McMahan, "The basis of moral liability to killing," *Philosophical Issues*, 15 (2005): 386–405.

[15] If this scenario does not seem compelling, one can imagine a number of similar cases with minimal moral responsibility.

[16] The language in this sentence tries to maneuver between two sets of views. First there are those who think there is no such thing as potential liability – *x* amount of harm is sufficient to avert the threat and one is sufficiently morally responsible to say that one is liable to that amount of harm *or not*. Second there are those who think there is such a thing as a potential liability to harm; where *x* amount of harm is required to avert the threat, one's moral responsibility is not sufficient to explain or account for that much harm, but nonetheless one is morally liable to the lesser amount of harm since that amount of harm *plus y* amount of harm (which can be justified otherwise) is sufficient to avert the threat.

[17] Jonathan Quong, "Killing in Self-Defense," *Ethics* 119 (2009) no. 1: 507–37.

circumstances, we ought not to evaluate the extent of permissible harm in comparison to (or in the light of) the harm we would impose on a fully culpable person in the same circumstance, but instead we ought to compare the relative responsibility and thus relative liability to harm between the relevant actors in the case. In our minimally responsible driver case, since there is an indivisible threat of death, we have to ask who is *more* morally responsible and thus more liable to harm – in this case death. On this view, in cases when we can divide the harm between the morally responsible and the fully innocent we ought to do so, but in cases like ours where that is not an option, the relative moral responsibility is all that matters and is sufficient to justify killing the minimally responsible driver. This sort of an answer to the previous question carries a number of problems, including the failure to make sense of differing intuitions in cases of 100 culpable murders and 100 minimally responsible threats taken in succession.[18] If we accept the relative moral responsibility argument, we would be justified in killing all of them in both scenarios. But this seems at least on the first pass wrong; in the case of 100 murderers waiting in line with a gun to kill me, it seems plausible that I would be permitted to kill them all in return, but this does not seem to be the case with the 100 minimally responsible drivers.[19]

So now we seem to be saddled with another problem: while it still remains unclear what could explain how in spite of varying responsibility for threatened harm we can justify the same amount of defensive harm (namely death in the case of lethal self-defence against the murderer and against the driver), now we also have a further worry. If moral responsibility for the threatened harm and liability are sole grounds for justifying lethal self-defence, then what could possibly explain why we are justified in killing a vast number of fully culpable aggressors but not a large number of minimally responsible threateners?[20]

I think and have argued, like a number of other scholars, that we ought not to accept the view that it is the relative differential in moral responsibility between the victim and threatener that explains why we are justified in imposing lethal harm on the threatener.[21] Those that rely on relative differential in moral

---

[18] Jeff McMahan develops this worry in a number of papers emerging from the talk "The Relevance to Proportionality of the Number of Aggressors," available at www.youtube.com/watch?v=VKM1Cb8txJo.

[19] McMahan, see previous footnote. Jovana Davidovic, "Proportionate Killing: Using Traditional Jus in Bello Conditions to Model the Relationship Between Liability and Lesser Evil Justifications for Killing in War," in *Weighing Lives: Combatants and Civilians in War*, eds. Jens Ohlin, Claire Finkelstein and Larry May, Oxford: Oxford University Press, 2017.

[20] It is important to note that these questions are question about what we ought to do (all things considered), not simply questions about what would be a proportionate action.

[21] Bazargan, "Killing Minimally Responsible Threats"; Davidovic, "Proportionate Killing"; McMahan, "Proportionate Defence," available at www.laws.ucl.ac.uk/wp-content/uploads//12/Colloquium-paper_Jeff-McMahan.pdf; and "Liability, Proportionality and the Number of Aggressors," available at http://jeffersonmcmahan.com/wp-content/uploads/2012/11/Liability-Proportionality-and-the-Number-of-Aggressors.pdf.

responsibility between the innocent bystander and driver seem to think that liability justification is exhaustive. But there are good reasons to think that it is not, and that instead we ought to rely on a combination of liability and lesser evil justifications to make sense of the problems of minimal moral responsibility.

A fourth possible solution to the problem of minimally responsible threatener relies on both liability and lesser evil justifications. Most individualist scholars who rely on both types of justification for killing minimally responsible threats suggest that the additional harms to such threats accumulate faster than to the innocent victim. One way to make sense of the solutions that rely on lesser evil and liability justification is to think of all the harms to a potentially liable individual, beyond that to which she is potentially liable, in the same way as one would consider harms to non-liable individuals, so that both considerations of narrow and (a kind of) wide proportionality apply to most combatants (since in most cases they will be less than culpable or even fully morally responsible). I explain this in what follows.

One is acting narrowly proportionate when the harm that one imposes on another who is liable to be harmed does not exceed one's moral responsibility for that harm. Of course this is at a minimum a two-dimensional proportionality, the smaller the harm for which one is morally responsible and the smaller one's moral responsibility for that harm, the lesser amount of harm we can impose on that person. Conversely, even the smallest amount of moral responsibility for a great harm might be sufficient to impose a rather large amount of harm in an attempt to avoid the greater harm. The question of course is in what sense is liability to harm proportionate or related to moral responsibility for that harm. On one hand, the proportionality calculation (between liability and moral responsibility) might for its analysis compare this moral responsibility to that of a fully culpable individual committing the same act. On the other hand, the proportionality calculation might appeal to the moral responsibility of others in our scenario. I am using the term "amount" of moral responsibility to compare the moral responsibility of the threatener to that of a fully culpable individual threatening the same amount of harm, and not in the relative sense, that is, moral responsibility compared to that of others involved, namely because then the threatener's moral responsibility would always (when others are innocent) be 100 per cent, as we have already seen. On this view, liability instead depends on the level of moral responsibility for the threat of harm. It follows then that the minimally morally responsible threat in the driver case is *potentially liable* to some level of harm but *not liable to be killed*. It does not follow, however, that on this account we would never be justified in killing a minimally responsible threat, all it means is that *liability justification* is not sufficient to explain why and when we are justified in killing a minimally responsible threat. This is exactly why the driver is only potentially liable to some level of harm. If the amount of harm that needs to be imposed is greater than the harm that the liability justification can account for, then the driver is only liable to that harm if the harm above that can be justified in some other way.

On this view, we should think of the harm above and beyond the harm to which the driver is potentially liable as the same sort of harm that one would impose on the innocent. In other words, we might in cases of minimally responsible threats apply *first* the narrow proportionality analysis and *then* something akin to the wide proportionality analysis. However, the amount of harm that would need to be imposed on the person that is liable to some amount of harm is simply smaller in cases of minimally responsible threats, assuming that the harm of death is equal since the harm that needs to be imposed is that of death minus the harm to which one is liable. This then explains why, even though a minimally responsible threat is not liable to be killed to avert a lethal threat they are posing, they nonetheless might be justifiably killed in those circumstances when the harm of death is equal between the threat and innocent victim. It also explains why we quickly "run out of" justification for such killing. If we think of the harm above that to which one is liable as having to be justified as a lesser evil, then even two minimally responsible threats might not be justifiably killed if they are posing the same threat to the same fully innocent victim in succession. Ultimately, it seems that when there is an inescapable threat of harm that has to be distributed somehow, there are morally better and worse ways to distribute such harm; and liability analyses do not seem sufficient to explain them. Lesser evil calculations can help make sense of why one is justified in imposing harm beyond that to which minimally morally responsible threat is liable.

IV Comparing Traditional and Individualist Accounts of *in Bello* Proportionality

Individualists argue that justice *in bello* depends on both narrow and wide proportionality, just like in ordinary circumstances. Traditional scholars reject that claim, partly, because they hold that individualist accounts of proportionality can guide neither individual behaviour nor law. If a theory suggests rules that cannot govern behaviour (because they are, for example, overly complicated, or people are unlikely to comply with them) we have to conclude, orthodox scholars argue, that law ought to look elsewhere and that that theory is wrong. I think both of those conclusions are mistaken. Much more will be said about the legal dimension of *in bello* proportionality in a later chapter.[22] What I want to focus on here is the view that moral analysis of actions in war, which fails to give straightforward guidance to law, is wrong. The main reason individualist analysis cannot be directly "translated" into law is that it requires too many in-the-field evaluations about justification for war, justification for the particular action and the enemy's reasons for fighting in that particular war or engagement. How could we possibly expect combatants to use a theory or a

---

[22] See Chapter 14, this volume, by Adil Haque, on this topic.

set of principles which require so much data that the combatants have no access to, critics ask?

It seems odd to think that the suggestion that proportionality in war functions in its heart the same way as proportionality in ordinary circumstances is in any way meant to suggest that laws ought to require proportionality calculations that work like the previous examples and are required of individuals at each step. Laws as well as rules for combatant behaviour in the field ought to take the morally salient aspects of the previous analysis, "churn" them through and with institutional facts and decide what is most likely to result in the morally preferable result. But note that if we take the individualist account seriously, the morally preferable result is not simply to limit the harm in war; it is to limit the unjustified harm in war to the greatest extent. Which laws, rules and behavioural conditioning are most likely to result in morally preferable outcomes in war (understood in individualist terms) is not an armchair discussion; it should rely on psychological, sociological and historical analyses.

Individualist and traditional accounts give substantively different answers to difficult moral questions regarding proportionality (and what counts as a morally preferable outcome) in war. Consider the previously mentioned Israeli attacks on police officers during Operation Cast Lead, during which some 240 police officers were killed. Even though Israel claimed that the police officers were legitimate targets since Hamas recruited some of them, the attacks were nonetheless deemed disproportionate by the UN Fact-Finding Mission on the Gaza Conflict.[23] The Mission concluded that the attacks did not strike an acceptable balance between the anticipated military advantage (killing police officers who are members of Palestinian armed groups) and the loss of civilian lives (both other police officers and members of the public in the vicinity).[24]

The attacks on police stations present a particularly interesting case for trying to compare the tools that the traditional and individualist Just War theories have to offer. It is likely that both types of theories would conclude that the attacks on police stations in general would not be permitted, but their reasons for saying so and the consequences of their differing analyses should be of particular interest to us.

The traditional Just War theory, which is likely at the heart of the report, argues that the ratio of police officers who are combatants and police officers who are not, together with the risk to other civilians in the vicinity, made the attacks on the police disproportionate. Further, the fact that the police stations are civilian buildings gave extra reasons to call the attacks unjustified and against international law.

This, according to an individualist scholar, misses out on a number of morally salient considerations, whose examination should not only be seen as an interesting armchair endeavour, but which has consequences for the way

---

[23] Goldstone Report.   [24] Goldstone Report, 18.

we treat such attacks and compensation for such attacks. The Mission's investigation had found that some, not insignificant, number of police officers were recruited by or were supporters of Hamas or other Palestinian armed groups. It clearly does not follow that they are or were fully culpable combatants, or that they were anything more than minimally responsible agents. This is particularly important because the Mission actually found that "many" of the officers had some relationship with Hamas or Palestinian armed groups. It seems then that the Mission's conclusion rested more on the claim that the buildings were civilian and that officers were at the time acting in their civilian capacity. Further it seems that the Mission's conclusion, in line with traditional Just War theory, also rested on the fact that the Israelis could not have known the proportions of Hamas supporters vs. innocent police officers and as such acted irresponsibly and indiscriminately. While all of those considerations are morally salient, it is also the case that we have good reasons to think that the large numbers of police officers who would have counted as combatants in the view of traditional Just War theory are minimally responsible, for a number of reasons – including that they were likely to continue acting in their civilian capacity, thus not presenting a threat. Even if a vast majority of the police officers had been supporters of Hamas, there would be good reasons to think that they were only minimally responsible threats and as such that attacks on them could only be justified by some vast benefit on the other end. According to traditional Just War theory, all of those police officers who were Hamas supporters or recruits should be "free" in our calculations of proportionality, so that whether or not the attack was justified would depend on the military advantages on the other end weighed against the police officers who count as civilians (and other civilians in the vicinity). According to individualist theory, more would be required on the military advantage side for the proportionality condition to be met – simply because all the extra harms to those police officers who were only minimally responsible would have to be justified via the good on the military advantage side as well.

In addition, it is not only the threshold of proportionality that is different between the two theories; the consequences of failing the proportionality condition are also different. On individualist terms, the extra harms imposed on those who are minimally or partially responsible are harms that might need to be compensated since even if they are outweighed by lesser evil calculus, they are nonetheless violations of rights.[25]

Furthermore, if we take individualist theories seriously, the good on the other (military advantage) side would have to be a moral good, not simply a military advantage. That means that we would need to establish not simply that such attacks will bring us closer to military victory but that there is some morally weighty aim that such attacks serve (e.g. saving more civilians, incapacitating

---

[25] Not all individualist scholars hold this view of course.

an unjust aggressor, limiting terrorist's abilities to strike). The relevance of this distinction (between evaluating military advantage in morally neutral terms and in morally salient terms) is particularly striking in the Mission's analysis of Israel's mortar shelling of al-Fakhura junction in Jabaliyah next to UNRWA school, which was sheltering well over a thousand people. According to the report:

The Israeli armed forces launched at least four mortar shells. One landed in the courtyard of a family home, killing 11 people assembled there. Three other shells landed on al-Fakhura Street, killing at least a further 24 people and injuring as many as 40. The Mission examined in detail statements by Israeli Government representatives alleging that the attack was launched in response to a mortar attack from an armed Palestinian group . . . In drawing its legal conclusions on the attack on al-Fakhura junction, the Mission recognizes that, for all armies, decisions on proportionality, weighing the military advantage to be gained against the risk of killing civilians, will present very genuine dilemmas in certain cases. The Mission does not consider this to be such a case. The firing of at least four mortar shells to attempt to kill a small number of specified individuals in a setting where large numbers of civilians were going about their daily business and 1,368 people were sheltering nearby cannot meet the test of what a reasonable commander would have determined to be an acceptable loss of civilian life for the military advantage sought.[26]

Note that the acceptable loss of civilian lives according to traditional Just War theory could shift based on the relationship between the military advantage sought and the overall military aim considered neutrally. In other words, if for some reason killing those few individuals would have brought Israel significantly closer to military victory (than it did), the risk to civilians might be acceptable. And this would be the case regardless of the moral standing of its overall cause for war. Individualist theories provide a more robust explanation of why the shelling of the al-Fakhura junction is disproportionate, being able to compare the threat of lethal harm to civilian lives to other civilian lives (directly or indirectly). In its concluding remarks the Mission's Report states the following:

In the framing of Israeli military objectives with regard to the Gaza operations, the concept of Hamas' "supporting infrastructure" is particularly worrying as it appears to transform civilians and civilian objects into legitimate targets. Statements by Israeli political and military leaders prior to and during the military operations in Gaza indicate that the Israeli military conception of what was necessary in a war with Hamas viewed disproportionate destruction and creating maximum

---

[26] Goldstone Report, 20.

disruption in the lives of many people as a legitimate means to achieve not only military but also political goals.[27]

Note again that the report has to rely on claiming that it was the political goals (which are not according to traditional Just War theory justified aims) that are problematic and the underlying cause as well as an explanation behind why Israeli tactics should be deemed disproportionate. But the problem does not rest solely on the fact that the Israeli military also pursued political goals and used them in proportionality calculations, it lies also in the vague and morally neutral understanding of what counts as a military advantage or a military goal. If we were to require that the advantage sought be morally justifiable, not just militarily justifiable, we would not only have stricter rules, but we would also have a significantly more robust explanation of why such actions are disproportionate. That explanation would not only be theoretically sturdier, but it would also have a meaningful expressive advantage over traditional theories because it would cohere with intuitions that the public and combatants have about what grounds moral permissibility to harm.

V Necessity *in Bello*

Finally, we turn to the related *in bello* condition of necessity. To start we ought to distinguish between a number of appeals to the concept of necessity that appear both earlier and in much of the literature on Just War theory. Necessity *in bello* is military necessity traditionally; it is a claim that an aim one is pursuing must be militarily as opposed to politically or morally necessary. This condition is often also understood as a minimal force requirement that says that even if some amount of overall force is proportionate, if it is not necessary then it is not justified. No gratuitous harm is allowed. Necessity *in bello* is distinct from the notion of necessity (internal to liability) discussed earlier.[28]

Traditional necessity *in bello* requires that we show that a particular military operation in war, which will destroy property or kill combatants and civilians, is necessary for the achievement of the overall military aim. If our troops need to cross a river and have a number of options to do so with the same likelihood of success, but one requires destroying a dual-use factory and killing two civilians, while the other requires only destroying a small cache of weapons and possibly killing some combatants, even if both options are deemed to be

---

[27] Goldstone Report, 24.

[28] Necessity, which is internal to liability, discussed earlier, is a different concept. As already mentioned narrow proportionality focuses on harm that one can impose on those who are liable to be harmed. Liability to harm is not like desert; if the harm does not need to be imposed to avert the unjustified threat, then one is not liable to such harm or to that extent of harm. This is what we mean when we say that necessity is internal to liability.

proportionate to the aim of crossing the river (because of its military impor-tance)m it would not be permissible that we take the first option – simply because it is not necessary to kill two civilians to achieve that aim. This is why this *in bello* condition is often also understood as a condition that requires that we use the minimum force to achieve our aim. Given that in orthodox Just War theory proportionality is a lesser evil calculation and focuses solely on civilian deaths and the destruction of civilian property, necessity calculations too are solely lesser evil (quite literally) calculations; but while proportionality evalu-ates the value of our aim vs. the cost of our actions, necessity condition evaluates the cost of alternative actions for the achievement of the same aim.

The *in bello* necessity condition understood in this way faces a number of difficulties. First, the condition seems to ignore the distinction between those liable to harm and those who are not, or at least an individualist would worry that it does. An action might seem to meet a condition of necessity, but if it is likely going to harm combatants, who are according to a careful individualist analysis not liable to harm, then an alternative that harms fewer combatants might be preferable (remember that in orthodox Just War theory combatant lives are "free" in such calculations). Second, it ignores the likelihood of success. An action might look to meet the condition of necessity, but it might have a lower chance of success than another proportionate action, which might impose more harm (and thus be precluded by the simple notion of necessity *in bello*) but have a significantly greater chance of success. This has led some scholars to propose a necessity condition, which is more sensitive to likelihood of success.

Ultimately, it seems that paying attention to moral responsibility for the threat of unjustified harm also affects whether or not we ought to see the necessity condition as meaningful and how best to understand the requirement of minimal force so as to achieve the morally preferable outcomes. After all, if the end for which we are fighting is unjust, then the fact that some action is necessary for achieving that aim does not seem to make such an action morally permissible.

In conclusion, there is no doubt that proportionality and necessity ought to play a role in deciding whether an action is morally permissible or justified both in everyday circumstances and in war. Whether we ought to understand proportionality and necessity *in bello* through the lens of traditional or indivi-dualist Just War theory should not be solely or even primarily decided based on the likelihood of implementation of such theory, but the reasons we have to accept either analyses. Only after we have done that can we ask what is the best set of rules, laws and training that would result in morally preferable outcomes, understood and supported by one of these theories or some third alternative.

10 Weighing Civilian Lives in War: Domestic versus Foreign

Saba Bazargan-Forward

I Introduction

When we wage war, we do so to achieve aims. The aims for which we fight and the means by which we achieve those aims must satisfy the constraint of proportionality. The constraint states that the harms for which we are responsible in that armed conflict cannot be outsized relative to the harms that the armed conflict prevents. All things being equal, civilian deaths ought to receive substantial weight in the proportionality calculation. The issue I address here is this: ought we to weigh the deaths of civilians on the enemy's side (i.e., enemy civilians) as heavily as the deaths of our own civilians (i.e., domestic civilians)?[1]

Here is the type of case I have in mind. Suppose that we are fighting in furtherance of a just aim in accordance with the constraints of necessity. The only way to save the lives of domestic civilians is by targeting enemy military installations. Doing so, however, will collaterally kill enemy civilians. Whether this is permissible – that is, whether it is permissible to collaterally kill in order to save lives – depends, of course, on the number killed and the number saved. But it also depends on the comparative weight these lives receive in the proportionality calculation.

I argue that the lives of domestic and enemy civilians should not receive equal weight in our proportionality calculations. Rather, the lives of enemy civilians should receive less (though certainly not zero) weight in comparison to the weight that domestic civilians receive. That is, the lives of enemy civilians ought to be "partially discounted" relative to the lives of domestic civilians. We ought to partially discount the lives of enemy civilians for the following reason (or so I argue). When our military wages a just war, we as civilians vest our right to self-defense in our military. This permits our military to weigh our lives more heavily. Before arguing for this view I first explain why recent accounts attempting to show the opposite – that enemy civilians ought to be weighed more heavily – are mistaken. I begin, though, by laying out several caveats clarifying the scope of the discussion.

---

[1] For a groundbreaking discussion of this issue, see Thomas Hurka, "Proportionality in the Morality of War," *Philosophy & Public Affairs*, 33 (2005) no. 1: 34–66.

II   Caveats

First, I only consider cases in which we are warring in furtherance of a just aim satisfying the constraint of necessity. This assumption might seem overly restrictive, but there are good reasons to adopt it. The issue I am addressing here is how heavily we should comparatively weigh the deaths of enemy civilians versus domestic civilians when calculating whether a military act or aim satisfies the proportionality constraint. If the war we are fighting is unnecessary for achieving the aim in question, then military violence aiming at protecting domestic civilians will unavoidably fail to satisfy the necessity constraint as well, since there is by hypothesis a peaceful way to achieve that end: by ceasing to aggress against the enemy. Indeed, we are morally required to cease hostilities because, by hypothesis, the war we are fighting is unjust. Since in such cases we already know that engaging in military violence as a means to saving domestic civilians is unjust on the grounds that it fails the necessity constraint, determining whether it also fails to satisfy the constraint of proportionality is largely otiose. For this reason I restrict my discussion of weighing civilian lives to cases in which we are warring in furtherance of a just aim in accordance with the necessity constraint.

Second – and as a corollary of the first – I only consider cases in which our adversary is engaging in military violence in furtherance of an unjust aim or, alternatively, in furtherance of a just aim unjustly. After all, if the adversary were acting in furtherance of a just aim justly, resisting it would be unjust, in which case attempting to ascertain whether doing so violates proportionality would again be otiose.

Third, I assume that our aim in undertaking military violence is either to save civilian lives on our side or to secure some equally weighty interest[2] – and that doing so does not substantially promote any other unjust aims. More specifically, either (1) there are no such unjust aims or (2) there are unjust aims but the pursuit of the just aim does not substantially contribute to (nor is it substantially contributed by) the pursuit of the unjust aim. This assumption is largely to keep the discussion tractable.

III   Beneficiary's Burden Principle

Some have argued (correctly, in my view) that standards for imposing risks on enemy civilians ought in general to be more stringent than the standards for imposing risks on domestic civilians.[3] Specifically, in cases where (1) imposing a risk is necessary to bring about a substantial benefit and (2) the benefits

---

[2] The sovereignty of a legitimate state might qualify as such as a good. See Cécile Fabre and Seth Lazar, eds., *The Morality of Defensive War*, Oxford: Oxford University Press, 2014.
[3] Jeff McMahan, *Killing in War*, New York: Oxford University Press, 2009, pp. 74–75, 215.

accrue to domestic civilians, it is worse to impose that risk on enemy civilians than it is to impose that risk on domestic civilians.

To see why this is so, consider the following case. Suppose we are constructing a massive power plant (either a hydroelectric dam or a nuclear power plant) that will benefit all domestic civilians in the region. There is a small but nontrivial chance of a catastrophic malfunction causing massive destruction. Still, for any given domestic civilian she is better off (in the evidence-relative sense[4]) with the power plant. There are, though, two ways to build the power plant. One method will channel the destruction in the event of a catastrophic malfunction toward the domestic civilian population. The other method will channel the destruction away from the domestic population and toward the people of a bordering country. Both will result in roughly the same harm. Given that one of the two methods must be chosen, we ought to choose the first. It is worse for the potential costs of a benefit to be imposed on those to whom that benefit is not expected to accrue than on those who are antecedently expected to benefit. The standard of risk imposition in a case such as this applies more stringently to the foreign population because they are not expected to benefit from the risk-imposing activity.

How does this result apply to warfare? It suggests that we can gamble with the lives of domestic civilians in ways that we cannot with enemy civilians when the benefits of winning the gamble accrue solely to the domestic civilians.

Suppose, then, that a domestic civilian population resides along the border of a country with which we are at war. That population is at risk of enemy bombardment. We can cripple the enemy's ability to do so by destroying one of two enemy military installations. We are in a position to choose either. One of the installations is close to our border; destroying it risks collateral harm to the very same civilians who are threatened by enemy bombardment. The other is near enemy civilians; destroying it risks collateral harm to them. Suppose further that, despite the collateral harms that will result when we target the enemy installation, any given domestic civilian in that area is nonetheless made better off (in the evidence-relative sense) should we target that installation than if we do nothing, given the otherwise imminent threat of enemy bombardment. It is morally better, then, to target the military installation near our own border because for *either* choice the expected benefits accrue solely to our civilians – not theirs. And it is unfair to shift the costs of that benefit to those who are not expected to be made better off by that benefit.

As in the power plant example, there are asymmetric standards of risk-imposition between war and domestic civilian life. It is worse to impose risks on enemy civilians given that it is solely domestic civilians who are expected to enjoy the benefit of imposing that risk. Let us call this the

---

[4] Derek Parfit, *On What Matters*, Oxford: Oxford University Press, 2011, pp. 150–51, n. 18.

Beneficiary's Burden Principle

When a beneficial event carries unavoidable risks and when we can choose where those risks will fall, it is worse to impose those risks on the individuals who are not beneficiaries of that event than to it is to impose those risks on those who are indeed beneficiaries of that event.

This principle, even if correct, will rarely militate in favor of granting extra weight to the lives of enemy civilians. Notably, it does not apply to cases in which we have to decide between imposing a risk on enemy civilians and accepting a risk to our own – the very sort of case we began with. Such a case is not one in which we have reason to decide who bears the costs of an expected benefit accruing to our civilians. Rather, it is simply a case of deciding where a harm should fall. So even if we are correct in thinking that there are asymmetric standards of risk-imposition in cases where the benefits of that risk accrue asymmetrically, this claim simply does not help adjudicate between options when we have to decide whether to cause harm to enemy civilians or allow harm to befall our own.

To the extent that the Beneficiary's Burden Principle does indeed apply to war, it will tend to do so in favor of partially discounting the lives of enemy civilians when we wage a just war, in that the enemy civilians will receive comparatively less weight in the calculation of proportionality than domestic civilians will. This is because civilians often benefit from the military as an institution – it provides defense against foreign aggression. Of course, it is not always the case that the people derive a net benefit from their military. Exceptions include all-too-common instances in which the military is used to enforce the oppressive policies of their government thereby subjugating the people it is tasked with protecting. But I focus, for the moment, on cases in which the people benefit from the protection their military provides. In such cases, forming and maintaining a formidable military force carries with it a risk – the risk that the institution will morally malfunction by impermissibly aggressing rather than defending. When that risk manifests – when a country's military unjustly aggresses – the civilians who have so far benefited from the protection that military force provides have a duty to see to it as far as they can that the costs of this protection are not imposed on those who are not beneficiaries of that protection.[5] This is just an application of the Beneficiary's Burden Principle.

Of course, when a country goes to war unjustly, civilians are typically ill situated to shift the costs of that aggression away from the civilians of the country against which their military is aggressing. Doing so will often involve insurmountable coordination problems. But the country against whom their military is aggressing is in a position to vicariously discharge that duty by

---

[5] Jeff McMahan makes this sort of argument in *Killing in War*, pp. 74–75, 215.

partially discounting the lives of enemy civilians in cases where doing so will save the lives of domestic civilians. This is precisely the sort of case we started off with. By doing so, our military effectively does for enemy civilians what they are otherwise morally required to do but cannot: namely, shift the costs of their morally malfunctioning military away from the civilians of the country against which their military is aggressing, and back toward those who have up until now benefited from the protection that military affords. By partially discounting the lives of enemy civilians in cases where doing so saves the lives of domestic civilians, we effectively enforce the application of the Beneficiary's Burden Principle.

An upshot is that to the extent the Beneficiary's Burden Principle is relevant to warfare, it militates in favor of weighing the lives of enemy civilians less than the lives of domestic civilians. In this way, forming and maintaining a military is like building a beneficial but risky power plant; if the risk manifests, the costs should go to those who have benefited so far. They should not be shifted to those who have not.

This being said, a "principle of efficiency" might overwhelm the principle of fairness underlying the Beneficiary's Burden Principle. Suppose that if the costs of the malfunctioning benefit are shifted to third parties, those costs would lessen in that either (1) the number of victims would increase but the amount each suffers would be much smaller or (2) the total amount of harm would decrease. In these cases, the totality of reasons might require that we shift the costs to third parties. But in deciding whether to do so, the unfairness of that option receives its due weight, even if it is outweighed. In this way, the Beneficiary's Burden Principle is still operative even in cases where it makes sense to shift the costs of the benefit to third parties.

One might raise an objection, though, about what counts as benefiting from the military. Suppose that an adventuristic government has authorized its military to engage in numerous unjust conflicts over the past few decades. This might be burdensome to the country's own population in two ways.

First, fighting numerous unjust wars will divert state funds that might have gone to public welfare. Suppose this makes the people worse off than they would have been if their country had not waged these numerous unjust wars. It might seem, then, that the Beneficiary's Burden does not apply in the way I have suggested because the people do not in fact benefit from their military. But this does not follow. The relevant counterfactual by which to determine whether the people benefit from the military is not one in which the military does not wage unjust wars, but rather one in which the military does not exist. It is not unreasonable to conclude that a military that diverts funds toward unjust wars is still better for the people of that country compared to the absence of a military altogether, especially if that country has aggressive neighbors. So long as the people are made better off all things considered relative to the absence of the military, they count as beneficiaries, and thus they have a duty to absorb some of the costs of that benefit; a failure to do so unfairly shifts that cost to third parties. Accordingly, the victims of their country's unjust aggression can – within limits – permissibly weigh enemy civilians less than domestic civilians in the proportionality calculation where doing so saves the lives of domestic civilians.

But there is another more direct way the people might be made worse off when their government wages unjust wars – they might be maimed, killed, or otherwise immiserated. When a large enough portion of the population suffers in this way, the Beneficiary's Burden Principle does not apply in that it does not permit us to discount the lives of enemy civilians when we are waging a just defensive war against their country. Doing so has a high chance of discounting the lives of those who have *not* relevantly benefited from their military. In such a case, we have no duty to vicariously discharge on their behalf – specifically, no duty to prevent imposing the costs of their morally malfunctioning military on third parties. This accords, I believe, with intuitions in this case: the enemy civilians have already paid the price of their country's unjust military adventurism. Partially discounting their lives would overburden them.

A result is that the application of the Beneficiary's Burden Principle is highly contingent. In the just wars we wage where enemy civilians have up until now benefited from their military, we are permitted to partially discount the weight their lives receive in the proportionality calculation when doing so is necessary to save lives on our side. This permission is derived from a permission to vicariously discharge a duty that they have to refrain from shifting the cost of their morally malfunctioning military onto third parties. But determining whether the enemy civilians have in fact benefited, and the degree to which they have done so (which might impact the degree of risk they are required to absorb) is empirically difficult.

There, is, though, a more reliable basis for thinking that we are permitted to partially discount the lives of enemy civilians when we wage a just war. I turn to this next.

IV   Agent-Relative Permissions and Fiduciary Duties

There are both agent-relative and agent-neutral reasons. A reason is agent-relative if it ineliminably refers to the person to whom the reason applies. A reason is agent-neutral if it does not ineliminably refer to the person to whom the reason applies. To use a canonical example, suppose you are walking through the woods when you chance upon a child drowning in a pond. You can easily save her. The reason you have is agent-neutral in that it is a reason applying to anyone capable of saving the child. You just happen to be in the right place at the right time, so the reason contingently picks out you. But now suppose that the child is your daughter. You still have an agent-neutral reason to save her since you have an agent-neutral reason to save *any* drowning child.

But because she is your daughter, you also have an agent-relative reason to save her because she is *your* child. The special relation you bear to her gives you a reason to save her – a reason that makes ineliminable reference to the child's parents.

If agent-neutral reasons, such as the reason to promote overall well-being, are left unchecked, they will overwhelm our lives by forcing us to abandon our personal projects that fail to maximize the overall good. These personal projects are partly constitutive of our practical identity. They are our ground level, long-term commitments which, from our own point of view, make our lives worth living and our actions worth undertaking. To threaten these commitments is to threaten, in a real sense, who we are. An account of morality forcing us to abandon suboptimal personal projects is neither psychologically plausible nor normatively desirable.

To address this worry, several philosophers have argued that agent-neutral reasons are defeasible – specifically, by a certain type of agent-relative reason yielding an agent-relative *permission* to act in accordance with our personal projects. There are, at the broadest level of generalization, two types of arguments in favor of agent-relative permissions: derivative and non-derivative arguments.

According to derivative arguments for agent-relative permissions, consequentialist reasons to make things go impersonally best ground agent-relative permissions to give special weight to personal projects. This is because a doctrine forcing us to abandon any and all suboptimific personal projects would be psychologically devastating to its adherents, thereby failing to maximize the impersonal good. In this respect consequentialism is partially self-effacing; we are permitted to act *as if* there is no requirement to maximize the impersonal good because deliberating from that standpoint is more likely to maximize the impersonal good. Peter Railton is best known for this kind of argument for agent-relative permissions.[6]

According to the most popular non-derivative arguments for agent-relative permissions, our moral permission to pursue personal projects without regard for whether doing so makes thing go impersonally best is grounded either in (1) the intrinsic personal value manifest in the permitted project or in (2) the more general value of having "space" in which to pursue our personal lives free from the tyranny of the impersonal point of view. Thomas Nagel is the most well-known proponent of the first view; Samuel Scheffler is the most well-known proponent of the second.[7]

Thomas Nagel points out that from an impersonal point of view, we determine whether we should act in accordance with a personal project by evaluating it

[6] Peter Railton, "Alienation, Consequentialism, and the Demands of Morality," *Philosophy & Public Affairs*, 13 (1944) no. 2:134–71.

[7] Thomas Nagel, *The View from Nowhere*, Oxford: Oxford University Press, 1989; Samuel Scheffler, *The Rejection of Consequentialism*, Oxford: Oxford University Press, 1982.

solely according to whether there are agent-neutral reasons to act in accordance with that project. Most personal projects will be sub-optimific and will thus fail the test. But he argues that personal projects generate their own values, intelligible only from the point of view of the individual adopting that personal project – that is, only from a personal point of view. These values are real; they speak in favor of acting in accordance with the project, though only for those whose project it is. Accordingly, the reasons those values generate are agent-relative, in that they ineliminably reference the bearer of the personal project generating the reason. Thus agent-neutral reasons do not exhaust the reasons you have to undertake the various pursuits that you value – whether it is child raising, mountain climbing, or stamp collecting. Agent-neutral reasons, then, are defeasible: a sufficiently important agent-relative reason can provide an all-things-considered justification for undertaking ends for which there are agent-neutral reasons to reject.

This does not mean, however, that our personal projects are inviolable. My personal project of collecting designer jeans will yield an agent-relative reason not to ruin mine by wading into a pond to save a drowning child. But the values that this personal project generates are simply not important enough to outweigh the agent-neutral reasons to save the child. This is one way that personal projects are violable, even assuming a framework in which such projects generate agent-relative reasons. In this case the agent-relative reasons are "still there" – they count in the moral calculus – but ultimately the agent-neutral reason to save the child carries the day.

Samuel Scheffler also worries about the tyranny of agent-neutral reasons – that they threaten to overwhelm our personal lives. But Scheffler's strategy is to argue that each of us has an agent-relative prerogative to refrain from doing what makes things go impersonally best. This gives us space to pursue our impersonally sub-optimific projects. The prerogative is agent-relative in that each person has a special permission to pursue her own sub-optimific projects; this reason does not extend to a permission to help others pursue their sub-optimific projects. On this view, the value of a protected space of conduct is defeasible. This prerogative to act sub-optimifically does not allow us to pursue just any personal projects. Some projects – such as those aiming at rights violations – ought not to be protected on the ground that they are not the sorts of projects that we should have freedom to pursue.

Whether we take Scheffler's, Nagel's, or some other non-derivative or derivative account of what grounds agent-relative reasons, they all have at least one thing in common: they permit each individual to give extra weight to her own life over the life of a stranger when deciding between the two (provided that she has done nothing to waive or forfeit her right to life).

So, for example, I might have an agent-relative permission to save my own life rather than the lives of two strangers. But this agent-relative permission to give extra weight to my own life does not provide an otherwise uninvolved third party with a permission to save my life over the lives of two other strangers. But it is possible, or so I argue, to vest an agent-relative permission in a third party, thereby permitting that party to give the extra weight to your life that you are permitted to give. Put differently, the right to act in accordance with an agent-relative permission to give extra weight to your own life can function as a *fiduciary* right – a right that belongs to you, but which you have vested in someone else who can thereby vicariously discharge that right on your behalf.

Suppose you and two others are drowning and your bodyguard can either save you or the two others; she is permitted to save you. A bodyguard can act in this sub-optimific way even though her own life and ground-level interests are not at stake because her charge has vested his agent-relative permission to give his own life extra weight in the bodyguard.

But why believe that agent-relative permissions, which are generally thought to be ineliminably first personal, can function as a fiduciary right? Examining the role that agent-relative permissions play helps answer this.

Agent-relative permissions are important practically in that they allow us to live recognizably independent lives. They are also important normatively (as I pointed out) in that they manifest our status as self-originating sources of ends. Because these agent-relative protections are so important, there is reason to think that we possess the power to recruit others to help us further these protected ends.[8] This is why the bodyguard in whom I vest my right to self-defense has an agent-relative reason to give extra weight to *my* life. The claim that we cannot legitimately ask others for assistance in furtherance of the ends that agent-relative protections vouchsafe belies the supposed importance of those protections if it turns out that those from whom we ask assistance – such as the bodyguard – are not permitted to give extra weight to those supposedly protected ends. (Indeed this restriction against vesting our agent-relative permissions in others is especially unfair to the severely handicapped. Such a restriction prohibits them practically from giving their own ends the extra weight that they are entitled to give those ends. This is especially troubling when we consider that such protections manifest our status as persons.)

If what I have argued is correct, it is possible (by means that I have not articulated here) to vest our right to self-defense in others. Something like this is what happens when our country wages a just defensive war. Our soldiers are fighting on our behalf in the sense that they are relevantly like our bodyguards. Inasmuch, we vest in them our right to give our lives extra weight (or, put alternatively, to partially discount the weight that lives of enemy civilians receive) in cases where our soldiers have to weigh our lives against the lives of enemy civilians.

---

[8] Cécile Fabre makes a similar point in Cécile Fabre, *Cosmopolitan* War, Oxford: Oxford University Press, 2012, pp. 201–2.

If this is correct, then soldiers waging a just war can partially discount the lives of enemy civilians in the calculation of proportionality when they are acting in furtherance of the goal of saving the lives of domestic civilians. This does not entitle them to target enemy civilians, of course. But it does suggest that soldiers waging a just war are permitted to inflict more collateral harms that just war ethicists might have thought, when doing so is necessary to save the lives of domestic civilians.

Against this, one might raise the following point: though an individual who has not waived or forfeited her right can refrain from saving two to save herself, no such individual can permissibly kill an innocent – even collaterally – to save herself. Since we have no such right, we cannot vest such a right in soldiers fighting on our behalf. So it seems that soldiers fighting a just war cannot partially discount the lives of enemy civilians they collaterally kill in furtherance of saving our own lives after all.

It is true that an individual cannot collaterally kill an innocent when necessary to save her own life. But we need not think otherwise to show that those in whom we have vested our right to self-defense can partially discount the weight of enemy civilians. Suppose that the agent-relative reason I have to weigh my own life more heavily permits me to multiply the value of my life by 1.2. Or, put alternatively, it permits me to partially discount the weight of the lives of other innocents by multiplying the value of those lives by 0.8. Now suppose that I am permitted to kill an innocent only if doing so is necessary to avert 50 times the amount of weighted harm that the killing consists in. (These numbers are largely arbitrary – the same point can be made by filling in different values.) I would therefore not be permitted to kill an innocent even if doing so saves me, because the amount of good it does is only 1.2 times greater. But suppose that 42 people have vested their right to life in a body-guard. Now suppose that the only way that the bodyguard can save the lives of those 42 people is by killing an unjust aggressor – but doing so will collaterally kill one by-standing innocent person. Now, if each of these 42 has vested in the bodyguard their right to multiply the weight that their lives receive by 1.2., then this means that the bodyguard can multiply the value of the 42 by 1.2, which is 50.4. The bodyguard then does indeed avert more than 50 times the weighted harm that the collateral killing of the innocent consists in. Put differently, a stranger cannot kill one to save 42; but a bodyguard can, even though none of those 42 is individually permitted to collaterally kill one to save herself.

The lesson is that even if a vested fiduciary right to weigh a life more heavily is not strong enough to warrant killing an innocent collaterally to save the individual who vested that fiduciary right, it can still affect the permissibility of inflicting collateral deaths when the numbers get high enough. And this is precisely what happens in war.

If this is correct, we are indeed permitted to partially discount the value of the lives of enemy civilians provided that we are waging an unjust war with an aim of saving the lives of domestic civilians. Note that if we are waging an unjust war, we are not permitted to do this discounting because we in general have no agent-relative permission to grant extra weight to our own lives when the individuals in whom we vested that right precipitate the threat to our lives. For example, suppose that we hire a bodyguard who against our wishes proceeds to endanger our lives by attacking our neighbors; they can repel the attack only by inflicting collateral damage on us. Though we too are victims here, the bodyguard cannot defend us by discounting the lives of the neighbors on our behalf. This is not because we have contributed to the bodyguard's aggression and thereby forfeited our defensive rights. (We can stipulate that there is no sense in which we caused the bodyguard to attack the neighbors; she did so for her own reasons and would have done that anyway.) Rather, the reason the bodyguard cannot discount the value of the neighbors' lives in defending us is that the bodyguard is the one who wrongly created the situation in which we need to be defended in the first place. This invalidates the duty to discharge the vested right of self-defense for the same reason that individuals in general cannot permissibly invoke a right of self-defense against justified aggression: there is no permissible defense against justified defense. Since the bodyguard unjustly aggressed, she can no longer invoke the *vested* right of self-defense, since doing so would, in effect, give her a right to defend against justified defense. The individuals who vested the right in the bodyguard can, however, exercise their right of self-defense directly since it is not they who unjustly aggressed; nor are they (by hypothesis) responsible for their bodyguard's aggression.

It is impossible, then, for us to vest a right of self-defense in an unjust aggressor when that aggressor is the one who created the situation endangering our rights in the first place. So if I am correct in characterizing the military as an institution in which we have vested a right to self-defense, that vested right provides a permission to vicariously discount the value that enemy civilians lives receive (or, put differently, augment the weight that domestic lives receive) in situations where the military has to decide between collaterally harming enemy civilians and allowing harms to befall domestic civilians. But this is only if the military has not wrongly created the situation in which the lives of the domestic civilians are in danger in the first place – that is, only if the military is not fighting in furtherance of unjust aims, or just aims unjustly.

V   Implications

Note that the argument I have presented in favor of the view that we can partially discount the weight of enemy civilians when waging a just war does not rely on an agent-relative permission to weigh the lives of co-nationals more heavily. It is not, for example, because the Turkish military is protecting fellow Turkish nationals that they are permitted to augment the value that their lives receive in the proportionality calculation. There is nothing special about sharing nationality per se. Rather, it is because Turkish nationals have vested their right to self-defense in their country's military that the latter is permitted to augment the value that their lives receive, by acting vicariously in accordance with the fiduciary right of self-defense.

Thomas Hurka considers a permission grounded in co-national partiality and rightly casts doubt on how much weight it can bear – though I am even more pessimistic about its prospects than he is.[9] Suppose an American must choose between saving 100 American nationals or 105 French nationals; it is absurd to claim that the American in virtue of sharing the same background as the victims is permitted to save the fewer number of lives. But if what I have argued is correct, an American *soldier* might indeed be permitted to save her own civilians, not because she is permitted to be biased in favor of Americans, and not because they share a background and culture, but because those American have antecedently vested in her an agent-relative permission to weigh their lives more heavily. In theory, this right could be vested in anyone of any background – it just so happens that it tends to be done in accordance with national identity. But this concomitance tempts the spurious view that it is national partiality rather than something else – namely, vested rights – that grounds the permission soldiers have to grant the lives of domestic civilians extra weight.

So the permission to weigh the lives of domestic civilians more heavily is jurisdictional, in the way that the obligations of police officers or firefighters are jurisdictional; the duties pertain to a particular population not because they share a common background but because it is that population that vested the relevant fiduciary rights. An important upshot of these grounds for giving extra weight to the lives of domestic civilians is that, unlike grounds of co-national partiality, it is fully compatible with the sort of cosmopolitan approach to the morality of war animating post-Walzerian, revisionist treatments.

Consider the following real-life example. In 1980, Iraq under Saddam Hussein launched an unprovoked invasion of Iran in the midst of the chaos following Iran's Islamic revolution. Iraq had two ultimate aims: to prevent the spread of Iran's revolutionary fervor to Iraq's long-suppressed Shia majority and to gain control over Iran's natural resources (specifically those in Khuzestan) as well as the Arvand River waterway. Iran had, at first, just one ultimate aim: to repel Iraq's attack.[10] Presumably this aim was just; regardless of the legitimacy of the nascent Islamic regime in Iran, the people had a right

---

[9] Hurka, "*Proportionality in the Morality of War.*"

[10] Iran had a chance to end the war in 1982 by accepting antebellum borders. Its failure to do so suggests that the war thereafter no longer had a just aim. For more on the ethics of wars whose aims change over time, see Saba Bazargan, "Morally Heterogeneous Wars," *Philosophia* 41 (2013) no. 4: 959–75.

not to suffer under the brutal heel of Hussein's anti-Shia totalitarianism. But whether the defensive war satisfied the constraint of proportionality is less clear. The war cost the lives of hundreds of thousands of civilians, on both sides. Perhaps the cost to Iranian lives was worth it for the Iranians, in that it is preferable to bear those costs than to suffer indefinitely under Hussein's anti-Shia totalitarianism. But the issue is whether the benefits of waging a successful defensive war against Iraq was worth it considering that it also cost the lives of hundreds of thousands *of Iraqi* civilians. If what I have argued is correct, the Iranian military was morally permitted to weigh the lives of its own civilians more heavily than the lives of Iraqi civilians because Iranian civilians possessed a right to self-defense vested in the military. The military was discharging that right on behalf of its civilians by repelling an invading army that would have otherwise violated the basic rights of countless Iranian civilians in perpetuity. Accordingly, the agent-relative permission that the Iranian civilians possessed – a permission to weigh their own well-being more heavily – was passed on to their military. This does not itself prove that Iran's decision to defend itself against Iraq satisfied proportionality, but it does suggest that the bar to doing so is less stringent that it might first appear. A consequence is that defensive wars, such as Iran's, might be easier to justify than what some pacifists have assumed.

In spite of all that I have argued here, I do not suggest that we voice to military and civilian leaders the view that they are permitted to give extra weight to the lives of domestic civilians when they wage just wars because (1) they presumably believe this already (albeit for the wrong reasons), and (2) they probably already overvalue the lives of domestic civilians over foreign civilians, given that many seem to recognize only prudential reasons to avoid collateral damage.[11] Our task should be to scale back the degree to which they discount the lives of foreign civilians. But if what I have argued here is correct, the degree to which they ought to scale back is not as great as it might seem: when fighting a just war justly, the military has an obligation to weigh more heavily the lives of domestic civilians.

---

[11] See Neta C. Crawford, *Moral Responsibility for Collateral Damage in America's Post-9/11 Wars*, Oxford: Oxford University Press, 2013.

11 Drone Warfare and the Principle of Discrimination

Eric Joseph Ritter

The increased use of uninhabited aerial vehicle systems (UAVS), known as drones, in modern warfare, is filled with paradoxes. Drone technology shields soldiers from harm, for example. And yet as legal scholar Paul Kahn has written, this very ethical motivation brings about the troubling military consequence in which one side of a war assumes all or most of the risk of being injured or killed. Scholars often call this an "asymmetric" war, and it is troubling not just because accomplishing a military objective may begin to resemble a video game under these circumstances but also because mutual assumption of risk, for traditional Just War theorists, is a necessary condition for acquiring the right to kill. A soldier acquires the right to kill only in virtue of needing to defend his/herself against harm, according to traditional Just War theory. So without the need to defend themselves against the threat of harm, it can be hard to see what gives individual soldiers the right to kill. Objections abound to the premises of this paradox,[1] but it's hard to shake this import at least: that an ethical obligation like shielding soldiers from harm can have unforeseen, problematic, and even contradictory consequences.

Another paradox of the increasing use of drones in armed conflict is a function of the secrecy of drone strikes.[2] Drones can be launched from thousands of miles away, strike, and then disappear almost instantly, leaving only a heap of rubble where minutes earlier a building, or a person, stood. The element of surprise is an essential military strategy. And yet that very sense of surprise and physical distance from the battlefield – which when presented on a high-definition screen does not necessarily feel so far away for the drone operators – separates the two

---

[1] For one set of objections, see Daniel Statman, "Drones and Robots: On the Changing Practice of Warfare," in *The Oxford Handbook of the Ethics of War*, eds. Seth Lazar and Helen Frowe, Online Publication October 2015. The premises of this paradox are fundamentally rejected by many "revisionist" Just War theorists, who don't think that both sides of an armed conflict are equally positioned with respect to the right to use lethal force. In short, soldiers fighting on the unjust side of the war, for revisionists, never acquire the right to kill, even in self-defense. My aim in this chapter is to say as little as possible about the principle of discrimination, or about drone strikes, that depends on assumptions peculiar either to a revisionist or to a classical Just War theorist. When this isn't possible, I explicitly call attention to either "traditional" or "revisionist" Just War theory.

[2] For a useful discussion of the secrecy of drones, see John Kaag and Sarah Kreps, *Drone Warfare*, United Kingdom: Polity Press, 2014, especially ch. 3.

sides physically and psychologically and opens up space for propagandists to redescribe drone strikes in their own terms, potentially recruiting people to join the ranks of the very armed group that drones strikes attempt to dismantle. It's not just that the secrecy of drone strikes has trade-offs; it's also that the most ethical of intentions in drone warfare – to strike quickly, precisely, and accurately – can lead to unethical consequences.

A full discussion of drone strikes – involving *ad bellum* and *post bellum* questions, involving a discussion of collateral damage – is impossible here. This chapter focuses on the narrow but vexed question of how to apply the *in bello* principle of discrimination to potential targets of drone strikes, that is, on the question of who counts as a "combatant" and a "noncombatant" in drone warfare. This is one among many unsettled questions surrounding drone strikes, but it is also an essential one because the principle of discrimination is pivotal to both international humanitarian law (IHL) and to the just war principles embedded in that law. In fact, the principle of distinction, as international lawyers refer to it, is often called *the* fundamental principle of IHL and Just War theory.[3] And yet – as this chapter shows – there is still tremendous controversy surrounding who may be targeted, if anyone, by drone strikes. In this chapter I argue that drone strikes conducted in one kind of armed conflict – non-international armed conflicts (NIAC) outside areas of active hostilities – stretch the principle of discrimination past the point of recognition. More specifically I argue that the two or three conceptual options for understanding who is caught in the scope of a drone offered by Just War theorists insufficiently capture the plurality of cases encountered in a drone war. As a consequence, I believe that the principle of discrimination, the pillar of Just War theory, cannot set meaningful restraints on some of the drone strikes the United States currently carries out. When there is "uncertainty over what kinds of people get counted as noncombatants in the first place,"[4] a principle that forbids the targeting of noncombatants has little use.

I Brief Background and History

The U.S. practice of drone warfare consists of two broad stages: a monitoring stage, in which drones hover undetected in the air above intended surveillance targets, and a second, lethal, striking stage.[5] Drones may be used for one or both of these purposes and, in fact, were first designed just for surveillance.

---

[3] Jelena Pajic, "Extraterritorial Targeting by Means of Armed Drones: Some Legal Implications," *International Journal of the Red Cross* 96 (2015) no. 893: 1-40, p. 19.

[4] Christian Enemark, "Unmanned Drones and the Ethics of War," in *Routledge Handbook of Ethics and War: Just War Theory and the 21st Century*, eds. Fritz Allhoff, Nicholas G. Evans, and Adam Henschke, New York: Routledge, 2013, p. 335.

[5] For a technological history of drones, see Paul J. Springer, *Military Robots and Drones: A Reference Handbook*, California: ABC-CLIO, 2013. The BARD center for the study of the drone also offers good introductory material. See their "The Drone Primer: A Compendium of Key Issues," http://dronecenter.bard.edu/publication/the-drone-primer

Designed and built in the 1980s and 1990s as a surveillance technology, the Central Intelligence Agency (CIA) and/or U.S. military did not begin fitting hellfire missiles onto Reaper and Predator UAV systems until after 9/11.[6] In this chapter, the term "drone warfare" is used to refer to both combined stages of this form of armed conflict: the surveillance of individuals on monitors hundreds to thousands of miles away and the eventual practice of targeting such individuals with lethal force.

It is perhaps obvious to say that each drone strike, whether or not justified, leaves rubble and destruction in its wake. And actual drone strikes carried out by the U.S. military and the CIA are usually cloaked in secrecy. The Bureau of Investigative Journalism, a left-leaning independent organization based in London, is arguably the best source for information on drone strikes carried out by the United States; the *Long War Journal* and the New America Foundation are two other sources with excellent reputations among scholars and journalists. The written work of philosophers occasionally gives the impression that if we can only get our principles right the world will fall into place. But I would argue that the philosophical exercise of constructing realistic examples of drone strikes from which to extract and test principles is parasitic on the work of journalists, whose role it is to report only what can be confirmed as fact. These organizations also, of course, help hold both sides of armed conflicts accountable to public opinion.

The domestic legal justification of drone strikes in the United States is the Authorization for the Use of Military Force, or AUMF, issued by the United States more than fifteen years ago, in the wake of 9/11.[7] The AUMF authorizes the use of force against "Al-Qaeda, the Taliban, and associated forces."[8] After initially announcing the hunt for suspected terrorists as a global war on terror, the United States has since characterized the use of drones as a non-international armed conflict between the United States and the armed non-state groups mentioned earlier, among others. A non-international armed conflict is an armed conflict between a state and a non-state group, or between several non-state groups, and is distinguished from an international armed conflict between two sovereign states. The full list of the groups the United States is fighting remains classified.[9]

The United States conducts drone strikes in at least two significantly different kinds of non-international armed conflicts – an important detail often missed by

---

[6] Springer, *Military Robots and Drones*, Chapter 1.

[7] (AUMF), Pub. L. 107-40, 115 at. 224, adopted by Congress in S.J. Res. 23 on September 14, 2001 and signed by President George W. Bush on September 18, 2001, available at www.gpo.gov /fdsys/pkg/PLAW-107publ40/html/PLAW-107publ40.htm.

[8] AUMF.

[9] Cora Currier, "Who Are We at War With? That's Classified," *ProPublica*, July 26, 2013, available at www.propublica.org/article/who-are-we-at-war-with-thats-classified.

philosophically minded Just War theorists. The first context, as Jelena Pejic of the International Red Cross explains, is exemplified by the current U.S. conflict in Afghanistan.[10] In 2001, the United States began an international armed conflict in Afghanistan against a number of armed non-state groups, and the destruction carried out by both sides of this conflict has resulted in the displacement of hundreds of thousands of people. But in June of 2002, the United States began collaborating with the Afghan government against a variety of non-state groups, a conflict in which "armed forces of one or more States fight alongside the armed forces of a host State in its territory against one or more organized armed groups."[11]

The United States also conducts drone strikes in countries such as Yemen, Somali, and Pakistan, with or without the permission of the host government. These drone strikes are "extraterritorial" in another sense: they are a form of military-political intervention within the borders of a state without the collaboration (or not always) of that host state's government. This is the second type of non-international armed conflict in which the United States conducts drone strikes and is even more controversial than the first. The Obama administration launched 473 of these strikes, by its own count, from 2009 to the end of 2015, so around 67 per year.[12] While the United States maintains that it has a right to national self-defense that trumps an individual nation-state's right to sovereignty, carrying out a missile strike within the territory of a nonbelligerent state is controversial. Legally speaking such a strike may count as an act of war between the United States and that nonbelligerent host state in which the strikes take place, even if the host state is itself fighting against an armed group within its borders. Thus the legality of these strikes – as well as the morality of them – is a topic of controversy. This chapter is focused primarily on this (second) type of drone strike outside areas of active hostilities, although some of what I hope to convey – especially about the failure of the traditional marks of combatant status to apply to drone warfare – is also applicable to the first kind of drone warfare.

Drones are not "just a tool of war, one among many," alongside airplanes and tanks, machine guns, and nuclear weapons.[13] Primarily because of the specific form of extraterritorial non-international armed conflict that drones have made possible – in which specific individuals are surveilled and pursued

---

[10] Pajic, "Extraterritorial Targeting by Means of Armed Drones," pp. 15-17.   [11] Ibid., p. 15.

[12] Executive Order, *United States Policy on Pre- and Post-Strike Measures to Address Civilian Casualties in U.S. Operations Involving the Use of Force*. The White House, Office of the Press Secretary, July 1, 2016. This executive order established a principle of disclosing this type of drone strikes on a yearly basis. It's not clear whether this executive order will be followed by future U.S. presidents who continue to engage in drone warfare.

[13] Statman, "Drones and Robots."

into the boundaries of another sovereign state – I think drone technology has initiated a unique kind of digital-surveillance–based armed conflict.

Finally, to conclude this brief background section, a caveat is in order. The empirical and historical research conducted for this chapter was restricted to drone strikes carried out by the CIA or the U.S. military. Israel, Britain, France, and other countries have also launched drone strikes in non-international armed conflicts, but this chapter focuses on the current use of the drones by the United States.

II   The Principle of Discrimination

The very nature of drone strikes described above brings the horror of war to the forefront. To put it bluntly, since the nature of a drone strike is to select specific targets, we are confronted with the question of who, if anyone, our ethical judgments allow us to target with a lethal, guided missile strike. Even after that decision is made, moreover, there is the equally difficult decision of deciding on the timing of the strike, which is essential to minimizing or eliminating unintended or predictable innocent casualties. Both choices – who can be targeted and when – call for a kind of moral evaluation.[14] Moral evaluation is not a property of drone technology but of the people who employ drone technology.

The just war tradition offers one important framework for forming these moral evaluations, and in Western thought, the principle of discrimination central to the just war tradition has been the starting point for the moral evaluation of the question of who can be killed in war.[15] But drone strikes complicate not just the answer to this question; they also complicate the terms of the question itself, as we will see.

Many of the clearest formulations of the principle of discrimination come from international lawyers. The International Committee of the Red Cross (ICRC) formulates the principle of distinction as follows, using the legal term "civilian" rather than "noncombatant"[16]: "The parties to the conflict must at all times distinguish between civilians and combatants. Attacks may only be directed against combatants. Attacks must not be directed against civilians."[17] As the ICRC phrasing makes clear, the principle of discrimination distinguishes between two classes of individuals in wartime and states, "the only appropriate object of force in a conflict are combatants."[18] Likewise, the principle of

---

[14] Even fully automated weapons systems, which are not the subject of this essay, require human programming in order to determine criteria for who and when to strike.

[15] See John Mark Mattox's chapter in this volume for a discussion of the early origins of Just War theory in the 4th century writings of St. Augustine of Hippo.

[16] See David Rodin, "Terrorism without Intention," *Ethics* 114 (2004) no. 4, p. 758.

[17] International Committee of the Red Cross, Rule 1, Principle of Distinction Between Civilians and Combatants.

[18] Rodin, "Terrorism without Intention," p. 758.

discrimination distinguishes between civilian objects and military objectives, where military objectives must serve some definite military advantage.

Although there are many questions which may arise here, the most important point to make for our purposes is that, according to both treaty and customary international law, civilians are at all times protected against direct attack except "unless and for such time as they take a direct part in hostilities."[19] As we shall see in the next section of this paper, the "direct participation" loophole for attacking noncombatants is the key interpretive issue when it comes to understanding the application of the principle of discrimination to drone warfare. And neither the Geneva Conventions nor the Additional Protocols provide a definition of this key phrase: direct participation in hostilities.[20] But before discussing this issue, there are a few more general remarks to make about the principle of discrimination.

Intentional attacks directed against civilians, even as a means to a military end, are expressly prohibited by the principle of discrimination. The aerial attacks on London, Hiroshima, Nagasaki, Dresden, and Hamburg seem to be what the twentieth-century interpreters of Just War theory and the drafters of the 1949 Geneva Convention had in mind in forming the modern understanding of Just War theory. The principle of discrimination as understood since that era would clearly prohibit those attacks, in so far as civilians or noncombatants were directly and intentionally targeted as a means to a military end.

Yet collateral damage is not always a violation of the principle. Indirect harm against noncombatants or their property may be permitted according to the typical interpretation of the discrimination principle, so long as such harm is not the intended military goal. Many disagree. Michael Walzer thinks, for example, "two intentions" are required – a distinct intention to target only combatants and a distinct intention to avoid harm to civilians. It is not enough to simply aim at a military target; one must also, additionally, take precautions to avoid civilian casualties, he says.[21] How much precaution will be a complex judgment and highly complex-dependent. Part of that context is psychological and includes the general moral sensibility to the harm of unintended or avoidable civilian deaths.[22]

In sum, then, the principle of discrimination, as it has been understood since the Second World War, forbids attacks on civilians who may nevertheless have some responsibility for sustaining the war effort. Thus not all persons on the

---

[19] Additional Protocol I, Art. 51(3) and Additional Protocol II, Art. 13(3).

[20] Pajic, "Extraterritorial Targeting by Means of Armed Drones," p. 19.

[21] This refers to the doctrine of double effect. See Michael Walzer, "Terrorism and Just War," *Philosophia* 34 (2006) no. 4, pp. 3–4.

[22] This will also involve other *in bello* principles, notably the idea that lethal force is permissible only when killing in war is necessary for a military goal that is itself necessary – the principle of necessity or limited force.

enemy side of a war effort can be targeted or killed in war, but only a part. And when we sense that this idea is ignored or not treated with respect, we believe that an injustice has occurred. This responsiveness to the unnecessary loss of human life reveals that the boundary between combatants/civilians and non-combatants outlined by the principle of discrimination marks a *moral* differ-ence – it pertains to who can be the justified object of lethal force. It does not, or need not, correspond to a strict factual difference between soldiers and civi-lians. For this reason, when thinking about the sorts of restraints on lethal force that the principle of distinction can be shown to demand in drone warfare, many Just War theorists tend to use the terminology of "noncombatants" and "combatants" rather than "civilians" and "soldiers."

But how do we draw the line between combatants and noncombatants? Think of soldiers stationed at a neutral port, sleeping on board a ship, as was the case of the crew members of the USS Cole killed at the port of Adan in 2000 by al-Qaeda, the year before 9/11. Are soldiers unengaged in combat function at a given time x still combatants?

This is a deeply divisive question but an essential one for taking a position on the morality of many drone strikes. The disagreement hinges largely on whether combatant function extends outside of the window of time during which a person takes up arms. As for the USS Cole killings by al-Qaeda, David Rodin thinks that the crew members were noncombatants because "they were in port on a routine friendly visit and were not involved in any combat function at the time."[23] On this view, the servicemen murdered on the USS Cole were both soldiers *and* noncombatants, members of an armed force and yet at a given time x lethal force was impermissibly used against them. On this view there is a rough *moral* equivalence between civilians, on the one hand, and soldiers who are at some given time noncombatants on the other hand, despite the fact that civilians are in nonmoral respects quite different from noncombatants.

The classical account of combatant status, as well as the Geneva Conventions, have a different view of whether solders are at all times non-combatants. "Simply by fighting," Michael Walzer writes in *Just and Unjust Wars*, all combatants have "lost their title to life and liberty."[24] Combatants on both sides of the war have lost their title to life and liberty, for Walzer, as soon as they take up arms against another state or another organization; this reflects the contractual model of traditional just war theory in which natural rights are exchanged for the right to employ force. In exchange for acquiring the right to kill, on this view, all combatants may be killed without restraint, and the fact that soldiers are *also* civilians – husbands, wives, mothers and fathers – is what makes killing in war tragic, but not immoral.

---

[23] Rodin, "Terrorism without Intention," p. 758.
[24] Michael Walzer, *Just and Unjust Wars: A Moral Argument with Historical Illustrations*, New York: Basic Books, 2006, p. 136.

I am raising the question of whether soldiers can sometimes be noncombatants not in order to solve the problem now but to show the stakes of the practice of targeted killing by drones. Those stakes can be put in the form of a dilemma. If soldiers are not always combatants – if they can shed their social role at home, at night, or on the weekend – then killing a soldier at the wrong time will amount to an act of premeditated murder, that is, to an act of extralegal, orchestrated killing. But if soldiers are always combatants, even at home, at night, and on the weekends, then U.S. soldiers as well as members of enemy groups targeted by drones strikes would be liable to being attacked all the time – even, for example, when not deployed in a combat function. So either some U.S. drone strikes count as acts of murder or all soldiers, including U.S. soldiers, never shed combatant status.

To avoid having to choose either horn of this dilemma, the Bush Administration attempted to place the members of the non-state armed groups it was fighting into the legally fraught third category of "unlawful combatants." Lawyers for the Bush Administration argued that because suspected terrorists had failed to distinguish themselves from the civilian population, they had lost the protections of combatant status – and they could be detained indefinitely without POW status in secret prisons all across the globe, including Guantanamo Bay. As Claire Finkelstein points out, the in-between status of suspected terrorists who were neither clearly combatants nor noncombatants "renders obscure who can be legitimately targeted, who can be detained, as well as the justification for targeting or detaining, the extent of the duty to seek capture before killing, and, more generally, whether detainees in the war on terror should fall under the protections traditionally extended to prisoners of war."[25]

The stakes of the problem of who counts as combatant in a drone war are perhaps now becoming clear. The targeting of noncombatants is murder; the targeting of combatants is killing in war. Without a way to reliably tell the difference, we risk collapsing murder and war, which all forms of Just War theory I am acquainted with aim to prevent.

In the next few sections, we will examine possible criteria for combatant status in a drone war, progressing from traditional marks and features of combatants to the most recent guidance issued by the International Red Cross. Ultimately I don't think any of these criteria establish a bright line between combatants and noncombatants in a drone war.

III Wearing Uniforms and Carrying Arms

Drone strikes present grave challenges for distinguishing combats from noncombatants. During the initial stages of a drone strike, possible targets are monitored

---

[25] Claire Finkelstein, "Targeted Killings as Preemptive Action," in *Targeted Killings: Law and Morality in an Asymmetric World*, eds. Claire Finkelstein, Jens David Ohlin, and Andrew Altman, Oxford: Oxford University Press, 2013, p. 158.

for weeks or even months; U.S. intelligence officers meanwhile, sometimes from across the globe, gather evidence against them. Intelligence officers monitor video footage, interpret the metadata of cell-phone communication, examine browser histories and emails and much more all through fiber-optic cables buried under the Atlantic, with data reportedly running through military bases in Germany.

In various ways, these persons and activities monitored by drone technology do not fall neatly into the categories of combatant or noncombatant. The most obvious way in which this is true is the lack of uniforms or other insignia worn by persons plotting attacks against the United States or its allies; and CIA officials responsible for drone strikes also do not wear uniforms. But the problem is far deeper than simply the presence or absence of insignia or even the role that insignia play in determining combatant status.

The 1977 Additional Protocols to the Geneva Convention, which tried to include liberation forces and guerrilla forces under combatant status who were fighting within the territory of a sovereign state against that sovereign state, already recognized that some combatants may not have uniforms. The 1977 Protocol I states that a person "shall retain his status as combatant" provided that he "carries arms openly in military situations."[26] So here the mark of carrying arms openly in military situations was proposed as a distinguishing mark of combatant status. But characterizing combatant status in terms of carrying arms openly will not be useful for drone warfare. First of all, a person who is not actively plotting against the United States might carry a weapon. But perhaps more importantly, it is likely that the intended targets of drone strikes – high-level persons in the armed groups the U.S. is fighting – do not always carry arms. The geopolitical situation which the drafters of the Additional Protocols had in mind – a non-international armed conflict in which one armed group tries to seize power within a single sovereign state – resulted in criteria for combatant status which aren't useful for deciding on combatants in the contemporary geopolitical situation involving drone warfare.

IV Imminent Threats

Perhaps the next best criterion for establishing combatant status is the concept of imminent threats. Grounding combatant status in the doctrine of imminent threats would be appealing because self-defense is a widely accepted ground for lethal force. Moreover, the official *ad bellum* legal justification for drone strikes in the AUMF leans heavily on the concept of imminent threats.

What does it mean to pose an imminent threat? Although the details are controversial, the basic idea might take the form of a conditional: *if* an act X is

---

[26] 1977 Geneva Protocol 1, Section II, Article 44. Furthermore, the combatant must carry arms openly both (1) during each military engagement and (2) "during such time as he is visible to the adversary while ... engaged in a military deployment preceding the launching of an attack in which he is to participate."

not prevented, then the immediate consequence would be a loss of life or serious injury. Questions come up when pinpointing the "immediacy" and "certainty" of the predicted consequences. If the harmful consequences are far enough in the future, then a threat cannot be characterized as imminent. In addition, if it's not clear whether a person will in fact carry out an attack or not, and the threat has a lower probability of being carried out, then a threat also cannot be characterized as imminent.

There is room for individual judgment here – and there will be disagreement about particular cases. But if we take an IED maker as an example, we immediately see a problem with linking combatant status to the doctrine of imminent threats. The only person who poses an imminent threat in the case of an IED is the person who actually detonates the device. The person in charge of orchestrating the attack may pose a threat, but it won't be an imminent threat, since it is temporally removed from the impending harm. And the IED maker who does not set off the actual devices, as we will see later in this chapter, will never pose an imminent threat. It seems that tying combatant status to imminent threat would limit harm to those persons who have been ordered to carry out an attack, which is neither militarily smart, since higher-ups are more pivotal to an enemy organization, nor morally sound, since responsibility for such events is surely spread over a number of agents.

We should also note that an individual who has merely given signs of wanting or planning to execute a terrorist act or an individual who has already committed an act of terrorism in the past does not pose an imminent threat. Killing someone such as the American citizen and preacher al-Awlaki does not imminently save lives; rather, such a judgment relies on prediction of risk or even more problematically, on desert for a prior crime.

Scholars generally agree that the imminent threat standard fails to justify drone strikes. That is, the question is not whether most targets of drone strikes pose imminent threats. They do not. But the disagreement comes in at what happens next. As Altman states, the disagreement "concerns the permissibility of the practice insofar as it extends beyond the imminent-explosion type of case."[27] The question is whether those targets who do not pose imminent threats can be targeted, and if so, then on what grounds?

At this juncture, those who wish to justify drone strikes typically now try to find a principle that "extends the preventive privilege to a number of cases in which the anticipated harm is non-imminent."[28] But I don't think the question to ask here is: "Should the principle of distinction cover the cases of preemptive but non-imminent threat that we *already* think are justified?" The point is not to rationalize or reinforce an existing belief but to determine a fair standard and then test our beliefs against that standard. Perhaps the International Red

[27] Andrew Altman, "Introduction" in *Targeted Killings*, eds. Finkelstein, Ohlin, and Altman, p. 8.
[28] Finkelstein, "Targeted Killing as Preemptive Action," p. 162.

Cross, which published its Interpretive Guidance on the question of who counts as a combatant in drone strike, can provide us with such a standard.

V   Direct Participation in Hostilities

The principle of discrimination as understood in international humanitarian law does allow for a small subset of civilians to be targeted —that is, for a small subset of civilians to lose their protections under the law. A civilian loses his/ her protection against direct attack when, and for as long as, he or she "directly participates" in hostilities, but the civilian does not, in doing so, gain combatant status.[29] Perhaps this idea might adequately regulate drone strikes. Unfortunately, however, neither the Geneva Conventions nor the Additional Protocols to the Geneva Convention offer a precise definition of direct participation in hostilities.

To remedy this, the International Committee of the Red Cross, with an eye toward the ongoing drone strikes carried out by the United States, published its Interpretive Guidance on how to understand this key phrase — "direct participation" — in 2009. The Guidance is long and complex; it is probably non-binding on the parties to the Geneva convention; and it also provoked a series of critiques in the New York University Journal of International Law and Politics following its publication.[30] Nevertheless, as a widely distributed and carefully devised document in international law, the interpretive guidance is important to examine here, if for no other reason than that it provides an accepted starting point. It should also be noted that the ICRC's recommendations were put in place *after the fact*, that is, in order to keep pace with the changing social practice of drone warfare. Thus the unstated main aim of the guidance was to understand who may be targeted by a drone strike against an organized, non-state, armed group.

The Guidance sought to establish criteria for both "membership in armed group" and, for those persons who are not members of an armed group, to establish criteria for what counts as "direct participation in hostilities." Thus the ICRC Guidance distinguished between two different *kinds* of combatants[31]: (1) members of non-state armed forces and (2) civilians who directly participate in hostilities. The first criterion (membership) allows for lethal force in virtue of belonging to a group; the second (direct participation) allows for lethal force in virtue of specific conduct. Membership is in turn predicated on a "continuous combat function" in which a member directly participates in hostilities. Thus for both kinds of combatants the key term is direct participation.

---

[29] AP I, Art. 51(3) and AP II, Art. 13(3).

[30] See *New York University Journal of International Law and Politics*, 42 (2010) no. 3, available at: http://nyujilp.org/print-edition/

[31] Legally speaking, "combatants" may not be the right word here. The non-state party to a non-international armed conflict is not entitled to combatant status according to IHL.

Let us briefly examine both of these categories of combatants, but before doing so, we should make a general but essential point. By claiming that a human being can lose their protected status in one of two ways – either by assuming a continuous combat function in an organized armed group or by directly participating in hostilities – the ICRC's interpretive guidance made the category of "combatant" quite complex, with several criteria which be determined to be in place to meet combatant status. This is only a reason to reject those criteria if there is *too* much room for human judgment, however.

The first kind of combatant status is based on membership. To establish membership in an armed group the ICRC leaned on the criteria of "continuous combat function." There are two observations to make here. First, the Obama Administration offered a different way of characterizing membership in the executive order issues in July 2016.[32] We don't have space to examine these differences here. But it should be remembered that the AUMF is vague about *which* armed groups the United States is at war with, as previously said, and the full list of such groups remains classified. Thus there is a double-pronged question: "what counts as membership in a group" and "which groups can be targeted?". Moreover, as we saw with the soldiers aboard the USS Cole, linking combatant status tightly to any kind of membership in an armed group is controversial. For it may be the case that soldiers at a given time x – at home with their families; sleeping at night – are not combatants, as David Rodin thinks. And if some soldiers are not combatants, then all criteria for combatantcy which depend on membership fail. There will be disagreement on this last point, but it is nevertheless a third point at which human judgment is needed – all merely within the membership criterion for combatant status.

As for the conduct-based criterion for combatant status provided by the ICRC, to count as an act of direct participation in hostilities, a specific action must fulfill all of the following, technical, criteria. Paraphrasing a bit, such an act must: (1) adversely affect the military operations or military capacity of a party to an armed conflict or inflict death or destruction on the persons or objects protected; (2) there must be a direct causal link between the act and the harm likely to result; and (3) the act must be specifically designed to directly cause the required threshold of harm in support of a party to the conflict.[33] These criteria are designed to distinguish between some acts which are liable to the use of lethal force, and other acts, which despite occurring in the context of an armed conflict, do not meet the threshold of combatant status and are not liable to lethal force.

---

[32] Executive Order, *United States Policy on Pre- and Post-Strike Measures to Address Civilian Casualties in U.S. Operations Involving the Use of Force.*

[33] Nils Melzer, Interpretive Guidance on the Notion of Direct Participation in Hostilities under International Humanitarian Law, ICRC, Geneva, 2009 (Interpretive Guidance), available at: www.icrc.org/eng/resources/documents/article/review/review-872-p991.htm.

The very need for such technicalities is of course evidence that the old criteria for combatant status on which the principle of discrimination formerly depended – wearing insignia; carrying arms openly; posing a clear and immediate threat – are no longer useful. But just because our way of waging war has changed does not mean that the principle of discrimination does not provide enough guidance on how to regulate those changes. The question is: do these criteria, however technical they are, solve the interpretive question at issue here – and give us a "bright line" between combatants and noncombatants in drone warfare?

The only way to answer this question is to test the ICRC's definition of direct participation. But how to test it? For the test to be exhaustive, we would have to test every likely situation in which a drone strike *could* be called for. This is impossible, so we must choose a particular example to examine with the standard the ICRC has provided. The choice of example will be very important, then, so how do we select examples? One approach would be to start from the case of someone who we think *ought* to be targetable. We would then expand the criteria for combatant status to cover this case, adjusting our principles to accord with immediate moral sensibilities. But the question will then come up: what's the basis for our previously settled sense that such a person is liable to lethal force? Without settling this former question, we risk merely rationalizing our beliefs; that is, we risk confirming, rather than testing, out attitudes with our reasons. But we do not want to simply confirm our previously formed opinions but instead to bring them into the public space of reasons and test them. How then do we choose a case that will genuinely test the strength of the ICRC's interpretive guidance?

One approach, following the work of legal scholar and philosopher Jeremy Waldron, proposes that any rule we use to determine combatant status ought to be acceptable to us even when "used by those we rightly regard as our enemies."[34] That is, Waldron suggests that any version of the principle of discrimination we endorse should be a neutral principle, endorsable by both sides of an armed conflict. This is an inheritance of the Kantian categorical imperative, of course: I ought to act only according to a maxim that I could, at the same time, generalize into a universal rule. Waldron encourages us to test principles in this way for two reasons: both to better understand our own principles and to ensure that any rule we endorse does not fall into the wrong hands where it could be used against us. In what follows we will use Waldron's approach to test the results of the ICRC's guidance against the case of an IED maker.

VI   Testing the ICRC's Criteria: The Case of the IED Maker

Some find the ICRC's criteria for combatant status too restrictive on the use of lethal force. Mark Maxwell, a staff judge advocate of the U.S. Army V Corps in

---

[34] Jeremy Waldron, "Justifying Targeted Killing with a Neutral Principle," in *Targeted Killings*, eds. Finkelstein, Ohlin, and Altman, p. 118.

Wiesbaden, Germany, has argued that these criteria count too many individuals as noncombatants and in fact place too many constraints on counterterrorism activity. "After 9/11," Maxwell writes, "the complexion of warfare changed and a gap developed between what the state of the law is and what it should be."[35] Accordingly, he writes, "the next generation of the law of war must make sense in the context of the ongoing armed conflict and not be so onerous that it makes categorizing individuals as belligerents virtually impossible."[36]

Maxwell focuses on the example of an IED maker who is responsible for the assembly, construction, purchase, or smuggling of an IED but not for its planting and detonation. Would the IED maker count as a combatant under the ICRC's interpretive guidance?

The interpretive guidance on the direct participation in hostilities leaves little doubt that the targeting of IED makers would be prohibited.[37] The full account of the ICRC's rationale cannot be given here, but the basic claim is that IED makers, unlike planters or detonators of the device, "do *not* cause that harm directly."[38] Direct harm, in turn, is defined as a "harm brought about in one causal step."[39] So directness has both a causal and temporal component, in which direct harm is both causally responsible and temporally near the moment of harm. But as we saw earlier when examining the "imminent threat" criterion for combatant status, an IED maker is neither fully responsible for, nor the last person to bring about, the harm.

Maxwell's objection to the ICRC's guideline is interesting. He thinks, in effect, that such a distinction does not consider both sides of the war equally, placing "U.S. soldiers at grave risk."[40] The reason is that a state attempting to target known or suspected terrorists has more to prove: it must prove not only that an individual is a member of an organized armed group but also that such an individual directly participates in hostilities. And yet, Maxwell thinks that U.S. soldiers do not face this "additional hurdle" to combatant status under the laws of war.[41] A U.S. soldier may be killed, Maxwell suggests, simply in virtue of his or her membership in the military, and the additional requirement of "direct participation" does not apply. Thus the two sides are situated unequally: "If an individual is a member of an organized armed group, then his function

---

[35] Mark Maxwell, "Rebutting the Civilian Presumption: Playing Whack-a-Mole Without a Mallett," in *Targeted Killings*, eds. Finkelstein, Ohlin, and Altman, p. 49.

[36] Ibid., p. 59. Here "belligerents" is meant as the legal term for combatants.

[37] ICRC Guidance 2009, p. 1022.   [38] Ibid., p. 1022.

[39] Ibid., p. 1021. Maxwell's discussion of the issue is in "Rebutting the Civilian Presumption," p. 51. John Kaag and Sarah Kreps also offer a worthwhile discussion of the issue.

[40] Maxwell, "Rebutting the Civilian Presumption," p. 44.

[41] Ibid., pp. 50–52.

with that group must be established . . . for a member of the U.S. armed forces, that function is assumed."[42]

But even putting aside the open-ended list of *which* specific groups the U.S. is fighting, Maxwell's view is thus that the functional equivalent of the IED maker in the United States Army would be liable to attack. But is this true? If we follow Waldron and devise a neutral principle that would entitle us to count IED makers as combatants, we would formulate something like:

Individuals who design, manufacture, produce, or construct lethal weapons for a war count as combatants and can be targeted with lethal force in war.[43]

When generalized in this way, the moral differences between the IED maker and the weapons manufacturer is no longer relevant. And this seems right; the IED maker and drone technology engineer both offer "analogous . . . benefits" to their respective side of the war.[44] Such a person contributes to a war and may even be necessary for it, and yet the principle of discrimination as crafted in the twentieth century expressly forbids targeting them. After the Second World War there was a general consensus that workers in munitions factories and civil engineers of weapon systems were not liable to lethal force, even if their support of the conflict was clear – even if these noncombatants were in no sense "innocent" of all wrongdoing. The principle of discrimination made the bold, arguably unintuitive step of forbidding intentional and direct attacks on this class of people, despite the fact that such persons are not without guilt or taint. If Maxwell's proposals were drawn into international law, then at least some participants of the war effort in the United States would count as combatants whom we at least used to not want to be combatants: factory workers, military engineers, and others.

This position does not seek to make morally equivalent an IED maker who has a malicious intent to cause serious bodily harm (or death) to soldiers and a munitions factory worker in the United States. The two may have completely different intentions and views of who is permitted to live in relative peace on this earth. But this difference in moral status is not relevant from a neutral perspective.

We should take a step back at this juncture and note just how deep the disagreement is here. Maxwell thinks IED makers should count as combatants. I disagree. But I don't just disagree that such persons count as combatants. If I use the language of just war theory to describe my disagreement with Maxwell, then I will be forced to say that I believe targeting an IED maker is targeting a noncombatant. Targeting a noncombatant is prosecutable under international law; it is a form or murder, and in some cases, especially in a

---

[42] Ibid., p. 52.

[43] Or more controversially: individuals who have implicitly consented to the ideology of their party to the war by designing and engineering lethal weapons that are a necessary part of that war can be targeted with lethal force.

[44] Executive Order, *United States Policy on Pre- and Post-Strike Measures to Address Civilian Casualties in U.S. Operations Involving the Use of Force.*

neutral zone, targeting noncombatants is terroristic. So by rejecting the claim that an IED maker is a combatant I have been forced to say that such a person is a civilian or noncombatant, and that a drone strike which targeted him/her is an act of terrorism. I may be prepared to say this in some cases, for example, if credible sources such as the Bureau of Investigative Journalism reported that a person who did not intend to harm civilians has been intentionally, unnecessarily or carelessly hit by a drone strike. But in general I don't want to call borderline cases acts of terrorism or murder: such a characterization is inaccurate and extreme. Yet left to the choice between combatants and noncombatants – however much the Bush Administration tried, they failed to convince the international community of scholars and journalists that a third category exists in just war theory – I am forced to say that such a strike targets noncombatants. For this reason, the conceptual dilemma (or trilemna if we count direct participation) offered by Just War theory is inadequate to the plurality of circumstances encountered in the scopes of a drone. When we expand this problem to an open-ended list of persons who are neither soldiers, nor civilians, nor even clear members of an organized armed group, but who bear some degree of responsibility for the maintenance of a group that is an enemy to the United States, we see that the terms combatant and noncombatant are inadequate to regulate the plurality of scenarios involving a choice of who can ethically be struck by a drone and killed. The terms "combatant" and "noncombatant" are thus inappropriately applied to drone wars.

VII Conclusion

This chapter has argued, one, that there is no bright line between combatants and noncombatants in a drone war, and two, that the two or three conceptual options for naming persons caught in the scope of a drone offered by Just War theorists insufficiently capture the plurality of cases encountered in a surveillance-based drone war.

One might object: isn't it in the nature of a standard to measure unlike cases? Couldn't we just continue to refine the criteria of combatant status and direct participation, along the lines of the ICRC's interpretive guidance, to determine who can be targeted by a drone strike within the language of Just War theory? I don't think this is a good idea. One reason is that there is too much ambiguity with regard to how to determine membership in an armed group, whether such membership automatically makes one a combatant, and, with regard to the current drone war, which armed groups are targetable. Another reason is that an extra-territorial drone war waged outside of any zone of active hostilities resembles law enforcement in its evidence-gathering, judgment, and prosecution of individual persons. It is outside the scope of this chapter to determine how well suited the law-enforcement paradigm would be as a regulatory framework for drone strikes, but there is much work already being done with this proposal, and more is required.

I want to end instead with two different points. The lethal drone strikes being carried out at the time of the writing of this chapter in the Middle East are being framed principally through the vocabulary of Just War theory, that is, as aimed at "combatants" rather than "noncombatants." I think there is good reason to demand more precise information than these labels can provide about the criteria being used to determine who is targetable. There will be room for genuine disagreement as to who is "guilty," and even more disagreement as to whose guilt merits a death sentence. But these are deeply needed conversations.

My last point has to do with the relation between social norms and social practices. Again taking inspiration from the thinking of Jeremy Waldron,[45] in my view, the social practice of drone warfare erodes the norm against targeted and intentional killing outside of clear war zones, that is, the norm against a new form of international assassination. If the threat of terroristic attacks against the U.S. and its allies is so great that this norm must be given up, then the only honorable way to give up this norm is with full self-consciousness of the stakes of the situation. As philosophers have apparently long known, the fact that drone strikes do in fact take place must not be taken as evidence that they should.

[45] Waldron, "Justifying Targeted Killing with a Neutral Principle," Ch. 4.

Part IV

Just War and International Legal Theory

Part IV

Just War and International Legal Theory

12 *Jus ad Bellum*

Larry May

International law shares with the Just War tradition many core ideas. But the most important is that war should not be initiated unless there is a just cause, principally understood in terms of self-defense. And in international law, as in the Just War tradition, self-defense is narrowly circumscribed by considerations of necessity and proportionality, among others. *Jus ad bellum* primarily concerns the use of force in initiating armed conflict. In this chapter I will explore the main contours of the idea of justified war in international law and also draw contrasts with the Just War considerations we have already examined in previous chapters.

There are significant areas of overlap and mutual influence between *jus ad bellum* international law and Just War theory today. Self-defense is the most widely recognized justification for engaging in war. Indeed, there are great controversies about whether anything other than self-defense can justify recourse to war. As we will see, international court decisions have interpreted the UN Charter Article 2, section 4's broad prohibition on the use of force as having a major exception in Article 51's articulation of an inherent right of individual or collective self-defense. As I will explain, self-defense exceptions to the prohibition on the use of force by states against other states are severely limited. But there is wide agreement in international law that at least until the UN has acted States have the right to use lethal force in self-defense.

The main international law texts on the use of force are Article 2, section 4, and Article 51 of the Charter of the United Nations. I will begin by examining these texts and then turn to case law and commentary that have refined understanding of the principles governing the use of force. So, in Section I, I provide an analysis of Article 2, section 4, and Article 51. In Section II, I examine a case that has had profound implications for the understanding of the use of force, that of Nicaragua. In Section III, I look at two other cases that have been highly influential. In Section IV, I examine how individuals have been treated in international criminal law when *jus ad bellum* norms have been violated. And finally, I draw out some of the parallels between debates about the use of force in international law and in the Just War tradition. Some of the ideas discussed briefly in this chapter, such as the idea of necessity, will get more developed discussion in other chapters.

I The UN Charter and the Use of Force

The Charter of the United Nations was ratified in the immediate aftermath of World War II. Since at the time that war was thought to be justified to stop the Nazi's global attacks as well as the Holocaust, it is interesting that the Charter talks about the initiation of war as being justified in only a very narrow range of cases. Perhaps, though, people were thinking of World War I, which was roundly condemned. Or maybe they were simply exhausted from fighting two massive wars within just a few decades of each other. In any event, the UN Charter set up a legal framework concerning *jus ad bellum*, the conditions for the legal justification of initiating war.

The Charter of the United Nations had as one of its most important goals to eliminate war. It is often commented that realizing this goal is no closer now than it was in 1945 when the Charter was drafted.[1] But it is also true that the Charter sets severe restrictions on initiating war, specifically in changing the burden of proof concerning justifying recourse to war, *jus ad bellum*.

The Preamble to the 1945 Charter of the United Nations begins in the following broad and evocative manner:

We the Peoples of the United Nations [are] Determined to save succeeding generations from the scourge of war, which twice in our lifetime has brought untold sorrow to mankind, and to reaffirm faith in fundamental human rights, in the dignity of and worth of the human person, in the equal rights of men and women and of nations large and small.

Notice that the first thing mentioned is "to save succeeding generations from the scourge of war." And notice also that war is associated with the term "scourge" already giving the reader the idea that war is not a favored institution. Of course, the point to emphasize in general is that the United Nations was established to save people from the scourge of war, especially as war had undermined human rights, seemingly implying that war as it had been known should end with the founding of the United Nations.

Article 1 of the United Nations Charter lists the following as the first purpose and principle of the United Nations:

To maintain international peace and security, and to that end: to take effective collective measures for the prevention and removal of threats to the peace, and to the suppression of acts of aggression or other breaches of the peace, and to bring about by peaceful means, and in conformity with the principles of justice and international law, adjustments or settlement of international disputes or situations which might lead to a breach of peace.

---

[1] See for example Mark Janis and John E. Noyes, *International Law: Cases and Commentary*, St. Paul: West Law, 1997, p. 419.

The first purpose and principle of the United Nations is to maintain the peace and by implication to avert war. Of course it is also true that maintaining the peace could involve the suppression of acts of aggression, and that a suppression effort could lead to the use of war to stop an aggressing State from attacking one of its neighbor States. But notice that the Charter says that stopping aggression is to be done "by peaceful means." Again this was in direct response to the two world wars that had just been fought.

Article 2, section 4, of the United Nations Charter is a bold statement seemingly prohibiting States from initiating war:

All members shall refrain in their international relations from the threat or use of force against the territorial integrity or political independence of any state, or in any other manner inconsistent with the Purposes of the United Nations.

This article only seemingly outlaws all initiation of war because of the effect on Article 2, section 4, of Article 51, which reads in its first half as follows:

Nothing in the present Charter shall impair the inherent right of individual or collective self-defense if an armed attack occurs against a Member of the United Nations, until the Security Council has taken measures necessary to maintain international peace and security.

We can see that self-defense is given pride of place as the just cause that could justify a State in using force against another State. So, like Just War theory, international law contemplates self-defense as one, if not the, just cause to wage war.

There has been much debate about how Article 2, section 4, and Article 51 are supposed to fit together. Some suggest that the use of the word "inherent" is the key to Article 51 as establishing its priority over Article 2, section 4, and hence of the acceptance of wars fought in self-defense.[2] Others have argued that "until" is the key to Article 51; this seems to give only a very limited right of unilateral action on the part of even those States that have been attacked, namely a right limited to the time until the UN acts.[3]

I believe it is important also to examine the second part of Article 51 for help in interpreting its meaning:

Measures taken by Members in the exercise of this right of self-defense shall be immediately reported to the Security Council and shall not in any way affect the authority and responsibility of the Security Council under the present Charter to take at any time such action as it deems necessary in order to maintain or restore international peace and security.

---

[2] See John Yoo, "Using Force," *The University of Chicago Law Review* 71 (Summer 2004) no. 3: 729–97.

[3] See Eugene V. Rostow, "Until What? Enforcement Action or Collective Self-Defense," *American Journal of International Law* 85 (1991) no. 3: 506–16.

The meaning here is by no means crystal clear, but it seems to say that even the inherent right of self-defense does not impede the right of the United Nations to act to maintain or reestablish the peace. It thus appears that the key to the whole of Article 51 is not to give States a blanket self-defense exception to Article 2, section 4's prohibition on waging war; it is to reaffirm that if war is to take place, it is only under the auspices of the United Nations, which would have dramatically changed the nature of war as it had been known. This is the promise of the Charter, or at least one interpretation of that document.

I believe we should in addition examine the beginning of Chapter VII of the Charter concerning threats to the peace and acts of aggression. Article 24, section 1 asserts that the Security Council has "primary responsibility for the maintenance of international peace and security." Any use of force that is legitimate under the UN Charter has to be recognized and authorized by the Security Council. The only exception is if self-defense is needed and the United Nations has not acted.

Article 39 is one of the most important lynchpins in my interpretive argument since it takes out of the hands of States the decision about whether to go to war. This article asserts that

The Security Council shall determine the existence of any threat to the peace, breach of the peace, or act of aggression, and shall make recommendations, or decide what measures shall be taken in accordance with Articles 41 and 42, to maintain or restore international peace and security.

The United Nations here arrogates to itself the determination of whether the acts of one State are a threat to the peace that would require action by the United Nations through its member nations or the temporary acts of self-defense by one nation. And here the United Nations again reaffirms that it is the institution that decides what measures should be taken and by whom, even in cases of self-defense.

Article 40 lists the actions short of the use of armed force that the United Nations can employ, including "interruption of economic relations." Article 41 specifies that the United Nations will use "action by air, sea, or land forces as may be necessary to maintain or restore international peace and security" if Article 40 measures have failed. The effect of these two articles, in combination with Article 39, is to greatly restrict what States can do in terms of initiating acts of war. It thus seems that one clear way to interpret Article 51 is merely as an emergency provision, where a State can act in self-defense only if the United Nations is not acting and only until the United Nations can react. On this interpretation, war as the world had known it, where States decided unilaterally when and whether to initiate war, was thus virtually outlawed.

There is though an exception for joint action by States under the auspices of the Security Council. Indeed some have argued that there is a requirement that States band together to address systematic human rights abuses. The use of force in such cases could be labeled a "just war." But I would argue that the kind of force envisioned in Articles 55 and 56 of the Charter, for instance, are not recognizably instances of "war" as this term has been employed over the centuries. Note that Articles 55 and 56 are grouped under Chapter IX, which has the title "International Economic and Social Co-operation" not under a title concerning the use of force. The kind of cooperation that is required is not primarily that of military force.

And so, even humanitarian intervention initiated by a single State seems not to be countenanced in international law. And for this reason, the Charter can be read, not uncontroversially, to outlaw all use of force not sanctioned by the Security Council, even as there is a section of the Charter that seems to allow for armed conflict in cases of self-defense. Indeed, Article 42 states:

> Should the Security Council consider that measures provided for in Article 41 would be inadequate or have proved to be inadequate, it may take such action by air, sea, or land forces as may be necessary to maintain or restore international peace and security. Such action may include demonstrations, blockade, and other operations by air, sea, or land forces of Members of the United Nations.

This reference to force is to a collective use of armed force by States authorized by the Security Council. But we see here a clear articulation of one of the key conditions of *jus ad bellum* that we will explore later: war is justified only when nonviolent means "would be inadequate or have proved to be inadequate."

II   The International Court of Justice's Nicaragua Case

To better understand how recourse to war is treated in international law, we can turn to the International Court of Justice's (ICJ) cases interpreting Article 2, section 4, and Article 51 of the UN's Charter. This is an especially rich source of how to understand the Charter since the ICJ is itself an organ of the United Nations. In what follows I will look at the most important cases on this topic from the ICJ: first, the Nicaragua case from 1986. I will later look at other important *jus ad bellum* cases: the Nuclear Weapons case from 1996, and the Palestinian Wall case from 2004.

The Nicaragua case grew out of the following political situation, according to the ICJ judgment of June 27, 1986:

> The United States of America is using armed force against Nicaragua and intervening in Nicaragua's internal affairs, in violation of Nicaragua's sovereignty, territorial integrity, and political independence and of the most fundamental and universally accepted principles of international law. United States armed forces and intelligence personnel have mined Nicaragua's ports and conducted air and naval attacks on targets within the territory of Nicaragua and within its territorial waters, including attacks on oil storage tanks, port facilities and merchant ships.

The United States has also created an army of more than 10,000 mercenaries – many of whom served the former dictator Anastasio Somoza Debayle – installed them in base camps in Honduras along the border with Nicaragua, trained them, paid them, supplied them with arms, ammunition, food, and medical supplies, and directed their attacks against human and economic targets inside Nicaragua, The United States has acknowledged spending more than US $70,000,000 on these illegal activities since 1981.[4]

Here we find the central ideas of failure to satisfy *jus ad bellum*: violations of "sovereignty, territorial integrity, and political independence" by one state against another state. The principles that were violated are said to be "the most fundamental and universally accepted principles of international law."

The United States responded to the charges by claiming that it was supporting a legitimate rebellion in Nicaragua – claiming that the Nicaraguan government was not a legitimate government and its sovereignty should not be recognized or protected. In addition, the United States claimed that it was acting for the collective self-defense of states in the Americas, in the Organization of American States, that were being threatened by Nicaragua's violent government. So, the case had competing claims of self-defense – Nicaragua's claim that the United States and its allies were threatening Nicaragua, and the U.S. claim that Nicaragua was threatening states in the collective security organization. Here we have a conflict between individual state self-defense and collective state self-defense, which will prove useful to examine to understand how *jus ad bellum* is conceptualized in international law.

Concerning the larger issues at play, in a preliminary decision about the mining of Nicaragua's harbor by the United States from 1984, the ICJ favorably cited Nicaragua's claim "that there is no generalized right of self-defense."[5] Here, undoubtedly, a difference between a generalized and a particularized right of self-defense was contemplated. And then in the 1986 main judgment concerning the merits of Nicaragua's case against the United States, the ICJ made several important points.

In the ICJ's 1986 Nicaragua (merits) case, the Court held that the principles concerning the use of force articulated in Article 2, section 4, of the UN Charter have a "binding character." Hence, states are required to abstain "from the threat or use of force against the territorial integrity or political independence

---

[4] *Case Concerning Military and Paramilitary Activities in and Against Nicaragua (Nicaragua v. United States of America)*, International Court of Justice, Merits, Judgment of 27 June 1986, paragraphs 6–7.

[5] *Case Concerning Military and Paramilitary Activities in and Against Nicaragua (Nicaragua v. United States of America)*, International Court of Justice, Jurisdiction of the Court and Admissibility of the Application, Judgment of 26 November 1984, paragraph 92.

of any State."[6] The Court goes on to discuss Article 51's exception to the prohibition on the use of force as a result of considerations of self-defense. The clearest case of justified use of force in self-defense is "in the case of an armed attack which has already occurred."[7] For self-defense to justify the use of force by state A against state B, there has to have been an armed attack against state A by state B. In addition, the attack must meet requirements of being of sufficient "scale and effects" to be more than a mere "frontier incident."[8]

The category of armed attack is severely limited by the Court in the Nicaragua merits case. And before self-defensive use of force can be justified, the state must have "immediately" notified the United Nations that it has been subject to an armed attack.[9] There is controversy about why the ICJ spends so much time in the Nicaragua case on this notification requirement. At least one plausible explanation is that even in cases of self-defense, a state must not act solely on its own. Requiring notification of the United Nations is not the same as requiring approval, but the requirement of notification signals that justified use of force for self-defense is not to be unilateral, or at least not beyond a temporary action taken until the UN can act.

Of perhaps even more importance is that the ICJ for the first time clearly differentiated acts that are armed attacks and acts that fall short of being armed attacks. And the ICJ stipulated that when acts fall short of being armed attacks, the attacked state does not have an inherent right to use force against the attacking state. In such cases, states have a right of nonintervention, but a right that does not rise to the level of the right of self-defense, and for which there is no inherent right to use force against the state that violates the right of nonintervention. The Court here worries that if there is an inherent right to use force against another state, such a rule would admit of "serious abuses."[10] Similarly, respect for sovereignty would also not justify the use of force that would otherwise constitute an abridgement of Article 2, section 4.

Even in cases of self-defense, the ICJ is clear that the "inherent right" of self-defense is not unlimited. Principles of international humanitarian law, which require that acts be both necessary and proportionate to the attack, are clear restrictions on even what is called an "inherent right" (in French the term used is *doit naturel* – natural right). But when such an inherent right is not applicable, "the criteria of necessity and proportionality take on a different significance."[11] The Court is clear that if the strict requirements of an armed attack are not met, then it will be much harder to satisfy necessity and proportionality requirements in justifying the use of retaliatory force. Here is the Court's summary:

---

[6] *Case Concerning Military and Paramilitary Activities in and Against Nicaragua (Nicaragua v. United States of America)*, International Court of Justice, Merits, Judgment of 27 June 1986, paragraph 188.

[7] Ibid., paragraph 194.   [8] Ibid., paragraph 195.   [9] Ibid., paragraph 200.

[10] Ibid., paragraph 202.   [11] Ibid., paragraph 237.

On the legal level, the Court cannot regard response to an intervention by Nicaragua as such a justification. While an armed attack would give rise to an entitlement of collective self-defense, a use of force of a lesser degree of gravity cannot ... produce any entitlement to collective counter-measures involving the use of force.[12]

The ICJ's interpretation of the UN Charter makes it very difficult, although not impossible, to justify recourse to war.

III   The Nuclear Weapons and Palestinian Wall Cases

In the ICJ's Nuclear Weapons case from 1996, the Court at one point seemed to go back on its earlier idea that there is no generalized right of self-defense:

The Court cannot lose sight of the fundamental right of every State to survival, and thus to its right to resort to self-defense, in accordance with Article 51 of the Charter, when its survival is at stake. Nor can it ignore the practice referred to as a "policy of deterrence," to which an appreciable section of the international community adhered for many years.[13]

Yet, earlier in this advisory opinion the Court said the following:

The entitlement to the resort to self-defense under Article 51 is subject to certain restraints. Some of these restraints are inherent in the very concept of self-defense ... [such as] the conditions of necessity and proportionality.[14]

It thus seems that states have a particularized right of self-defense but not one that is generalized and unlimited. The Article 51 right is not a right that allows any measures at all when self-defense is at issue. Indeed the Court said that "States do not have unlimited freedom of choice of means in the weapons they use."[15]

The highly controversial penultimate decision of the ICJ Nuclear Weapons case shows how tentative the Court is about its view of the justifiability of initiating war even in self-defense, and also how the Court nonetheless refuses to rule out the possibility of justification of such a war in the future. Here is the reasoning for the decision in regard to one of the issues:

By seven votes to seven, by the President casting the deciding vote,

It follows from the above-mentioned requirements that the threat or use of nuclear weapons would generally be contrary to the rules of international law applicable in armed conflict, and in particular the principles and rules of humanitarian law;

---

[12] Ibid., paragraph 249.
[13] *Legality of the Threat or Use of Nuclear Weapons*, International Court of Justice, Advisory Opinion of 8 July 1996, paragraph 96.
[14] Ibid., paragraphs 40 and 41.   [15] Ibid., paragraph 78.

However, in view of the current state of international law, and of the elements of fact at its disposal, the Court cannot conclude definitively whether the threat or use of nuclear weapons would be lawful or unlawful in an extreme circumstance of self-defense, in which the very survival of the State would be at stake.

Here the ICJ addresses the possibility that all nuclear weapons attacks are illegal but backs away from an absolute ban; instead, it says that their use is contrary to international law today even in cases of self-defense.

Another case to consider is the ICJ's 2004 Palestinian Wall case. The Court gives the same nuanced reading of Article 2, section 4, as in the two previous ICJ cases we have examined. The Court also reaffirmed the idea that "No territorial acquisition resulting from the threat or use of force shall be recognized as legal."[16] The Court then responds to Israel's contention that its building of a wall that cut into parts of Palestine was important for "military exigencies," largely related to stopping Palestinian insurgents from mounting attacks on Israeli citizens. The Court argues that the restrictions on the movement of Palestinians must meet a high threshold consideration:

It is not enough that such restrictions be directed at the ends authorized; they must be necessary for the attainment of those ends. As the Human Rights Committee put it, they "must conform to the principle of proportionality" and "must be the least intrusive instrument amongst those which might achieve the desired result."[17]

It should be noted that Article 51 was said not to be relevant to the case because Israel was not responding to a direct threat from another state.[18]

Nonetheless, in the ICJ's Wall case, the Court endorses a substantial limitation on self-defense claims, or a state of necessity, which might allow for the justified use of force or recourse to war. Even though the Court recognizes that Israel has various legitimate security demands to respond to, including "numerous indiscriminate and deadly acts of violence against its population," the construction of the wall is said not to be justified because the Court is "not convinced that the construction of the wall along the route chosen was the only means to safeguard the interests of Israel against the peril which it has invoked as its justification for that construction." Notice that the ICJ here sets a high threshold for satisfying the principle of necessity, even in a case where self-defense of Israel's citizens is at stake. It is not enough for a state to claim that it is necessary that it take a certain aggressive action.

[16] *Legal Consequences of the Construction of a Wall in the Occupied Palestinian Territory,* International Court of Justice, Advisory Opinion of July 9, 2004, paragraph 87.
[17] Ibid., paragraph 136.   [18] Ibid., paragraph 139.

IV   Prosecuting Individuals for Violations of *Jus ad Bellum*

In international criminal law, prosecutions of individuals for *jus ad bellum* violations have occurred, although these prosecutions have been rare. At least in part this is because of the difficulty of seeing how an individual could be guilty for committing what is really a crime of a state, the crime of aggression as the crime against *jus ad bellum* has been known since the Nuremberg trials. When we consider prosecutions of individuals for initiating unjust or aggressive war, matters get more complicated – we should be more lenient than if we are considering whether the state itself should be subject to sanctions. The reason for this is well stated in the Ministries Case at Nuremberg:

Obviously, no man may be condemned for fighting in what he believes is the defense of his native land, even though his belief be mistaken. Nor can he be expected to undertake an independent investigation to determine whether or not the cause for which he fights is the result of an aggressive act of his own government. One can be guilty only where knowledge of aggression in fact exists, and it is not sufficient that he have suspicions that the war is aggressive. Any other test of guilt would involve a standard of conduct both impracticable and unjust.[19]

The American Military Tribunal sitting at Nuremberg held that we should not expect individual defendants to be responsible for doing a full-scale investigation to determine whether their states are engaging in aggressive or defensive war.

Nonetheless, in this respect consider the case of Admiral Doenitz who was successfully prosecuted at Nuremberg for the crime of aggression. Doenitz was, by the end of World War II, the highest-ranking naval officer in the Third Reich, and met regularly with Adolph Hitler to plan aggressive naval operations against Allied countries in the final years of the war. Doenitz never denied his role in the war effort and boasted that he shared with Hitler the goals of that war, including the subjugation of Germany's neighbors. In considering his case, I focus on the act requirement of the crime of aggression, as well as possible defenses to that element.

Doenitz and Admiral Erich Raeder were the only naval officers tried before the International Military Tribunal at Nuremberg. As was well documented, the Nazi regime used the Navy as an integral and essential element in the waging of aggressive war against its neighbors as well as against Great Britain and the United States. Indeed, the heads of the Navy were some of Hitler's closest advisors during the war. Doenitz was also responsible for one of the Nazis' most effective weapons during the war, the development of the U-boats, submarines designed with faster engines and better snorkels than in any

---

[19] "The Ministries Case Judgment," *Trials of War Criminals Before Nuremberg Military Tribunals Under Control Council Law No. 10*, vol. 14, p. 337.

other navy, which operated in packs in attacking military convoys and merchant fleets. Doenitz commanded the submarine division of the Nazi Navy at the outbreak of the war and played an integral part in the initiation and waging of that war.[20] But one of the central questions in the trial was whether or not this participation was sufficient to establish the *actus reus* element in his prosecution for the crime of waging aggressive war.

We can divide this question into two parts: first, what were the acts that Doenitz is accused of committing that contributed significantly to the war effort; and second, what considerations made these acts guilty ones? Doenitz's case is seemingly an easy one for the prosecution since there is little if any disagreement about what Doenitz did during the war. I here confine myself to his acts of participation in the war of aggression rather than the alleged war crimes perpetrated by Admiral Doenitz.[21] Doenitz did not deny that he gave speeches regularly exhorting the men under his command to pursue the aims of war as vigilantly as they could, and to do so to achieve the aims of the Third Reich. Doenitz did not deny that he had indeed sent U-boats to destroy military convoys and even merchant fleets in the Atlantic. And Doenitz did not deny that he continued to wage war long after it became clear that the war was hopeless and that Germany could not achieve its aims.[22]

Three distinct acts were thought to link Doenitz to the state aggression of the Nazi regime. First, the prosecution charged that Doenitz played a major role in directing the aggressive war by ordering U-boats to attack neutral ships. Second, the prosecution claimed that Doenitz acted in a way that participated in the war of aggression by accepting his appointment as commander in chief of the Navy. And third, the prosecution contended that Doenitz conspired with others to plan the aggressive war, at least after his commission as commander in chief. In all three charges, Doenitz's acts are characterized as satisfying the *actus reus* element of the crime against peace and the waging of aggressive war; in all three charges, as we just briefly saw, Doenitz denied that his involvement constituted aggression.

Let us examine the prosecution's claim that Doenitz committed guilty acts by ordering attacks on neutral ships and hence engaged in acts that directly participated in the waging of aggressive war, and thus violated the conditions of *jus ad bellum*. It was well known that using military ships to attack neutral ships was an act of war. And the prosecution claimed that Doenitz was actively engaged in "building up the U-boat arm"[23] so that "it can fight and strike."[24] There is also evidence presented that Doenitz ordered U-boats to move into

---

[20] See the description of Karl Doenitz in Eugene Davidson, *The Trial of the Germans*, New York: Macmillan, 1966 [reprinted by University of Missouri Press, 1977], pp. 392–426.

[21] Doenitz was tried and convicted of war crimes, such as ordering German sailors not to rescue enemy sailors whose ships were sinking, and in some cases of ordering his sailors to fire on these enemy sailors in life rafts.

[22] Davidson, *The Trial of the Germans*, pp. 415–19.   [23] Vol. 4, p. 229.   [24] Ibid., p. 230.

proximity of England and to sink British ships and that these ships left their harbor long before war was declared. This evidence is supposedly meant to show that Doenitz was indeed directing his ships to sink British ships as part of the first stage of war against Great Britain in 1939.[25] The idea seems to be that Doenitz's forces were the cutting edge of the first strike of the aggressive war against Great Britain, and that his commands were an essential component of that first strike.

The second charge was that Doenitz "took part in the planning and execution of aggressive war against Poland, Norway, and Denmark."[26] But what specific acts did Doenitz commit? According to the prosecution, Doenitz received an order from Admiral Raeder, then commander in chief of the Navy, for the invasion of Poland, the sixth copy of which was delivered to Doenitz. Doenitz is then accused of having issued an order to U-boats to carry out the general order for the invasion of Poland.[27] In addition, documents were presented to show that Doenitz sent memos to Raeder concerning the best way to invade Norway from the sea, which included the flying of the British flag on German U-boats until the boats had landed.[28] Here we have Doenitz seemingly actively engaged in the planning phase of the aggressive war against Norway, as well as against Poland.

Third, the conspiracy charge mainly concerned *mens rea* rather than *actus reus*. But this charge also concerns *actus reus* in a sense, namely, that some of Doenitz's acts can be seen as sufficient participation in aggressive war to make him liable since he was aware that these acts, in conjunction with others, would constitute aggression. The chief evidence brought against Doenitz to establish the conspiracy charge was that he, along with other high-ranking members of Hitler's staff, met regularly and discussed plans to invade Poland and Norway, for instance. The prosecution contended that Doenitz not only knew about the plan to invade Norway but also actually participated in that plan as well as in its execution.

There may be a just cause to engage in some wars that turn out to be aggressive because of how first strike and provocation are understood. This is relatively clear in cases of contemporary warfare such as the use of long-range missiles. States trying to defend against the possible use of long-range missiles may not be able to wait for an imminent threat and hence may act aggressively but may nonetheless act on a just cause for war in a broadened construal of just cause. We might even wonder whether there is a tight connection between what counts as aggressive war and what counts as just cause for initiating war. If aggression means something like not based in self-defense, then as we will see certain wars may have a just cause, such as a humanitarian cause, and are hence justified and yet aggressive.

---

[25] Ibid., p. 231.   [26] Ibid., p. 230.   [27] Ibid.   [28] Ibid., p. 231.

Humanitarian wars fall into the class of those wars that in some cases could be aggressive, but for which in some other cases it might be appropriate to say that there is a just cause sufficient for not allowing prosecutions to go forward. At least in part this could be because of the ambiguity or lack of clarity in the idea of defense of others. Defense of others could include not merely states that have been invaded, but subgroups within a state that are being persecuted. And there is evidence that the United Nations has sometimes discussed events in just this way. Indeed, the UN's at least tacit acceptance of NATO's war waged against Serbia to stop it from persecuting its Kosovar Albanian minority population is a case in point. We should not expect even most military and political leaders to be able to determine such close calls.

One proposal is that "just cause" be easier to prove, and aggression be correspondingly harder to prove, in international criminal proceedings against individual defendants than in discussion of possible sanctions against states for illegal use of force. In particular, in criminal proceedings I would widen the understanding of just cause to include any basis for going to war covered by most instances of defense of self or others, whereas I would restrict the idea in its use outside of international criminal law only to individual or collective self-defense, not to consideration of defense of others.

Very serious problems of knowledge concern whether it is true that a state is in need of military help when the state in question is not one's own, but a state in another part of the world. By widening the idea of just cause for prosecutions and narrowing it for state sanctions, we can better deal with the hard cases, where provocation occurs, or where the confrontation of terrorist groups or other groups causing a humanitarian crisis calls for intervention in the form of war. These cases are still hotly debated in international law, as well as in Just War theory.

V International Law and Just War Theory

As in the international law of *jus ad bellum*, in contemporary Just War theory self-defense is also seen as the main "just cause" to which one can appeal to show that a war is a just war and that initiating it is justified. The main example used today is of a country that is invaded by another country with malicious motives. War fought in defense of innocent others is often also accepted as a just war, but there is, as in international law, debate about whether and when such wars are to count as just.

A second similarity is that the responsibilities of individuals, rather than institutions such as the state, are increasingly at the center of the debates over war. The rise of international criminal law has propelled the individual defendant and victim into the forefront of issues in international law. This has effectively been a sea change in that in prior times the interactions of states were the main focus of international law, as the name (inter-national) implies.

Since Nuremberg, the idea has been that the best way to deter illegal wars is to deter the individuals who typically start those wars.

Just as international criminal law has arisen to focus on individual culpability, so in Just War theory there has been a strong turn toward individual liability for waging unjust war. This has also been somewhat of a sea change, since earlier Just War theory often relieved the individual of blame and focused on the blameworthiness of the state that starts an immoral war. This approach is often connected to the advance of human rights, as has also been true in international law. The rights of individuals to defend themselves, and the liabilities of those who abridge the rights of others, have been of paramount concern especially among the so-called revisionist Just War theorists.

And a third similarity is that the nonlethal use of force is clearly preferred to war, so much so that humanitarian intervention is viewed somewhat skeptically. And while many theorists defend wars of humanitarian intervention, war fought in defense of other states is much less acceptable than war fought in defense of one's own state. In international law, many today see wars of humanitarian intervention as violations of the "sovereignty, territorial integrity, and political independence" (to quote the Nicaragua opinion) of the target state, even though it may be oppressing its own citizens.

In Just War theory, starting a war so as to aid others is regarded somewhat more positively than in international law. But controversy certainly continues about how wars of humanitarian intervention should be regarded from the moral point of view that characterizes Just War theory. Here issues of last resort are much more difficult to determine when the intervention is for the sake of others' defense rather than for one's own self-defense.

Fourth, one of the main points of disagreement between contemporary Just War theorists and international law scholars concerns the relevance of sovereignty to their debates about war. Many contemporary moral and political philosophers argue that sovereignty only matters if the state in question is a protector, not a violator, of human rights. Sovereignty in and of itself is morally neutral. From this standpoint, the Just War theorists have more trouble than do international law scholars in defending even most cases of state self-defense since so many states are not protectors of human rights on balance.

In international law, lethal force may be used for the collective self-defense of a group of states, or for the single defense of just one state. Loss of sovereignty for a state is like loss of life for an individual, so some wars are legal in *jus ad bellum* terms that are not needed to protect against the loss of human life. But lethal force does still have to satisfy necessity and proportionality constraints.[29]

Another debate that could be constructed between Just War theorists and international law scholars concerns what follows from a finding that a person

---

[29] See Chapter 14, this volume, by Adil Haque, on this topic.

has started or participated in starting an unjust war. Revisionist Just War theorists argue that a person participating in an unjust war is liable to be killed. Culpability is different from liability, to be sure, but there is nonetheless a loss of the right not to be attacked or killed on the part of the person who starts or participates in starting an unjust war.

In international criminal law, by contrast to Just War theory, those who start or participate in starting an illegal war are subject to severe punishment – but this stops short of capital punishment. In the international law of force, lethal force may be used but a necessity condition must be satisfied. For some Just War theorists who still subscribe to the principle of last resort, the two traditions come closer together than if a narrower meaning is given to necessity.

Some disagreement exists about whether or not international law and Just War theory have common roots, a different question than whether they have overlapping positions and sympathies. Some argue that both modern forms of Just War theory and of international law originate in the writing of Hugo Grotius in the early seventeenth century. But for Just War theorists this is only true if one is discussing secular Just War theory. International law scholars often say that until there were full-fledged nation-states, in the middle of the nineteenth century, international law properly conceived did not arise.

Yet, there is no denying that both of these theoretical and practical perspectives have borrowed from each other over the centuries – indeed one sign of this is that the terminology is often the same. And it has been common for many Just War theorists to rely on real cases drawn from international law, just as it is beginning to be true that some international law scholars are drawing on the hypothetical examples employed by Just War theorists. All in all, there is mutual influence and common positions taken such that it makes sense to look at international law in Just War terms, as we will continue to do in the other chapters of this section of the *Handbook*.

13 The Basic Structure of *Jus in Bello*

Jens David Ohlin

Introduction

International law imposes restrictions on the conduct of hostilities in warfare – restrictions that are typically referred to as *jus in bello*. The term *jus in bello* refers both to ethical constraints which are the domain of philosophers and legal constraints which are the domain of international lawyers.[1] The present chapter seeks to elucidate and critique the basic structure of *jus in bello* in international law to see how much the current legal regime embodies deeper principles emanating from Just War theory.

Section I discusses the basic building blocks of *jus in bello* in international law and explains its relationship to *jus ad bellum* and international human rights law (IHRL). It then outlines the key principles and prohibitions of *jus in bello* and explains which actions are lawful – and which are prohibited – under international law. At issue are the core principles of necessity, humanity, and proportionality, as well as more specific prohibitions against particular tactics and methods of warfare, including perfidy and causing unnecessary suffering. Section II then outlines the enforcement mechanisms available to ensure that *jus in bello* restrictions are followed in practice. The enforcement strategies include criminal prosecutions when breaches occur, but other non-penal mechanisms are sometimes equally important. Finally, Section III shifts towards normative critique by outlining the basic requirements that a system of *jus in bello* ought to embody, and then testing the current legal regime against that ideal picture. The key requirements that will be defended include transparency, reciprocity, reducing suffering for civilians, and reducing suffering for combatants. The resulting evaluation suggests that today's international law is morally defensible, although incremental alterations to the regime are both permitted and welcomed. By logical extension, this entails the conclusion that calls for a radical reworking of *jus in bello* are either unnecessary or misguided. The resulting conclusion paints the picture of a modestly more humane horizon to which international law should direct itself.

---

[1] In the domain of international law, *jus in bello* is sometimes referred to as international humanitarian law (IHL) or the law of armed conflict (LOAC).

I The Current Legal Regime

The centerpiece of the current legal regime is the conceptual independence of *jus in bello* and *jus ad bellum*. The *jus ad bellum* regime determines whether or not the state's decision to exercise military force is legitimate. Generally speaking, with few exceptions, military force is permitted only when exercised in self-defence pursuant to Article 51 of the UN Charter, or when exercised pursuant to a binding Security Council authorization, under Chapter VII of the UN Charter, as part of a collective effort to restore international peace and security. These are the only two exceptions to the general prohibition on the use of military force codified in Article 2 of the UN Charter.[2] *Jus ad bellum* determinations are separate from the *jus in bello* legal analysis, so that both the aggressor state and the victim state are subject to the same legal restrictions regarding the conduct of warfare. Consequently, it is not necessary to first resolve any *jus ad bellum* controversies before turning to *jus in bello* specifics. Even the victim state must abide by the laws of war in fighting off an unjust invasion; conversely, the aggressor state is not prohibited from using the same lawful tactics during its illegal war of aggression. As is discussed in greater detail in Section III, the conceptual independence of *jus ad bellum* and *jus in bello* promotes the goals of transparency and reciprocity.

The relationship between *jus in bello* and human rights law is more complicated to articulate, in part because the exact status of their interplay is still deeply contested among lawyers today.[3] There are several different models for understanding the relationship between the two bodies of law. The first might be called field pre-emption, which would suggest that human rights law does not apply during situations of armed conflict, and in its place is substituted a legal regime, international humanitarian law (IHL), specifically designed to regulate the behaviour of belligerents and to protect civilians from the horrors of warfare.[4] The second model might be called rule pre-emption, which is more limited and suggests that the *field* of human rights law continues to apply during armed conflict – indeed running parallel to IHL – but that in the case of a conflict between two particular rules of IHRL and IHL, the more specific rules of IHL should govern.[5]

---

[2] The prohibition against the use of force is recognized in customary law as one of the pillars of the international legal system, going at least as far back as the Peace of Westphalia and has obtained the status of *jus cogens*. For a discussion, see Thomas Weatherall, *Jus Cogens: International Law and Social Contract*, Cambridge: Cambridge University Press, 2015, p. 224.

[3] See Jens David Ohlin, "Introduction: The Inescapable Collision" in *Theoretical Boundaries of Armed Conflict and Human Rights*, ed. Jens David Ohlin, Cambridge: Cambridge University Press, 2016, p. 4.

[4] See Oona Hathaway et al., "Which Law Governs During Armed Conflict? The Relationship Between International Humanitarian Law and Human Rights Law," *Minnesota Law Review* 96 (2012) no. 6, p. 1895.

[5] See Marko Milanovic, "The Lost Origins of *Lex Specialis*: Rethinking the Relationship between Human Rights and International Humanitarian Law," in *Theoretical Boundaries*, ed. Ohlin, pp. 78, 103.

This model is sometimes referred to as *lex specialis*, after the legal maxim *lex specialis derogate legi generali*, a loose canon of interpretation that suggests that the more specific law, tailored or designed for the situation, is usually crafted with the goal that it will prevail over more basic and general legal pronouncements.[6] The final model is a rather extreme one: that IHL and IHRL remain in force and should be co-applied, always, without any submission of human rights norms to the primacy of the laws of war. I shall not comment on the validity of this last model, except to say that one thing the model must do is demonstrate how the human right not to be killed is consistent with the privilege of combatancy that allows soldiers to kill each other during armed conflict.[7]

Part of the problem with harmonizing IHL and IHRL stems from the fact that the two regulatory regimes arguably have different normative foundations, though there are some bridges and commonalities between them. Human rights law is based on the concept of dignity, in the Kantian sense of that term, and codifies the inherent moral worth that attaches to each human being, person, or rational agent. The codification of these rights was solidified in multilateral conventions that codify promises among states to ensure and protect these rights.[8] In contrast, IHL is based on the goal of reducing suffering in war through reciprocal constraints, between belligerent states, to limit methods of warfare. One could argue that civilians are protected under IHL because their right to life must be respected, thus making human rights the more primary conceptual foundation for *jus in bello*. But as the analysis in this chapter demonstrates, the actual law in this area complicates the picture tremendously. Civilians can be killed as collateral damage; more importantly, soldiers are human beings yet *jus in bello* permits their summary killing. Whatever the conceptual ground is for *jus in bello*, the most that can be said is that it is buoyed by human rights principles.[9] But it would be inaccurate to label human rights law as more primary than the law of war; the latter arguably has a

---

[6] This issue is discussed in Marko Milanovic, "Norm Conflicts, International Humanitarian Law, and Human Rights Law" in *International Humanitarian Law and International Human Rights Law*, ed. Orna Ben-Naftali, Oxford: Oxford University Press, 2011, p. 98.

[7] Some scholars have suggested that the right not to be killed applies to arbitrary killings, and that killings performed consistent with the laws of war would be non-arbitrary and therefore not in violation of human rights law. This solution is only available in cases where the human right to life is limited to arbitrary deprivations, such as the International Covenant on Civil and Political Rights. In contrast, the European Convention on Human Rights does not include the term "arbitrarily" in its Article 2 right-to-life provision. See Gloria Gaggioli and Robert Kolb, "A Right to Life in Armed Conflicts? The Contribution of the European Court of Human Rights," *Israel Yearbook of Human Rights* 37 (2007) no. 115, pp. 134–36.

[8] For a history of the modern human rights movement, see Samuel Moyn, *The Last Utopia: Human Rights in History*, Cambridge: Harvard University Press, 2012.

[9] David Luban argues that as a historical matter, IHL and IHRL flow from different sources, but that "human rights thinking" has now influenced the current state of IHL. See David Luban, "Human Rights Thinking and the Laws of War," in *Theoretical Boundaries*, ed. Ohlin, pp. 48–50.

separate conceptual justification based in a quasi-consequentialist (or perhaps instrumental) desire to reduce suffering in war, which distinguishes it from the deontological foundation for human rights. The most that can be said is that the rules of IHL, if complied with, will reduce the number of unjust killings (from the vantage point of human rights) in war, without necessarily eliminating all of them.[10] IHL is a pragmatic enterprise of suffering *reduction*, as opposed to suffering *elimination*. IHRL has much loftier ambitions.

IHL applies to armed conflicts, regardless of whether they are classified as international or non-international armed conflicts. International armed conflicts (IACs) involve the use of force between nation-states. In contrast, non-international armed conflicts (NIACs) involve conflicts that are "not of an international character." The paradigmatic example of a NIAC is a civil war or other internal conflict between a government and a rebel force; typically the rebel force is fighting for control and aspires to rule the state as its government, either over the entire territory of the state or some subset of it. However, NIAC has other possible flavours. For example, one might involve a conflict between two non-state actors, such as two rebel forces fighting each other. The most controversial flavour is an extra-territorial NIAC between a state government and a non-state terrorist organization whose members are located on the territory of a third state. Although one might consider this an IAC because it crosses international boundaries, most lawyers instead refer to this as a NIAC because one party is a non-state actor.[11] In any event, the rules of IHL apply regardless of how the conflict is classified, though the *codified* rules for NIACs are relatively sparse.[12] However, almost all legal scholars concede that most of the IHL rules regarding IACs now apply, as a matter of customary international law, to NIACs as well, a process of harmonisation that was surely accelerated by the jurisprudence of the ad hoc tribunal for the former Yugoslavia.

Turning now to the core proscriptions of IHL, the key legal concepts include necessity and proportionality. The principle of necessity is defined broadly in IHL and operates more as a license than as a constraint.[13] It permits soldiers to kill enemy soldiers at will because killing the enemy is, as a whole, "necessary" for winning the war. In this sense, international law's use of the term "necessity" is quite far from our common-sense notion of unnecessary killings. Our gut intuition is that an unnecessary killing is any killing that is not absolutely

---

[10] On this issue, see Adil Haque, "Laws for War," in *Theoretical Boundaries*, ed. Ohlin, p. 44 (concluding that IHL can "serve soldiers well by helping them indirectly avoid objectively impermissible killing").

[11] See *Hamdan v. Rumsfeld*, 548 U.S. 557, 630 (2006) (applying Common Article 3 to the armed conflict with al-Qaeda).

[12] The IHL rules applicable to NIAC are contained in Common Article 3 of the Geneva Conventions, sometimes referred to as the "Miniature Convention," and Additional Protocol II to the Geneva Conventions.

[13] Francis Lieber, "Instructions for the Government of Armies of the United States in the Field," General Order No. 100, article 60 (24 April 1863) [hereinafter Lieber Code].

necessary to win the war. However, international law generally evaluates particular tactics, not specific incidents, and views the killing of enemy soldiers as generally within the ambit of the principle of necessity.[14] In other words, the principle of necessity in international law does not require soldiers to stand back and ask whether every battlefield killing meets a strict necessity requirement and is truly necessary to win the war. Finally, it was once thought that necessity could also operate as an exception to generally applicable prohibitions, so that extreme actions could be committed if they were required by military necessity.[15] This understanding of necessity – as an exception to generally applicable prohibitions – has fallen by the wayside over the past century and generally does not apply today.[16]

The principle of proportionality governs the killing of non-combatants during military operations. Civilians can never be made the object of attack, though it is permissible for them to be killed as collateral damage during an attack against a lawful military target, provided that civilian casualties are not disproportionate to the value of the anticipated military advantage gained from striking the primary military target.[17] In applying the rule of proportionality, there is little formal or binding guidance about how to weigh the value of military advantage and then engage in the required balancing that the rule presupposes, though there are plenty of proposals for how the balancing and weighing should be conducted.[18] Complicating matters is that there is grave uncertainty and disagreement over what counts as an intentional or non-intentional attack against a group of civilians – terms that have a particular technical meaning in criminal law that is not always stable across diverse legal cultures.[19] It is particularly controversial how to treat targeting mistakes that are reckless, for example, attacking forces who believe they are attacking a legitimate military target but in fact are bombing civilians and their mistake is reckless (in the sense that they were aware of the risk of mistake but pursued the

---

[14] For more discussion of the principle of necessity, see David Luban, "Military Necessity and the Cultures of Military Law," *Leiden Journal of International Law* 26 (2013) no. 2, pp. 341–42.

[15] See John Fabian Witt, *Lincoln's Code: The Laws of War in American History*, New York: Free Press, 2012, p. 184 (noting that Francis Lieber believed that although military necessity could justify almost anything, torture was beyond the pale).

[16] See Scott Horton, "Military Necessity, Torture, and the Criminality of Lawyers," in *International Prosecution of Human Rights Crimes* , eds. Wolfgang Kaleck et. al., New York: Springer, 2007, pp. 169–83.

[17] Yoram Dinstein, *The Conduct of Hostilities under the Law of International Armed Conflict*, 3rd edn, Cambridge: Cambridge University Press, 2016, p. 154.

[18] One example is contained in Adil Haque, "A Theory of Jus in Bello Proportionality," in *Weighing Lives in War: Combatants & Civilians*, eds. Jens David Ohlin, Claire Finkelstein, and Larry May, Oxford: Oxford University Press, 2017, p. 188 (arguing that "incidental harm on civilians is objectively proportionate only if it prevents substantially greater harm to the attacking force or to its civilians over the remainder of the conflict").

[19] For an extensive discussion of this issue, see Jens David Ohlin, "Was the Kunduz Hospital Attack a War Crime?" *Opinio Juris* (1 May 2016) (including comments).

attack anyway).[20] In some legal cultures, intent includes recklessness, while in other legal cultures intentional conduct and reckless mistakes are viewed as different categories.[21] What is certain is that Additional Protocol I now imposes on states the obligation to take all feasible measures to reduce collateral damage – a legal requirement that arguably goes well beyond the older prohibition against causing disproportionate collateral damage to civilians.[22]

Civilians are not the only ones protected by the laws of war. Soldiers are also protected when they are *hors de combat* either from injury or capture. The basic idea is simple: captured soldiers in the custody of the enemy, or injured soldiers receiving medical treatment, are outside the zone of combat and become the functional equivalent of protected civilians again. The rule is obvious although the philosophical rationale can be expressed in different ways, and in many ways is the mirror image of the principle of necessity, which permits summary killing of soldiers in all other situations. One possibility, articulated by Walzer, is that soldiers are subject to summary killing because their training and role in the "war convention" make them dangerous, that is, agents of killing and death.[23] The "war convention" is Walzer's phrase, since adopted by the philosophical literature, to refer to the basic structure of international law's regulatory enterprise for war. Soldiers on both sides of the conflict are subject to summary killing, but civilians are immune from direct targeting, regardless of whether they belong to the just or unjust side of the conflict. In that sense, the war convention creates a division of labour between civilians and soldiers, where soldiers gain the "right" to engage in combatancy but also acquire a reciprocal liability to be attacked at any time. If Walzer's argument that soldiers are dangerous is correct (it is deeply contested in the philosophical literature),[24] then it would stand to reason that soldiers regain their right to life once they are no longer threatening or dangerous. And soldiers who are detained by the enemy or receiving medical treatment are paradigmatic examples of soldiers who are not threatening.

Finally, *jus in bello* restricts tactics and methods of warfare. Perfidy is outlawed – a prohibition that stands in need of conceptual justification. The classic

---

[20] As an example, see Matthew Rosenberg, "Pentagon Details Chain of Errors in Strike on Afghan Hospital," *New York Times* (29 April 2016), available at www.nytimes.com/2016/04/30/world/asia/afghanistan-doctors-without-borders-hospital-strike.html?_r=0

[21] This issue is examined in greater detail in Jens David Ohlin, "Targeting and the Concept of Intent," *Michigan Journal of International Law* 35 (2013) no. 1: 79–130.

[22] Protocol Additional to the Geneva Conventions of 12 August 1949, and Relating to the Protection of Victims of International Armed Conflicts, 8 June 1977, 1125 U.N.T.S. 3 (hereinafter cited as Additional Protocol I), art 57 ("take all feasible precautions in the choice of means and methods of attack with a view to avoiding, and in any event to minimizing, incidental loss of civilian life, injury to civilians and damage to civilian objects"). Although the United States is not a state party to Additional Protocol I, most scholars view this provision as representative of customary law.

[23] Michael Walzer, *Just and Unjust Wars*, New York: Basic Books, 2000, p. 145.

[24] For a discussion of the various objections, see Gabriella Blum, "The Dispensable Lives of Soldiers," *Journal of Legal Analysis* 2 (2010) no. 1: 69–124.

example of perfidious killing is feigning civilian or protected status to lure the enemy into confidence but then betraying that confidence by killing them. Examples include pretending to be a civilian, pretending to be injured and *hors de combat*, and pretending to surrender – all as ruses to engage in lethal action with the element of surprise. The obvious and most frequent philosophical justification for the ban on perfidious killing is a simple consequentialist one: if soldiers are worried that "civilians" and soldiers who appear to be *hors de combat* are acting perfidiously, no one will be willing to give them the benefit of the doubt and refrain from killing them.[25] The result will be a radical increase in lethal violence against civilians. Under this rationale, the individuals most harmed by perfidious attacks are the future civilians who might be endangered by the mistrust that will exist between them and soldiers who come upon them and worry that their protected status is illusory. However, there is also a deeper philosophical position, this one articulated by Kant: "dishonest stratagems" make the return to peace more difficult because their use will carry over after the war.[26] Kant's unhappiness with lying is no surprise here, given his views on the subject, although its effect on the law of war is a bit more surprising.[27] However, Lieber understood his Kant, was well versed in "Perpetual Peace" specifically, and adopted it as the rationale for the prohibition on perfidious killing when it came time to author his code.[28]

Finally, the prohibition of weaponry falls into two broad categories. The first is weapons that cause unnecessary suffering, which generally means that some aspect of the weapon increases suffering to the victim without increasing its lethality.[29] In those cases, use of the weapon is simply designed to make the enemy soldier suffer more – a result that could only be motivated by vengeance or sadism, neither of which are appropriate motivations in warfare. However, suffering that is merely incidental to lethality is never considered unnecessary, unless the attacking force has at its disposal an equally efficacious method of warfare that causes less pain.[30] As a matter of normative theory, one might ask whether soldiers should be required to take on reasonable risks in their use of

---

[25] For example, see Neil C. Rowe, "Perfidy in Cyberwarfare," in *Routledge Handbook of Ethics and War: Just War Theory in the 21st Century*, eds. Fritz Allhoff, Nicholas G. Evans, and Adam Henschke, New York: Routledge, 2013, p. 399 ("the key casualty of perfidy is trust").

[26] Immanuel Kant, "Perpetual Peace: A Philosophical Sketch," in *Kant: Political Writings*, ed. Hans Reiss, trans. H.B. Nisbet, Cambridge: Cambridge University Press, 1970, p. 93.

[27] See Immanuel Kant, "On a Supposed Right to Lie from Altruistic Motives," in *Immanuel Kant: Critique of Practical Reason and Other Writings in Moral Philosophy*, trans. Lewis White Beck, Chicago: University of Chicago Press, 1949.

[28] Witt, *Lincoln's Code*, p. 182. For a more in-depth discussion of this point, see Jens David Ohlin, "Sharp Wars Are Brief," in *Weighing Lives in War*, eds. Ohlin, May, and Finkelstein.

[29] Additional Protocol I, article 35 ("It is prohibited to employ weapons, projectiles and material and methods of warfare of a nature to cause superfluous injury or unnecessary suffering").

[30] For a discussion of this issue, see Gary D. Solis, *The Law of Armed Conflict*, 2nd edn, Cambridge: Cambridge University Press, 2016, pp. 291–92. See also *Advisory Opinion on the Legality of the Threat or Use of Nuclear Weapons* [1996] ICJ Rep. 226, para. 78 (noting that unnecessary suffering involves a harm "greater than that avoidable to achieve legitimate military objectives").

alternate weapons that cause less suffering – a viable moral position – but such a norm is probably not one that can fairly be read into the current text of today's law.

The second category involves weapons that are *malum prohibitum* – usually explicitly by a negotiated convention. Examples include chemical weapons, biological weapons, and, on some accounts, nuclear weapons.[31] Landmines and cluster munitions have also been the subject of international campaigns for prohibition.[32] Usually the rationale for the ban is that the weapon is inherently indiscriminate or could harm the environment in ways that will impact the civilian population. For example, it is nearly impossible to program a biological or chemical weapon to target only enemy soldiers but spare all civilians. Moreover, given the unpredictable ways that these weapons spread, it may be difficult or impossible to ensure that civilian deaths are not disproportionate. However, instead of simply relying on the principle of proportionality to do its regulatory work, international lawyers instead take a more categorical approach.

The case of nuclear weapons requires special note. The International Court of Justice ruled in its 1996 Advisory Opinion that the use of nuclear weapons was per se illegal under international law because the weapons were inherently indiscriminate; that is, their use would inevitably harm civilians as well as legitimate military targets.[33] The decision prompted a fierce dissent from Judge Schwebel, who argued that tactical nuclear weapons on isolated battlefields, or in the ocean, might be detonated in a controlled manner in an area where civilians were not located.[34] In such situations the weapons would not be indiscriminate nor would they violate the principle of proportionality. Furthermore, Judge Schwebel took aim at the court's claim that *threatening* to use nuclear weapons – a key element of Cold War and post–Cold War geopolitical strategy – was also a violation of *jus in bello*. In particular, Schwebel noted that American threats (albeit insincere threats) to use nuclear weapons during the Gulf War as a response to a possible Iraqi deployment of biological or chemical weapons, successfully dissuaded Saddam Hussein from using his biological and chemical weapons.[35] This ought to be counted as a great success rather than a violation of *jus in bello*. Finally, the court refused to extend its analysis to cases of so-called existential self-defence, that is, whether a nation is permitted to use or threaten to use nuclear weapons to defend itself from existential destruction.[36]

---

[31] See e.g. Convention on the Prohibition of the Development, Production, Stockpiling and Use of Chemical Weapons, Geneva, 3 September 1992, 1974 U.N.T.S. 45.

[32] Convention on the Prohibition of the Use, Stockpiling, Production and Transfer of Anti-Personnel Mines and on Their Destruction, 18 September 1997, 2056 U.N.TS. 211.

[33] *Advisory Opinion on the Legality of the Threat or Use of Nuclear Weapons*, [1996] ICJ Rep. 226.

[34] Dissenting Opinion of Vice-President Schwebel, p. 320.   [35] Ibid, p. 324.

[36] *Advisory Opinion on the Legality of the Threat or Use of Nuclear Weapons*, p. 266 ("However, in view of the current state of international law, and of the elements of fact at its disposal, the

Perhaps what is most special about the current state of *jus in bello* is not what is prohibited but what is still permitted. Killing the enemy, indeed killing a massive number of enemy soldiers, is permitted. Also, killing civilians is also permitted as long as it is under the rubric of collateral damage and does not violate the principle of proportionality or other requirements to take feasible precautions to reduce collateral damage. Finally, some other behaviour, such as spying, is not technically a violation of the international law of war, though to the extent that spying is conducted by an unprivileged belligerent, it can be prosecuted as a violation of domestic law and – nothing in international law prevents a state from proceeding domestically against an enemy spy caught during the course of the armed conflict.[37] This might have some practical consequences for where and how a spy is prosecuted – before a military commission or a regular civilian court.

The overall picture that emerges from *jus in bello* is an activity – the conduct of war – that is only lightly regulated by international law. The goal of *jus in bello* is to make war more humane, for combatants and civilians, but the behaviour of the belligerents is not so heavily restricted as to make it impossible for them to pursue the war effort. The restriction of war per se, at least under some circumstances, is the conceptual purview of the *jus ad bellum* regime, not *jus in bello*; the latter legal regime accepts, as a basic fact, that the belligerents are engaged in an armed conflict and that killing is an integral part of that endeavour.[38]

II   Enforcement

We now turn to the question of enforcement, perhaps one of the thorniest problems in the law of war. Much attention is given to international criminal prosecutions, justifiably so, but the question of enforcement is much larger

Court cannot conclude definitively whether the threat or use of nuclear weapons would be lawful or unlawful in an extreme circumstance of self-defence, in which the very survival of a State would be at stake"). This final passage in the opinion was confusing, in part because it is unclear if it is a statement regarding *jus in bello* (the subject of the rest of the opinion) or rather self-defence under *jus ad bellum*, which is a different topic. Also, even the scope of the exception is a bit unclear: does it apply to situations in which the nation will be physically destroyed and all of its inhabitants will be killed in a genocide, or does it also refer to situations where the life of the "nation" is at stake because the state will be defeated but its occupants will survive to life under occupation? These are quite different factual scenarios.

[37] See Richard Baxter, "So-Called 'Unprivileged Belligerency': Spies, Guerrillas, and Saboteurs," in *Humanizing the Laws of War: Selected Writings of Richard Baxter*, eds. Detlev F. Vagts et. al., Oxford: Oxford University Press, 2013, pp. 37, 44.

[38] It may be the case that pacifism is a legitimate answer to this moral tension. However, whatever the merits of pacifism as a moral doctrine, it is not deeply interwoven into the fabric of international law. For a discussion of pacifism, see Larry May, *Contingent Pacifism: Revisiting Just War Theory*, Cambridge: Cambridge University Press, 2015.

than prosecutions before international tribunals. This section canvasses and evaluates the different options for *jus in bello* enforcement.

A number of ad hoc international tribunals, most notably those for Rwanda and the former Yugoslavia, have or have had jurisdiction to prosecute violations of the laws and customs of warfare. In addition, the permanent International Criminal Court (ICC) includes jurisdiction for war crimes, as do various hybrid or regional courts, including the Special Court for Sierra Leone, the Extraordinary Chambers of the Courts of Cambodia (ECCC), and the Bosnian War Crimes court.[39] The international tribunals tend to focus on those "most responsible" as targets for prosecution, which generally means military and political leaders who are higher up in the chain of authority and therefore most responsible for the *jus in bello* violations.[40] The concentration on leadership-level defendants is necessitated by scarcity of institutional resources.[41] With a limited number of trials they can conduct, tribunals have tended to prioritise among defendants, starting with those at the top of the political or military hierarchy. Street-level perpetrators, if they will be prosecuted at all, will be prosecuted before regional or domestic criminal tribunals. For example, the Bosnian War Crimes court has tried and convicted many street-level perpetrators, and the Gacaca courts in Rwanda prosecuted and punished thousands of individual perpetrators charged with individual acts of violence.[42]

In the case of leadership-level defendants, the prosecution must demonstrate some connection between the defendant and the perpetrators who physically performed the killings that constituted a violation of *jus in bello*, such as killing innocent civilians or prisoners of war (POWs). A number of new legal doctrines have emerged in recent years to make these connections. For example, the International Tribunal for the Former Yugoslavia (ICTY) and the International Criminal Tribunal for Rwanda (ICTR) have applied the doctrine of Joint Criminal Enterprise (JCE), a conspiracy-like doctrine that seeks to link all participants in a joint plan or endeavour to commit international crimes.[43]

---

[39] The official name of the court is the War Crimes Chamber of the Court of Bosnia and Herzegovina. For a discussion, see Sarah Williams, *Hybrid and Internationalised Criminal Tribunals: Selected Jurisdictional Issues*, Oxford: Hart Publishing, 2012.

[40] See Kai Ambos, "Ius Puniendi and Individual Criminal Responsibility in International Criminal Law," in *Research Handbook on the International Penal System*, eds. Róisín Mulgrew and Denis Abels, Northampton, MA: Edward Elgar, 2016, pp. 57–79.

[41] For a discussion, see Elies van Sliedregt, "The Curious Case of International Criminal Liability," *Journal of International Criminal Justice* 10 (2012) no. 5: 1171–88.

[42] See Mark A. Drumbl, "Punishment, Postgenocide: From Guilty to Shame to Civis in Rwanda," *New York University Law Review* 75 (2000): 1221–326. Many defendants languished in jail for years waiting to be prosecuted before domestic courts; once the trials were conducted in the Gacaca system, many observers criticised their lack of rigorous procedures.

[43] See Antonio Cassese, *International Criminal Law*, Oxford: Oxford University Press, 2003, p. 187.

Under the doctrine, all participants of the JCE are equally culpable for the crimes carried out by the JCE, regardless of who physically performs the killings. Recent cases have broadened its application so that leadership-level defendants might participate in a leadership-level JCE that then intersects with a street-level JCE consisting of physical perpetrators.[44]

The ICC does not apply the JCE doctrine and instead applies the Control Theory of Perpetration.[45] Under the Control Theory, leadership-level defendants who jointly control the crime, that is, are in a position to determine whether or not the crime is carried out, are defined as the principal co-perpetrators, whereas those who carry out the crime but do not control it are instead defined as mere accomplices. It might be odd to suggest that the physical perpetrator does not "control" the crime, but the intuition can be vindicated by suggesting that the true leader in control of the crime would simply reassign the task to a different subordinate if the first would-be perpetrator refuses the task. In that sense, a physical perpetrator might not fully be in control over whether or not the crime occurs.

The Control Theory has given rise to various sub-categories and confusing doctrinal combinations. Indirect perpetration involves the leadership-level defendant controlling the crime by having a subordinate complete the crime.[46] In this sense, the defendant has "indirectly" perpetrated the crime. One special version of indirect perpetration is the German doctrine of *Organisationsherrschaft*, which involves the use of an organization or "organized apparatus of power" to carry out the crime.[47] In that special case, the instrument of the indirect perpetration is not a single individual but rather an entire bureaucratic agency, such as a militia, army, or civilian government organization; the leader uses the organization as the instrument to commit his or her crimes. Finally, courts have sometimes combined co-perpetration and indirect perpetration to form indirect co-perpetration, which involves two or more individuals who work together, as in a junta, and control separate organizations that are then used to carry out the international crimes.[48]

---

[44] See e.g. *Prosecutor v. Brdjanin*, Appeals Judgment, ICTY Case No. IT-99-36, 3 April 2007; *Prosecutor v. Popovic et al.*, Trial Judgment, ICTY Case No. IT-05-88, 10 June 2010, para. 1029; *Prosecutor v. Krajisnik*, Appeals Judgment, ICTY Case No. IT-00-39, paras. 225–26.

[45] Neha Jain, "The Control Theory of Perpetration in International Criminal Law" *Chicago Journal of International Law*, 12 (2011), p. 157.

[46] See Stefano Manacorda and Chantal Meloni, "Indirect Perpetration versus Joint Criminal Enterprise: Concurring Approaches in the Practice of International Criminal Law?" *Journal of International Criminal Justice* 9 (2011) no. 1: 159–78; Florian Jessberger and Julia Geneuss, "On the Application of a Theory of Indirect Perpetration in Al Bashir: German Doctrine at The Hague?" *Journal of International Criminal Justice* 6 (2008) no. 5: 853–69.

[47] See Thomas Weigend, "Perpetration through an Organization: The Unexpected Career of a German Legal Concept," *Journal of International Criminal Justice* 9 (2011) no. 1: 91–111.

[48] See *Prosecutor v. Germain Katanga and Mathieu Ngudjolo Chui*, Decision on Confirmation of Charges, Pre-Trial Chamber, ICC-01/04–01/07–3269, 30 September 2008, para. 492. For analysis of the doctrine of indirect co-perpetration, see Jens David Ohlin, "Second-Order

Both JCE and the Control Theory are relatively recent entries onto the legal landscape compared to the doctrine of command responsibility, which was used after World War II to prosecute General Yamashita before a military commission for atrocities committed by Japanese troops under his command. Yamashita's trial was convened in Manila in 1945 by the American military; his conviction for war crimes was based on the killings of noncombatant civilians during the Japanese invasion of the Philippines. The Supreme Court of the United States later ratified the use of the command responsibility doctrine, thus enshrining the doctrine into positive law,[49] although not without some controversy.[50] Under the doctrine, a military commander or civil leader is responsible for the crimes committed by his or her subordinates. To prevent the doctrine from degenerating into strict liability, a few doctrinal limitations apply. The commanders must have tolerated the crimes by either failing to investigate their commission or failing to prosecute soldiers under their command who committed the offenses.[51]

There is some confusion over whether command responsibility is a mode of responsibility, such that the commander is responsible personally for the atrocities committed by others, or whether it is a separate offence based on the underlying principle of dereliction of duty.[52] It is often referred to as a mode of responsibility, but it is a bit odd that the commander should be held responsible for crimes committed before the point in time when the lack of punishment occurred. This suggests that either backward causation occurred (which is impossible) or that causation is not an element of the mode of responsibility at all (an equally implausible statement). One solution, recently adopted by the German domestic legal system, is to consider command responsibility as a cluster concept with two flavours: one a separate offence based on dereliction of duty and the other a mode of responsibility in cases where causation is established.[53]

Linking Principles: Combining Vertical and Horizontal Modes of Liability," *Leiden Journal of International Law* 25 (2012): 771–97.

[49] See *In re Yamashita*, 327 U.S. 1 (1946).

[50] In dissent, Justice Murphy complained that Yamashita was charged with an "unrecognized crime" because "international law makes no attempt to define the duties of a commander of an army under constant and overwhelming assault, nor does it impose liability under such circumstances for failure to meet the ordinary responsibilities of command." 327 U.S. at 29. Whether or not this statement was true in 1945, it is certainly the case that today international law *does* impose this liability.

[51] For a general discussion of the doctrine, see Guénaël Mettraux, *The Law of Command Responsibility*, Oxford: Oxford University Press, 2009.

[52] This tension is best described by, and resolved in, Darryl Robinson, "How Command Responsibility Got So Complicated: A Culpability Contradiction, Its Obfuscation, and a Simple Solution," *Melbourne Journal of International Law* 13 (2012) no. 1 (arguing that the doctrine should require causation and should be considered a mode of responsibility).

[53] For a discussion of this solution, see Kai Ambos, "Joint Criminal Enterprise and Command Responsibility," *Journal of International Criminal Justice* 5 (2007) no. 1: 159–83.

All of this being said, the greatest avenues for *jus in bello* enforcement reside outside the system of international criminal prosecutions. Most militaries across the globe have at their disposal robust mechanisms for internal discipline, including courts martial and other forms of criminal responsibility for not just atrocities but also more pedestrian breakdowns of command discipline. Although scholars naturally focus on situations where crimes are committed by and with the consent of military leaders (where self-enforcement is unlikely to occur), it is important to remember that, as Louis Henkin famously said, almost all nations obey almost all international law almost all of the time.[54] Military forces usually comply with *jus in bello* and when they do not, the first line of enforcement is with their own commanders, and then failing that, domestic prosecutions before national courts. International tribunals are generally a last resort.

In situations where domestic enforcement is not a possibility, the other avenue for enforcement is international pressure from non-governmental organisations that will "name and shame" states that violate *jus in bello*.[55] These organisations will engage in fact-finding missions and produce reports regarding ongoing violations. In some situations the evidence collected will be held for eventual prosecution in an international arena,[56] but even when no prosecution occurs, fact finding is important to apply international pressure through a decentralised system of enforcement through pressure and out casting.[57]

The last mechanism of enforcement is the controversial question of reprisals. This form of self-enforcement was once more common than it is today. State parties to an armed conflict will threaten to conduct a reprisal against a state that violated *jus in bello* to pressure that state into complying with the law in the future. So, for example, if one state killed 100 civilians or 100 POWs illegally, the victim state might respond by committing a reprisal: killing 100 POWs in response. The message would then be clear: If you violate *jus in bello*

---

[54] Louis Henkin, *How Nations Behave: Law and Foreign Policy*, 2nd edn, Columbia University Press/Council on Foreign Relations, 1979, p. 47.

[55] See generally H. Richard Friman, ed., *The Politics of Leverage in International Relations: Name, Shame, and Sanction*, Springer, 2015.

[56] Several groups are currently collecting evidence regarding atrocities committed in Syria. See Ben Hubbard and David D. Kirkpatrick, "Photo Archive Is Said to Show Widespread Torture in Syria," *New York Times* (January 21, 2014), available at www.nytimes.com/2014/01/22/world/middleeast/photo-archive-is-said-to-show-widespread-torture-in-syria.html

[57] The International Committee of the Red Cross (ICRC) studies and explains *jus in bello* but does not actively engage in direct naming and shaming during the court of a conflict because the practice might harm its mission of providing humanitarian assistance to victims of the armed conflict, a mission that requires that it has state cooperation from both sides of the conflict to operate on their territory. For a discussion of this and related issues, see Steven R. Ratner, "Behind the Flag of Dunant: Secrecy and the Compliance Mission of the International Committee of the Red Cross," in *Transparency in International Law*, eds. Andrea Bianchi and Anne Peters, Cambridge: Cambridge University Press, 2013, p. 297.

again, we will respond in kind. It is a violent form of self-help in the absence of a viable enforcement mechanism on the ground. Reprisals continued to exist in practice and in the literature through World War II.[58]

However, the legality of reprisals has undergone a significant shift since the end of World War II, and their continued legality is now very much in question.[59] The underlying philosophical issue here is deep and has to do with the conceptual foundation for *jus in bello*. At one time *jus in bello* obligations were viewed as reciprocal obligations between states, as are many obligations under general international law. Under this view, one party's breach of the obligation would release the other party from having to perform its part of the "bargain," much as a breach of contract would release the other party of the contract from having to perform under the deal. Now, however, the "reciprocal" worldview has broken down in favour of a newer portrait that gives greater significance to the individual who is protected by the *jus in bello* regulation. In the past, the individuals were regarded as mere third-party beneficiaries, at the most, in a reciprocal relationship between two state parties. Now, however, individuals have a central role in our modern system of human rights, which remains in force even if one party to the arrangement has failed to live up to its obligations. The failure to comply with *jus in bello* can no longer be justified by the appeal to *tu quoque* – if you did, so can I.[60] The era of reciprocity for *jus in bello* has now passed.

III The Basic Requirements of a Legal System of *Jus in Bello*

This section pivots more explicitly to normative assessment of international law. It briefly outlines the requirements for a just system of *jus in bello*, based on four goals, and then assesses international law against those standards. The four proposed goals are reciprocity, transparency, reduction of suffering for civilians, and reduction of suffering for soldiers. The analysis in this section largely vindicates the basic structure of *jus in bello* in international law but also suggests avenues for progressive development of the law.

First, *jus in bello* should be based on reciprocity. By reciprocity I do not mean reciprocity of *behaviour*, which was discussed in the last section. Belligerents

---

[58] For example, German forces carried out a reprisal in the Ardeatine Caves, on 24 August 1944, near Rome, in response to attacks against the Germans that were carried out by Italian partisans. The officers involved were later tried and convicted before a British military tribunal in 1945. However, the court's decision gave various reasons for its conclusion that the reprisals constituted war crimes, including the number of prisoners killed but notably did not state that reprisals were categorically illegal under international law. For a discussion of the case, see Giorgio Resta and Vincenzo Zeno-Zencovich, "Judicial 'Truth' and Historical 'Truth': The Case of the Ardeatine Caves Massacre," *Law & History Review* 31 (2013) no. 4, p. 843.

[59] See Andrew D. Mitchell, "Does One Illegality Merit Another? The Law of Belligerent Reprisals in International Law," *Military Law Review* 170 (2001): 155–77.

[60] Solis, *The Law of Armed Conflict*, p. 124.

engaged in an armed conflict should be required to follow the dictates of *jus in bello* even if the other side of the conflict ignores them. The rationale for this position can be both deontological or consequentialist. The deontological argument is straightforward: civilians and other protected persons have a right not to be subjected to inhumane treatment, and the fact that other civilians (on the other side) were mistreated is no reason to think that they have forfeited their own rights. As for consequentialist arguments, one can immediately see that if lack of respect for *jus in bello* should absolve the other side of their obligations, the result will be a quick race to the bottom – a moral disaster.

But one can talk of reciprocity in terms of obligations, that is, that both sides of the subject are reciprocally subject to the same normative standards, no matter what. They are reciprocally applied to both sides – a common currency that each side gets to spend when it engages in warfare. Revisionist Just War theorists have suggested that the right to engage in combatancy is predicated on the soldier's participation in a just war effort.[61] If the overall war effort is unjust, such as a crime of aggression, then the soldier has no right to engage in acts of belligerency; his acts of battlefield killings are, in fact, examples of unjust killings. This view of the "deep morality" of warfare suggests that *jus in bello* should not be reciprocal but rather should be conceptually dependent on more primary considerations of *jus ad bellum*. At least one argument in favour of this approach is that the justness or unjustness of the overall endeavour would be an essential consideration of a self-defence analysis under domestic criminal law, such that an unjust aggressor in criminal law has no right to engage in self-defence against his target's defensive force, unless of course the original target has unjustly escalated the situation.[62] If self-defence in criminal law requires consideration of the justness of the overall endeavour, why should not warfare require the same thing?

Without taking a stand on this philosophical position, suffice it to say that even revisionist Just War theorists such as Jeff McMahan conclude that there may be pragmatic considerations for why the "war convention" should require reciprocal application of the rules of *jus in bello*, independent of *jus ad bellum*.[63] First, soldiers may be unable to adequately assess whether they are fighting for an unjust (or illegal) endeavour, at least in hard cases. In situations where the UN Security Council has issued a binding resolution under Chapter VII condemning the war as illegal under international law, that may provide a useful clue, but most cases of unlawful force are not explicitly condemned in this fashion.

---

[61] See Jeff McMahan, "The Ethics of Killing in War," *Philosophia* 34 (2006) no. 1: 23–41.

[62] Ibid, p. 31.

[63] Jeff McMahan, "The Ethics of Killing in War," *Ethics* 114 (2004), p. 730 ("The formulation of the laws of war is a wholly different task, one that I have not attempted and that has to be carried out with a view to the consequences of the adoption and enforcement of the laws or conventions").

Furthermore, the ICJ, though it has jurisdiction to render decision on use of force questions, often defers to the Security Council and even if it does not defer would not be capable of issuing a determination on a timely basis for individual soldiers to make decisions regarding their participation. Also, many cases of armed conflict are hard cases where even the lawyers engage in substantial disagreement; this is not to say that hard cases have no right answers, but rather that it may be unreasonable to expect individual soldiers to ascertain the right answer in the absence of institutional mechanisms with jurisdiction to immediately provide those answers.

As an overall matter, McMahan is sympathetic to the suggestion that based on current prevailing conditions our *legal* system with a reciprocally applied *jus in bello* may do a better job of lowering cases of atrocities and unjust killings, and that dismantling the reciprocal nature of *jus in bello* might have overall negative consequences.[64] Part of the stability of the war convention is that its reciprocal application helps with the process of ensuring that it is complied with as much as possible, a factor that is surely morally relevant.

This notion of reciprocity is closely tied to the second goal, transparency. In the absence of the needed institutional resources described earlier, *jus in bello* must be constructed in such a way that it can be self-applied by, first, the participants in the armed conflict themselves, and second, the world community at large. This is the only enforcement available in most armed conflicts, since prosecutions before international tribunals are few and far between. The most important constraining work will be done by the world community that reacts when *jus in bello* is violated, and that means that the rules of *jus in bello* need to be transparent and easily applied in the real world, in the absence of complex factual and legal determinations better suited to a courtroom determining a criminal or tort case. Consider the following examples. First, causation is a notoriously complex question and domestic law has the luxury of engaging in complex assessments of causation during lengthy trials, which are well suited to parsing out complex causal chains. However, the law of war is usually adjudicated outside of the courtroom and therefore should – and indeed does – place a premium on legal rules that do not require such complex factual and legal investigation. Second, the applicability of IHL, at least for non-international armed conflicts, is often assumed to be based on the geography of armed conflict, so that IHL only applies (allegedly) in NIACs in so-called hot battlefield situations, and not outside the zone of combat.[65] Now I do not believe that this is an advisable or even accurate statement of the law, but it is one that is frequently said to be the rule regarding IHL's application. The opposite rule would be that IHL applies whenever a killing or attack is causally

---

[64] Ibid.

[65] See Mary Ellen O'Connell, "Combatants and the Combat Zone," *University of Richmond Law Review* 43 (2009), p. 845.

connected to the non-international armed conflict, regardless of the location in which it takes place. However, one reason people are suspicious of this latter possibility is that a functional standard might be less transparent to the actors involved. Using a more basic territorial standard – "only on hot battlefields" – has the benefit that the participants themselves and the world community at large can more immediately discern if IHL applies. Whether or not this should be dispositive is unclear. But it is certainly true that *jus in bello* places a premium on transparency and abhors complex legal rules that require secret information to investigate or adjudicate.

We now turn to the third goal to which *jus in bello* should be directed: reducing suffering in war for civilians. The rationale for the importance of this goal is that civilians are, as a class, relatively innocent, although there may be some civilians who are morally culpable for making causal contributions to unjust war efforts. But the vast majority of civilians are morally blameless and it would be a good thing if war were to reduce the number of civilian casualties. Moreover, to the extent that there is civilian suffering in war, there is no evidence that this burden is more often borne by morally culpable civilians. In fact, the very opposite seems true: when civilians suffer in war, it is usually civilians who have nothing to do with the war effort. Therefore it would count as a moral benefit if *jus in bello* were constructed in such a way as to reduce civilian suffering.

On this score, *jus in bello* takes a moderate, incrementalist approach. Collateral damage is restricted but not prohibited. The restriction, as noted earlier, is embodied in two basic rules: (1) the rule against causing disproportionate collateral damage and (2) the affirmative obligation to take all feasible precautions to reduce collateral damage and harm to civilians. Nonetheless, these rules still sanction a huge number of civilian deaths that are envisioned but not purposeful, as long as they are not disproportionate and there is no feasible alternative for avoiding the deaths. So civilians still suffer in war.

Could *jus in bello* be constructed with more demanding norms? One thing is for certain: a rule preventing collateral damage entirely would be tantamount to a rule *contra bellum* entirely, since it is almost impossible to conduct a war in the modern sense without harming at least some civilians.[66] Would this be morally bad or morally beneficial? Two points are important to make here. First, a rule of *jus in bello* that essentially makes war impossible to conduct would be a *jus in bello* that is completely ignored by the world's major powers, and thus it would fail on grounds of enforcement – it would produce results that are morally bad. Second, even if we assume that the rule could be enforced and would be complied with, a rule that makes war essentially impossible would do two things: it would come dangerously close to outlawing all unjust

---

[66] This issue is discussed in David Lefkowitz, "Collateral Damage," in *War: Essays in Political Philosophy*, ed. Larry May, Cambridge: Cambridge University Press, 2008, p 164.

wars but also would outlaw all *just* wars as well. And this consequence is something that is too often ignored. Some wars are morally bad but some wars are pursued to redress moral disasters, whether slavery, genocide, or unjust occupation and cultural oppression. If war is outlawed either explicitly or implicitly, it is outlawed for both just and unjust wars alike, and it is difficult to tell whether this would be morally beneficial or not.

The fourth and final goal for *jus in bello* is to reduce suffering in war for soldiers while still permitting belligerents to pursue an armed conflict. The reason this goal is important is that soldiers have moral rights too – although certainly not the same rights as civilians. But to the extent that the war convention places the burdens of warfare on the shoulders of combatants, it would seem that there is a distributional concern regarding the harms of war that fall disproportionately on soldiers. For some, this burden is one voluntarily taken, but many nations – even Western liberal nations – still have mandatory military service or the draft, thus negating the plausible argument that soldiers have voluntarily accepted the burdens that come with their participation in the war machine. For these reasons, it is imperative to reduce the burdens as far as possible, even if it is impossible to eliminate them. Therefore, soldiers should suffer as little as possible, and risk death as little as possible, if such a thing is ever consistent with the goal of engaging in warfare.

Unfortunately, the current state of *jus in bello* does little to limit the suffering of soldiers. They are protected from unnecessary suffering, but unnecessary suffering is defined rather narrowly, because if a weapon produces more suffering but is marginally more effective than its natural alternative, it arguably is still permitted because it confers a military advantage.[67] Soldiers cannot be executed as POWs, nor even criminally punished if they satisfy the demands for privileged belligerency. However, they are subject to summary killing at almost any time, as long as they are not *hors de combat*, even if they are not particularly dangerous. So the proverbial naked or sleeping soldier can be killed at any time. Also, fleeing soldiers are subject to mass killing, particular from aerial bombardment, because there is no codified legal duty that requires attacking forces to forgo lethal force when doing so will result in an inhumane level of casualties to enemy soldiers.[68] Historically, this last rule has been justified by the fact that fleeing soldiers might regroup and attack later, and there is no requirement that soldiers should forgo force and let the enemy decide when it is most convenient for them to engage in battle. Indeed, the whole point of winning the war is that one side forces tactical confrontations at times and places when it is strategically inconvenient for the enemy. If the enemy is permitted to retreat with total immunity, the strategic balance of power will never change, and war will be reduced to a series of symbolic skirmishes, none of which trigger a final resolution to the conflict.

---

[67] Solis, *Law of Armed Conflict*.   [68] Blum, "Dispensable Lives of Soldiers," p. 70.

So there is clearly room for progressive development of *jus in bello*. Although *jus in bello* scores high as a legal system based on principles of transparency and reciprocity, and it does a good job of protecting civilians, it leaves soldiers relatively unprotected. The question is what changes, if any, could be codified that would make warfare more humane for soldiers. In the space that remains, I briefly outline a few possibilities that would protect soldiers without necessarily unwinding the entire war convention or the concept of warfare itself.

The first possibility is that attacking forces could be subject to a requirement to use the least harmful level of force to accomplish the mission. This would entail, under some circumstances, capturing instead of killing.[69] In other circumstances, it would entail injuring rather than killing the enemy. Killing would then be a last resort if the other two non-lethal options are not feasible or have already been exhausted and not succeeded. There are several arguments in favor of this approach. To name just one, the requirement to limit lethal force to situations of "last resort" would accord with a classical requirement of Just War theory that war – and killing – are justified only as a last resort.[70] Of course, in most works of classical Just War theory, the last resort criterion is a requirement of *jus ad bellum* rather than *jus in bello*; that is, a nation can only resort to war when it is the last resort and all other avenues of securing its safety have been exhausted.[71] However, it is occasionally referenced as a requirement of killing *simpliciter*, and it might be said that soldiers should only be entitled to kill their professional brethren when it is a last resort.[72]

Some believe that the law already imposes this kind of restriction.[73] As I have argued elsewhere, I believe this reading of the relevant treaties is overly optimistic and improperly elevates a few idealistic statements that were made during the negotiation process into actual law, when in fact these sentiments were never codified in the final treaties.[74] Even if this were the law, it is unclear in how many circumstances it would apply since there is almost always a greater risk or inconvenience to attacking forces to disable or capture the enemy as opposed to using lethal force.[75] So if the requirement is that capture or injuring the enemy is only required when it can be accomplished without bearing additional risk or is inconvenient, then the requirement may come perilously close to being a null set – a requirement that should occupy

---

[69] See Jens David Ohlin, "The Duty to Capture," *Minnesota Law Review* 97 (2013): 1268–342.

[70] See e.g. Grotius, *De Jure Belli ac Pacis (On the Law of War and Peace)* 175 (1625) (Frances W. Kelsey trans., 1925).

[71] Ibid.

[72] See e.g. Thomas Aquinas, *Summa Theologica* Pt. II-II, Qu. LXIV, art. 6, at 1464 (Fathers of the Dominican Province, trans., Benziger Bros. 1948).

[73] See Ryan Goodman, "The Power to Kill or Capture Enemy Combatants," *European Journal of International Law* 24 (2013), p. 819.

[74] Ohlin, "Sharp Wars Are Brief."

[75] International Committee of the Red Cross, *The Use of Force in Armed Conflicts: Interplay between the Conduct of Hostilities and Law Enforcement Paradigms* (2013), p. 17.

philosophers and lawyers but will never change actual tactical operations on the ground.

But it is certainly the case that the law could move in this direction in the future, and the question is whether it would be advisable to do so. The way to make the requirement meaningful would be to require attacking forces to bear a *reasonable risk* in order to, in some circumstances, use non-lethal force, which might involve either disabling or capturing the enemy instead of simply killing them. As a practical matter, soldiers would be required to consider some non-lethal alternatives if doing so were consistent with overall objectives and only involved the imposition of reasonable risks to the attacking force.[76] Of course, what counts as a "reasonable" risk is squishy and would have to be cashed out in greater detail. It would require a fact-dependent analysis at the tactical level and should be judged relative to the standard of a "reasonable commander" under the same circumstances. But the basic idea is sound: attacking forces could be required to exhaust non-lethal alternatives first and the fact that doing so would require them to take on a modicum of additional risk would not, by itself, defeat the normative requirement.

If the law were to evolve in this direction, military force would still allow attacking forces to pursue the war effort and would not hamstring military forces and force them into a situation of prolonged stalemate. The only difference is that some soldiers might be captured or injured rather than killed, when the non-lethal measures would not change the overall strategic balance of the conflict. All things considered, this would be a modest but real change to the character of military operations. However, we should be clear that international law does not currently impose this requirement. If it were to do so in the future, however, *jus in bello* would do a better job of making warfare more humane for soldiers.

Conclusion

This chapter has outlined the basic structure of *jus in bello* by first examining the basic prohibitions that apply in international law. It then outlined the complex and sometimes unique mechanisms used to enforce *jus in bello*, many of which involve processes and methods that are not typically used in domestic legal systems. Because of this fact, there is a temptation here to view *jus in bello* as insufficiently law-like, in part because some of the enforcement mechanisms look alien; the ones that look conventional are limited in scope and do not cover the field entirely. The temptation is to then compare this type of enforcement against the paradigm of enforcement that reigns in domestic law, and to find *jus in bello* enforcement wanting. While indeed *jus in bello*

---

[76] This proposal is developed in Jens David Ohlin and Larry May, *Necessity in International Law*, Oxford: Oxford University Press, 2016, p. 230.

enforcement should be strengthened going forward, it is a mistake to conclude that *jus in bello* does not qualify as "law" simply because it does not measure up against the supposed "standard" for law-governed activities that emerges from domestic law. Put simply, there is no reason to supposes that domestic law should set the standard against which all other forms of law should be judged and defined as law. Instead, one should recognize that enforcement comes in many flavours, and indeed that enforcement itself is not the be-all-and-end-all of the rule of law. Once we have jettisoned the idea of law as the commands of the sovereign backed up by coercive threats, what remains are alternative definitions.[77] The practice of warfare is constrained by *jus in bello*, and Henkin's edict that most nations follow international law applies as much to *jus in bello* as it does to general international law. Soldiers operating in most armed conflicts view themselves as constrained by *jus in bello* and conduct themselves accordingly. Today's world is beset with violations of *jus in bello*, which are terrible indeed, but they are *violations* nonetheless, not evidence that *jus in bello* is not law.

---

[77] See J. L. Austin, *The Province of Jurisprudence Determined* (1832), p. 15.

14 Necessity and Proportionality in International Law

Adil Ahmad Haque

International law constrains both the resort to military force and the conduct of hostilities. In both contexts, principles of necessity and proportionality limit the lawful use of lethal violence. The content of these principles is controversial, however, both within each context and across contexts. This chapter aims to illuminate these controversies and suggest how they should be resolved.

International lawyers often refer to the legal norms constraining the resort to military force as the *jus ad bellum* or *jus contra bellum* and to the legal norms constraining the conduct of hostilities as the *jus in bello*. Infelicitously, philosophers use the same terms to refer to the moral norms to which these legal norms quite imperfectly correspond. To minimize confusion, I refer to the first set of legal norms as the *law of force* and to the second set of legal norms as the *law of armed conflict* (although many refer to the latter as *international humanitarian law*).

I The Law of Force

The primary source of the contemporary law of force is the United Nations Charter, a multilateral treaty to which almost all states are parties. Many experts contend that the UN Charter's provisions regulating the use of force reflect *jus cogens*, that is, peremptory norms of customary international law from which no derogation is permitted.[1]

The UN Charter requires states to settle their international disputes by peaceful means and prohibits states from using military force on the territory of other states.[2] This general prohibition has three narrow exceptions. First, the UN Charter does not prohibit the use of force with the consent of the territorial state, although such force may be constrained by other legal norms.[3] Second, the UN Security

---

[1] See e.g. Reports of the International Law Commission to the General Assembly, 21 U.N. GAOR Supp. No. 9, pt. II, U.N. Doc. A/6309/Rev.l (1966), reprinted in [1966] 2 Y.B. Int'l L. Comm'n 172, at 247, U.N. Doc. A/CN.4/SER.A/1966/Add.l. But see James A. Green, "Questioning the Peremptory Status of the Prohibition of the Use of Force", Michigan Journal of International Law 32 (2011) no. 2, p. 215.

[2] UN Charter, arts 2(3) and 2(4).

[3] See e.g. Report of the Special Rapporteur on extrajudicial, summary or arbitrary executions, Study on Targeted Killings, para 37, U.N. Doc. A/HRC/14/24/Add.6 (May 28, 2010) (by Philip Alston).

Council may authorize member states to use military force on the territory of other states if necessary to maintain or restore international peace and security.[4] Finally, states retain an inherent right to use military force in individual or collective self-defence if an armed attack occurs, until the UN Security Council takes measures necessary to maintain international peace and security.[5]

Importantly, by recognizing the *inherent* right of self-defence, the UN Charter incorporates by reference limitations on the right of self-defence arising from customary international law, including necessity and proportionality.[6] While conventional international law is codified in written treaties whose words may be quoted and parsed, customary international law arises from the convergent practice and legal opinion of states.[7] Accordingly, the principles of necessity and proportionality in the law of force have no canonical formulation, and their content can only be determined through close examination of state practice and opinion. Rather than attempt such close examination here, I simply present and discuss the most important positions in the field.[8]

II Necessity in the Law of Force

Necessity in the law of force roughly corresponds to the just war principle of last resort (*ultima ratio*). As we will see later, the use of more force than necessary to repel or prevent an armed attack is legally constrained by the proportionality principle, not by the necessity principle. Additionally, the necessity constraint in the law of force should not be confused with the necessity justification in the law of state responsibility, which has no application to the use of force.[9]

In its strictest formulation, necessity in the law of force provides that states may only use military force in self-defence "when peaceful means have reasonably been exhausted, or when diplomatic enterprises would clearly be futile,"[10] This strict formulation of necessity coheres well with a strict interpretation of

---

[4] UN Charter, art 42.   [5] UN Charter, art 51.

[6] See e.g. Legality of the Threat or Use of Nuclear Weapons, Advisory Opinion (1996) ICJ Reports 226, 245 para 41; Military and Paramilitary Activities in and against Nicaragua (Nicaragua v. United States of America) (1986) ICJ Reports 14, 94 para 176.

[7] Roughly, a norm of customary law arises when states generally accept that such a legal norm governs their conduct (*opinio juris*) and generally behave accordingly (*usus*).

[8] See generally, Jens David Ohlin and Larry May, *Necessity in International Law*, Oxford: Oxford University Press, 2016; Michael Newton and Larry May, *Proportionality in International Law*, Oxford: Oxford University Press, 2014.

[9] See e.g. Articles on the Responsibility of States for Internationally Wrongful Acts, in Report of the International Law Commission on the Work of Its Fifty-third Session art. 25, U.N. GAOR, 56th Sess., Supp. No. 10, at 43, U.N. Doc. A/56/10 (2001), annexed to G.A. Res. 56/83 (Dec. 12, 2001).

[10] Tom Ruys, *"Armed Attack" and Article 51 of the UN Charter*, Cambridge: Cambridge University Press, 2010, p. 95. See also United States Department of Defense, *Law of War Manual* (2015) 1.11.1.3.

self-defence as a whole. On this strict interpretation, states may only use military force in self-defence "if an armed attack occurs," that is, once an armed attack begins or while an armed attack is ongoing. In such circumstances, the attacking state has clearly renounced peaceful means of settling its disputes, while the UN Security Council has evidently failed to take measures necessary to maintain international peace and security. Military force is therefore necessary to intercept an incipient armed attack or to repel an ongoing armed attack. Accordingly, "there seems to be an almost irrebuttable presumption here that such a use of force in self-defense would pass the test of necessity."[11]

The strict formulation of necessity is under increasing pressure, as the triggering condition for the right of self-defence has been called into question. First, some states now claim that it may be lawful for a state to use military force in self-defence *before* any armed attack occurs if that state determines that an armed attack is imminent or will occur if not forcibly prevented. Second, many states now claim that it is lawful for a state to use military force in self-defence *after* an armed attack ends if that state determines that further armed attacks are imminent or will occur if not forcibly prevented.

In such cases, it cannot be presumed that peaceful means will fail, or that the UN Security Council will not or cannot take measures necessary to maintain or restore international peace and security. At the same time, some contend that states anticipating future armed attacks need not bear the risk of exhausting peaceful means when doing so will make forcible measures less likely to succeed should peaceful means fail. Arguably, states should weigh the risk of using unnecessary force (a "false positive") against the risk of not using necessary force (a "false negative") and use force when the risk of restraint outweighs the risk of action.[12] On the other hand, if states systematically overestimate the costs and risks of diplomacy and underestimate the costs and risks of military action, then the strict interpretation of necessity may prove a necessary corrective to these cognitive biases.

One international incident that elicited relevant *opinio juris* involved a 1981 Israeli strike on an Iraqi nuclear reactor. The UN Security Council unanimously condemned the strike as a "clear violation of the [UN] Charter."[13] For its part, the United States stated that its position "was based solely on the conviction that Israel had failed to exhaust peaceful means."[14] By way of contrast, in 2015, the United States appeared to peacefully resolve its dispute with Iran over the latter's nuclear program. In this context, it was alleged that military force was immediately necessary to prevent Iran from fortifying its nuclear facilities,

---

[11] Dapo Akande and Thomas Liefländer, "Clarifying Necessity, Imminence, and Proportionality in the Law of Self-Defense", *American Journal of International Law*, 107 (2013) no. 3, p. 564.

[12] See Noam Lubell, "The Problem of Imminence in an Uncertain World" in *The Oxford Handbook of the Use of Force in International Law*, ed. Marc Weller, Oxford: Oxford University Press, 2015.

[13] SC Res. 487 (1981) of 19 June 1981.   [14] United Nations Yearbook (1981), p. 276.

thereby making forcible measures less likely to succeed should negotiations fail. The apparent success of negotiations suggests that peaceful resolution of disputes is possible even between adversary states.

In an important case, the International Court of Justice (ICJ) considered the use of military force in response to repeated armed attacks. In 1987, a missile struck a Kuwaiti oil tanker, reflagged to the United States. The United States attributed the attack to Iran and three days later attacked two Iranian oil complexes. In 1988, a U.S. warship struck a mine in international waters. Four days later, the United States simultaneously attacked and destroyed two Iranian oil complexes. In both cases, the United States claimed self-defence. The ICJ found insufficient evidence that Iran was responsible for the two attacks. Importantly, assuming Iranian responsibility for the sake of discussion, the ICJ was "not satisfied that the attacks on the platforms were necessary to respond to these incidents," noting, "there is no evidence that the United States complained to Iran of the military activities of the platforms."[15] This passage suggests that states must make reasonable efforts to resolve disputes by peaceful means, even after armed attacks occur and even if future armed attacks are anticipated.

In the same case, the ICJ wrote, "One aspect of these criteria [of necessity and proportionality] is the nature of the target of the force used avowedly in self-defence" and found that the oil platforms were not "legitimate targets for an armed action in self-defence."[16] To some scholars, these passages suggest that "it is not sufficient that the target is a legitimate military objective," such as a combatant or military facility. Instead, military force "should in principle be directed at the source(s) of the armed attack(s)."[17] On this view, the law of force may regulate not only whether force may be used but also what targets may be attacked, a domain traditionally reserved for the law of armed conflict.[18]

Finally, a growing number of states claim that it is lawful to use military force against a non-state armed group operating from the territory of another state, even if the acts of the group are not attributable to the territorial state, if the territorial state is "unwilling or unable" to prevent that armed group from launching armed attacks.[19] In my view, the necessity of non-consensual force involves both the necessity to use force and the necessity to proceed without consent. Accordingly, the intervening state must make reasonable efforts to obtain the consent of the territorial state, even if the territorial state is unwilling or unable to suppress the armed group itself.

---

[15] *Oil Platforms (Islamic Republic of Iran v. United States of America)*, Judgment (2003) ICJ Reports 16, 196, para 76.

[16] Ibid. 195–97, para 74.   [17] Ruys, "*Armed Attack*", p. 108.

[18] See also UK Ministry of Defense, *Law of Armed Conflict Manual*, Oxford University Press, 2005 2.8.1.

[19] See e.g. Brian Egan, "International Law, Legal Diplomacy, and the Counter-ISIL Campaign: Some Observations," *International Law Studies* 92 (2016), p. 241.

III   Proportionality in the Law of Force

Like necessity, the principle of proportionality in the law of force is not found in any treaty but resides instead in customary international law. Unfortunately, state practice and opinion remain confused and fractured, with substantial support for three very different approaches.

On one approach, proportionality requires that defensive force must be comparable in its scale and effects to that of the armed attack to which it responds. The ICJ seemed to adopt this position in the *Oil Platforms* case, in which it found, "As a response to the mining, by an unidentified agency, of a single United States warship, which was severely damaged but not sunk, and without loss of life," the United States launch an extensive military operation "which involved, *inter alia*, the destruction of two Iranian frigates and a number of other naval vessels and aircraft" in addition to the attacks on two oil complexes at issue in the case. The ICJ found that "neither 'Operation Praying Mantis' as a whole, nor even that part of it that destroyed the Salman and Nasr platforms, can be regarded, in the circumstances of this case, as a proportionate use of force in self-defence."[20]

This strict, "quantitative" approach fits alongside the strict interpretation of self-defence according to which force may be used only to halt or repel an incipient or ongoing armed attack, thereby meeting force with force in a discrete encounter. However, this approach will not appeal those who believe that force may be used after an armed attack ends to prevent or deter future attacks. In such cases, the force necessary to prevent future attacks may be greater in scale and effects than the initial attack.

Accordingly, on a second approach, proportionality requires only that the scale and effects of defensive force must be no greater than necessary to repel or prevent an armed attack. Some judges, several experts, and many scholars favour this "instrumental" or "functional" approach.[21] On this view, international law never prevents states from taking effective defensive measures.

In my view, exclusive reliance on the "instrumental" approach is unsustainable. Suppose that a non-state armed group G launches a series of armed attacks against State A from the territory of State T. Each attack harms a small number of persons in State A, but any defensive response sufficient to stop these attacks would collaterally kill hundreds of civilians in State T. Under the instrumental approach, such a defensive response by State A would be "proportionate." This result seems inconsistent with the object and purpose of

---

[20] *Oil Platforms*, at 197–99, para 77.

[21] See e.g. *Legality of the Threat or Use of Nuclear Weapons, Advisory Opinion*, Dissenting Opinion of Judge Higgins (1996) ICJ Reports 226, 583, para 5; Roberto Ago, Addendum to the Eighth Report on State Responsibility, UN Doc A/CN.4/318, Add 5–7, *Yearbook of the International Law Commission* (1980) 69–70, para 121; Judith Gardham, *Necessity, Proportionality, and the Use of Force by States*, Cambridge: Cambridge University Press, 2004.

the modern law of force, which is not only to protect states from unlawful force but also "to save succeeding generations from the scourge of war."[22] Accordingly, humanitarian values should inform both the law of force and the law of armed conflict.

Now suppose that State T is unable to quickly prevent group G from launching armed attacks against State A from State T's territory. Perhaps State T, seeking to minimize harm to its civilians, plans and begins a ground campaign against G that will take weeks or months to succeed. However, State T does not consent to State A's use of force on its territory out of concern for its civilians. If State A attacks group G in State T, killing hundreds of State T's civilians, then international law should permit State T to use force against State A, in defence of its territory and civilian population. Yet, under international law, "there can be no self-defense against self-defense."[23] In my view, we should avoid this conflict of rights by rejecting the instrumental approach and finding State A's use of defensive force disproportionate.

Accordingly, on a third approach, proportionality compares the harm inflicted by defensive force with the harm prevented by defensive force.[24] This "weighing" or "balancing" approach parallels the view in Just War theory that the resort to military force, even if necessary to repel or prevent armed attacks, is morally proportionate only if it does more good than harm. The ICJ seemed open to this approach in its *Nuclear Weapons* advisory opinion, in which it noted that the "extremely strong risk of devastation" associated with nuclear weapons may limit the extent to which states "can exercise a nuclear response in self-defence in accordance with the requirements of proportionality."[25]

Moreover, the third approach appears to inform state practice and *opinio juris*. As David Kretzmer observes, "in the reaction of states and commentators to specific cases of force used in self-defence, the damage caused plays a major role in descriptions of the force as disproportionate."[26] Similarly, Tom Ruys notes that "defensive action resulting in large numbers of civilian casualties has [i]nvariably evoked strong negative reactions from the international community and has frequently been condemned by the Security Council and/or the General Assembly."[27]

In *DRC v. Uganda*, the majority seemed to combine the second and third approaches, observing that "the taking of airports and towns many hundreds of kilometres from Uganda's border would not seem proportionate to the series of

---

[22] United Nations Charter, preamble.

[23] *US v Von Weizsaecker et al* (Ministries Case) (Nuremberg, 1949), 14 NMT 314, 329.

[24] See e.g. U.S. Dep't of Defense, *Law of War Manual* 3.5.1.

[25] *Nuclear Weapons*, paras 41–44 (majority opinion).

[26] David Kretzmer, "The Inherent Right to Self-Defence and Proportionality in *Jus Ad Bellum*," *European Journal of International Law* 24 (2013), p. 279.

[27] Ruys, "*Armed Attack*", pp. 121–22. Note that these statements typically refer to the scale and effects of entire campaigns, invoking the law of force, not to particular strikes, which would invoke the law of armed conflict.

transborder attacks it claimed had given rise to the right of self-defence, nor to be necessary to that end."[28] Apparently, these actions were both unnecessary and disproportionate to the end of preventing future transborder attacks. Writing separately, Judge Kooijmans more clearly combined the second and third approaches:

> Not by any stretch of the imagination can this action [occupying Kisangani airport] or any of the subsequent attacks against a great number of Congolese towns and military bases be considered as having been necessitated by the protection of Uganda's security interests. These actions moreover were grossly disproportionate to the professed aim of securing Uganda's border from armed attacks by anti-Ugandan rebel movements.[29]

In Judge Kooijmans's view, these actions were both unnecessary to protect Uganda's security interests and grossly disproportionate to Uganda's professed defensive aim.

On some views, "a *jus ad bellum* proportionality analysis might consider the harm suffered by enemy military forces in the fighting."[30] Accordingly, the best combination of the "instrumental" and "balancing" approaches may be that harm inflicted on enemy military forces must be no greater than necessary to prevent or repel their armed attack, but that harm inflicted on civilians must be outweighed by the harm that the armed attack would inflict if not prevented.

The Law of Armed Conflict

Like the law of force, the law of armed conflict derives from both treaty and custom. The most important treaties are the four Geneva Conventions of 1949 and their Additional Protocols, many provisions of which are widely accepted as reflecting customary international law. The law of armed conflict touches on many issues, including the treatment of prisoners of war, civilian internees, the wounded, the sick, the shipwrecked, and even the dead. However, our interest lies in the law governing "attacks," that is, "acts of violence against the adversary, whether in offence or in defence."[31]

Under the law of armed conflict, "civilians shall enjoy general protection against dangers arising from military operations . . . unless and for such time as

---

[28] *Armed Activities on the Territory of the Congo (Democratic Republic of the Congo v. Uganda)*, Judgment (2005) ICJ Reports 168, 223, para 147. On an alternative reading, the actions by Uganda were disproportionate in their scale and effects to the transborder attacks that had already occurred, and unnecessary to the defensive end of preventing future attacks.

[29] *Armed Activities on the Territory of the Congo*, Separate Opinion of Judge Kooijmans, 2005 ICJ Reports 168, 306, para 34.

[30] See e.g. U.S. Dep't of Defense, *Law of War Manual* 3.5.1.

[31] Protocol Additional to the Geneva Conventions of 12 August 1949, and relating to the Protection of Victims of International Armed Conflicts, 8 June 1977 (Protocol I), art 49.

they take a direct part in hostilities."[32] To give effect to this general protection, the law of armed conflict lays down a number of specific rules, of which three are most relevant here. First, civilians shall not be the object of attack. Second, all feasible precautions must be taken to avoid, and in any event to minimise, harm to civilians (*the precautions rule*). Finally, attacks which may be expected to cause incidental harm to civilians which would be excessive in relation to the concrete and direct military advantage anticipated are prohibited (*the proportionality rule*). We focus on the precautions rule, which essentially prohibits causing unnecessary collateral harm to civilians, as well as the proportionality rule. However, we begin with the elusive concept of "military necessity."

With respect to combatants, the law of armed conflict prohibits the use of weapons of a nature to cause superfluous injury or unnecessary suffering to opposing combatants.[33] Some experts argue that this prohibition extends to unnecessarily killing opposing combatants, when killing would yield no military advantage or when capture would yield the same military advantage.[34] Although morally compelling, the better view seems to be that this rule prohibits inflicting injury or suffering on opposing combatants that is unnecessary to kill or physically incapacitate them but does not prohibit killing or physically incapacitating them as such.[35]

IV Military Necessity

Military lawyers often refer to *military necessity* as a legal principle underlying and pervading the law of armed conflict. On some views, military necessity is a permissive principle that provides legal authority for acts of violence in armed conflict.[36] On other views, military necessity is a restrictive principle that provides legal constraints on acts not prohibited by specific legal rules.[37] Both views are important and influential, although both rest on unstable foundations.

Interestingly, military necessity is not defined in any treaty. The most influential formulation of military necessity comes from a U.S. Army General Order, issued at the height of the American Civil War. The General Order is widely referred to as the "Lieber Code," after its principal drafter, Francis Lieber. According to the code: "Military necessity, as understood by modern civilized nations, consists in the

---

[32] Protocol I, art 51.   [33] See e.g. Protocol I, art 35(2).

[34] See e.g. Ryan Goodman, "The Power to Kill or Capture Enemy Combatants," *European Journal of International Law* 24 (2013), p. 819.

[35] See e.g. Michael N. Schmitt, "Wound, Capture, or Kill: A Reply to Ryan Goodman's 'The Power to Kill or Capture Enemy Combatants'," *European Journal of International Law* 24 (2013), p. 860; Jens David Ohlin, "The Duty to Capture," *Minnesota Law Review* 97 (2013), p. 1268.

[36] See e.g. U.S. Dep't of Defense, *Law of War Manual* 2.2.1 ("*Military necessity* justifies actions, such as destroying and seizing persons and property").

[37] See e.g. UK Ministry of Defense, *Law of Armed Conflict Manual* 2.2.1 ("the use of force which is not necessary is unlawful, since it involves wanton killing or destruction").

necessity of those measures which are indispensable for securing the ends of the war, and which are lawful according to the modern law and usages of war."[38] By the terms of this definition, measures are militarily necessary only if they are lawful. However, measures are not lawful in virtue of military necessity. Measures derive their lawfulness not from military necessity but "according to the laws and usages of war," that is, according to the specific legal rules that other provisions of the code purport to list. On this literal reading, military necessity is not a source of legal authority or even part of the law of war.

Nevertheless, many scholars argue that, according to the code, military necessity is an independent source of legal authority, based on the following passage:

Military necessity admits of all direct destruction of life or limb of armed enemies, and of other persons whose destruction is incidentally unavoidable in the armed contests of the war; it allows of the capturing of every armed enemy, and every enemy of importance to the hostile government, or of peculiar danger to the captor; it allows of all destruction of property, and obstruction of the ways and channels of traffic, travel, or communication, and of all withholding of sustenance or means of life from the enemy; of the appropriation of whatever an enemy's country affords necessary for the subsistence and safety of the army, and of such deception as does not involve the breaking of good faith either positively pledged, regarding agreements entered into during the war, or supposed by the modern law of war to exist.

According to these scholars, these acts are lawful because they are "admitted" or "allowed" by military necessity. However, as we have seen, the better view is that military necessity "admits" or "allows" these acts because they are lawful (i.e. not prohibited) according to the law and usages of war.

To see this more clearly, consider another provision of the code, which states that "There exists no law or body of authoritative rules of action between hostile armies, except that branch of the law of nature and nations which is called the law and usages of war on land."[39] It follows that hostile armies are legally free to do whatever the law and usages of war on land do not specifically prohibit. We do not need the concept of military necessity to explain this result, which follows from the general proposition that states are legally free to do what no specific rule of international law prohibits them from doing.[40]

Other scholars argue that according to the code, military necessity is an independent source of legal constraints, based on the following passage:

Military necessity does not admit of cruelty – that is, the infliction of suffering for the sake of suffering or for revenge, nor of maiming or wounding except in fight,

---

[38] Instructions for the Government of Armies of the United States in the Field, General Order No. 100, art. 14 (April 24, 1863).

[39] Ibid., art. 40.

[40] See generally *The S.S. Lotus* (France v. Turkey) (Judgment), 1927 P.C.I.J. (series A) No. 10.

nor of torture to extort confessions. It does not admit of the use of poison in any way, nor of the wanton devastation of a district. It admits of deception, but disclaims acts of perfidy; and, in general, military necessity does not include any act of hostility which makes the return to peace unnecessarily difficult.[41]

According to these scholars, these tactics are unlawful because military necessity does not "admit" them. However, as we have seen, the better view is that military necessity "does not admit" of these tactics because these tactics are not "lawful according to the modern law and usages of war." Accordingly, cruelty, poison, perfidy, and wanton violence are all specifically prohibited in other articles of the code, by reference to the laws of war rather than to military necessity.[42]

Almost a century after the Lieber Code, the American Military Tribunal at Nuremberg wrote that "Military necessity permits a belligerent, subject to the laws of war, to apply any amount and kind of force to compel the complete submission of the enemy with the least possible expenditure of time, life, and money."[43] As before, by the terms of this definition, military necessity permits force only if that force is lawful. However, force is not lawful because it is militarily necessary. Instead, every amount and kind of force is "subject to the laws of war," with which military necessity is partially contrasted.

Importantly, the tribunal repeatedly states that "international law is prohibitive law."[44] On this view, "the law relating to the conduct of hostilities is primarily a law of prohibition: it does not authorize, but prohibits certain things."[45] Accordingly, international law tolerates but does not necessarily endorse what it does not specifically prohibit.[46] It is in this weak sense that belligerent states are "permitted" to use force subject to the laws of war. Again, we do not need the concept of military necessity to explain this result.

As the tribunal observed, the laws of war specifically prohibit the destruction or seizure of property "unless such destruction or seizure be imperatively demanded by the necessities of war."[47] It was in this context that the Tribunal wrote: "The destruction of property to be lawful must be imperatively demanded by the necessities of war ... There must be some reasonable connection between the destruction of property and the overcoming of the enemy

---

[41] General Order No. 100, art. 16.   [42] See id., arts 56, 70, 44, 65.

[43] *US v. List* (American Military Tribunal, Nuremberg, 1948), 11 NMT 1230, at 1253.

[44] Ibid. at 1247, 1252, 1256. See also ibid. at 1236.

[45] International Committee of the Red Cross, Commentary on the Additional Protocols of 8 June 1977 to the Geneva Conventions of 12 August 1949 (ICRC/Martinus Nijhoff 1987) para 2238. See also Richard R Baxter, "So-Called 'Unprivileged Belligerency': Spies, Guerillas, and Saboteurs," *British Yearbook of International Law* 28 (1951), p. 324.

[46] Indeed, the tribunal condemned reprisals against civilian hostages as "a barbarous relic of ancient times" and bemoaned the "complete failure on the part of the nations of the world to limit or mitigate the practice by conventional rule." *US v. List* at 1249, 1251.

[47] Ibid. at 1296.

forces."[48] In context, this passage does not support the view that military necessity is a general source of either legal authority or legal constraint. As the tribunal noted, other legal rules "make no such exceptions to [their] enforcement."[49]

Today, specific legal prohibitions contain exceptions for cases of military necessity, public necessity, medical and investigative necessity, as well as the necessity of providing for the civilian population.[50] However, "The[se] prohibitions ... control, and are superior to military [or other] necessities of the most urgent nature except where the [prohibitions] themselves specifically provide the contrary."[51] Accordingly, military necessity, public necessity, medical and investigative necessity, and so forth are not free-standing sources of legal authority or constraint. On the contrary, they are best understood as non-legal concepts that must be incorporated into specific legal rules to have any legal effect.

V Precautions in Attack

In its most general form, the precautions rule requires that "in the conduct of military operations, constant care shall be taken to spare the civilian population, civilians and civilian objects."[52] Accordingly, "all feasible precautions must be taken to avoid, and in any event to minimise, incidental loss of civilian life, injury to civilians and damage to civilian objects."[53] While the proportionality rule sets an upper limit on the harm that attackers may inflict on civilians in pursuit of some military advantage, the precautions rule requires attackers to inflict even less harm on civilians whenever feasible.

The precautions rule generates a number of sub-rules. Attacking forces must "do everything feasible to verify that targets are military objectives" – to avoid mistakenly targeting civilians.[54] Similarly, attacking forces "must do everything feasible to assess whether the attack may be expected" to inflict excessive harm on civilians.[55] More distinctively, attacking forces must "take all feasible precautions in the choice of means and methods of attack with a view to avoiding, and in any event to minimizing, incidental loss of civilian life, injury to civilians and damage to civilian objects."[56] In particular, "effective advance warning shall be given of attacks which may affect the civilian population, unless circumstances do not permit."[57] Finally, "when a choice is possible

---

[48] Ibid. at 1253–54.   [49] Ibid. at 1256.   [50] See e.g. Protocol I, arts 34(4)(b), 63(5), 70(3)(c).

[51] Ibid. at 1296.

[52] Protocol I, art 57(1); International Committee of the Red Cross, *Customary International Humanitarian Law*, vol. 1, Cambridge: Cambridge University Press, 2009, 51.

[53] ICRC, *Customary IHL* 51.

[54] Protocol I art 57(2)(a) (emphasis added); ICRC, *Customary IHL* 55.

[55] ICRC, *Customary IHL* 58.

[56] Protocol I art 57(2)(a)(ii); ICRC, *Customary IHL* 56. See also Protocol I art 57(4).

[57] Protocol I art 57(2)(c); ICRC, *Customary IHL* 62.

between several military objectives for obtaining a similar military advantage, the objective to be selected shall be that the attack on which may be expected to cause the least danger to civilian lives and to civilian objects."[58]

Feasible precautions are "those precautions which are practicable or practically possible, taking into account all circumstances ruling at the time, including humanitarian and military considerations."[59] Presumably, "taking into account" both the humanitarian considerations in favour of taking a precaution and the military considerations against taking that precaution means balancing the former against the latter.[60] If the former outweigh the latter, then the precaution is required. Conversely, if the latter outweigh the former, then the precaution is not required.

Importantly, on this view, "it is reasonable to require military forces to assume some degree of risk to avoid collateral damage and incidental injury. They do so regularly. By this analysis, the greater the anticipated collateral damage or incidental injury, the greater the risk they can reasonably be asked to shoulder."[61] For example, in 2013, the U.S. Joint Chiefs of Staff took the position that "circumstances permit" effective advance warning of an attack when "any degradation in attack effectiveness is outweighed by the reduction in collateral damage [e.g.] because advanced warning allowed the adversary to get civilians out of the target area."[62] On this sensible view, attackers must weigh the military reasons to attack without warning against the humanitarian reasons to give advance warning. If the latter outweigh the former, then advance warning must be given; if not, then not.

Two years later, in a disturbing turn of events, the U.S. Department of Defense *Law of War Manual* declared that "if a commander determines that taking a precaution would result in operational risk (i.e., a risk of failing to accomplish the mission) or an increased risk of harm to their own forces, then the precaution would not be feasible and would not be required."[63] It seems that, according to the manual, "feasible" means "risk free." Far from "taking into account" both humanitarian and military considerations, the manual seems to disregard or exclude the former when they conflict with the latter – as they almost always do.

As a matter of law, the manual is almost certainly wrong on both counts.[64] As one international group of experts concluded, "whereas a particular course of action may be considered non-feasible due to military considerations (such

---

[58] Protocol I art 57(3); ICRC, *Customary IHL* 65.   [59] ICRC, *Customary IHL* 54, 70.

[60] Michael N. Schmitt, "Precision Attack and International Humanitarian Law," *International Review of the Red Cross* 87 (2005) no. 859, p. 462.

[61] Ibid.

[62] United States Joint Chiefs of Staff, Joint Targeting (Joint Publication 3–60) (January 13, 2013) A-5.

[63] US Dep't of Defense, *Law of War Manual* (2015) 5.3.3.2.

[64] See generally, Adil Ahmad Haque, "Off Target: Selection, Precaution, and Proportionality in the DoD Manual," *International Law Studies* 92 (2016).

as excessive risks to aircraft and their crews), some risks have to be accepted in light of humanitarian considerations."[65] Similarly, A.P.V. Rogers writes that "military necessity cannot always override humanity. In taking care to protect civilians, soldiers must accept some element of risk to themselves."[66] Rogers quotes British Defense Doctrine, which stated that "there may be occasions when a commander will have to accept a higher level of risk to his own forces in order to avoid or reduce collateral damage to the enemy's civil population."[67]

My own view is that the humanitarian consideration in favour of taking a precaution is that doing so will reduce the marginal risk of harming civilians.[68] Similarly, the military consideration against taking a precaution is that doing so will increase the marginal risk of allowing opposing forces to harm attacking forces or civilians in current or future military operations, including as a result of mission failure. Importantly, there is a substantial moral asymmetry between doing harm and allowing harm. Unlike allowing harm, doing harm infringes another person's physical integrity (or, in some cases, something else to which she has a right) while making her worse off than she would have been in your absence. These facts make doing harm morally worse, or harder to justify, than allowing harm.[69] Accordingly, on my view, attacking forces should take a precaution unless the reduced marginal risk of harming civilians is substantially outweighed by the increased marginal risk of allowing harm to themselves or to other civilians.

VI   Proportionality in the Law of Armed Conflict

The proportionality rule prohibits attacks "which may be expected to cause incidental loss of civilian life, injury to civilians, damage to civilian objects, or a combination thereof, which would be excessive in relation to the concrete and direct military advantage anticipated."[70] While the precautions rule regulates *how* armed forces may pursue a particular military advantage, the proportionality rule regulates *whether* a particular military advantage may be pursued or must be abandoned.

---

[65] Program on Humanitarian Policy and Conflict Research, *Commentary on the HPCR Manual on International Law Applicable to Air and Missile Warfare* (2010) 39.

[66] A.P.V. Rogers, "Conduct of Combat and Risks Run by the Civilian Population" (1982) Military Law and Law of War Review 310.

[67] British Ministry of Defence, *JWP 0–01 British Defence Doctrine* (1996).

[68] See Adil Ahmad Haque, *Law and Morality at War*, Oxford: Oxford University Press, 2016, chap. 7; Seth Lazar, "Necessity in Self-Defense and War," *Philosophy and Public Affairs* 40 (2012) no. 1, p. 43.

[69] See Warren S. Quinn, "Actions, Intentions, and Consequences: The Doctrine of Doing and Allowing" ," *Philosophical Review* 98 (1989): 287–312; Helen Frowe, "Killing John to Save Mary: A Defense of the Moral Distinction between Killing and Letting Die," in *Action, Ethics, and Responsibility*, eds. Joseph Keim Campbell, Michael O'Rourke, and Harry Silverstein, Cambridge: MIT Press, 2007.

[70] Protocol I, art 51(5). See also ICRC, *Customary IHL* 46.

The most challenging question raised by the proportionality rule is how to balance civilian harm against military advantage. Before turning to that question, let us briefly review other key elements of the proportionality rule.

First, civilian losses are excessive in relation to military advantage just in case the former exceed, outweigh, or are unjustified by the latter.[71] Strangely, it is sometimes suggested that civilian losses are "excessive" in relation to military advantage only if the former substantially outweigh the latter.[72] This suggestion has no obvious basis in language or logic. In ordinary language, "excessive" simply means "exceeding" or "going beyond" some normative standard.[73] Moreover, it seems illogical to concede that the humanitarian considerations against an attack outweigh the military considerations in favour of the attack yet insist that the attack is permissible.

Second, international law prohibits attacks which may be *expected* to cause civilian losses which would be excessive in relation to the military advantage *anticipated*. In other words, the lawfulness of an attack depends not on its actual consequences but on its reasonably foreseeable consequences.[74] According to the International Criminal Tribunal for the former Yugoslavia,

> In determining whether an attack was proportionate it is necessary to examine whether a reasonably well-informed person in the circumstances of the actual perpetrator, making reasonable use of the information available to him or her, could have expected excessive civilian casualties to result from the attack.[75]

Attackers must do everything feasible to assess whether an attack will cause excessive civilian losses and to cancel or suspend an attack if it becomes apparent that it will do so.[76]

Third, only military advantages that are *concrete* and *direct* can legally justify civilian losses. A military advantage is "any consequence of an attack which directly enhances friendly military operations or hinders those of the enemy" such as disabling opposing combatants, destroying their equipment, denying them opportunities to attack, and creating opportunities to attack them.[77] By contrast, "forcing a change in the negotiating position of the enemy only by

---

[71] See U.S. Dep't of Defense, *Law of War Manual* 2.4.1.2.

[72] See e.g. Geoffrey S. Corn, Laurie R. Blank, Chris Jenks, and Eric Talbot Jensen, "Belligerent Targeting and the Invalidity of a Least Harmful Means Rule," *International Law Studies* 89 (2013), p. 536.

[73] See e.g. *Merriam-Webster Dictionary* (defining "excessive" as "exceeding what is usual, proper, necessary, or normal"); *Oxford English Dictionary* ("More than is necessary, normal, or desirable").

[74] Cf. *Commentary on the HPCR Manual* 91 ("The standard is objective in that expectations must be reasonable").

[75] ICTY, *Prosecutor v. Galić*, Judgment, IT-98–29, Trial Chamber, December 5, 2003, para 58.

[76] Protocol I arts 57(2)(a)(iii) and 57(2)(b); ICRC, *Customary IHL* 58 and 60.

[77] *Commentary on the HPCR Manual* 45.

affecting civilian morale does not qualify as military advantage."[78] A military advantage is concrete only if it is substantial and clearly identifiable. A military advantage is direct only if it is proximately caused, either without further intervening agency (as with the destruction of weapons to prevent their future use) or with reasonably foreseeable intervening agency (as with strikes intended to lead an adversary to divert troops or resources away from one's true objective).

It has been claimed that military advantages are concrete and direct only if they are "relatively close" to the attack in space and time, and that advantages "which would only appear in the long term should be disregarded."[79] However, it seems clear that the destruction of weapons in a factory or armoury would yield a concrete and direct advantage even if the weapons had not been sent to the front lines for many weeks. Accordingly, a concrete and direct advantage "may or may not be temporally or geographically related to the object of the attack" so long as it is "foreseeable by the [attacker] at the relevant time."[80]

When the achievement of a military advantage requires coordinated attacks, the proportionality rule compares the harm expected and the military advantage anticipated from the operation as a whole.[81] Paradigmatically, it may be necessary to destroy several bridges to prevent the movement of troops or supplies. The military advantage of destroying any one bridge may be trivial if the opposing force could simply use one of the other bridges. Accordingly, we should compare the advantage anticipated and the harm expected from destroying all the bridges.

Fourth, it is sometimes claimed that "Remote harms resulting from [an] attack do not need to be considered in a proportionality analysis."[82] On the contrary, unlike military advantages, civilian losses need not be concrete and direct, let alone relatively close in space and time, to fall under the proportionality rule. Placing a mine or improvised explosive device in a civilian area may kill or injure civilians days, weeks, or months later. Similarly, destroying bridges or roads necessary to bring food or medicine to a civilian population may predictably result in civilian deaths when existing supplies run out.[83] Such foreseeable remote harms must be considered in a proportionality analysis.

Fifth, an attack may be rendered disproportionate by loss of civilian life, injury to civilians, or damage to civilian property. Other negative consequences

---

[78] Ibid.   [79] ICRC, Protocol I Commentary para 2209.

[80] International Criminal Court, Elements of Crimes n. 36.

[81] See e.g. UK Ministry of Defense, *Law of Armed Conflict Manual* 5.33.5; ICRC, Protocol I Commentary para 2218.

[82] U.S. Dep't of Defense, *Law of War Manual* 5.12.3.

[83] See ICTY, *Prosecutor v Prlic*, Judgment, IT-04-74, Trial Chamber, May 29, 2013, paras 1582–84.

of an attack may render the attack morally impermissible all things considered but will not render an attack legally disproportionate.[84]

Finally, attacks may be rendered disproportionate by a combination of loss of civilian life, injury to civilians, and damage to civilian property. A complete account of the proportionality rule therefore requires an account of how to measure the disvalue of death, injury, and property damage and then aggregate such losses across persons.

Civilian Harm and Military Advantage

On its face, the proportionality rule seems to call for a comparison between two incommensurable values – civilian losses and military advantage – irreducible to any more basic value.[85] Although perhaps incommensurable, civilian losses and military advantages seem roughly or imprecisely comparable. Certainly, we often make confident proportionality judgments in extreme cases. For example, the ICRC writes that "the presence of a soldier on leave obviously cannot justify the destruction of a village. Conversely, if the destruction of a bridge is of paramount importance for the occupation or non-occupation of a strategic zone, it is understood that some houses may be hit, but not that a whole urban area be leveled."[86] Similarly, the Israeli High Court writes that "shooting at [a sniper firing on soldiers or civilians] is proportional even if as a result, an innocent civilian neighbor or passerby is harmed. That is not the case if the building is bombed from the air and scores of its residents and passersby are harmed."[87]

Henry Shue proposes that we can improve our proportionality judgments by sorting particular military advantages and civilian losses into rough categories along the following lines:

Level	Military Advantage	Civilian Losses
1	Important	Moderate
2	Compelling	Severe
3	Decisive	Catastrophic

---

[84] For three partially conflicting approaches to environmental damage, compare Protocol I, art 55(1); Rome Statute, art 8(2)(b)(iv); and ICRC, *Customary IHL* 143.
See also Eliav Lieblich, "Beyond Life and Limb: Exploring Incidental Mental Harm under International Humanitarian Law," in *Applying International Humanitarian Law in Judicial and Quasi-Judicial Bodies: International and Domestic Aspects*, eds. Derek Jinks, Jackson Nyamuya Maogoto, Solon Solomon, The Hague: TMC Asser, p. 185.

[85] See e.g. A.P.V. Rogers, *Law on the Battlefield*, New York: Manchester University Press, 1996, p. 17; Michael N. Schmitt, "The Principle of Discrimination in 21st Century Warfare," *Yale Human Rights and Development Law Journal* 2 (1999), p. 151.

[86] ICRC, Protocol I Commentary para 2214.

[87] HCJ 769/02, Pub. Comm. Against Torture in Israel v. Gov't of Israel, Judgment, Dec. 11, 2005, para 46.

According to Shue, "it is excessive to inflict civilian losses of a category higher than the category of military advantage anticipated."[88] On this view, an attacking force may inflict moderate civilian losses in pursuit of an important, compelling, or decisive military advantage; severe civilians losses in pursuit of a compelling or decisive advantage; and catastrophic civilian losses only in pursuit of a decisive military advantage.

Shue does not attempt to fix the boundaries of each category, but he imagines that the task of doing so would proceed along parallel tracks, with military experts categorizing military advantages according to military standards and "morally sensitive" individuals categorizing civilian losses according to moral standards. Independent moral judgment would then be exercised to sort the categories created by the two groups into three (or more) levels. Each level would then contain categories of losses and advantages that are roughly equal in moral weight.

For their part, Thomas Hurka and Jeff McMahan reject the view that civilian losses and military advantages are incommensurable values on the grounds that military advantages have no intrinsic value at all.[89] On their view, military advantages have instrumental or derivative value only if they contribute to the achievement of a just cause. Conversely, a military advantage that contributes to an unjust cause has no moral value and therefore cannot morally justify inflicting civilian losses. On this view, every harm that unjust combatants inflict on civilians is *morally* disproportionate. Moreover, the *legal* rule of proportionality has no morally intelligible content when applied to the conduct of unjust combatants.

My own view is that the value of a military advantage lies in the harm to soldiers and civilians that its achievement will prevent in current or future military operations. As discussed at the end of the previous section, there is a substantial moral asymmetry between doing harm and allowing harm. Accordingly, on my view, expected civilian harm is excessive if the anticipated military advantage will not prevent or enable one to prevent opposing forces from inflicting substantially greater harm on one's own forces or civilians in current or future military operations. Simply put, an attack is proportionate only if it will foreseeably prevent substantially more harm to attacking forces or civilians than it will foreseeably inflict on civilians.[90]

---

[88] Henry Shue, "Proportionality in War," in *The Encyclopedia of War*, ed. Gordon Martel, 2012, p. 7. For a similar approach, see Jason D. Wright, "'Excessive' Ambiguity: Analysing and Refining the Proportionality Standard," *International Review of the Red Cross*, 94 (2012), p. 852.

[89] See Thomas Hurka, "Proportionality in the Morality of War," *Philosophy and Public Affairs* 33 (2005) no. 1, p. 34; Jeff McMahan, "Proportionality and Necessity in *Jus in Bello*" in *The Oxford Handbook of the Ethics of War*, eds. Helen Frowe and Seth Lazar, Oxford: Oxford University Press, 2016.

[90] See Haque, *Law and Morality at War*, chap. 8.

My interpretation of the proportionality rule applies symmetrically to all parties to a conflict, independently of their war aims, yet all parties have decisive moral reasons to obey it. Just combatants who violate the proportionality rule will act wrongfully, while unjust combatants who violate the proportionality rule will act even more wrongfully than they would if they obeyed the proportionality rule. The moral function of the law of armed conflict is to help all combatants, just and unjust alike, more closely conform to the moral reasons that apply to them.[91] For unjust combatants, full conformity is generally impossible and partial conformity is the most that they can achieve so long as they continue to fight at all. However, given the moral stakes of armed conflict, even partial conformity is most welcome.

[91] Ibid., chap. 2.

15 Humanitarianism: Neutrality, Impartiality, and Humanity

Elizabeth Lanphier

During warfare it is not only the combatants who are present on the battlefield. Civilians, auxiliary or paramilitary workers, journalists, and humanitarian actors are potentially on or near the sites of the conflict. Humanitarian workers have a mandate to provide *impartial* and *neutral* emergency assistance to all sides of the conflict, prioritizing the greatest humanitarian needs, regardless of the recipients of such aid being on the just or unjust side of war. Increasingly, this humanitarian assistance also positions itself as *independent* of any state action. While historically medical relief to combatants was provided largely by militarily affiliated medics, or organized national societies, contemporary humanitarian aid is often international and independent in nature. This emphasizes the perceived neutrality and impartiality of such actors, while posing challenges to creating "humanitarian space" for apolitical actors, primarily nongovernmental organizations (NGOs), to respond to the humanitarian suffering produced by the political and legal actions of war.

The first section of this chapter provides a brief history of the presence of humanitarian action in warfare, the codification of protections for humanitarian workers, and some key debates in the Just War literature that emerge around humanitarianism.[1] In the second section I sketch a short history of the contemporary political and legal positions toward humanitarianism during warfare, primarily as an *in bello* consideration.[2]

The third and fourth sections of the chapter shift to a paradox that arises in contemporary humanitarian aid: that aid is on the one hand legally and politically recognized as neutral and impartial, and that on the other hand humanitarianism takes its mandate from a humanism in which duties toward humanity appear to supersede legal and political status. The third section explores the concepts of neutrality and impartiality and how they apply to

---

[1] This chapter alternately uses the terms "humanitarian actors," "agencies," and "organizations" to refer to independent bodies providing humanitarian aid (often as nongovernmental organizations, or NGOs). This is importantly distinct from the concept of "humanitarian intervention," or state military intervention justified by "humanitarian" reasons.

[2] However the missions of many humanitarian agencies expand beyond conflict zones, and some do not enter into conflict zones at all but provide aid in response to natural disasters, epidemics, endemics, neglected diseases, food insecurity, or *post bellum* reconstruction efforts.

humanitarian aid. That humanitarianism is appealing to a moral duty, rather than a legal or political one, creates an asymmetry between the source of humanitarian agencies' obligation to aid and the protections and rights afforded by legal and political initiatives to do so. In the fourth section, I suggest that humanitarian aid exists in a paradoxical realm between politics and morals, in which the principle of neutrality may be impossible for humanitarian actors to uphold if they are to remain consistent with their mandate to serve human dignity.

I Humanitarianism on the Battlefield

The primary focus of this chapter is contemporary humanitarian action in conflict settings. Such aid is unique for its independent humanitarian status. However the history of medical aid on the battlefield dates back to ancient Greece. The Greek army traveled with medical staff, influencing the Roman army to take on a similar practice of traveling with an organized medical service to care for wounded soldiers both on the battlefield and in established army field hospitals.[3] Michael Walzer has suggested that medical staff embedded with military forces has "almost always been taken to be immune – ever since the Middle Ages."[4] According to Walzer, medical staff both "patch up soldiers and return them back into battle" and "relieve human suffering." It is this second role, as relievers of suffering, that grants medics membership in the category of "the larger human community" instead of the army, and therefore affords them immunity.[5] Even though many of these medics were traveling with and organized by the armed forces they were medically attending, according to Walzer's argument, their medical aid was part of a human cause, not a military one.

During the American Civil War, Walt Whitman wrote a series of poems set on the battlefield, including "The Wound Dresser," which documents his experiences as a civilian medical support person tending to soldiers wounded in battle. Whitman was supporting combatants, yet set apart from them. He was a witness to and provider of relief from suffering, but not taken to be a party to the conflict.[6] Concurrent to Whitman's battlefield nursing care, the first Geneva Conventions were being held, which would establish formal, internationally recognized immunity for and protections of medical staff in conflict zones.

The International Committee of the Red Cross (ICRC) was formed out of an idea developed by Henry Dunant, a Swiss businessman involved in charitable organizations in his home country, who had encountered the brutal conditions

---

[3] See "The Military Medicine of Ancient Rome," in *Science and Its Times*, eds. Neil Schlager and Josh Lauer, vol. 1, Detroit: Gale, 2001.

[4] Michael Walzer, "Response to Jeff McMahan," *Philosophia* 34 (2006): 19–21, p. 20.   [5] Ibid.

[6] Walt Whitman, "The Wound Dresser," *Leaves of Grass*, New York: The Modern Library Publishers, 1921: 263–65.

of soldiers wounded during combat in the 1859 Battle of Solferino. Dunant, like Whitman, published an account of what he witnessed as *A Memory of Solferino* in which he proposed that volunteers from all states should be trained to provide relief to those wounded in combat, and that an international treaty should be created to establish protections for the wounded and sick, as well as those who cared for them during war.[7]

A conference was organized in Geneva in 1863 around Dunant's vision for an international cadre of trained volunteer relief personnel and international protections. At this meeting the ICRC was established to act as a coordinating body for national relief organizations, though over time the ICRC developed an independent identity and direct operations. Following this 1863 conference, the Geneva Committee convened with 16 represented states in August 1864 to propose a convention that would protect wounded and sick combatants, as well as those who provided medical care to them. Article 1 designated that "ambulances and military hospitals shall be recognized as neutral, and as such, protected and respected by the belligerents as long as they accommodate wounded and sick," while Article 2 extended this neutrality to military "hospital and ambulance personnel."[8] A symbol was established, the red cross on a white background, to universally indicate those individuals and sites protected by the Convention.[9]

The 1864 document likewise protected combatants when wounded or sick, regardless of the nation to which they belonged. It indicated that they should be "collected and cared for," with those unfit for continued service being repatriated, and those who could be fit for continued service to abstain from further military duty "for the duration of hostilities."[10] This is a crucial point on which contemporary medical humanitarian aid diverges from these original Geneva Conventions. On one view of neutrality, mandating that soldiers wounded and healed in battle abstain from further combat ensures that those providing medical relief are indeed attending to human suffering and are not contributing to the war efforts of either a just or unjust side of a conflict by patching up soldiers who will be sent back out to fight.

Yet on another view of neutrality, which I discuss further later, one might say that contemporary humanitarian medical workers, especially those affiliated with the ICRC and Doctors Without Borders/Medecins Sans Frontieres (MSF), are establishing impartiality by not involving themselves with which side the wounded fighters originated from, or to which they will return. These organizations embody Article 6 of the 1864 Conventions insofar as they collect and care for the wounded and sick, regardless of their nationality or military membership. But to fully realize their organizational impartiality, they must

[7] Henry Dunant, *A Memory of Solferino*, Geneva: ICRC, 1939.
[8] International Committee of the Red Cross, "Geneva Conventions," August 22, 1864.
[9] Ibid., Article 7.   [10] Ibid., Article 6.

also refrain from taking a position regarding the identity or affiliations of their patients, as well as their patients' activities after receiving medical care. A question arises then, if this view of impartiality can be consistent with the objectives of neutrality. The revised Geneva Conventions of 1906 removed the provision to repatriate the wounded and sick, converting it to a mere recommendation.

The Conventions of 1906 were ratified by 35 states and replaced the 1864 Conventions.[11] The 1906 Conventions expanded definitions of and terms of care and burial for the wounded, sick, and dead and included maritime operations. Additionally, the 1906 Conventions were the first to recognize nonmilitary medical personnel. Article 10 designates "the personnel of volunteer aid societies, duly recognized and authorized by their own governments" as also bound by the same terms "upon condition that the said personnel shall be subject to military laws and regulations."[12] Such independent "aid societies" are to be identified with the same red cross on white background emblem, indicating their immunity and neutrality; the emblem is to be issued by a "competent military authority."[13]

With the 1929 Geneva Conventions, the protections expanded to include considerations for prisoners of war, in addition to the wounded, sick, and sanitary personnel who had been addressed in earlier iterations of the Conventions. However it is with the 1949 Conventions, drafted in light of the experience of World War II, that the Conventions were further expanded to explicitly address civilians during war. The original 1949 Conventions were broken into four parts: I on the Wounded and Sick in the Armed Forces in the Field; II on the Wounded, Sick and Shipwrecked of Armed Forces at Sea; III Prisoners of War; and IV Civilians. Additional commentaries and protocols have since further amended the 1949 Conventions including in 1977, 1993, and 2005.

In extending the Conventions to certain civilian protections, especially civilians in territories occupied during a conflict, the 1949 Conventions commit the occupying territories to allow for relief efforts on behalf of civilians in said occupied lands either by "States or by impartial humanitarian organizations such as the International Committee of the Red Cross," whose activities "shall consist, in particular, of the provision of consignments of foodstuffs, medical supplies and clothing." Furthermore, it is required that "all Contracting Parties shall permit the free passage of these consignments and shall guarantee their protection."[14]

---

[11] The 1906 Conventions remained in effect until 1970, although new Conventions were again drafted in 1929 and then 1949. However, because not all states ratified the Conventions of 1929 and 1949, the 1906 Conventions remained in force until all states signed on to the updated 1949 conventions, which were finally ratified in 1970.

[12] International Committee of the Red Cross, "Geneva Conventions," July 6, 1906.

[13] Ibid., Article 20.

[14] International Committee of the Red Cross, "Geneva Conventions," August 12, 1949, Article 59.

Thus the 1949 Geneva Conventions expressly protect the rights of safe passage and protection for humanitarian relief efforts by both state and independent humanitarian actors on and off the battlefield, whose beneficiaries are combatant and noncombatant parties, and whose scope expands beyond mere medical aid. Furthermore, the Conventions prescribe that "in adopting measures of health and hygiene and in their implementation, the Occupying Power shall take into consideration the moral and ethical susceptibilities of the population of the occupied territory."[15] Not only is it a legal and political obligation for the occupying power to concern itself with the "health and hygiene" of the occupied population, but it looks like a *moral* duty to do so, one that appeals to the dignity and humanity of the occupied persons.

It might appear as if, in practice, aid agencies failed to fully respect the dignity and humanity of occupied persons during World War II. The ICRC has since admitted its failures to fully uncover the facts of what was occurring in deportation and concentration camps, to adequately visit or monitor camps, or to address the suffering and executions taking place in the camps.[16] In light of these recognized failures, the ICRC reestablished its mandate and independence, particularly its political independence from Switzerland, and its coherence as an acting body beyond merely coordinating national societies of the Red Cross.[17] Next I take up how these changes to the Geneva Conventions and the ICRC in light of World War II developed in the contemporary humanitarianism of the second half of the twentieth and beginning of the twenty-first centuries, with the rise of independent actors such as ICRC and MSF at the forefront of providing what is taken to be impartial, neutral, humanitarian relief in the most urgent conflict zones.

II   Contemporary Humanitarian Action in Conflict Zones

The ICRC was established in 1863 but has developed since then from being an organizing body for national Red Cross societies into a freestanding agency with its own mandate for humanitarian action. The Geneva Conventions of 1949, and their subsequent Additional Protocols of 1977, committed signatories to allow their own national agencies to adopt principles in accordance with those of the Red Cross. The ICRC has seven "fundamental principles" including the guiding principle of humanity, which is connected to the complementary principle of

---

[15] Ibid., Article 56.

[16] These points were raised in an address on November 4, 2002, by François Bugnion, then the ICRC's director for international law and cooperation, at the International Red Cross and Red Crescent Museum. See François Bugnion, "Dialogue with the Past: The ICRC and the Nazi Death Camps," ICRC, 2002.

[17] Ibid.

impartiality; the related concepts of neutrality and independence; and, finally, the implementing principles of voluntarism, unity, and universality.[18]

In 1991 the United Nations (UN) established the UN Department for Humanitarian Affairs and declared that "humanitarian assistance must be provided in accordance with the principles of humanity, neutrality and impartiality,"[19] essentially adopting the first three of the ICRC principles as the standard for all humanitarian action recognized by the UN and its member states, and providing the most widely accepted standards for humanitarian action today.[20]

These principles of humanity, impartiality, and neutrality are what in turn grant humanitarian actors immunity in conflict zones in accordance with the Geneva Conventions' requirements to respect the activities of humanitarian actors, including allowing their safe passage through conflict zones. Individuals, buildings, and goods designated with the red cross, red crescent, or other identified symbol of their humanitarian status, are to be recognized by states and belligerent forces as immune from attack.[21]

However, this does not mean that all states and conflicting parties openly welcome humanitarian presence, nor necessarily respect their impartiality. Humanitarian actors talk about the need to negotiate "humanitarian space" during armed conflicts.[22] This space is both literal and figurative, being a physical place where humanitarian agencies can establish their activities including the setup of a hospital, trauma center, clinic, or refugee camp but also a figurative sense of safe passage, protection, and immunity. Both literal and figurative aims of "humanitarian space" are lofty goals, which as I discuss later, may not be possible to achieve.

While international law protects humanitarian actors, "it does not guarantee humanitarian agencies unfettered access to war zones; rather access entails negotiations between parties to the conflict and humanitarian agencies."[23] Negotiations for humanitarian space already fall within the realm of the political, as negotiations between state (or non-state militarized) actors. And

---

[18] International Committee of the Red Cross, "The Fundamental Principles of the International Red Cross and Red Crescent Movement," Geneva: ICRC, 2015. According to Jean Pictet, who provided a commentary on the ICRC principles in 1979 that continues to be referenced by the ICRC currently, the principles can be arranged in a pyramid with "humanity" at the top, accompanied by "impartiality," from which the five remaining principles necessarily follow.

[19] UN General Assembly Resolution 46/182, December 19, 1991.

[20] See Fiona Terry, *Condemned to Repeat? The Paradox of Humanitarian Action*, Ithaca: Cornell University Press, 2002, p. 18.

[21] Organizations such as MSF or Action Against Hunger (ACF) each have their own unique, but recognized logo to set apart not only their humanitarian status but also their independence from other humanitarian actors such as the ICRC or branches of the UN.

[22] Terry, *Condemned to Repeat?*, p. 19.

[23] International Committee of the Red Cross, "The Fundamental Principles of the International Red Cross and Red Crescent Movement," 2015, p. 13.

the co-opting of aid for political purposes may lie behind why and how humanitarian access is granted, cut off, or manipulated by the political, conflicting parties.[24] According to the ICRC, its fundamental principles provide a tool when negotiating its presence in conflict zones: the principles are concrete tools to "gain the respect and trust of people during wars – when they are naturally suspicious and communities can be torn apart."[25]

One such negotiation humanitarian actors often face is whether or not to speak out about what they witness in the course of providing humanitarian relief. Organizations working in conflict zones encounter grave suffering, but they may also be in a unique position to witness the manipulation of aid, mass atrocities, or war crimes that occur during the conflict. Whether silence about what they witness is necessarily built into the principles of humanity, impartiality, and neutrality, or if it may at times be at odds with these principles, is a tension among humanitarian actors. The ICRC describes the principle of neutrality as one in which "in order to enjoy the confidence of all, the Movement [ICRC] may not take sides in hostilities or engage at any time in controversies of a political, racial, religious or ideological nature."[26] And they hasten to add: "neutrality is often mistakenly taken to mean passivity or indifference. But not taking sides in a conflict does not mean being indifferent. Neutrality in fact enables [the ICRC] to put the Principles of humanity and impartiality into action."[27] Although individual ICRC workers may not be indifferent to the suffering to which they are attending, nor the actions they witness in the course of providing aid, they interpret neutrality to require refraining from taking any outward position that might suggest that they have taken a stance on a controversy or a side of a conflict.

However the ICRC notes: "neutrality does not mean the Movement will stay silent on issues of grave humanitarian concern," and it has been committed to taking action to "prevent the cruelty and abuse that can arise in armed conflict." For the ICRC neutrality takes the form of communicating directly with those "taking part in the hostilities, reminding them of their obligations under humanitarian law."[28] Neutrality may not be passivity, but in this iteration, any form of speaking out is directed at "all sides to a conflict"[29] to adhere to international law, rather than targeting particular abuses observed on one side of the conflict, which will only be communicated to the parties in question, in confidence, but without any form of external or international accountability.

---

[24] The ICRC provides an example of the manipulation of aid in Afghanistan during the U.S. invasion of Afghanistan following the attacks on the United States on September 11, 2001, noting how military personnel purposefully dressed as civilians and drove vehicles similar to the white vehicles used by humanitarian agencies, co-opting this recognized symbol of neutral, impartial, and immune humanitarian activity. See "The Fundamental Principles," p. 18.

[25] Ibid., p. 12.   [26] Ibid., p. 40.   [27] Ibid., p. 42.   [28] Ibid., p. 44.   [29] Ibid., p. 45.

This vision of neutrality held by the ICRC led to the creation of the NGO Doctors Without Borders/Medecins Sans Frontieres in 1971 during the Biafra War in Nigeria. On one account, several French medics working with the ICRC during the Biafra War "rebelled at the ICRC's insistence on absolute public discretion even when faced with the worst atrocities."[30] This team of doctors determined that speaking out only in confidentiality or to "all sides" of a conflict about the general requirement to respect international law was insufficient. Such an interpretation of neutrality failed to meet the humanitarian demands of humanitarian aid. They subsequently broke away from the ICRC to form their own, independent, neutral and impartial NGO.

The MSF Charter crafts its own triumvirate of principles composed of medical ethics, independence, and impartiality. In the discussion of impartiality MSF intertwines the concept of neutrality but then adds two additional principles not reflected in the ICRC charter: bearing witness and accountability. The latter is primarily an internal accountability of its own actions and finances, which are accountable to donors and beneficiaries alike.[31] The principle to "bear witness" derives from the original French MSF Charter's principle of *témoignage*, which has the dual sense of both witnessing and testifying. Bearing witness is to not only stand in solidarity with those who are suffering but also to actively speak out about what one has witnessed, as a way to call to action those who cannot see firsthand what humanitarian actors witness. Through the principle of *témoignage*, MSF is not only calling for adherence to international law by those parties to the conflict, but it is also raising awareness among individuals, nation-states, and organizing bodies such as the UN about "extreme need and unacceptable suffering" and when aid is insufficient, diverted, or abused.[32]

This view of impartiality and neutrality as interconnected with a mandate to speak out; bear witness; and provide testimony to suffering, human rights abuses, war crimes, and breeches in international law casts into relief the very definition of political neutrality. Aid may be impartially distributed according to where the humanitarian needs are perceived to be greatest, irrespective of whether beneficiaries are the just or unjust combatants (or complicit civilians) of a conflict, and regardless of nationality, religion, ethnicity, or any other identifying group affiliation. Yet this impartiality need not be connected to neutrality. The ICRC and MSF charters equate the two, as mutually necessary conditions. However they enact this neutrality quite differently in practice, which is a reflection of their divergent definitions of the term.

In the next section, I discuss in detail the concepts of neutrality and impartiality. In the final section I suggest how these terms yield a paradoxical

[30] David Rieff, *A Bed for the Night: Humanitarianism in Crisis*, New York: Simon and Schuster Paperbacks, 2002, p. 27.

[31] See MSF Charter, available at www.doctorswithoutborders.org/about-us/history-principles /charter.

[32] Ibid.

situation for humanitarian actors who are at once attempting to carve out humanitarian space as an apolitical arena, motivated by obligations toward humanity, and the nonideal realities of humanitarian agencies acting in the face of all-too-political conflicts, in which it is impossible to extricate themselves from a political space entirely.

III Neutrality and Impartiality

This chapter focuses on medical humanitarian assistance to parties wounded in conflict zones, who are often, though not always, combatants. Such medical assistance to combatants places humanitarian workers in a unique position of potentially aiding both just and unjust combatants. This assistance is often framed as a humanitarian commitment to neutrality and impartiality, two distinct but often interlocking concepts that are the focus of the rest of this chapter.

However, it should be noted that humanitarian assistance during wartime may cover a range of services including, but not limited to, provisions of temporary shelter to civilians displaced by warfare, food rations to civilians whose food supplies have been reduced or cut off because of conflict, as well as medical care to noncombatants, especially when normal health systems and infrastructure have been disrupted by the conflict. It may be the case that providing medical care to combatants helps position humanitarian agencies to also provide these forms of emergency relief to a much larger pool of noncombatants. Yet this is not to suggest that noncombatants are excluded from being just or unjust parties to war.

There is a debate within the Just War literature regarding civilian complicity, particularly whether civilians are complicit for the actions of their government or military when on the unjust side of war. Jeff McMahan claims that "no one can be liable to be harmed *merely* by virtue of membership in a group and that the same arguments that establish this claim also show that no one can be morally immune from being harmed simply by virtue of membership in a group, such as the group of civilians."[33] So there is an argument that civilians on the unjust side of war are not immune to harm because of their status as civilians. Yet their contribution as noncombatants in the actions of their state's (unjust) war may render them accountable for their individual actions. Such individual contributions may not meet a requisite threshold of complicity, if they did not intend for their actions to result in the collective action of war.[34]

Cécile Fabre offers a divergent view that does not hinge complicity on the collective act but holds individual noncombatants accountable for their individual acts.[35] Helen Frowe understands noncombatants to be potentially *liable*

---

[33] Jeff McMahan, *Killing in War*, Oxford: Oxford University Press, 2009, p. 210.

[34] See Christopher Kutz, *Complicity: Ethics and Law for a Collective Age*, Cambridge: Cambridge University Press, 2007.

[35] See Cécile Fabre, "Guns, Food, and Liability to Attack in War," *Ethics* 120 (2009): 36–63, p. 61.

to attack, but that this liability does not necessarily entail permissibility to be attacked, all things considered. She notes that there are, however, instances in which killing a noncombatant will "serve the purpose of the just war" and that if the noncombatant "is liable to be killed, killing the non-combatant is not wrong."[36] Although not the primary focus of this chapter, humanitarian aid that provides relief to noncombatants faced with humanitarian crises brought about by war tends to assume that part of what entitles these civilians to aid is their noncombatant status, which would render both the aid providers and civilians immune from being unjust actors of war. However, it is worth noting that even if noncombatants were considered unjust actors complicit in warfare, the principles of impartiality and neutrality would still apply.

It is likely the case that in medical relief facilities established by humanitarian actors in conflict zones, relief organizations would be attending to emergency medical needs of combatants and noncombatants alike, wounded in battle or in the crossfires of warfare. That humanitarian agencies, which understand their actions to be independent, impartial, and neutral, attend to *any* of the most urgent needs that enter into their hospital compound is important to their perceived impartiality and neutrality.

The dictionary definitions of impartiality and neutrality provide a starting place from which to pinpoint the conceptual similarities and differences in these two terms. Impartiality is "freedom from prejudice or bias; fairness,"[37] while neutrality is "an intermediate state or condition, not clearly one thing or another; a neutral position, middle ground."[38] More specifically applicable to war, neutrality is "a neutral policy or attitude between contending parties or states; abstention from taking any part in a war between other states" and "the state or condition of not being on any side."[39] When applied to humanitarian assistance in the context of just and unjust wars, we might say that impartiality is providing care for any person in need, *regardless* of her participation in the just or unjust side of war. This does not require that the impartial party not recognize a beneficiary's status as just or unjust combatant; it simply requires that this status not influence the provision of care.

On the surface it may appear most simple for humanitarian actors to remain impartial if they do not seek to know who their beneficiaries are, and indeed the principle of impartiality would allow for an organization to remain ignorant of whether it was attending to civilians or combatant, and which side of the

---

[36] See Helen Frowe, "Non-Combatant Liability in War," in *How We Fight: Ethics in War*, eds. Helen Frowe and Gerald Lang, Oxford: Oxford University Press, 2014, p. 187.

[37] "impartiality, n." OED Online, September 2016, Oxford University Press, available at www.oed.com/view/Entry/92114.

[38] "neutrality, n." OED Online, September 2016, Oxford University Press, available at www.oed.com/view/Entry/126461.

[39] Ibid.

conflict those civilians or combatants were on. Many organizations clearly designate that weapons are not allowed in clinics and hospitals or on any NGO compound or facility. This means that active combatants are asked to leave their weapons at the door if they are seeking treatment or accompanying another patient; unless someone is in a uniform designating them as a particular combatant, their exact origin may remain unknown. However, strategically, it is unlikely that an aid organization is not largely aware of who its beneficiaries are. Identifying particular populations in need is often how NGOs determine where to establish their hospitals and services. And it is often in support of the principle of impartiality that an organization may choose to work in particular settings and among certain beneficiary populations to clearly communicate it is providing impartial treatment to multiple sides of a conflict.

Neutrality appears to require knowledge of whom one is treating, what side of a conflict one is on, and what one's role is to consciously take a middle-ground position, in which one abstains from taking a position or side in the conflict. One way of parsing the distinction between impartiality and neutrality is according to moral versus political or legal grounds. Impartiality entails moral commitments to equal access to treatment indiscriminate of the group membership or identity of potential beneficiaries. It expands beyond one's mere membership in a group affiliated with a party to a conflict; it includes race, ethnicity, religion, gender, and so on.[40] Neutrality, on the other hand, is particularly applicable to contexts in which a conflict, whether civil or interstate, is occurring, or perhaps contexts where humanitarian assistance is in response to social exclusion. Neutrality might best be understood as *political* neutrality, and as a political category compared to the moral category of impartiality.

Impartial aid provided for humanitarian reasons does not necessarily entail neutrality. By providing impartial medical care, aid workers may be acting in ignorance of their beneficiary's combatant or political status entirely. Neutrality never enters the picture. However, whether or not aid is knowingly neutral, it may be complicit.[41] Humanitarian workers are potentially aiding, and restoring to the battlefield, soldiers on the unjust side of a conflict, whether or not one knows her beneficiaries to be unjust combatants.

Impartiality, therefore, already risks complicity of humanitarian actors when their aid knowingly or unknowingly supports the unjust side of a conflict. This complicity, however, is an unintended but foreseeable consequence of the humanitarian mandate to attend to individuals based on need, and free from prejudice. Whether the complicity of humanitarian workers ought to be subject to sanctions, or they should be considered to be, all things considered, doing

---

[40] The principle of impartiality would be part of humanitarian assistance whether in a conflict or non-conflict setting. Race, ethnicity, nationality, religion, and gender should not influence the provision of aid in response any form of humanitarian disaster.

[41] For a further consideration of this topic, see Larry May, *Contingent Pacifism*, Cambridge: Cambridge University Press, 2015, pp. 125–27.

more good than harm in their complicit actions, is open to debate.[42] The unintended complicity of humanitarian aid workers may be increased when that aid is neutral, in addition to being impartial. To uphold the principle of neutrality, humanitarian workers are necessarily aware of the political affiliations of their beneficiaries and commit to abstaining from taking a stance on their politics or the conflict in which they are engaged.

Of course, adhering to the principles of impartiality and neutrality does not mean that humanitarian workers must remain silent regarding what they witness in the course of providing assistance. It simply means that they cannot take a stance. Yet at times, the line between reporting the sheer facts of what an aid agency has witnessed in its hospitals during a conflict and expressing a view on the conflict can be blurry. MSF includes "bearing witness" as a key element of its charter, stating, "the principles of impartiality and neutrality are not synonymous with silence. When MSF witnesses extreme acts of violence against individuals or groups, the organization may speak out publicly."[43] In such instances, the organization retains a right to take a stance not on conflict, but on the gross abuses of war or conflict. While the organization may remain neutral vis-à-vis the just and unjust sides of war, it will not remain neutral to potential war crimes or crimes against humanity.

The organization further states that it "may seek to bring attention to extreme need and unacceptable suffering when access to lifesaving medical care is hindered, when medical facilities come under threat, when crises are neglected, or when the provision of aid is inadequate or abused."[44] In instances where its operations are blocked by one or both sides of a conflict or other political actors and actions, MSF will refrain from remaining entirely neutral and will speak out. While it may aim for neutrality when this neutrality affords them (relatively) safe access to populations to provide care, when its aid is hindered, co-opted, or abused, a neutral position is futile. Neutrality becomes an empty principle when it does not ensure unimpeded access to and sufficient care for populations most in need. When adequate care is no longer possible as a result of the manipulation of aid, lack of security for aid workers, or a concern for humanitarian complicity in abuses, humanitarian operations must cease. In such extreme cases bearing witness may be the only humanitarian option that remains.

Yet it is more frequently the case that humanitarian aid can be sufficiently provided in a conflict setting. And in such humanitarian operations neutrality

---

[42] May holds that humanitarian workers' "complicity is not of the sort that makes them liable to be severely sanctioned" (May, *Contingent Pacifism*, 127), while Frowe has suggested that they are potentially liable to be killed (Frowe, "Non-Combatant Liability in War"). Lepora and Goodin take an all-things-considered view that four aspects of complicity contribute to a calculation of the overall moral blameworthiness of complicity (Chiara Lepora and Robert E. Goodin, *On Complicity and Compromise*, Oxford: Oxford University Press, 2013, pp. 97–98).

[43] See MSF Charter.   [44] Ibid.

presents precarious consequences, which need to be carefully, and continually, navigated. Taking a neutral stance to sustain the provision of humanitarian assistance can have at least two types of harmful outcomes. One, as already alluded to, is complicity in wrongdoing. Maintaining neutrality may lead to increased complicity. Another potential harm occurs when an organization decides that the complicity entailed by neutrality is too great and elects to break from neutrality in favor of speaking out. This can result in the organization losing access to beneficiary populations when host countries block entry of humanitarian workers into their territory through the refusal of visas or travel permissions, when belligerent parties fail to guarantee safe passage of aid workers or supplies into conflict zones where they are to otherwise be granted immunity, or when aid workers are directly targeted by any party of the conflict with violence or other threats.

There are two significant cases of humanitarian neutrality and complicity in wrongdoing during World War II that I take as examples in this chapter. One is the case of the ICRC and the Nazi concentration camps during the war. The ICRC has, in the years since WWII, reflected on its own actions and shortcomings and has been critiqued for its noted failures to protect Jews from the genocide perpetrated by the Nazi regime. The ICRC attempted to provide relief by delivering food parcels to prisoners of war, monitoring the escalating situation in the camps, and recording missing persons. It used formal channels to negotiate behind the scenes with officials but did not speak out about the growing atrocities of the war and holocaust, of which it was aware.[45] However, as François Buignon reflected in 2002: "the failure was, above all, that of the ICRC's inability – or unwillingness – to fully recognize the extent of the tragedy that was unfolding, and to confront it by reversing its priorities and taking the risks that the situation demanded."[46] How else could the ICRC have more fully recognized the unfolding tragedy? Possibly be revoking its former priority, to remain neutral, and reverse this position in favor of taking the risk to speak out. Buignon further notes, "after the war, criticism of the ICRC focused mainly on the issue of public condemnation," but he wonders "to what extent is this failure attributable to the ICRC itself?"[47] In other words, was the ICRC uniquely accountable in this way and complicit in this failure? Buignon wonders: "Should the ICRC have denounced the genocide? In what way? And by addressing whom?"[48]

The ICRC maintained its mandate of neutrality and continued to carry out the actions it could, which were insufficient in the face of genocide, though nonetheless reduced some suffering and resulted in some lives saved. Had the ICRC spoken out sooner (and the question remains, spoken out to whom? International

---

[45] François Bugnion, "Dialogue with the past: The ICRC and the Nazi death camps" ICRC, 2002, available at www.icrc.org/eng/resources/documents/misc/6ayg86.htm
[46] Ibid.   [47] Ibid.   [48] Ibid.

media? International state representatives or leaders?), would any additional suffering have been reduced? The counterfactual is not dispositive for an alternate outcome. It could be the case that the same or more suffering and death could have occurred, and the only difference would be a mitigated sense of institutional complicity on the part of the ICRC had it spoken out. These are the questions that humanitarian actors face when negotiating their humanitarian objectives with their principles of impartiality and neutrality, their own potential complicity in wrongdoing, and the possible but uncertain benefits they can provide to populations in need.

A similar set of questions faced MSF in the second significant case of neutrality and humanitarian action I consider here. Just over fifty years after the ICRC was faced with genocide by the Nazi regime, MSF was working in Rwanda both in the lead up to the 1994 genocide and in the refugee camps following the genocide. As the mass killings scaled up in Rwanda, in which the Hutu majority population sought out and killed the minority Tutsi population, international political actors pulled away from any form of military intervention. In light of the absence of a political response, a humanitarian response was futile at best, and harmful at worst, acting as a cover for the political failure to intervene in the crisis when Western governments could point to their "support" for Rwanda by the presence of international aid workers from their respective nations on the ground in Rwanda.[49]

However, without earnest international political support, most aid agencies evacuated from Rwanda aside from the ICRC and some MSF doctors who remained to work alongside the ICRC.[50] MSF leadership at the time spoke out about the need for political intervention, which David Rieff characterized as a warning that "in the absence of some political resolution, the humanitarian aid that was so needed in many places in Rwanda risked wrongly being seen as a solution to the crisis."[51] Although humanitarian assistance was necessary in response to a growing humanitarian crisis, it was in no way sufficient. The Rwanda crisis was born first and foremost out of a political conflict, which required a political response. And this political response was a necessary condition for the provision of humanitarian aid. Although humanitarian assistance is responding to an imperative of human dignity that transcends the political, political negotiations and protections are nonetheless crucial to the safe and adequate provision of a humanitarian response.

Following the initial massacre of the genocide, NGOs were able to reassert a presence in Rwanda and refugee camps that mixed civilian and militia populations were established in then-Zaire. Chiara Lepora and Robert Goodin describe the situation following the initial 1994 massacre of up to one million people in Rwanda in the span of approximately one hundred days as follows: "Having first committed genocide against the Tutsi, the FAR (Rwandan Armed Forces)

---

[49] Rieff, *A Bed for the Night*, pp. 164–66.   [50] Ibid., p. 164.   [51] Ibid., p. 167.

soon began using the refugee (mainly Hutu) population in various ways: as a source of income and power in their own right; as a lure for international assistance and legitimation; and as protection against those who might punish or retaliate against the FAR for genocide."[52]

A further question then arises: what role did humanitarian actors, who had initially set up and subsequently maintained these camps, play as complicit in the manipulation and further atrocities carried out by the FAR? To provide any assistance in Rwanda, NGOs had to "acknowledge, interact with and contribute to those perpetrators of genocide" in order to intervene on a "purely humanitarian basis."[53] Again, assistance in the name of the humanitarian duty to rescue is not immune from the political context. To provide relief to those who were the targeted victims of genocide, humanitarian agencies were also providing aid to the unjust perpetrators of the conflict. Yet when the genocide was in full force, the absence of political actors with whom humanitarian agencies could negotiate their neutrality rendered the aid organizations powerless. No international political actors were available to monitor the situation, and the political power on the ground in Rwanda was a government that MSF worker Alex de Waal characterized as one "whose *raison d'etre* was the infliction of suffering."[54] It is impossible for any humanitarian organization committed to the relief of suffering to negotiate under the auspices of neutrality with a state whose entire existence was to cause mass suffering. As Fiona Terry has remarked in a striking parallel to the formulation from de Waal: "the raison d'etre of humanitarian assistance is the alleviation of suffering."[55]

Neutrality requires politics. It is, after all, largely political neutrality that humanitarian agencies are committing to observe when they negotiate their presence in conflict zones. Yet humanitarian actors also stake a claim to their neutrality in something beyond politics: in human dignity, and the intrinsic worth of each human life. The humanitarian worker has a duty to humanity, a duty that provides both the justification for humanitarian presence, action, and protection and the source of tension when a state or states engaged in a political conflict are asked to accommodate and protect a higher-order right to life in the name of humanity[56]. It is this humanity, which, because of the nature of armed conflict, is often directly threatened in war or other political state actions. And perhaps to appeal to humanity in the face of political conflict is itself a political statement. Where the principle of humanity is being eroded in the course of a violent conflict, staking one's place as responding to human dignity and the diminishing of suffering cannot be a neutral claim.

---

[52] Lepora and Goodin, *On Complicity and Compromise*, p. 131.   [53] Ibid., p. 133.
[54] Rieff, *A Bed for the Night*, p. 166.   [55] Terry, *Condemned to Repeat?*, p. 16.
[56] However this "duty" on the part of the humanitarian aid organization or worker is only invoked in response to the absence of a political actor meeting the duty to protect from suffering. For more on this point, see Henry Shue, *Basic Rights: Subsistence, Affluence, and U.S. Foreign Policy*, Princeton: Princeton University Press, 1996.

Rieff has argued that MSF, for example, may never have been truly neutral to begin with. He cites an internal debate within the organization according to which some wish to "remove the commitment of neutrality from the charter," arguing that the organization "had always been political."[57] This inherent political nature of humanitarian aid may be one of the conceptual paradoxes of an impartial duty to rescue. Such a duty is always already responding to, and therefore acknowledging, suffering, harm, and wrongdoing, often either perpetrated or overlooked by a political actor. How it could ever be neutral to begin with is the puzzle.

IV The Paradox of Aid

Part of what appears paradoxical about humanitarian aid is that it participates in both the political realm and a pre-political realm. Walzer has described one puzzle of humanitarian aid to be whether it is a duty, kindness, or both.[58] He notes that if humanitarian assistance responds to people in truly desperate circumstances, then the provision of aid is a matter of justice, and a form of duty. Yet often aid is framed as charity – a good but not a duty.[59] If humanitarian assistance is supererogatory, then on what grounds can humanitarian actors stake an unalienable right to provide assistance that would obligate warring political parties to permit them safe passage and protection to carry out their work in conflict zones? It appears that the rights of humanitarian actors who have a duty to rescue and relieve suffering is necessarily in opposition to the rights of conflicting parties to engage in war, the very enactment of which will entail at least a temporary increase particularly in combatant and possibly civilian suffering. That warring parties therefore have an obligation to ensure humanitarian actors access to beneficiary populations and guarantee that they can safely provide care in line with their duty to humanity is at odds with the conflicting parties' political interests in waging war.

Such a duty to relieve suffering and provide medical assistance neutrally to all combatants on both sides of a conflict may infringe on the interests of both sides of a conflict equally as the victory of either side arises through the administering of suffering and death to the other parties' combatants. Yet arguably humanitarian assistance is only in opposition to the legal and moral rights of one side of the conflict: the just side. Humanitarian workers, acting under the rubric of neutrality, will necessarily be aiding unjust combatants as well. However, the unjust side of the conflict does not have a moral right to kill or inflict suffering on its opponent; its very status as unjust combatant implies that

[57] Ibid., p. 308.

[58] Michael Walzer, "On Humanitarianism: Is Helping Others Charity, or Duty, or Both?," *Foreign Affairs* 90 (2011) no. 4, p. 69.

[59] If we were to follow Kant's reading of the duty to charity, it is an imperfect duty and therefore one has an obligation to be charitable but no particular duty in any given circumstance to provide assistance.

killing its opponent is unjustified. It therefore appears to be a problem for humanitarian neutrality that it not only protects but also promotes aiding and respecting the rights of care for both sides of the conflict, which both sides, just and unjust, of a conflict are required to honor by granting humanitarian actors immunity.

As already noted, humanitarian aid is "concerned with preserving the dignity of humanity."[60] In this way, it might be viewed as a pre-political category, for humanity transcends political categorization, rights, and affiliations in favor of a "universal ethic founded on the conviction that all people have equal dignity by virtue of their membership in humanity."[61] The category of membership in humanity overrides the categories of political membership. Humanitarian actors aim to carve out "humanitarian space," a space that exists outside of the political, in which to conduct their work.[62] Terry notes this concept of "humanitarian space" is more of an ideal than a reality, as such separation of the humanitarian from the political sphere "is seldom possible in practice." Such a separation may in fact be impossible, in practice. If membership in humanity is a universal category, and if each individual human has the human right to statehood as the UN Declaration of Human Rights asserts, then all particular members within the category of humanity will also be members of a political category, though not necessarily of any specific political category.[63]

This remains a paradox then for humanitarian neutrality. Humanitarian aid is always appealing to a duty derived from a pre-political source, yet the very negotiation for an apolitical "humanitarian space" is necessarily negotiated among political actors. And the beneficiaries, who are being aided for their membership in humanity, are nonetheless also members of political communities.[64] Rieff has suggested that the concept of "humanitarian space," in which humanitarian action is strictly autonomous and neutral, is merely "wishful thinking," and cannot in fact be realized: "Soldiers ... are not going to do what relief workers want. Instead they are going to expect, in the case of any serious disagreement, that relief workers will do what they tell them to do."[65] While the Geneva Conventions protect medical and humanitarian workers in conflict zones, this on-paper protection does not entail a force field of immunity and guaranteed safety inside a secure humanitarian space for humanitarian

---

[60] Terry, *Condemned to Repeat?*, p. 17.

[61] Ibid., p. 19. And see Rony Brauman, "L'assistance humanitaire international," *Dictionnaire de philosophie morale et politique*, ed. Monique Canto-Sperber, Paris: Presses Universitaire de France, 1996, p. 96.

[62] Ibid. And see Daniel Warner, "The Politics of the Political/Humanitarian Divide," *International Review of the Red Cross* 833 (March 1999): 109–18.

[63] UN General Assembly Resolution 217A, Article 15, December 10, 1948.

[64] Barring cases of statelessness, which provides an added layer of complexity in that those who are deemed stateless are particularly vulnerable because they do not have a status as political member.

[65] Rieff, *A Bed for the Night*, p. 328.

workers who are nonetheless subject to the political interests and decisions of the combatants and governments among whom they are working.

Part of the paradox then is that on the one hand, humanitarian action entails legal protections, codified in international treaties, by state actors in wartime. Yet on the other hand, humanitarian aid is appealing to a moral, not legal or political, duty and calling. There is an asymmetry between the source of the obligation to aid and the protections and rights to do so, which states, as well as non-state actors in war, can choose to not respect through either limiting humanitarian access or not guaranteeing immunity and protection of humanitarian workers. This asymmetry leads to a problem of rights and obligations. Humanitarian actors seek the right to free movement and access to populations out of a human duty to relieve suffering. But they seek this access and protection from political actors, who, during wartime, are operating against those very humanitarian principles of dignity and relief of suffering by eroding human dignity through warfare and inflicting suffering.

The principles of neutrality and impartiality are witness to this paradox of aid, and the moral duties and political compromises that delivery of aid entails. The risks of not remaining neutral reveal an uneasy compromise at the heart of humanitarian relief in conflict settings. By serving all of humanity there is not a clear political standing for aid workers. It is a moral standing, and one that can all too easily fail to be respected. A question then follows whether there is an obligation to remain neutral, or if instead one ought *not* have the right to remain neutral in the face of human suffering, given the moral foundation of humanitarian action.

The reality of aid work is that the moral call to supply aid may be connected to the moral call to not remain neutral: to speak out, to recognize wrongs, to hold accountable those who have committed harms. Patching up those who are victims of such harms responds to the immediate suffering of particular individuals, but remaining neutral does not necessarily address the universal harm done to humanity, to which the humanitarian aid worker is also morally responsive.

With regard to Just War theory, impartiality to provide aid to all sides of the conflict is distinct from remaining neutral toward unjust acts and actors in war. Arguably, it is part of the moral responsibility to which humanitarian aid responds to bring to light unjust acts committed during war. But this entails a risk of tragedy interwoven with the charity: there can be no guarantee of safety or protected humanitarian space when your aim is to address the needs caused by war, in which at least one warring party is unjust. Perhaps, as I have tried to argue, neutrality in humanitarian action is an impossible ideal, incompatible with the human dignity that morally motivates humanitarian action.

16 The Challenge to the Laws of War by Islamic Jihad

Shannon Fyfe

The term "Islam" means "submission and obedience to God," but it also means "peace."[1] This conflicts with the way we tend to view Islamic terrorists, who claim to be quite concerned with the former and do not seem at all concerned with the latter. Modern militant Islamic terrorists rely on their interpretations of Islamic law to glorify, encourage, and justify violent acts as *jihad*, or as their religious obligation to go to war.[2] M. Cherif Bassiouni argues that "jihad as political violence has become nothing more than a revolutionary doctrine to legitimize the self-proclaimed aims of those who engage in it."[3] While the *jihadists* justify terrorism through religious doctrine, their actions fly in the face of international laws of war. The conflict is striking between the historical and normative stance of Islam on Just War theory and the claims made today by Islamic terrorists. In this chapter, I confront the impact of this disconnect between Islam and terrorism on international law.

Section I begins with an examination of the historical and legal basis of Islamic laws of war, particularly with respect to the imperative of struggling to achieve a global Muslim faith. Section II turns to the Islamic understanding of *jus ad bellum* and *jus in bello*, both textually and in practice. In the following section, I consider the unique position of Islamic nation-states in the international community. Finally, Section IV takes up the current challenge posed by Islamic terrorism to international laws of war, and I argue that these terrorist groups cannot reasonably justify their aims or their practices with Islam and jihad.

I Islamic Law and Jihad

In this first section, I set up the basis for the Islamic laws of war, exploring sources of law, international relations, types of jihad, and the roles and obligations of states and individuals under Islamic law.

---

[1] Ahmed Al-Dawoody, *The Islamic Law of War: Justifications and Regulations*, New York: Palgrave Macmillan, 2011, p. 47.

[2] See Donald Holbrook, "Using the Qur'an to Justify Terrorist Violence: Analysing Selective Application of the Qur'an in English-Language Militant Islamist Discourse," *Perspectives on Terrorism* 4 (2010) no. 3.

[3] M. Cherif Bassiouni, "Evolving Approaches to Jihad: From Self-Defense to Revolutionary and Regime-Change Political Violence," *Journal of Islamic Law and Culture* 10 (2008) no. 1, p. 63.

Islamic Law

According to Islamic legal theory, "only God, as the source of ultimate author-ity, has knowledge of the perfect law."[4] This divine law (*sharia*) was intended to be universally applied to all people, to ensure the peace and security of the world. Much like the concept of natural law in Western legal theory, because it is only fully known by God, Islamic law is neither definite nor settled as a body of law for humans. Several main sources are used to discover *sharia* law. We will focus on the Quran, which is the book containing God's word as revealed to Muhammad, and the *sunnah*, which are the deeds and practices of Muhammad. Because these are primary, textual sources, they are the best sources of legal norms to use when assessing jihad.

The main source of Islamic law is the Quran, which means "reading" or "recitation."[5] The Quran is the holy book of the Islamic faith and is considered to be the word of God as revealed to Muhammad. Since only God knows the divine law, the Quran is the "earthly record" of the universal divine law, as it was communicated to Muhammad.[6] The words of God were not transmitted to Muhammad all at once, but "in stages and in accordance with incidents faced by the Muslim community."[7] Thus the law that can be derived directly from the Quran is limited, and it does not account for most of the law in Islam.[8]

The word *sunnah* literally means "a clear path or a beaten track," but it often refers to an established practice or course of conduct.[9] It existed prior to Islam and was associated with the conduct of both individuals and nations alike.[10] As such, some Islamic scholars include the traditions of Muhammad's companions and successors as part of the *sunnah*, and others include the system of cus-tomary law that existed in pre-Islamic Arabia.[11] Islamic law did not abolish all of the customs that existed prior to Muhammad's lifetime, and Muhammad accepted many customs as part of his own practices and traditions.[12] But the

---

[4] Majid Khadduri, *War and Peace in the Law of Islam*, Clark, NJ: The Lawbook Exchange, 2006, p. 23.

[5] Mohammad Hashim Kamali, *Principles of Islamic Jurisprudence*, The Islamic Text Society, 1991, p. 22.

[6] Khadduri, *War and Peace in the Law of Islam*, pp. 24–25.

[7] Imran Ahsan Khan Nyazee, *Islamic Jurisprudence*, Islamabad: International Institute of Islamic Thought, 2000, p. 158.

[8] Ann Black, Hossein Esmaeili, and Nadirsyah Hosen, *Modern Perspectives on Islamic Law*, Northampton, MA: Edward Elgar, 2013, 11.

[9] Kamali, *Principles of Islamic Jurisprudence*, p. 47.

[10] Wael B. Hallaq, *The Origins and Evolution of Islamic Law*, Themes in Islamic Law, Cambridge: Cambridge University Press, 2005, p. 46.

[11] See, e.g., Mohd Hisham Mohd Kamal, "Meaning and Method of the Interpretation of Sunnah in the Field of Siyar: A Reappraisal," in *Islam and International Law: Engaging Self-Centrism from a Plurality of Perspectives*, eds. Marie-Luisa Frick and Andreas Th. Müller, Leiden: Martinus Nijhoff Publishers, 2013.

[12] Ibid., p. 65.

technical term *sunnah*, as the source of Islamic law, refers to the practices of Muhammad. The *sunnah* of Muhammad does not merely reflect the consistent practices of a particular man within his community. Rather, Muhammad's practices constitute exemplary conduct, and they hold great normative weight as part of Islamic law.[13]

The divine law of Islam "established its own order of right and wrong, embodying its own justice, as the correct and valid one."[14] This resulted in a "universalist aspiration" for the faith, a goal of peace through the establishment of the correct religious doctrine all over the world.[15] Yet this religious aim has a clear political implication, as we will see shortly.

Muslim Actors and Obligations

Islamic law regulates both the obligations of individuals to God and the relations among Muslims. Certain rights and obligations are institutional, while others attach to the individual: "Although in Islamic law the subject is the individual who is responsible before God to respect his laws, for some public matters, like war, which needs collective mobilization of human and material resources, the subject is the Muslim state."[16] Before turning to issues of war and peace between nations, we should identify the way Islamic law distinguishes between collective and individual obligations.

The individual is generally the subject of Muslim law. The aim of the individual Muslim is to achieve salvation, and the divine law shows the path to salvation through the imposition of certain obligations.[17] The basic articles of faith that constitute the obligations of individuals are the Five Pillars, which include faith, prayer, charity, fasting, and pilgrimage. These are duties that must be performed by individuals, such that an individual is liable to punishment for failing to perform a duty.[18]

But the early Muslim societies placed much more emphasis on the group than the individual. The rights and obligations of an individual were "always defined in terms of (though subordinate to) the community's interests."[19] Communities were seen as necessary for protecting individuals and ensuring their cooperation, because an individual by himself boasted "weakness and inability either to provide a livelihood or to protect himself against outsiders."[20] But society was not enough. A community needed legal authority to properly function. The Quran notes, "if it

---

[13] Hallaq, *The Origins and Evolution of Islamic Law*, p. 47.

[14] Khadduri, *War and Peace in the Law of Islam*, pp. 22–23.

[15] Christopher A. Ford, "Siyar-Ization and Its Discontents: International Law and Islam's Constitutional Crisis," *Texas International Law Journal* 30 (1995), p. 500.

[16] A. G. Dizboni, *Islam and War: The Disparity between the Technological-Normative Evolution of Modern War and the Doctrine of Jihad*, Lewiston, NY: E. Mellen Press, 2011, p. 91.

[17] Khadduri, *War and Peace in the Law of Islam*, p. 25.   [18] Ibid., p. 60.   [19] Ibid., p. 3.

[20] Ibid., p. 4.

were not for Allah checking [some] people by means of others, the earth would have been corrupted, but Allah is full of bounty to the worlds."[21] Early Islamic philosopher Al-Farabi "stressed the necessity of a society in which the individual could attain physical and moral satisfaction" when discussing the model state.[22]

Islam actually predated Hobbes in arguing for the existence of a sovereign authority, to which individuals gave up some of their rights for the sake of their protection.[23] The role of the Islamic state was thus instrumental. The Islamic state, which was "derived from and exercised on behalf of God, was potentially capable of governing the whole of mankind,"[24] and we can see this universalist aspiration as the Islamic state's obligation. The duty to establish Islam all over the world was the collective duty of all Muslims, rather than that of any one individual Muslim. The universalist aspiration could only be realized, however, if the Islamic state were able to interact with other communities and other states. The system of international law that governs Islamic foreign relations and war is known as *siyar*. I turn to each of these aspects of international law in the next two subsections.

International Relations

Since the aim of the Muslim world was to bring the entire world to the Islamic faith, the Muslim world consisted of two parts: the Muslim and the non-Muslim. The Muslim part of the world was known as *dar al-islam*, or the "domain of Islam," while the rest of the world was known as *dar al-harb*, or the "domain of war." Some Muslim scholars recognize a third division of the world, which is known as the *dar al-sulh*, meaning "domain of peace" or "domain of covenant."[25] This term refers to parts of the non-Muslim world that had entered into peace treaties with the Islamic state.[26]

The *dar al-Islam* referred to communities of Muslims but also included "non-Muslim communities, the *dhimmis* (protected people), whose separate communal laws and leaders were tolerated by the Islamic state as long as they did not

---

[21] Q. II, 251. All quotes from the Quran are from the Sahih International American Translation.

[22] Khadduri, *War and Peace in the Law of Islam*, p. 4.

[23] Khadduri notes that al-Farabi and Hobbes both argued that "isolated individuals agreed on a universal contract of submission to a ruler who is vested at once with exclusive power." Ibid., p. 9.

[24] Majid Khadduri, *The Islamic Conception of Justice*, Baltimore: Johns Hopkins University Press, 1984, p. 162.

[25] See, e.g., Al-Dawoody, *The Islamic Law of War*, p. 92; Onder Bakircioglu, *Islam and Warfare: Context and Compatibility with International Law*, New York: Routledge, 2014. Khadduri refers to this third division as temporary, because of the contractual nature of the division, even for those theorists who recognize the division at all. Khadduri, *War and Peace in the Law of Islam*, p. 144.

[26] These peace agreements involved the payment of a tax in return for military defense obligations of one sort or another, or arrangements for the exchange of goods or services. Al-Dawoody, *The Islamic Law of War*, pp. 93–94.

challenge Muslim sovereignty."[27] The *dhimmis* (mostly Christians and Jews) were permitted to retain their own religions, but they were required to pay a poll tax to the Islamic authority.[28] The *dar-al harb*, however, was the object, not the subject, of Islam, and it was the duty of the Imam, the head of the Islamic state, to extend the validity of its Law and Justice to the unbelievers at the earliest possible moment. The communities of the *dar al-harb* were regarded as being in a "state of nature," because they lacked the standard of justice granted to believers under the Islamic public order.[29]

The *dar al-harb* and the *dar al-islam* were considered to be in a potential state of war at all times, regardless of the existence of ongoing hostilities, because of the obligation of the *dar al-islam* to universalize Islam.[30] I now refer to this obligation to universalize Islam as *jihad*, and we take up this term in the next subsection.

Jihad

The Arabic word *jihad* means "to exert oneself" or in the context of Islam, "exertion of one's power in Allah's path, that is, the spread of the belief in Allah and in making His word supreme over this world."[31] The Quran states that the duty of Muslims is to "strive for Allah with the striving due to Him,"[32] and "believe in Allah and His Messenger and strive in the cause of Allah with your wealth and your lives."[33] While the term *dar al-harb* implies that the obligation to spread Islam involves war, the term *jihad* does not necessarily refer to war, because "exertion of one's power in Allah's path" could be achieved either peacefully or violently.[34] The Quran calls Muslims to "declare what you are commanded and turn away from the polytheists"[35] and to "fight them until there is no [more] *fitnah*[36] and [until] worship is [acknowledged to be] for Allah. But if they cease, then there is to be no aggression except against the

---

[27] Sohail H. Hashmi and James Johnson, "Introduction," in *Just Wars, Holy Wars, and Jihads: Christian, Jewish, and Muslim Encounters and Exchanges*, ed. Sohail H. Hashmi, New York: Oxford University Press, 2012, p. 10.

[28] ʿAbd Allāh Aḥmad Naʿīm, *Islam and the Secular State: Negotiating the Future of Shariʿa*. Cambridge, MA: Harvard University Press, 2008, p. 31.

[29] Khadduri, *The Islamic Conception of Justice*, p. 163.   [30] Ibid.

[31] Richard C. Martin, "The Religious Foundations of War, Peace, and Statecraft in Islam," in *Just War and Jihad: Historical and Theoretical Perspectives on War and Peace in Western and Islamic Traditions*, eds. John Kelsay and James Turner Johnson, Westport, CT: Greenwood Press, 1991, pp. 96–97.

[32] Q. XXII, 78.   [33] Q. LXI, 11.

[34] Khadduri, *War and Peace in the Law of Islam*, p. 55; *The Islamic Conception of Justice*, p. 164.

[35] Q. XV, 94.

[36] Meaning "disruption of society." See M. Cherif Bassiouni, *The Shariʿa and Islamic Criminal Justice in Time of War and Peace*, New York: Cambridge University Press, 2013, p. 218.

oppressors."[37] The struggle to expand the influence of Islam was meant "to establish peace with justice within a secure political order,"[38] but the peaceful and secure political order might only be established through war. Some verses of the Quran suggest that jihad will require a violent form of exertion: "O Prophet, fight against the disbelievers and the hypocrites and be harsh upon them. And their refuge is Hell, and wretched is the destination."[39]

There are several distinct types of jihad, some of which may involve overlapping obligations. I lay out each type briefly here, but I look more closely at what constitutes just cause for war in later sections. The first important distinction to be made is between personal jihad and political jihad. The former, *al-jihad al-akbar*, refers to a personal moral struggle and is considered to be the "greater" jihad.[40] Political jihad, or *al-jihad al-a ghar*, refers to an armed struggle of the state and is known as the "lesser" jihad.[41] Political jihad can be either domestic or international. Domestic jihad is fought against one or more of the following groups: (1) rebels or secessionists; (2) bandits, highway robbers, or pirates; (3) apostates; and (4) violent religious fanatics.[42] International jihad is fought against non-Muslim states. The terms *jihad al-kuffar* (jihad against unbelievers) and *jihad fi sabil Allah* (jihad in the path of God) are often used to refer to international jihad.[43] But because Muslims were historically or theoretically united under one state, "any *jihad* that occurred between the Islamic state and its enemies was a war between Muslims and their enemies," and this means that not every conflict was motivated by lack of Muslim faith.[44] Finally, there is a distinction between *jihad al-daf*, or defensive war, and *jihad al-talab*, which is aggressive war initiated by Muslims outside the Islamic state.[45]

Scholars disagree as to whether the duty of jihad was collective or individual. Al-Mawardi argued that the duty to initiate jihad is collective, while the duty becomes individual after hostilities have begun.[46] This seems plausible in light of the various types of jihad: an individual may have a duty to participate in *al-jihad al-a ghar* (lesser, political jihad), but as part of what he understands to be his individual duty of *al-jihad al-akbar* (greater, personal jihad). So the duty of an individual with respect to jihad could be seen to implicate the collective,

---

[37] Q. II, 193.

[38] John Kelsay, *Islam and War: A Study in Comparative Ethics*, Lousiville, KY: Westminster/ John Knox Press, 1993, p. 34.

[39] Q. IX, 73.   [40] Al-Dawoody, *The Islamic Law of War*, p. 76.   [41] Ibid.   [42] Ibid., p. 77.

[43] Ibid.   [44] Ibid.   [45] Ibid.

[46] Asma Afsaruddin, "The Siyar Laws of Aggression: Juridical Re-Interpretations of Qur'ānic Jihād and Their Contemporary Implications for International Law," in *Islam and International Law*, eds. Frick and Müller, Leiden: Martinus Nijhoff Publishers, 2013, citing Al-Mawardi, *al-Hawi al-kabir fi fiqh madhhab al-imam al-shafi'i radi allahu 'anhu wa-huwa sharh mukhtasar al-muzani*, vol. 14, ed. 'Ali Muhammad Mu'awwad and 'Adil Ahmad 'Abd al-Mawjud, Beirut: Daral-kutub al-'arabiyya, 1994, p. 180.

political jihad, but it might only directly involve the "religious and legal duty" that can be fulfilled "by the heart and tongue in combatting evil and spreading the word of God."[47]

As a collective duty, however, jihad falls on the state. Each believer was bound to fulfill his duty by "the hand and sword in the sense of participation in fighting."[48] If such a "duty is fulfilled by a part of the community it ceases to be obligatory on others; the whole community, however, falls into error if the duty is not performed at all."[49] Khadduri argues that this collective understanding of the duty of jihad results in two main benefits:

> In the first place, it meant that the duty need not necessarily be fulfilled by all the believers. For the recruitment of all the believers as warriors was neither possible nor advisable. Some of the believers were needed to prepare food and weapons, while the crippled, blind, and sick would not qualify as fighters. Women and children were as a rule excused from actual fighting, although many a woman contributed indirectly to the war effort. In the second place, the imposition of the obligation on the community rather than on the individual made possible the employment of the jihad as a community and, consequently, a state instrument; its control accordingly, is a state, not an individual, responsibility. Thus the head of the state can in a more effective way serve the common interest of the community than if the matter is left entirely to the discretion of the individual believer.[50]

So as a state doctrine, used to legitimate conquest, preemptive self-defense, and the use of force to promote political legitimacy,[51] a decision to participate in jihad could only be made effectively through an Islamic government. In Muhammad's time, he was the head of government, while Allah was the "titular head of the state and its source of governing authority."[52] The leaders of the Islamic state following Muhammad's death were called imams, and thus jihad as a state doctrine should only be declared by the imam who serves as the head or deputy head of state.[53]

In the next section, I turn to the realm of international jihad and consider the possible just causes for war under Islamic law.

II   *Jus ad Bellum* and Jihad

Jus ad bellum concerns the use of force in initiating armed conflict. The justice of a decision to go to war involves the consideration of various criteria, and the Islamic laws of war speak to several. Given our narrow focus on Islamic terrorism, I focus on the criteria of just cause and legitimate authority.

---

[47] Khadduri, *The Islamic Conception of Justice*, pp. 164–65.   [48] Ibid., p. 165.
[49] Khadduri, *War and Peace in the Law of Islam*, p. 60.   [50] Ibid., p. 61.
[51] Bassiouni, "Evolving Approaches to Jihad," p. 62.
[52] Khadduri, *War and Peace in the Law of Islam*, p. 10.   [53] Ibid., p. 94.

Just Cause

According to the Quran, as with nearly all texts underlying Just War theory, the most basic justification for going to war is in self-defense of life. The first Quranic reference to jihad as war is found in the Sura al-Haj[54]:

Permission [to fight] has been given to those who are being fought, because they were wronged. And indeed, Allah is competent to give them victory. [They are] those who have been evicted from their homes without right – only because they say, "Our Lord is Allah." And were it not that Allah checks the people, some by means of others, there would have been demolished monasteries, churches, synagogues, and mosques in which the name of Allah is much mentioned. And Allah will surely support those who support Him. Indeed, Allah is Powerful and Exalted in Might.[55]

The Quran also says "fight in the way of Allah those who fight you but do not transgress. Indeed. Allah does not like transgressors."[56] These verses appear to permit fighting in response to direct aggression, and the latter verse contains a proportionality restraint on fighting, which I return to in the next section. Islamic law also permits jihad in defense of others:

And what is [the matter] with you that you fight not in the cause of Allah and [for] the oppressed among men, women, and children who say, 'Our Lord, take us out of this city of oppressive people and appoint for us from Yourself a protector and appoint for us from Yourself a helper?"[57]

All of these verses are vague with respect to the scope of self-defense. Instances in which one is "wronged" or "oppressed" would certainly include threats to life. It appears that the Quran also permits the use of force in response to threats to territory and property. But these verses are not clear, on their faces, as to whether defense of the religion of the Islamic state would be within the permissible scope of justified reasons to fight. However, given our understanding of greater and lesser jihad, it is likely that the use of lesser jihad to maintain the Muslim faith through exertion (i.e., the object of greater jihad) would constitute a just cause for war. The reference in Q. 22:40 to "monasteries, churches, synagogues, and mosques" also suggests that defense of houses of worship might be more about defending religion against a violent adversary than the physical buildings.[58]

---

[54] See Adam L Silverman, "Just War, Jihad, and Terrorism: A Comparison of Western and Islamic Norms for the Use of Political Violence," *Journal of Church and State* 44 (2002) no. 1, p. 78.

[55] Q. XXII, 39–40.   [56] Q. II, 190.   [57] Q. IV, 75.

[58] See generally Asma Afsaruddin, "In Defense of All Houses of Worship? Jihad in the Context of Interfaith Relations," in *Just Wars, Holy Wars, and Jihads, ed. Hashmi.*

It might be said that Islamic justifications for offensive jihad are identical to those for defensive jihad: the duty to spread the Muslim faith all over the world. It could be argued that the negative duty to prevent an enemy from destroying Islam within the Islamic state is no different from the positive duty to promote the spread of Islam outside the Islamic state. But the Quranic evidence of this parity is not convincing. Some verses could possibly be interpreted as permitting offensive war:

Fight those who do not believe in Allah or in the Last Day and who do not consider unlawful what Allah and His Messenger have made unlawful and who do not adopt the religion of truth from those who were given the Scripture – [fight] until they give the jizyah willingly while they are humbled.[59]

However, this verse is contained in a chapter of the Quran that is focused on the conduct of hostilities, rather than the spread of Islam, so it is plausible to interpret this verse as limited by a general Quranic principle of nonaggression.[60] Another verse possibly permits offensive war: "And if they break their oaths after their treaty and defame your religion, then fight the leaders of disbelief, for indeed, there are no oaths [sacred] to them; [fight them that] they might cease."[61] Yet this looks more like the self-defense of religion. And other verses clearly encourage peace in light of a retreating enemy: "So if they remove themselves from you and do not fight you and offer you peace, then Allah has not made for you a cause [for fighting] against them,"[62] and "Allah does not forbid you from those who do not fight you because of religion and do not expel you from your homes – from being righteous toward them and acting justly toward them. Indeed, Allah loves those who act justly."[63] The Quran does not seem to provide a straightforward justification for offensive jihad.

The *sunnah* does not provide such a justification either. The first verses discussed in this section ("Permission [to fight] has been given to those who are being fought, because they were wronged," Q. 22:39–40) were revealed to Muhammad during a time of conflict with the Medians. Yet all of the hostilities that Muslims engaged in during Muhammad's lifetime were defensive in nature.[64] Quranic verse 9:29, noted earlier as a possible call for offensive jihad, refers to an incident that historical accounts of Muhammad's life identify as a "defensive act to stop the Byzantine advance from reaching Medina."[65] So there is no evidence from the *sunnah* that jihad is permitted for any reason other than self-defense, where self-defense includes defense against religious persecution.[66]

---

[59] Q. IX, 29

[60] Niaz A. Shah, *Self-Defense in Islamic and International Law: Assessing Al-Qaeda and the Invasion of Iraq*, New York: Palgrave Macmillan, 2008, p. 20.

[61] Q. IX, 12.   [62] Q. IV, 90.   [63] Q. LX, 80.

[64] Al-Dawoody, *The Islamic Law of War*, p. 39.   [65] Ibid., p. 65.   [66] Ibid., p. 83.

There have certainly been Islamic scholars, especially during specific historical periods, who have argued for the justification of aggressive jihad. Al-
Farabi, for instance, thought that certain instances of offensive jihad that
sought to promote human rights were permissible.[67] But as we are focused on
the Quran and *sunnah* in our analysis of *sharia*, we will not explore these
scholars as sources any further, and will instead move on to the *jus ad bellum*
criterion of competent authority.

Legitimate Authority

The use of force in Islam must take place pursuant to the commands of a
legitimate authority. However, the Quran and *sunnah* contain only indirect
evidence of the criteria for what (or who) constitutes a legitimate authority. The
Quran entrusts Muhammad with the authority to wage defensive jihad, as in the
verse that says "O Prophet, urge the believers to battle."[68] The Quran suggests
that Muhammad should consult with other Muslims but that he makes the final
decisions,[69] and that other Muslims are charged with obeying him as the
authority: "O you who have believed, obey Allah and obey the Messenger
and those in authority among you. And if you disagree over anything, refer it
to Allah and the Messenger, if you should believe in Allah and the Last Day.
That is the best [way] and best in result."[70]

The Quran also designates that issues of public safety, such as the possibility
of aggression, should be referred to Muhammad or his successor[71]: "And when
there comes to them information about [public] security or fear, they spread it
around. But if they had referred it back to the Messenger or to those of authority
among them, then the ones who [can] draw correct conclusions from it would
have known about it."[72] So if the Quran and *sunnah* indicate that Muhammad
held the authority to enter into jihad on behalf of the collective during his
lifetime, the authority should pass to whomever takes his place upon his death,
and this is the imam, or Muslim ruler, who is permitted to "invoke the jihad to
enforce his commands."[73] There is significant support in other parts of Islamic
law for this interpretation that places legitimate authority in the ruler of the
Islamic state, but again, we will here rely only on the Quran and *sunnah*.

However, if we consider the individual obligation of jihad, the determination
of legitimate authority looks more difficult to square with a single entity.
Despite the Quranic exhortations to obey authority, the *sunnah* obligates

---

[67] Khadduri, *The Islamic Conception of Justice*, p. 172, citing Al-Farabi, *Fusul Al-Madani:
Aphorisms of the Statesman*, ed. D. M. Dunlop, Cambridge, UK: University Press 1961,
pp. 146–47.
[68] Q. VIII, 65; see also Shah, *Self-Defense in Islamic and International Law*, pp. 21–22.
[69] Q. III, 159.   [70] Q. IV, 59.
[71] Shah, *Self-Defense in Islamic and International Law*, p. 22.   [72] Q. IV, 83.
[73] Khadduri, *War and Peace in the Law of Islam*, p. 78.

individuals to right wrongs, and by force if necessary.[74] This might permit jihad on the part of one individual, or on the part of a non-state actor. But the *sunnah* remains limited by the Quran, and therefore this would only be permissible if the Muslim ruler had not outlawed such jihad.[75]

Now that we have sketched out the main aspects of how jihad can be justifiably begun, we examine the manner in which permissible jihad must be waged.

III *Jus in Bello* and Jihad

Jus in bello restricts the means and methods of engaging in armed conflict, or *qital*. The justice of how to fight a war, like the justice of when to go to war, involves the consideration of various criteria. I focus on what the Islamic laws of war require with respect to proportionality and distinction.

Proportionality

The Quran limits the states of affairs in which fighting is permissible: "Fight in the way of Allah those who fight you but do not transgress. Indeed. Allah does not like transgressors."[76] This verse implies that Muslims should only fight in response to the particular threat posed by their enemies. Indeed, the verses that follow maintain that if the enemies cease fighting, they too should cease fighting, instead of inflicting violence as punishment: "And if they cease, then indeed, Allah is Forgiving and Merciful. Fight them until there is no [more] fitnah and [until] worship is [acknowledged to be] for Allah. But if they cease, then there is to be no aggression except against the oppressors."[77]

While the fighting continues, it is only just for Muslims to act in a way that is proportionate to the oppressive actions of their enemies. The Quran claims that "whoever responds [to injustice] with the equivalent of that with which he was harmed and then is tyrannized – Allah will surely aid him. Indeed, Allah is Pardoning and Forgiving."[78] Quranic verses "if you punish [an enemy, O believers], punish with an equivalent of that with which you were harmed. But if you are patient – it is better for those who are patient,"[79] and "we ordained for them therein a life for a life, an eye for an eye, a nose for a nose, an ear for an ear, a tooth for a tooth, and for wounds is legal retribution. But whoever gives [up his right as] charity, it is an expiation for him"[80] suggest that retribution against enemies must be limited by the proportionality principle, but that Muslims are encouraged to have mercy on their enemies if possible.

---

[74] L. Ali Khan, *A Theory of International Terrorism: Understanding Islamic Militancy*, Leiden; Boston: Martinus Nijhoff Publishers, 2006, p. 201.
[75] See ibid.   [76] Q. II, 190.   [77] Q. II, 192–93.   [78] Q. XXII, 60.   [79] Q. XVI, 126.
[80] Q. V, 45.

The first of these, verse 16:126, was revealed to Muhammad following a battle in which his uncle had been killed, and there was a need to prevent the Muslim fighters from killing excessively.[81] Thus the *sunnah* and Quran agree that conduct in war may not include excessive violence.

Distinction

The *jus in bello* principle of distinction is also contained in verse 2:190 of the Quran. Muslims may only fight against a particular group of persons: namely, those who are fighting against the Muslims. Other groups of persons are not permitted to be killed. The Quran says that Muslim fighters must "not kill the soul which Allah has forbidden, except by right. And whoever is killed unjustly – We have given his heir authority, but let him not exceed limits in [the matter of] taking life. Indeed, he has been supported [by the law].[82] Similarly, verse 6:151 forbids killing "the soul which Allah has forbidden [to be killed] except by [legal] right."[83] Notably, this legal distinction between combatants and noncombatants is limited to status with respect to the conflict, not citizenship: "non-combatants, whether Muslims or Dhimmis, are all citizens of the territory of Islam (*dar al-Islam*), the territory of peace. In principle, they are as such subject to all the rights and duties of citizenship, without distinction."[84]

Muhammad's *sunnah* confirms the legal requirement of distinguishing between combatants and noncombatants, as he prohibited targeting those who could not or did not fight: women, children, the clergy, the aged, the sick, and mercenaries.[85] Muhammad specifically advised Muslim fighters to do everything they could to aim at combatants rather than children the combatants were attempting to use as human shields.[86]

Yet the principle of distinction in the Islamic law of war is relevantly distinguishable from the modern doctrine of noncombatant immunity in Just War theory – Islamic law during Muhammad's lifetime required "all able-bodied men used to take part in war because there was no regular army to fight the enemy, and society as a whole contributed to the war effort."[87] It was accordingly the case that all such men, if taken prisoner by the enemy, and whether or not they had been actually participating in the fighting, could be

---

[81] Niaz A. Shah, *Islamic Law and the Law of Armed Conflict: The Conflict in Pakistan*, New York: Routledge, 2011, p. 36.

[82] Q. XVII, 33   [83] Q. VI, 151.

[84] Sobhi Mahmassani, "The Principles of International Law in the Light of Islamic Doctrine," *Recueil des Cours* 117 (1966), p. 261.

[85] See, e.g., Al-Dawoody, *The Islamic Law of War*, p. 111–16.

[86] Shah, *Islamic Law and the Law of Armed Conflict*, p. 35.

[87] Muhammad Munir, "Suicide Attacks: Martyrdom Operations or Acts of Perfidy?" in *Islam and International Law*, eds. Frick and Müller, p. 117.

executed or held for ransom.[88] It is not clear, however, that all able-bodied men were actually considered to be combatants.

With this understanding of jihad and the justice requirements for going to war and engaging in war under Islamic law, we can now explore the disconnect between modern Islamic terrorism and the Islamic laws of war.

IV   Islam and Challenges in Modern War

In this final section, I briefly examine the relationship between Islamic law and modern Islamic nation-states, before analyzing the relationship between Islamic law and Islamic terrorism.

Islamic Nation-States

Muslims today, despite their religious group membership, live in territory-based nation-states. Modern "Islamic nation-states," a term I use to refer to those states with "constitutions that entrenched Islam or Islamic law (sharia) as *a* source, *a* primary source or *the* primary source for legislation,"[89] are the closest parallel to the Islamic state referenced in *sharia* law. The Islamic state was a religious entity first and foremost, and was only thought of as a political entity in terms of its responsibility to protect individuals and communities. The head of state was a religious leader, not just a political leader. This is contrary to the religious and political underpinnings of many modern Western states. Therefore, to function within the modern global order, "Islam's previous role in governance had to be realigned and reconfigured to fit the emergence of the 'modern' nation-state."[90] As nation-states, these political entities are subject to the rules and norms of international law. So regardless of the influence of Islamic law on their constitutions or international relations policies, Muslim majority states must abide by international law, including international laws of war discussed in previous chapters in this volume.

A thorough discussion of the relationship between *sharia* law and nation-states is beyond the scope of this chapter. But I note that a state could abide by all four of the principles of just war discussed earlier and wage defensive jihad.[91] A state could of course fail to meet any one of these requirements, as I discuss in the next subsection on terrorism. But an Islamic nation-state

---

[88] Sohail H. Hashmi, "Jihad and the Geneva Conventions: The Impact of International Law on Islamic Theory," in *Just Wars, Holy Wars, and Jihads*, ed. Hashmi, p. 333.

[89] Dawood I. Ahmed and Moamen Gouda, "Measuring Constitutional Islamization: The Islamic Constitutions Index," *Hastings International and Comparative Law Review* 38 (2015), p. 14. Italics in original.

[90] Ibid., p. 16.

[91] At least as I have outlined defensive *jihad* in earlier sections. I do not address aggressive *jihad* on behalf of a nation-state here, nor do I address peaceful jihad in the sense of spreading the Muslim faith through a venue other than violence.

waging defensive jihad in accordance with *sharia* law will not necessarily pose a problem under international law or Just War theory.

Islamic Terrorism

Global terrorism is a rapidly growing problem for the international community and international law: 32,658 people were killed by terrorism in 2014, an 80 percent increase from the number killed in 2013 and the largest ever recorded.[92] Two groups were jointly responsible for 51 percent of all claimed global fatalities in 2014: Boko Haram and the Islamic State of Iraq and the Levant (ISIL).[93] Boko Haram has pledged allegiance to ISIL, and both groups seek to establish Islamic States in their respective areas of control, namely Nigeria and Iraq/Syria. Most of the deaths from terrorism occur in the countries of Afghanistan, Iraq, Syria, Nigeria, and Pakistan, which largely correlates with internal political violence.[94] Lone wolf terrorists are responsible for 70 percent of the terrorist attacks in Western countries, and 20 percent of these deaths are caused by terrorists inspired by Islamic jihad.[95]

The principles of *jus ad bellum* and *jus in bello* were historically intended to apply to conflicts between state actors. This generates a problem when we try to apply the Islamic or international laws of war to terrorism, as it is almost guaranteed that at least one party to the violence (terrorist or victim) will not be a state party. The principle of distinction is also difficult to navigate, as combatants must only direct acts of war at enemy combatants and are not permitted to directly target noncombatants. But the definition of a combatant is traditionally tied to a state party affiliation. Thus, when the terrorist or terrorist group is not a state party, it is not clear whether an individual terrorist is a combatant or a person engaged in combat who does not meet the definition of a combatant, or a noncombatant.

We also face a problem in attempting to define terrorism in the first place. As C.A.J. Coady notes when considering some of the various definitions that have been used by the Terrorism Research Center in the United States, the real issue is not about definitions.[96] Rather, the issue is about morality, but this still requires initial clarification of the right definition of terrorism.[97] One definition cited by the Terrorism Research Center is that terrorism is "the use or threatened use of force designed to bring about political change."[98] This definition is too broad

---

[92] "2015 Global Terrorism Index: Deaths from Terrorism Increased 80% Last Year to the Highest Level Ever; Global Economic Cost of Terrorism Reached All-Time High at US$52.9 Billion," *PR Newswire*, November 16, 2015.

[93] Ibid.   [94] Ibid.   [95] Ibid.

[96] C.A.J. Coady, "Terrorism and Innocence," *The Journal of Ethics* 8 (2004) no. 1, p. 38.

[97] Ibid.

[98] Brian Michael Jenkins, *The Study of Terrorism: Definitional Problems*, Santa Monica: RAND Corporation, 1980.

for the purposes of this chapter as it is concerned only with the intention behind the violent action and makes no reference to the actors, victims, or types of forceful acts that could constitute terrorism. A second option is that terrorism "constitutes the illegitimate use of force to achieve a political objective when innocent people are targeted."[99] This definition is clearer, limiting acts of terrorism to those in which a particular group of people (namely, innocent people) are targeted, but it still does not mention the type of force used or the actor wielding the violence. A third option is to define terrorism as "the premeditated, deliberate, systematic murder, mayhem, and threatening of the innocent to create fear and intimidation in order to gain a political or tactical advantage, usually to influence an audience."[100] This definition gives a clearer picture of what we generally think of as terrorism, getting closer to a specific purpose behind the acts and specific kinds of acts that would constitute terrorism, but it may in fact be too specific, and it leaves out the identity of the victims or the actors.

Coady ultimately defines terrorism as "the organized use of violence to attack non-combatants ('innocents' in a special sense) or their property for political purposes."[101] I agree with his approach to focusing on the victims as what make an act an act of terrorism, but I disagree with his decision to leave out threats of violence as acts of terrorism. I do not see any reason to distinguish between situations in which terrorists are successful from situations in which terrorists are unsuccessful for reasons that may amount to no more than sheer luck. So, the definition of terrorism I use is *the organized use of violence to target innocent noncombatants or their property for political purposes.*

Now that we have a definition of terrorism, I use each of the four just war principles discussed in the second and third sections of the chapter to analyze the permissibility of jihad by terrorists. I analyze al-Qaeda and ISIL as paradigm cases of collective jihad, as they are the most well-known terrorist groups operating today, at least in Western countries. The tactics ISIL and al-Qaeda use in service of their goals are violent, brutal, and largely directed at non-combatants. I also analyze instances of individual jihad that are purportedly inspired by terrorist groups.

Just Cause

I argued in the second section that the Quran and the *sunnah* do not provide a straightforward justification for offensive jihad. Therefore, I argue here that jihad on the part of terrorist groups can only be justified by *sharia* law if it can be classified as defensive jihad. Recall that a defensive jihad is one undertaken in defense of persons, property, or religion. The distinction between offensive

---

[99] Walter Laqueur, *The Age of Terrorism*, Boston: Little, Brown, 1987.

[100] James M. Poland, *Understanding Terrorism: Groups, Strategies, and Responses*, Englewood Cliffs, NJ: Prentice Hall, 1988.

[101] Coady, "Terrorism and Innocence," p. 39.

and defensive jihad, as with other instances of aggression, is often ambiguous. Acts of aggression that are said to be preemptive self-defense, for instance, are difficult to categorize depending on the surrounding circumstances.

Al-Qaeda claims that it exercised defensive jihad in its 9/11 attacks on the United States and its allies, on the ground that it was defending itself from the "usurpation of Muslim lands."[102] If hijacking planes and killing innocent civilians could be reasonably construed as an act that directly protected Muslim lands from being invaded through Western expansionism, then this argument might be plausible. But there is no evidence that the particular individuals who were killed on 9/11 were directly involved in Western intervention in Muslim countries. So claiming that killing these particular individuals was an act of self-defense is a stretch. Another tactic might be to claim that killing these individuals was a necessary step in an even more attenuated self-defense claim. Because Western "policy" cannot be attacked, in self-defense or otherwise, hijacking planes and crashing them into the World Trade Center and the Pentagon are the closest approximation. This argument is a weak one, given the lack of precedent in international or Islamic law for such a broad understanding of self-defense. But it could be plausible if made by a legitimate authority, rather than "a very tiny minority [of Muslims] representing none but themselves."[103]

So-called lone wolves will suffer from the same weaknesses in any claims of self-defense, but their arguments might carry even less weight. Individuals who take up the mantle of terrorist groups who have already declared jihad could appeal to their duties to fight once hostilities have begun. But as the individual jihad obligation is considered the greater jihad, while the collective jihad is the lesser jihad, this implies that individuals cannot justify their moral obligation to wage jihad on the basis that they were just "following orders." While they may argue that they are choosing to contribute to a collective effort, individual jihadists cannot rely solely on the self-defense justifications propounded by the terrorist groups they seek to follow. It is notable that lone wolves do not necessarily coordinate with the terrorist groups they claim to have been inspired by, but terrorist groups such as ISIL will take credit for the attacks nonetheless. This tactic appears to be even further removed from the possibility of a self-defense claim.

Legitimate Authority

International law, Islamic law, and traditional Just War theory were all crafted with an understanding that war occurs between states or other distinct communities. Thus the requirement that a legitimate or competent authority make

---

[102] ElSayed M.A. Amin, *Reclaiming Jihad: A Qur'anic Critique of Terrorism*, Nairobi, Kenya: The Islamic Foundation, 2015, p. 121.
[103] Ibid.

the decision to go to war assumes that a state will have a clear leader who can fill this role. Terrorist groups, on the other hand, are almost certainly non-state actors, so establishing legitimate authority will be more challenging. If only sovereign states with some level of international recognition can exercise legitimate authority and wage a just war, as was the case for many years, then this will also exclude non-state terrorist organizations. Even if we broaden the scope of legitimate authority to include leaders of large organizations, rather than just states, the lack of consensus among Muslims with respect to terrorism as part of jihad could undermine claims of legitimate authority.

Some scholars have recently argued that groups such as ISIL may actually constitute state actors.[104] There are several reasons why. First, ISIL identifies as a political entity, not just as a collective of like-minded people. Abu Bakr al-Baghdadi has been its leader since May 2010. It is highly organized as a top-down bureaucracy, divided into civil and military branches. And relatedly, ISIL has control over significant tracts of land. It looks as if ISIL may be able to meet the stricter standard for legitimate authority, given that it identifies as an independent state and claims jurisdiction over a bounded territory. However, self-identification is not sufficient for recognizing an entity as a state. Additionally, the territorial control looks to be crucial to this claimed designation. If ISIL were to lose its territory, it would look more like other terrorist organizations and would be less able to meet the stricter requirements to establish legitimate authority to conduct jihad.

Individual actors who engage in violence are likely incapable of meeting the requirements of legitimate authority. Under international law, individuals cannot "wage war." As noted, *sharia* law provides little justification for individuals to enact violent jihad alone. Because the *sunnah* obligating individuals to use force to correct wrongs is limited by the Quran, which tells individuals to obey authority, it looks like lone wolf attacks would require actual alignment with a permissible collective jihad, which might entail coordination and not just adoration. This means individual jihadists must utilize a group's legitimate authority, and I have already shown that this will be a challenging prospect.

Distinction

Distinction demands that only combatants may be targeted in jihad, and other groups are entitled to protection. But before we consider the victims of terrorism, the principle of distinction requires us to first identify the status of the terrorists themselves. Under traditional Just War theory, we need to be able to identify terrorists as combatants for them to be permitted to commit any acts of violence in pursuit of their just cause. So we must see if we can attach combatant privilege to terrorists.

---

[104] See, e.g., Audrey Kurth Cronin, "ISIS Is Not a Terrorist Group," *Foreign Affairs* 94 (2015) no. 2.

Based on the concept of jihad, it does seem plausible to attach combatant privilege to terrorists who are part of collective jihad acting in self-defense of the Muslim faith. Assuming the group meets the *jus ad bellum* requirements of just cause and legitimate authority, the members of a terrorist group could be combatants. Lone wolf terrorists have a higher bar to meet to be considered combatants with respect to jihad. They could only acquire combatant status through alignment with a permissible collective jihad with legitimate authority. Alternatively, there might be an argument for combatant status based on individual jihad. It could be that every single Muslim is a combatant of sorts, permitted to use violent means whenever necessary to follow along the path of Allah. But this means that all Muslims should lose the protections that come with noncombatant status, even those who are not participating in or supporting violence. If this is the argument terrorists want to use, it does not look good for a claim that they are acting in defense of the Muslim people.[105]

Even assuming we can attach combatant privilege to terrorists, which does seem plausible under Islamic law, there remains a fairness problem. The reason we care about identifying combatants is the principle of the moral equality of combatants, meaning each side of a conflict is equally privileged to kill and liable to be killed. Not only does the classification of Islamic terrorists as combatants create the problem that all nonviolent Muslims could also be classified as terrorists, but it creates a similar problem on the other side of the conflict. If all Muslims are combatants, and they are fighting jihad against all non-Muslims or all non-Muslims who are citizens of Western states with expansionist policies, the purpose of the combatant/noncombatant distinction disappears. Hardly anyone with protected status is left. And while this is the actual view of some terrorist organizations,[106] it looks like an absurd interpretation of the Quran and the *sunnah*.

It does not look like even the attenuated just cause of self-defense against Western expansionism could transform innocent civilians into combatants. So if we are able to classify terrorists as combatants and still preserve the existence of protected noncombatant status for some individuals, we might be able to justify

---

[105] Despite his regular use of the tactic, even Osama bin Laden recognized that targeting civilians has a negative impact on the cause of jihad, "distorting the image of the jihadis in the eyes of the umma's [Muslim community's] general public and separating them from their popular bases." Daniel Byman, *Al Qaeda, the Islamic State, and the Global Jihadist Movement: What Everyone Needs to Know*, New York: Oxford University Press, 2015, p. 155, quoting from *Letters from Abbottabad: Bin Laden Sidelined?*, Combating Terrorism Center at West Point, May 3, 2012, p. 13.

[106] Bassiouni notes, "jihadists conclude that there is no such thing as an innocent civilian, whether in the United States . . . or anywhere else, because their belief in the morality of their cause and the complicity of all who stand against them." Bassiouni, *The Sharī'a and Islamic Criminal Justice in Time of War and Peace*, p. 200. Osama bin Laden explicitly called for the targeting of civilians and combatants alike as early as 1998. See Alia Brahimi, *Jihad and Just War in the War on Terror*, New York: Oxford University Press, 2010, p. 174.

the unintentional death of many noncombatants in service of a jihad to defend the entire Muslim religion from Western policy. But at some point foreseen deaths of many noncombatants cannot be reasonably claimed as unintentional.

Proportionality

The proportionality requirement in jihad is inextricably tied up with the just cause and distinction requirements, as the results of an attack and the death of noncombatants must be proportionate to the direct advantage sought. If we take the attenuated view of self-defense against Western policy as just cause, discussed earlier, we could also construct an argument for the proportionality of almost any number of deaths caused by defensive jihad. The broad defense of an entire religion could theoretically justify extreme consequences. However, the proportionality requirement is also inextricably tied up with the distinction requirement. Killing many noncombatants may not be permissible, even if it were actually to defend the entire Muslim religion.

Additionally, certain tactics that have been used by terrorists and terrorist groups, such as the execution of captured noncombatants and the use of suicide bombers, cannot be reasonably tied to the just cause of self-defense against Western policy. These kinds of actions could only be tied to a narrower just cause, because they either explicitly target a noncombatant or indiscriminately attack knowing that many noncombatants would be killed. The impact of these actions clearly violates the principle of proportionality under *sharia* law.[107] For example, in light of the actions of the Afghan government, the Taliban might be justified in targeting civilians who directly support the Afghan government, or Western civilians who are directly supporting the use of drone strikes against the Taliban. Because this conflict is asymmetric, the "kind of low level and imprecise targeting of the Taliban may be proportional, and similarly may be necessary to inflict equal damage on the opponent."[108] But direct or indiscriminate targeting of Western civilians who have only indirectly supported their own governments (who have themselves supported the Afghan government) cannot be proportional.

Given the foregoing analysis of terrorists and terrorist groups under Islamic international law, their reliance on *sharia* law in justifying their violent acts is misplaced. The Quran and Muhammad's *sunnah* cannot justify the use of indiscriminate and unwarranted violence to defend the Muslim faith or territories, in defiance of international laws of war.

---

[107] See Bassiouni, *The Sharī'a and Islamic Criminal Justice in Time of War and Peace*, p. 197.
[108] Ibid., p. 242.

Afterword

Henry Shue

One of the great lost opportunities in contemporary moral philosophy is for the systematic moral assessment of the laws of war, domestic and international, especially the laws of armed conflict (LOAC) or international humanitarian law (IHL) – alternative names for the same body of international law – and for constructive proposals for their moral improvement.[1] Great energy is being poured by philosophers into the elaboration and perfection of what is sometimes called "the deep morality of war," which I have argued is an answer searching for a question.[2] Be that as it may even the proponents of the deep morality of war – to whom I refer loosely here as revisionists[3] – readily acknowledge that its principles usually cannot guide the action of morally conscientious agents engaged in war, who are instead advised in the end to follow not any conclusions of the deep morality itself, but LOAC/IHL. This means that contemporary revisionism is unable to serve the function traditionally served by *jus in bello*: to guide action during war. The advice to follow the law, not the supposed morality, is often presented as "merely pragmatic" and a terrible compromise. But if the advice is itself to be morally justified, the laws need at least to be morally acceptable – and the more morally acceptable, the better. And if a law is as morally acceptable as a law in the circumstances of war can be, following it is not merely the pragmatic action – it is the morally right action for the circumstances.[4] So moral assessment of law is morally central and highly valuable because it can provide guidance about the morally right action to take, which will sometimes be the legally right action.

Part IV of this book contains some beautiful examples of diverse types of this crucial enterprise of the moral examination of laws of war.[5] Adil Haque, for

---

[1] Henry Shue, *Fighting Hurt: Rule and Exception in Torture and War*, Oxford: Oxford University Press, 2016. I endorse this project explicitly in pp. 33–34 and attempt to conduct it in, for example, pp. 67–86 (U.S. domestic law), pp. 87–129 (U.S. domestic law), pp. 295–317 (LOAC), and pp. 330–47 (LOAC), and frequently elsewhere in *Fighting Hurt*.

[2] Shue, *Fighting Hurt*, pp. 401–28.

[3] For finer categories, see Seth Lazar, "Method in the Morality of War," in *Oxford Handbook of Ethics of War*, eds. Helen Frowe and Seth Lazar, Oxford: Oxford University Press, 2017.

[4] Shue, *Fighting Hurt*, pp. 469–93.

[5] It goes without saying that other sections of the book also contain valuable discussions. In this very brief section it seems more useful to be slightly less superficial in commenting on a few chapters than to be completely superficial about them all.

instance, shows in a splendid chapter how the application of some philosophical sophistication to the legal conception of proportionality makes better sense of a notion that philosophers tend initially to find alien. This seems much more useful than concocting, as some revisionist philosophers do, sophisticated substitute notions of moral proportionality that are inapplicable to all the unjust parties to war, which in the case of many wars are both sides.

Law requires a comparison between the expected military advantages of an attack and the civilian losses expected to result. Haque correctly notes that on the revisionist notion of proportionality what the law considers to be "military advantages have no intrinsic value at all." Consequently, "every harm that unjust combatants inflict on civilians is *morally* disproportionate. Moreover, the *legal* rule of proportionality has no morally intelligible content when applied to the conduct of unjust combatants." Haque is faithful to the legal conception of proportionality, however, and brings to bear the "substantial moral asymmetry between doing harm and allowing harm." He construes the achievement of military advantage as the prevention of harm – not allowing harm to be done by the adversary – (in line, I would suggest, with a conception of the justification of war as the prevention of evil) and construes civilian losses caused by one's own side as the doing of harm oneself. Because of the asymmetry of allowing and doing, "an attack is proportionate only if it will foreseeably prevent substantially more harm to [one's own] attacking forces or civilians than it will foreseeably inflict on civilians." The law phrases this as a requirement that expected civilian losses from an attack not be excessive in light of the expected military advantage of the attack. On Haque's interpretation the legal conception of proportionality "applies symmetrically to all parties to a conflict, independently of their war aims, yet all parties have decisive moral reasons to obey it." This is vastly better than the revisionist conception that tells an unjust party nothing about how to conduct the war (except not to conduct it at all, which is an option already rejected by it upon entering the war). There is much more to be said about proportionality, but this is an admirable way to proceed.[6]

Jens David Ohlin, on the other hand, employs moral considerations, not to interpret an obscure element already in LOAC/IHL, but to argue imaginatively for a specific proposal for the "progressive development" of these laws. It is well known that the primary purpose by far of the existing system of law is the protection of civilians. This is a primary reason why the inability of the revisionist conception of proportionality to make sense of constraining the

---

[6] Much more is said in a valuable debate between Haque and USAF Gen. [retired] Charles Dunlap about the new *Law of War Manual* issued by the U.S. Department of Defense in 2015 – see Adil Ahmad Haque, "Off Target: Selection, Precaution, and Proportionality in the DoD Manual," *International Law Studies* [U.S. Naval War College] 92 (2016): 31–84; and Charles J. Dunlap Jr., "The DoD *Law of War Manual* and Its Critics: Some Observations," *International Law Studies* [U.S. Naval War College] 92 (2016): 85–118.

conduct of the fighting by unjust parties is extremely unfortunate – it is failing to a considerable extent to accomplish the main goal of civilian protection. But notoriously international law has only peripheral and fairly inconsequential limits on harm to combatants. The existing legal system "leaves soldiers relatively unprotected. The question is what changes, if any, could be codified that would make warfare more humane for soldiers."

Ohlin proposes the principle that "attacking forces could be subject to a requirement to use the least harmful level of force to accomplish the mission."[7] This could be implemented by a three-step progression: "under some circumstances, capturing instead of killing. In other circumstances, it would entail injuring rather than killing the enemy. Killing would then be a last resort." The reference to last resort echoes the argument for his proposal about the conduct of war that Ohlin constructs by analogy with the requirement of last resort in the resort to war. His chapter also contains a valuable contrast between LOAC/IHL and international human rights law.

Space does not permit as much comment on the section's other chapters. Unlike the other four, Larry May's chapter focuses on the resort to war rather than the conduct of war; he tends to highlight similarities between law and morality while Haque and Ohlin highlight differences. May analyses the moral stakes in a fascinating and important group of legal cases: the ICJ's Nicaragua case, Nuclear Weapons case, and Palestinian Wall case, as well as the better-known Ministries case at Nuremberg. I am inclined to think that one of the similarities that May finds, the focus on the individual in international criminal law and the focus on individual liability in revisionist Just War theory, is undermined by the underlying radical differences in conceptions of responsibility, liability and culpability. But there is much here to consider.

In a refreshing departure from the usual, Shannon Fyfe compares the practice of Islamic terrorists, not to law heavily influenced by Christian conceptions of just war, but to the Islamic law that the terrorists claim is their own tradition.[8] She finds that "the *sunnah* and Quran agree that conduct in war may not include excessive violence" and concludes overall that the terrorists' "reliance on *sharia* law in justifying their violent acts is misplaced. The Quran

---

[7] I have made a proposal in a somewhat similar spirit, but mine applies a proportionality requirement to combatant losses on one's own side (rather than exclusively to civilian losses, as now) rather than imposing a minimisation requirement on combatant losses on the opposing side like Ohlin's – see Rule 2 in Shue, *Fighting Hurt*, p. 333. I quote Gen. Charles Dunlap's provocative statement in 2000 that "citizen soldiers" are "non-combatants in uniforms" – p. 335. The two suggestions are compatible, and each might save lives. On actual trends, see Neta Crawford, "Targeting Civilians and U.S. Strategic Bombing Norms," in *The American Way of Bombing: Changing Ethical and Legal Norms, from Flying Fortresses to Drones*, eds. Matthew Evangelista and Henry Shue, Ithaca, NY: Cornell University Press, 2014, pp. 64–86.

[8] A rare complementary analysis is Alia Brahimi, *Jihad and Just War in the War on Terror*, Oxford: Oxford University Press, 2010.

and Muhammad's *sunnah* cannot justify the use of indiscriminate and unwarranted violence to defend the Muslim faith or territories in defiance of international laws of war."

Like Fyfe, Elizabeth Lanphier does not tackle a topic that is one of the usual suspects in volumes on war and ethics, but she examines the conceptual framing of the practices of humanitarian organizations such as the ICRC and MSF which operate in war zones. Her focus is the extremely slippery question of the relation between neutrality and impartiality,[9] which she subtly analyzes, while noting that "even if noncombatants were considered unjust actors complicit in warfare [enough to be appropriately killed, as some revisionists claim], the principles of impartiality and neutrality would still apply" for the humanitarian organisations. Lanphier carefully and dialectically probes, through the cases of the ICRC in the Nazi concentration camps and MSF in the Rwandan genocide, the dangers implicit in neutrality, especially the dilemma between complicity on the part of the humanitarian actors from remaining publicly silent about atrocity and loss of access to the victims from speaking out, an issue on which ICRC and MSF have differed. Lanphier insightfully observes: "neutrality requires politics." So, I would suggest, does all ethics of war.

What all the chapters in Part IV have in common is that their authors have not indulged in the narrow specialisation – I do law, oh, I do philosophy – that plagues academic life and makes so much academic writing of so little use to people in the world who must make all-things-considered decisions. All these authors are knowledgeable about both morality and law, and they all struggle with the differences and similarities, the cross-fertilizations and the corruptions. Such rich analysis is what we need more of.

---

[9] A path-breaking book-length analysis of these concepts is Emily Paddon Rhoads, *Taking Sides in Peacekeeping: Impartiality and the Future of the United Nations*, Oxford: Oxford University Press, 2016, pp. 25–91. Rhoads argues that impartiality is a composite norm.

Bibliography

Advisory Opinion on the Legality of the Threat or Use of Nuclear Weapons, International Court of Justice Reports, 1996.

Advisory Opinion on the Legality of the Threat or Use of Nuclear Weapons, Dissenting Opinion of Judge Higgins, International Court of Justice Reports, 1996.

Afsaruddin, Asma. "In Defense of All Houses of Worship? Jihad in the Context of Interfaith Relations," in *Just Wars, Holy Wars, & Jihads: Christian, Jewish, and Muslim Encounters and Exchanges*, ed. Sohail H. Hashmi, New York: Oxford University Press, 2012, pp. 47–68.

"The Siyar Laws of Aggression: Juridical Re-Interpretations of Qur'ānic Jihād and Their Contemporary Implications for International Law," in *Islam and International Law: Engaging Self-Centrism from a Plurality of Perspectives*, eds. Marie-Luisa Frick and Andreas Th. Müller, Leiden: Martinus Nijhoff Publishers, 2013.

Ago, Roberto. Addendum to the Eighth Report on State Responsibility, UN Doc A/CN.4/318, Add 5–7, *Yearbook of the International Law Commission* (1980) 69–70.

Ahmed, Dawood I. and Moamen Gouda. "Measuring Constitutional Islamization: The Islamic Constitutions Index," *Hastings International and Comparative Law Review*, vol. 38, 2015.

Akande, Dapo and Thomas Lieflander. "Clarifying Necessity, Imminence, and Proportionality in the Law of Self-Defense," *American Journal of International Law*, vol. 107, no. 3, 2013.

Al-Dawoody, Ahmed. *The Islamic Law of War: Justifications and Regulations*, New York: Palgrave Macmillan, 2011.

Al-Farabi, Abu Nasr. *Fusul Al-Madani: Aphorisms of the Statesman*, ed. D.M. Dunlop, Cambridge: Cambridge University Press, 1961.

Al-Mawardi, Ali Ibn Muhammad. *Al-Hawi al-Kabir fi Fiqh Madhhab al-Imam al-Shafi'I radi allahu 'anhu wa-huwa Sharh Mukhtasar al-Muzani*, vol. 14, eds. 'Ali Muhammad Mu'awwad and 'Adil Ahmad 'Abd al-Mawjud, Beirut: Daral-kutub al-'arabiyya, 1994.

Alexander of Hales. *Summa theologica*, III, n. 466: *Utrum bellare sit licitum*, quoted in Gregory M. Reichberg, Henrik Syse, and Endre Begby eds., *The Ethics of War: Classic and Contemporary Readings*, Oxford: Blackwell Publishing Ltd., 2006.

Aloyo, Eaman. "Just War Theory and the Last of Last Resort," *Ethics and International Affairs*, vol. 29, no. 2, 2015.

Altman, Andrew. "Introduction" in *Targeted Killings: Law and Morality in an Asymmetrical World*, eds. Claire Finkelstein, Jens David Ohlin, and Andrew Altman, Oxford: Oxford University Press, 2012, pp. 1–8.

Ambos, Kai. "Ius Puniendi and Individual Criminal Responsibility in International Criminal Law," in *Research Handbook on the International Penal System*, eds. Róisín Mulgrew and Denis Abels, Cheltenham: Edward Elgar, 2016, pp. 57–79.

"Joint Criminal Enterprise and Command Responsibility," *Journal of International Criminal Justice*, vol. 5, no. 1, 2007, 159–83.

Amin, ElSayed M.A. *Reclaiming Jihad: A Qur'anic Critique of Terrorism*, Nairobi, Kenya: The Islamic Foundation, 2015.

Aquinas, Thomas. *Questions on Love and Charity*, ed. Robert Miner, New Haven: Yale University Press, 2016.

Summa Theologica, trans. Fathers of the English Dominican Province, New York: Benzinger Bros., 1948 [1265–74].

Aristotle. *The Politics and the Constitution of Athens*, ed. Stephen Everson, Cambridge: Cambridge University Press, 1996.

Arkin, Ronald C. "The Case for Ethical Autonomy in Unmanned Systems," *Journal of Military Ethics*, vol. 9, no. 4, 2010, 332–41.

Armed Activities on the Territory of the Congo (Democratic Republic of the Congo v. Uganda), Judgment (2005) ICJ Reports 168.

Armed Activities on the Territory of the Congo, Separate Opinion of Judge Kooijmans (2005) ICJ Reports 168, 306.

Arreguin-Toft, Ivan. "How the Weak Win Wars: A Theory of Asymmetric Conflict," *International Security*, vol. 26, no. 1, 2001, 93–128.

Augustine. *City of God*, trans. Henry Bettenson, London: Penguin Books, 1984.

City of God, trans. John Healey, ed. R.V.G. Tasker, London: J.M. Dent & Sons, 1945.

Confessions, trans. R.S. Pine-Coffin, New York: Penguin Books, 1981.

Contra Faustum XXIII, c. 74, cited in Alexander de Hales, *Summa theological seu sic ab origine dicta* "Summa fratris Alexandri," vol. 4, trans. Robert Andrews, Florence: Quaracchi, 1948, pp. 683–86.

Of the Morals of the Catholic Church XV.25, *The Nicene and Post-Nicene Fathers* [hereafter *NPNF*], Grand Rapids: Eerdmans Publishing Company, IV, 1994, p. 48.

On Free Choice of the Will I.V, trans. Anna S. Benjamin and L.H. Hackstaff, New York: Macmillan Publishing Company, 1964.

Questions on the Heptateuch 6.10, quoted in Louis J. Swift, *The Early Fathers on War and Military Service*, Wilmington: Michael Glazier, Inc., 1983, p. 135.

Austin, John L. *The Province of Jurisprudence Determined*, London: John Murray, Albemarle Street, 1832.

Ayala, Balthazar. *Three Books on the Law of War*, 2 vols., ed. John Westlake, trans. John Pawley Bate, Washington: Carnegie Institution, 1912 [1582].

Bacon, Francis. "Of Empire," in *The Essays or Counsels, Civil and Moral*, ed. Brian Vickers, Oxford: Oxford University Press, 1999 [1625], pp. 42–46.

Considerations Touching a Warre with Spaine. London: Imprinted, 1629 [1619].

Bakircioglu, Onder. *Islam and Warfare: Context and Compatibility with International Law*, New York: Routledge.

Barnes, Jonathan. "The Just War," in *The Cambridge History of Later Medieval Philosophy*, eds. Norman Kretzman, Anthony Kenny, and Jan Pinborg, Cambridge: Cambridge University Press, 1982, pp. 771–84.

Bassiouni, M. Cherif. "Evolving Approaches to Jihad: From Self-Defense to Revolutionary and Regime-Change Political Violence," *Journal of Islamic Law and Culture*, vol. 10, no. 1, 2008.

The Sharī'a and Islamic Criminal Justice in Time of War and Peace, New York: Cambridge University Press, 2013.

Baumgold, Deborah. "Pacifying Politics: Resistance, Violence, and Accountability in Seventeenth-Century Contract Theory," in her *Contract Theory in Historical Context: Essays on Grotius, Hobbes, and Locke*, Leiden: Brill, 2010, pp. 27–49.

Baxter, R. "So-Called 'Unprivileged Belligerency': Spies, Guerrillas, and Saboteurs," in *Humanizing the Laws of War: Selected Writings of Richard Baxter*, eds. D.F. Vagts et al., Oxford: Oxford University Press, 2013, pp. 37, 44.

Bazargan, Saba. "Killing Minimally Responsible Threats," *Ethics*, vol. 125, no. 1, 2014, 114–36.

"Morally Heterogeneous Wars," *Philosophia*, vol. 41, no. 4, 2013, 959–75.

Beckman, Gary. *Hittite Diplomatic Texts*, 2nd ed., Atlanta, GA: Scholars Press, 1999.

Bedau, Hugo Adam and Michael L. Radelet. "Miscarriages of Justice in Potentially Capital Cases," *Stanford Law Review*, vol. 40, 1987, 21–179.

Beitz, Charles. "Nonintervention and Communal Integrity," *Philosophy and Public Affairs*, vol. 9, 1980, 385–91.

Political Theory in International Relations, Princeton: Princeton University Press, 1979.

"The Moral Standing of States Revisited," in *Reading Walzer*, eds. Yitzhak Benbaji and Naomi Sussmann, New York: Routledge, 2013.

Bellamy, Alex J. *Just Wars: From Cicero to Iraq*, Cambridge: Polity Press, 2006.

Benbaji, Yitzhak. "Distributive Justice, Human Rights, and Territorial Integrity: A Contractarian Account of the Crime of Aggression," in *The Morality of Defensive Wars* eds. Fabre and Lazar, Oxford: Oxford University Press, 2014, pp. 159–84.

Black, Ann. Hossein Esmaeili and Nadirsyah Hosen. *Modern Perspectives on Islamic Law*, Northampton, MA: Edward Elgar, 2013.

Blom, Andrew. "Owing Punishment: Grotius on Right and Merit." *Grotiana*, vol. 36, 2015, 3–27.

Blum, Gabriella. "The Dispensable Lives of Soldiers," *Journal of Legal Analysis*, vol. 2, 2010, 69–124.

Borschberg, Peter. "'De Pace': Ein unveröffentlichtes Fragment von Hugo Grotius über Krieg und Frieden," *Zeitschrift der Savigny-Stiftung für Rechtsgeschichte*, vol. 113, no. 1, 1996, 268–92.

Brahimi, Alia. *Jihad and Just War in the War on Terror*, New York: Oxford University Press, 2010.

Brauman, Rony. "L'assistance humanitaire international," in *Dictionnaire de philosophie morale et politique*, ed. Monique Canto-Sperber, Paris: Presses Universitaire de France, 1996.

Brodie, Bernard. "More about Limited War," *World Politics*, vol. 10, no. 1, October 1957.

Buckle, Stephen. *Natural Law and the Theory of Property: Grotius to Hume*. Oxford: Clarendon Press, 1991.

Bugnion, François. "Dialogue with the Past: the ICRC and the Nazi Death Camps," ICRC, 2002.

Bull, Hedley. "The Importance of Grotius in the Study of International Relations," in *Hugo Grotius and International Relations*, eds. Hedley Bull, Benedict Kingsbury, and Adam Roberts, Oxford: Clarendon Press, 1990, pp. 65–93.

Byman, Daniel. *Al Qaeda, the Islamic State, and the Global Jihadist Movement: What Everyone Needs to Know*, New York: Oxford University Press, 2015.

Callimachi, Rukmini. "ISIS Remains Silent on Encrypted App," *New York Times*, June 12, 2016. www.nytimes.com/live/orlando-nightclub-shooting-live-upd ates/comment-on-a-terrorism, accessed July 25, 2016.

Carter, Jacoby Adeshei. "Just/New War Theory: Non-State Actors in Asymmetric Conflicts," *Philosophy in the Contemporary World*, vol. 16, no. 2, Fall 2009, 1–11.

Case Concerning Military and Paramilitary Activities in and against Nicaragua (Nicaragua v. United States of America), International Court of Justice, Jurisdiction of the Court and Admissibility of the Application, Judgment of 26 November 1984.

Case Concerning Military and Paramilitary Activities in and against Nicaragua (Nicaragua v. United States of America), International Court of Justice, Merits, Judgment of 27 June 1986.

Cassese, Antonio. *International Criminal Law*, Oxford: Oxford University Press, 2003.

Cavallar, Georg. *The Rights of Strangers: Theories of International Hospitality, the Global Community, and Political Justice since Vitoria*, Aldershot: Ashgate, 2002.

Chang, Ruth. "Introduction," in *Incommensurability, Incomparability, and Practical Reason*, ed. Ruth Chang Cambridge, MA: Harvard University Press, 1997, pp. 1–14.

Christopher, Paul. *The Ethics of War and Peace*. Upper Saddle River, NJ: Pearson/Prentice Hall, 2004.

Cicero, Marcus Tullius. *De Re Publica* III.xxiii, in Loeb Classical Library: Cicero XVI, *De Re Publica and De Legibus*, trans. Clinton Walker Keyes, Cambridge: Harvard University Press, 1928.

    On Duties, eds. M.T. Griffin and E.M. Atkins, Cambridge: Cambridge University Press, 1991.

Coady, C.A.J. "The Ethics of Armed Humanitarian Intervention," *Peaceworks*, United States Institute of Peace, 2002.

Morality and Political Violence, Cambridge: Cambridge University Press, 2008.

"Terrorism and Innocence," *The Journal of Ethics*, vol. 8, no. 1, 2004.

Coleman, Stephen. *Military Ethics: An Introduction with Case Studies*, Oxford: Oxford University Press, 2013.

Convention on the Prohibition of the Development, Production, Stockpiling and Use of Chemical Weapons, Geneva, 3 September 1992, 1974 U.N.T.S. 45.

Convention on the Prohibition of the Use, Stockpiling, Production and Transfer of Anti-Personnel Mines and on Their Destruction, 18 September 1997, 2056 U.N.T.S. 211.

Coppieters, Bruno et al. "Last Resort," in *Moral Constraints on War*, 2nd ed., eds. Bruno Coppieters and Nick Foton, Lanham, MD, and Plymouth: Lexington Books, 2008, pp. 139–54.

Corn, Geoffrey S., Laurie R. Blank, Chris Jenks, and Eric Talbot Jensen. "Belligerent Targeting and the Invalidity of a Least Harmful Means Rule," *International Law Studies*, vol. 89, 2013.

Crawford, Neta. *Accountability for Killing: Moral Responsibility for Collateral Damage in America's Post-9/11 Wars*. New York: Oxford University Press, 2013.

"Targeting Civilians and U.S. Strategic Bombing Norms," in *The American Way of Bombing: Changing Ethical and Legal Norms, from Flying Fortresses to Drones*, eds. Matthew Evangelista and Henry Shue, Ithaca, NY: Cornell University Press, pp. 64–86.

Cronin, Audrey Kurth. "Isis Is Not a Terrorist Group," *Foreign Affairs*, vol. 94, no. 2, 2015.

Darwall, Stephen. "Grotius at the Creation of Modern Moral Philosophy." *Archiv für Geschichte der Philosophie*, vol. 94, no. 3, 2012, 296–325.

Davidovic, Jovana. "Proportionate Killing: Using Traditional *Jus in Bello* Conditions to Model the Relationship between Liability and Lesser Evil Justifications for Killing in War," in *Weighing Lives: Combatants and Civilians in War*, eds. Jens Ohlin, Claire Finkelstein, and Larry May, Oxford: Oxford University Press, 2017, pp. 155–72.

Davidson, Eugene. *The Trial of the Germans*, New York: Macmillan, 1966, 392–426.

Dershowitz, Alan. *Why Terrorism Works: Understanding the Threat, Responding to the Challenge*, New Haven: Yale University Press, 2002.

Desch, Michael C. "Bush and the Generals," *Foreign Affairs*, May/June 2007.

Dinstein, Yoram. *The Conduct of Hostilities under the Law of International Armed Conflict*, 3rd ed., Cambridge University Press, 2016.

Dizboni, A.G. *Islam and War the Disparity between the Technological-Normative Evolution of Modern War and the Doctrine of Jihad*, Lewiston NY: E. Mellen Press, 2011.

Drumbl, Mark A. "Punishment, Postgenocide: From Guilty to Shame to *Civis* in Rwanda," *New York University Law Review*, vol. 75, 2000, 1221–326.

Dunant, Henry. *A Memory of Solferino*, Geneva: ICRC, 1939.

Dunlap, Charles J. Jr. "The DoD *Law of War Manual* and Its Critics: Some Observations," *International Law Studies* [US Naval War College], vol. 92, 2016, 85–118.

"Response to Jeff McMahan's 'The Moral Responsibility of Volunteer Soldiers,'" *Boston Review*, November 6, 2013.

Egan, Brian. "International Law, Legal Diplomacy, and the Counter-ISIL Campaign: Some Observations," *International Law Studies*, vol. 92, 2016, 235–241.

Enemark, Christian. "Unmanned Drones and the Ethics of War," in *Routledge Handbook of Ethics and War: Just War Theory and the 21st Century*, eds. Fritz Allhoff, Nicholas G. Evans, and Adam Henschke, New York: Routledge, 2013, pp. 327–37.

Fabre, Cécile. *Cosmopolitan War.* Oxford: Oxford University Press, 2012.

"Guns, Food, and Liability to Attack in War," *Ethics* vol. 120, 36–63.

"Cosmopolitanism and Wars of Self-Defense" in *The Morality of Defensive War*, eds. Fabre and Lazar, pp. 103–13.

"Rights, Justice and War: A Reply." *Law and Philosophy*, vol. 33, no. 3, 2014, 391–425.

Fabre, Cecile and Seth Lazar (eds.), *The Morality of Defensive War.* Oxford: Oxford University Press, 2014.

Fearon, James. "Rationalist Explanations for War," *International Organization* vol. 49, 1995, 379–414.

Finkelstein, Claire. *"Targeted Killing as Preemptive Action,"* in *Targeted Killings: Law and Morality in an Asymmetrical World*, eds. Claire Finkelstein, Jens David Ohlin, and Andrew Altman, Oxford: Oxford University Press, 2013.

Ford, Christopher A. "Siyar-Ization and Its Discontents: International Law and Islam's Constitutional Crisis," *Texas International Law Journal*, vol. 30, 1995.

Forde, Steven. "Hugo Grotius on Ethics and War," *American Political Science Review*, vol. 92, no. 3, 1998, 639–48.

Forester, Benjamin. "Water under the Straw: Peace in Mesopotamia," in *War and Peace in the Ancient World*, ed. Kurt A. Raaflaub, Oxford: Blackwell Publishing, 2007, pp. 66–80.

Freedman, Lawrence. "The First Two Generations of Nuclear Strategists," in *Makers of Modern Strategy: From Machiavelli to the Nuclear Age*, ed. Peter Paret, Oxford: Clarendon Press, 1986, pp. 735–78.

French, Shannon E. *The Code of the Warrior: Exploring Warrior Values, Past and Present*, 2nd ed., Lantham, MD and New York: Rowman & Littlefield, 2016.

Friman, H. (ed.). *The Politics of Leverage in International Relations: Name, Shame, and Sanction*, New York: Springer, 2015.

Frowe, Helen. *Defensive Killing*, Oxford: Oxford University Press, 2014.

"Killing John to Save Mary: A Defense of the Moral Distinction between Killing and Letting Die," in *Action, Ethics, and Responsibility*, eds. Joseph Keim Campbell, Michael O'Rourke, and Harry S. Silverstein, Cambridge, MA: MIT Press, 2010, pp. 47–66.

"The Moral Status of Combatants," in *The Ethics of War and Peace: An Introduction*, 2nd ed., London: Routledge, 2016.

"Non-Combatant Liability in War," in *How We Fight: Ethics in War*, eds. Helen Frowe and Gerald Lang, Oxford: Oxford University Press, 2014, pp. 172–187.

Gaggioli, G. and R. Kolb. "A Right to Life in Armed Conflicts? The Contribution of the European Court of Human Rights," *Israel Yearbook of Human Rights*, vol. 37, 2007, 115–136.

Galliott, Jai. "Uninhabited Aerial Vehicles and the Asymmetry Objection: A Response to Strawser," *Journal of Military Ethics*, vol. 11, no. 1, March 2012, 58–66.

Gardham, Judith. *Necessity, Proportionality, and the Use of Force by States*, Cambridge: Cambridge University Press, 2004.

Gentili, Alberico. *De Jure Belli Libri Tres*, 2 vols, eds. C. John and C. Rolfe, Oxford: Clarendon Press, 1933 [1598].

Gillespie, Alexander. *The Causes of War: Vol. I: 3000 BCE to 1000 CE*, Oxford: Hart Publishing, 2013.

Gladwell, Malcolm. *David and Goliath*, Boston: Back Bay Books, 2013.

Goodman, Ryan. "The Power to Kill or Capture Enemy Combatants," *European Journal of International Law*, vol. 24, 2013.

Gratian, *Concordia discordantium canonum* part II, causa 23, Question II, Canon 1, quoted in Frederick H. Russell, *The Just War in the Middle Ages*, Cambridge: Cambridge University Press, 1975.

Green, James A. "Questioning the Peremptory Status of the Prohibition of the Use of Force," *Michigan Journal of International Law*, vol. 32, 2011.

Grossman, David. *On Killing: The Psychological Cost of Learning to Kill in War and Society*, rev. ed., New York: Back Bay Books, 2009.

Grotius, Hugo. *The Rights of War and Peace*, 3 vols., ed. Richard Tuck, Indianapolis: Liberty Fund, 2005 [1625].

  "Commentarius in Theses XI": An Early Treatise on Sovereignty, the Just War, and the Legitimacy of the Dutch Revolt, ed. Peter Borschberg, Bern: Peter Lang, 1994.

  Commentary on the Law of Prize and Booty, ed. M.J. van Ittersum, Indianapolis: Liberty Fund, 2006.

  Mare Liberum, ed. Robert Feenstra, Leiden: Brill, 2009.

Haakonssen, Knud. "Hugo Grotius and the History of Political Thought." *Political Theory*, vol. 13, no. 2, 1985, 239–65.

Haggenmacher, Peter. *Grotius et la Doctrine de la Guerre Juste*, Paris: Presses Universitaires de France, 1983.

  "Grotius and Gentili: A Reassessment of Thomas E. Holland's Inaugural Lecture," in *Hugo Grotius and International Relations*, eds. Hedley Bull, Benedict Kingsburg, and Adam Roberts, Oxford: Clarendon Press, 1990, pp. 133–76.

  "Just War and Regular War in Sixteenth-century Spanish Doctrine," *International Review of the Red Cross*, vol. 32, no. 290, 1992, 434–45.

Hallaq, Wael B. *The Origins and Evolution of Islamic Law*, Themes in Islamic Law, Cambridge: Cambridge University Press, 2005.

Hamdan v. Rumsfeld, 548 U.S. 557, 630 (2006).

Hammurabi, *The Laws of Hammurabi* (c. 1750 BCE), in *Law Collections from Mesopotamia and Asia Minor*, 2nd ed., trans. and ed. Martha T. Ross, Atlanta: Scholars Press, 1997.

Haque, Adil. "Laws for War," in *Theoretical Boundaries of Armed Conflict and Human Rights*, ed. Jens David Ohlin, New York: Cambridge University Press, 2016.

"Off Target: Selection, Precaution, and Proportionality in the DoD Manual," *International Law Studies*, vol. 92, 2016.

"A Theory of Jus in Bello Proportionality," in *Weighing Lives in War: Combatants & Civilians*, eds. Jens David Ohlin, Claire Finkelstein, and Larry May, New York: Oxford University Press, 2017.

Hashmi, Solail. "Jihad and the Geneva Conventions: The Impact of International Law on Islamic Theory," in *Just Wars, Holy Wars, and Jihads: Christian, Jewish, and Muslim Encounters and Exchanges*, ed. Sohail H. Hashmi, New York: Oxford University Press, 2012, pp. 323–41.

Hashmi, Sohail H. and James Johnson, "Introduction," in *Just Wars, Holy Wars, and Jihads: Christian, Jewish, and Muslim Encounters and Exchanges*, ed. Sohail H. Hashmi, New York: Oxford University Press, 2012, pp. 3–21.

Hathaway, Oona et al. "Which Law Governs during Armed Conflict? The Relationship between International Humanitarian Law and Human Rights Law," *Minnesota Law Review*, vol. 96, 2012.

Heath, Malcolm. "Aristotle on Natural Slavery," *Phronesis*, vol. 53, no. 3, 2008, 243–70.

Hedges, Chris. *What Every Person Should Know about War*, New York: Free Press, 2003.

Henkin, Louis. *How Nations Behave: Law and Foreign Policy*, 2nd ed., New York: Columbia University Press/Council on Foreign Relations, 1979.

Hobbes, Thomas *On the Citizen*, ed. Richard Tuck, trans. Michael Silverthorne, Cambridge: Cambridge University Press, 1998 [1642].

The Elements of Law, Natural and Politic, ed. Ferdinand Tönnies, London: Frank Cass, 1969 [1640].

Leviathan, 3 vols., ed. Noel Malcolm, Oxford: Clarendon Press, 2012 [1651].

Holbrook, Donald. "Using the Qur'an to Justify Terrorist Violence: Analysing Selective Application of the Qur'an in English-Language Militant Islamist Discourse," *Perspectives on Terrorism*, vol. 4, no. 3, 2010.

Hornyak, Tim. "Korean Machine-Gun Robots Start DMZ Duty," C-Net, July 14, 2010, www.cnet.com/news/korean-machine-gun-robots-start-dmz-duty.

Horton, S. "Military Necessity, Torture, and the Criminality of Lawyers," in *International Prosecution of Human Rights Crimes*, eds. W. Kaleck et al., New York: Springer, 2007, pp. 169–83.

Hubbard, B. and D. D. Kirkpatrick. "Photo Archive Is Said to Show Widespread Torture in Syria," *New York Times*, January 21, 2014. www.nytimes.com/20 14/01/22/world/middleeast/photo-archive-is-said-to-show-widespread-tor ture-in-syria.html?_r=0, accessed July 1, 2016.

Hurka, Thomas. "Liability and Just Cause," *Ethics & International Affairs*, vol. 21, no. 2, 2007, 199–218.

"Proportionality and Necessity," in *War: Essays in Political Philosophy*, ed. Larry May, New York: Cambridge University Press, 2008.

"Proportionality in the Morality of War," *Philosophy & Public Affairs*, vol. 33, 2005, 34–66.

In re Yamashita, 327 U.S. 1 (1946).

International Committee of the Red Cross. *Customary International Humanitarian Law*, vol. 1, New York: Cambridge University Press, 2009.

Commentary on the Additional Protocols of 8 June 1977 to the Geneva Conventions of 12 August 1949, Dordrecht: Martinus Nijhoff, 1987.

The Use of Force in Armed Conflicts: Interplay between the Conduct of Hostilities and Law Enforcement Paradigms, 2013.

The Fundamental Principles of the International Red Cross and Red Crescent Movement, Geneva: International Committee of the Red Cross, 2015.

Jain, N. "The Control Theory of Perpetration in International Criminal Law," *Chicago Journal of International Law*, vol. 12, 2011.

Janis, Mark and John E. Noyes. *International Law: Cases and Commentary*, St. Paul: West Law, 1997.

Jenkins, Brian Michael. *The Study of Terrorism: Definitional Problems*, Santa Monica, CA: RAND Corporation, 1980.

Jessberger, F. and J. Geneuss. "On the Application of a Theory of Indirect Perpetration in Al Bashir: German Doctrine at The Hague?" *Journal of International Criminal Justice*, vol. 6, 2008, 853–69.

Johnson, James Turner. *Just War Tradition and the Restraint of War: A Moral and Historical Inquiry*, Princeton: Princeton University Press, 1981.

"Grotius' Use of History and Charity in the Modern Transformation of the Just War Idea," *Grotiana*, vol. 4, 1983, 21–34.

Kaag, John and Sarah Kreps. *Drone Warfare*, New York: Polity Press, 2014.

Kahn, Paul. "The Paradox of Riskless War," *Philosophy and Public Affairs Quarterly*, vol. 22, no. 3, summer 2002, 2–8.

Kalmanovitz, Pablo. "Early Modern Sources of the Regular War Tradition," in *The Oxford Handbook of Ethics of War*, eds. Seth Lazar and Helen Frowe, Oxford: Oxford University Press, 2016.

Kamal, Mohd Hisham Mohd. "Meaning and Method of the Interpretation of Sunnah in the Field of Siyar: A Reappraisal," in *Islam and International Law: Engaging Self-Centrism from a Plurality of Perspectives*, eds. Marie-Luisa Frick and Andreas Th Müller, Leiden: Martinus Nijhoff Publishers, 2013.

Kamali, Mohammed Hashim. *Principles of Islamic Jurisprudence*, The Islamic Text Society, 1991.

Kamm, Frances. *Ethics for Enemies*, Oxford: Oxford University Press, 2011.

Kant, Immanuel. "On a Supposed Right to Lie from Altruistic Motives," in *Immanuel Kant: Critique of Practical Reason and Other Writings in Moral Philosophy*, trans. Lewis White Beck, Chicago: University of Chicago Press, 1949.

"Perpetual Peace: A Philosophical Sketch," in *Kant: Political Writings*, ed. H.S. Reiss and trans. H. B. Nisbet, Cambridge: Cambridge University Press, 1970.

Kasher, Asa. "A Moral Evaluation of the Gaza War – Operation Cast Lead," *Journal of the Jerusalem Center for Public Affairs*, vol. 9, no. 18, February 4, 2010.

Keene, Edward. *Beyond the Anarchical Society: Grotius, Colonialism and Order in World Politics*, Cambridge: Cambridge University Press, 2002.

Kelsay, John. *Islam and War: A Study in Comparative Ethics*, Lousiville, KY: Westminster/John Knox Press, 1993.

Khadduri, Majid. *War and Peace in the Law of Islam*, Clark, NJ: The Lawbook Exchange, 2006.

Khan, L. Ali. *A Theory of International Terrorism: Understanding Islamic Militancy*, Leiden and Boston: Martinus Nijhoff Publishers, 2006.

King, Martin Luther Jr. "Racism and the World House," in *In a Single Garment of Destiny: A Global Vision of Justice*, ed. and intro. Lewis V. Baldwin, Boston: Beacon Press, 2012.

Kingsbury, Benedict and Benjamin Straumann. "Introduction," in *The Roman Foundations of the Law of Nations: Alberico Gentili and the Justice of Empire*, eds. Benedict Kingsbury and Bewnjamin Straumann, Oxford: Oxford University Press, 2010, pp. 1–18.

"Introduction," in *Alberico Gentili: The Wars of the Romans*, eds. Benedict Kingsbury and Benjamin Straumann, trans. David Lupher, Oxford: Oxford University Press, 2011.

Kretzmer, David. "The Inherent Right to Self-Defence and Proportionality in *Jus ad Bellum*," *European Journal of International Law*, vol. 24, 2013, 235–79.

Kutz, Christopher. *Complicity: Ethics and Law for a Collective Age.* Cambridge: Cambridge University Press, 2007.

"Democracy, Defense, and the Threat of Intervention," in *The Morality of Defensive War*, eds. Fabre and Lazar, Oxford: Oxford University Press, 2014, pp. 229–46.

"The Difference Uniforms Make: Collective Violence in Criminal Law and War," *Philosophy and Public Affairs*, vol. 33, 2005, 156–73.

Lango, John W. "Before Military Force, Nonviolent Action: An Application of the Generalized Just War Principle of Last Resort," *Public Affairs Quarterly*, vol. 23, no. 2, 2009.

Laqueur, Walter. *The Age of Terrorism*, Boston: Little, Brown, 1987.

Lazar, Seth. "Debate: Do Associative Duties Really Not Matter?" *Journal of Political Philosophy*, vol. 17, no. 1, 2009, 90–101.

"Method in the Morality of War," in *Oxford Handbook of Ethics of War*, eds. Seth Lazar and Helen Frowe, Oxford: Oxford University Press, 2016.

"National Defense, Self-Defense, and the Problem of Political Aggression," in *The Morality of Defensive War*, eds. Fabre and Lazar, Oxford: Oxford University Press, 2014, 11–39.

"Necessity in Self-Defense and War," *Philosophy & Public Affairs*, vol. 40, no. 3, 2012.

"War," *The Stanford Encyclopedia of Philosophy*, ed. Edward N. Zalta, Summer 2016.

Lee, Stephen. *Ethics and War: An Introduction*, Cambridge: Cambridge University Press, 2012.

Lefkowitz, David. "Collateral Damage," in *War: Essays in Political Philosophy*, ed. Larry May, New York: Cambridge University Press, 2008, 145–64.

Legal Consequences of the Construction of a Wall in the Occupied Palestinian Territory, International Court of Justice, Advisory Opinion of July 9, 2004.

Lepora, Chiara and Robert E. Goodin. *On Complicity and Compromise*, Oxford: Oxford University Press, 2013.

Lieber, Francis. "Instructions for the Government of Armies of the United States in the Field," General Order No. 100, April 24, 1863, [the Lieber Code].

Lieblich, Eliav. "Beyond Life and Limb: Exploring Incidental Mental Harm under International Humanitarian Law," in *Applying International Humanitarian Law in Judicial and Quasi-Judicial Bodies: International and Domestic Aspects*, eds. Derek Jinks, Jackson Nyamuya Maogoto, and Solon Solomon, Amsterdam: TMC Asser, 2014, pp. 185–218.

Luban, David. "Military Necessity and the Cultures of Military Law," *Leiden Journal of International Law*, vol. 26, 2013, 315–42.

Lubell, Noam. "The Problem of Imminence in an Uncertain World" in *The Oxford Handbook of the Use of Force in International Law*, ed. Marc Weller, New York: Oxford University Press, 2015, pp. 697–719.

Locke, John. "Second Treatise of Government," in *Locke: Two Treatises of Government*, ed. Peter Laslett, Cambridge: Cambridge University Press, 1988 [1690].

Luban, David. "Human Rights Thinking and the Laws of War," in *Theoretical Boundaries of Armed Conflict and Human Rights*, ed. Jens David Ohlin, New York: Cambridge University Press, 2016.

"Just War and Human rights," *Philosophy and Public Affairs*, vol. 9, no. 2, 1980: 160–81.

"Preventive War," *Philosophy and Public Affairs*, vol. 32, no. 3, 2004, 207–48.

Machiavelli, Niccolò. *The Prince*, eds. Quentin Skinner and Russell Price, Cambridge: Cambridge University Press, 1988 [1532].

Maddox, John Mark. "The Moral Limits of Military Deception," *Journal of Military Ethics*, 2002.

Saint Augustine and the Theory of Just War, London: Bloomsbury Publishing, 2006, 2009.

Mahmassani, Sobhi. "The Principles of International Law in the Light of Islamic Doctrine," *Recueil des Cours*, no. 117, 1966.

Malcolm X, "The Homecoming Rally of the OAAU," in *By Any Means Necessary*, ed. George Breitman, 134–37, New York, Pathfinder Press, 1970.

Manacorda, S. and C. Meloni. "Indirect Perpetration versus Joint Criminal Enterprise: Concurring Approaches in the Practice of International Criminal Law?" *Journal of International Criminal Justice*, vol. 9, 2011, 159–78.

Martin, Richard C. "The Religious Foundations of War, Peace, and Statecraft in Islam," in *Just War and Jihad: Historical and Theoretical Perspectives on War and Peace in Western and Islamic Traditions*, eds. John Kelsay and James Turner Johnson, Westport, CT: Greenwood Press, 1991, pp. 91–118.

Mautner, Thomas. "Grotius and the Skeptics," *Journal of the History of Ideas*, vol. 66, no. 4, 2005, 577–601.

"War and Peace," *British Journal for the History of Philosophy*, vol. 15, no. 2, 2007, 365–81.

Maxwell, Mark. "Rebutting the Civilian Presumption: Playing Whack-a-Mole without a Mallett," in *Targeted Killings*, eds. Finkelstein, Ohlin, and Altman, Oxford: Oxford University Press, pp. 31–59.

May, Larry. *After War Ends*, Cambridge: Cambridge University Press, 2012.

Aggression and Crimes against Peace, Cambridge: Cambridge University Press, 2008.

Contingent Pacifism: Revisiting Just War Theory, Cambridge: Cambridge University Press, 2015.

Crimes against Humanity: A Normative Account, Cambridge: Cambridge University Press, 2005.

Genocide: A Normative Account, Cambridge: Cambridge University Press, 2010.

War Crimes and Just War, Cambridge: Cambridge University Press, 2007.

McCready, Douglas. "Now More than Ever: Territorial Asymmetric Warfare, and the Just War Tradition," *Political Theology*, vol. 7, no. 4, 2006, 461–74.

McEvoy, Philip. "Law at the Operational Level," in *Ethics, Law, and Military Operations*, ed. David Whetham, Houndmills, Basingstoke, Hampshire; New York: Palgrave Macmillan, 2011, pp. 108–34.

McMahan, Jeff. "The Basis of Moral Liability to Defensive Killing," *Philosophical Issues*, vol. 15, 2005, 386–405.

"The Ethics of Killing in War," *Ethics*, vol. 114, 2004, 693–732.

"Just Cause for War," *Ethics and International Affairs*, vol. 19, 2005, 1–21.

"Just War," in *A Companion to Contemporary Political Philosophy*, vol. 2, eds. Robert Goodin et al., Chichester, UK: Wiley-Blackwell, 2012, pp. 669–77.

Killing in War, Oxford: Clarendon Press, 2009.

"The Morality of War and the Law of War," in *Just and Unjust Warriors: The Moral and Legal Status of Soldiers*, eds. David Rodin and Henry Shue, Oxford: Oxford University Press, 2008, pp. 19–43.

"The Moral Responsibility of Volunteer Soldiers," *Boston Review*, November 6, 2013.

"On the Moral Equality of Combatants," *Journal of Political Philosophy*, vol. 14, no. 4, 2006.

"Proportionality and Necessity in *Jus in Bello*," in *The Oxford Handbook of the Ethics of War*, eds. Helen Frowe and Seth Lazar, Oxford: Oxford University Press, 2016.

"Self Defense against Morally Innocent Threats," in *Criminal Law Conversations*, eds. Paul Robinson, Stephen Garvey, and Kimberly Kessler. New York: Oxford University Press, 2009.

"Targeted Killing: Murder, Combat, or Law Enforcement," in *Targeted Killings*, eds. Finkelstein, Ohlin, and Altman.

"War as Self-Defense," *Ethics & International Affairs*, vol. 18, 2004, 75–80.

McPherson, Lionel K. "Innocence and Responsibility in War," *Canadian Journal of Philosophy*, vol. 34, 2004.

"Is Terrorism Distinctively Wrong?" *Ethics*, vol. 117, 2007.

"The Limits of the War Convention," *Philosophy & Social Criticism*, vol. 31, 2005, 147–63.

"Response to Jeff McMahan's 'The Moral Responsibility of Volunteer Soldiers,'" *Boston Review*, November 6, 2013.

Meron, Theodor. "Common Rights of Mankind in Gentili, Grotius and Suarez," *The American Journal of International Law*, vol. 85, no. 1, 1991, 110–16.

Messenger, Charles. *Rommel: Leadership Lessons from the Desert Fox*, New York: Palgrave Macmillan, 2009.

Mettraux, G. *The Law of Command Responsibility*, Oxford: Oxford University Press, 2009.

Milanovic, Marko. "The Lost Origins of *Lex Specialis*: Rethinking the Relationship between Human Rights and International Humanitarian Law," in *Theoretical Boundaries*, ed. Ohlin, pp. 78–103.

Norm Conflicts, International Humanitarian Law, and Human Rights Law," in *International Humanitarian Law and International Human Rights Law*, ed. O. Ben-Naftali, New York: Oxford University Press, 2011, pp. 95–125.

"The Military Medicine of Ancient Rome," in *Science and Its Times*, eds. Neil Schlager and Josh Lauer, vol. 1, Detroit: Gale, 2001.

Mill, John Stuart. "A Few Words on Non-intervention," in his *Collected Works, Vol. XXI: Essays on Equality, Law, and Education*, ed. John M. Robson, Toronto: University of Toronto Press, 1984 [1859], pp. 109–24.

Miller, David. *National Responsibility and Global Justice*, New York: Oxford University Press, 2008.

"Territorial Rights: Concept and Justification," *Political Studies*, vol. 60, 2012, 252–68.

Mitchell, A.D. "Does One Illegality Merit Another? The Law of Belligerent Reprisals in International Law," *Military Law Review*, 2001, 155–77.

Moore, Margaret. "Collective Self-Determination, Institutions of Justice, and Wars of National Defense," in *The Morality of Defensive War*, eds. Fabre and Lazar, pp. 185–202.

Moyn, Samuel. *The Last Utopia: Human Rights in History*, Cambridge, MA: Harvard University Press, 2012.

Munir, Muhammed. "Suicide Attacks: Martyrdom Operations or Acts of Perfidy?" in *Islam and International Law: Engaging Self-Centrism from a Plurality of Perspectives*, eds. Marie-Luisa Frick and Andreas T. Müller, Leiden: Martinus Nijhoff Publishers, 2013, pp. 99–123.

Nagel, Thomas. *The View from Nowhere*, Oxford, Oxford University Press, 1989.

Na'īm, Abd Allāh Aḥmad. *Islam and the Secular State: Negotiating the Future of Shari'a*, Cambridge, MA: Harvard University Press, 2008.

Neff, Stephen C. *War and the Law of Nations: A General History*, Cambridge: Cambridge University Press, 2005.

Nellen, Henk. *Hugo Grotius: A Lifelong Struggle for Peace in Church and State, 1583–1645*, Leiden: Brill, 2014.

Newton, Michael and Larry May. *Proportionality in International Law*, Oxford: Oxford University Press, 2014.

Nicholas, Abe. "The Woes of an American Drone Operator," *Der Spiegel*, vol. 14, December 2002.

Nichols, John. "Remembering the Folly of 'Blank-Check' War and 'Escalation Unlimited,'" *Nation*, August 7, 2014.

Norman, Richard. *Ethics, Killing and War*, Cambridge and New York: Cambridge University Press, 1995.

Nyazee, Imran Ahsan Khan. *Islamic Jurisprudence*, Islamabad: International Institute of Islamic Thought, 2000.

O'Connell, Mary Ellen. "Combatants and the Combat Zone," *University of Richmond Law Review*, vol. 43, 2009.

O'Donnell, James D. "The Authority of Augustine," 1991 St. Augustine Lecture, Villanova University, November 13, 1991.

Ohlin, Jens David. "Introduction: The Inescapable Collision," in *Theoretical Boundaries of Armed Conflict and Human Rights*, ed. Jens David Ohlin, New York: Cambridge University Press, 2016, pp. 1–22.

"Second-Order Linking Principles: Combining Vertical and Horizontal Modes of Liability," *Leiden Journal of International Law*, vol. 25, 2012, 771–97.

"Sharp Wars Are Brief," in *Weighing Lives in War: Combatants and Civilians*, eds. Ohlin, Finkelstein, and May.

"Targeting and the Concept of Intent," *Michigan Journal of International Law*, vol. 35, 2013, 79–130.

"The Duty to Capture," *Minnesota Law Review*, vol. 97, 2013, 1268–342.

"Was the Kunduz Hospital Attack a War Crime?" *Opinio Juris*, vol. 1, May 2016.

Ohlin, Jens D. and Larry May, *Necessity in International Law*, Oxford: Oxford University Press, 2016.

Oil Platforms (Islamic Republic of Iran v. United States of America), Judgment (2003) ICJ Reports 16.

Olsthoorn, Johan. "Why Justice and Injustice Have No Place Outside the Hobbesian State," *European Journal of Political Theory*, vol. 14, no. 1, 2015, 19–36.

Onuma Yasuaki ed. *A Normative Approach to War: Peace, War, and Justice in Hugo Grotius*, Oxford: Clarendon Press, 1993.

Orend, Brian. *The Morality of War*, 2nd ed., Peterborough: Broadview Press, 2013.

Pagden, Anthony. *The Fall of Natural Man: The American Indian and the Origins of Comparative Ethnology*, Cambridge: Cambridge University Press, 1986.

Parfit, Derek. *On What Matters*, Oxford: Oxford University Press, 2011.

Piirimäe, Pärtel. "Alberico Gentili's Doctrine of Defensive War and Its Impact on Seventeenth-century Normative Views," in *The Roman Foundations of the Law of Nations: Alberico Gentili and the Justice of Empire*, eds. Benedict Kingsbury and Benjamin Straumann, Oxford: Oxford University Press, 2010, pp. 187–209.

Poland, James M. *Understanding Terrorism: Groups, Strategies, and Responses*, Englewood Cliffs, NJ: Prentice Hall, 1988.

Powell, Jonathan and Niall Rudd. *Editorial Preface to Niall Rudd's Translation of Cicero's* The Republic *and* The Laws, Oxford: Oxford University Press, 1998.

Program on Humanitarian Policy and Conflict Research, *Commentary on the HPCR Manual on International Law Applicable to Air and Missile Warfare*, 2010.

Prosecutor v. Brdjanin, Appeals Judgment, ICTY Case No. IT-99-36, April 3, 2007.

Prosecutor v. Galić, Judgment, IT-98-29, ICTY Trial Chamber, December 5, 2003.

Prosecutor v. Germain Katanga and Mathieu Ngudjolo Chui, Decision on Confirmation of Charges, Pre-Trial Chamber, ICC-01/04-01/07-3269, September 30, 2008.

Prosecutor v. Krajisnik, Appeals Judgment, ICTY Case No. IT-00-39.

Prosecutor v. Popovic et al., Trial Judgment, ICTY Case No. IT-05-88, June 10, 2010.

Prosecutor v Prlic, Judgment, IT-04-74, ICTY Trial Chamber, May 29, 2013.

Protocol Additional to the Geneva Conventions of August 12, 1949, and relating to the Protection of Victims of International Armed Conflicts, June 8, 1977 (Protocol I) art 49. 1125 U.N.T.S. 3.

Public Committee against Torture in Israel v. Government of Israel, Judgment, HCJ 769/02, December 11, 2005, para 46.

Quinn, Warren S. "Actions, Intentions, and Consequences: The Doctrine of Doing and Allowing," *Philosophical Review*, vol. 98, 1989, 287–312.

Quong, Jonathan and Joanna Firth, "Necessity, Moral Liability and Defensive Harm," *Law and Philosophy*, vol. 31, 2012.

Railton, Peter. "Alienation, Consequentialism, and the Demands of Morality," *Philosophy & Public Affairs*, vol. 13, no. 2, 1984, 134–71.

Ratner, Stephen R. "Behind the Flag of Dunant: Secrecy and the Compliance Mission of the International Committee of the Red Cross," in *Transparency in International Law* eds. A. Bianchi and A. Peters, New York: Cambridge University Press, 2013.

Rawls, John. *The Law of Peoples*, Cambridge, MA: Harvard University Press, 1999.

Reichberg, Gregory M. "Just War and Regular War: Competing Paradigms," in *Just and Unjust Warriors: The Moral and Legal Status of Soldiers*, eds. David Rodin and Henry Shue, Oxford: Oxford University Press, 2008, pp. 193–213.

"Preventive War in Classical Just War Theory," *Journal of the History of International Law*, vol. 9, no. 1, 2007, 5–34.

"Suárez on Just War," in *Interpreting Suárez: Critical Essays*, ed. Daniel Schwartz, Cambridge: Cambridge University Press, 2012, pp. 184–204.

"The Moral Equality of Combatants – A Doctrine in Classical Just War Theory?" *Journal of Military Ethics*, vol. 12, no. 2, 2013, 181–94.

Reichberg, Gregory M., Henrik Syse, and Endre Begby ed. *The Ethics of War: Classic and Contemporary Readings*, Oxford: Blackwell Publishing, 2006.

Resta, G. and V. Zeno-Zencovich, "Judicial 'Truth' and Historical 'Truth': The Case of the Ardeatine Caves Massacre," *Law & History Review*, vol. 31, 2013.

Rhoads, Emily Paddon. *Taking Sides in Peacekeeping: Impartiality and the Future of the United Nations*, Oxford: Oxford University Press, 2016.

Rieff, David. *A Bed for the Night: Humanitarianism in Crisis*, New York: Simon and Schuster, 2002.

Ripstein, Arthur. "Beyond the Harm Principle," *Philosophy and Public Affairs*, vol. 34, 2006, 215–45.

   Force and Freedom, Cambridge: Cambridge University Press, 2009.

Roberts, Adam and Richard Guelff. *Documents on the Laws of War*, 3rd ed. Oxford: Oxford University Press, 2000.

Robinson, Darryl. "How Command Responsibility Got So Complicated: A Culpability Contradiction, Its Obfuscation, and a Simple Solution," *Melbourne Journal of International Law*, vol. 13, 2012.

Rodin, David. "Ethics of Asymmetric War," in *The Ethics of War: Shared Problems in Different Traditions*, eds. Richard Sorabji and David Rodin, Aldershot, UK: Ashgate, 2006, pp. 153–68.

   "The Moral Inequality of Soldiers: Why *Jus in Bello* Asymmetry Is Half Right," in *Just and Unjust Warriors: The Moral and Legal Status of Soldiers*, eds. David Rodin and Henry Shue, Oxford: Oxford University Press, 2008, pp. 44–68.

   "The Myth of National Defense" in Fabre and Lazar (eds.), *The Morality of Defensive War*.

   "Terrorism without Intention," *Ethics*, vol. 114, 2004, 752–71.

   War and Self-Defense, Oxford: Clarendon Press, 2002.

Rogers, A.P.V. *Law on the Battlefield*, Manchester: Manchester University Press, 1996.

   "Unequal Combat and the Law of War," *Yearbook of International Humanitarian Law*, vol. 7, 2004, 3–34.

Rosenberg, M. "Pentagon Details Chain of Errors in Strike on Afghan Hospital," *New York Times*, April 29, 2016. www.nytimes.com/2016/04/30/world/asia/afghanistan-doctors-without-borders-hospital-strike.html, accessed July 1, 2016.

Rostow, Eugene V. "Until What? Enforcement Action or Collective Self-Defense," *American Journal of International Law*, vol. 85, no. 3, July 1991, 506–16.

Rousseau, J.J. "On the Social Contract," in *The Collected Writings of Rousseau*, vol. IV, eds. Roger D. Masters and Christopher Kelly, Hanover and London: University Press of New England, 1994 [1762], pp. 127–224.

Rowe, N.C. "Perfidy in Cyberwarfare," in *Routledge Handbook of Ethics and War: Just War Theory in the 21st Century*, eds. Fritz Allhoff et al., New York: Routledge, 2013.

Royal, General Benoit. *The Ethical Challenges of the Soldier: The French Experience*, Paris: Economica Press, 2010.

Russell, Frederick H. *The Just War in the Middle Ages*, Cambridge: Cambridge University Press, 1975.

Ruys, Tony. *"Armed Attack" and Article 51 of the UN Charter*, New York: Cambridge University Press, 2010.

Salter, John. "Hugo Grotius: Property and Consent," *Political Theory*, vol. 29, no. 4, 2001, 537–55.

Schaffner, Tobias. "The Eudaemonist Ethics of Hugo Grotius (1583–1645): Premodern Moral Philosophy for the Twenty-First Century?" *Jurisprudence*, vol. 7, no. 3, 2016, 478–522.

Schecter, A., L.C. Dai, L.T. Thuy, H.T. Quynh, D.Q. Minh, H.D. Cau, P.H. Phiet, N.T. Nguyen, J.D. Constable, and R. Baughman. "Agent Orange and the Vietnamese: The Persistence of Elevated Dioxin Levels in Human Tissues," *American Journal of Public Health*, vol. 4, April 1995, 516–22.

Scheffler, Samuel. *The Rejection of Consequentialism*, Oxford: Oxford University Press, 1982.

Schiff, Ze'ev and Ehud Ya'ari. *Israel's Lebanon War*, New York: Simon & Schuster, 1984.

Schmitt, Michael N. "Precision Attack and International Humanitarian Law," *International Review of the Red Cross*, vol. 87, 2005.

"The Principle of Discrimination in 21st Century Warfare," *Yale Human Rights and Development Law Journal*, vol. 2, 1999, 143–51.

"Wound, Capture, or Kill: A Reply to Ryan Goodman's 'The Power to Kill or Capture Enemy Combatants,'" *European Journal of International Law*, vol. 24, 2013.

Schmitt, Carl. *The Nomos of the Earth in the International Law of the Jus Publicum Europaeum*, trans. G.L. Ulmen, New York: Telos Press Publishing, 2003 [1950].

Schulzke, Marcus. "The Morality of Remote Warfare: Against the Asymmetry Objection to Remote Weaponry," *Political Studies*, vol. 64, no. 1 (2016), 90–105.

Schwartz, Daniel. "Late Scholastic Just War Theory," in *The Oxford Handbook of Ethics of War*, eds. Seth Lazar and Helen Frowe, Oxford: Oxford University Press, 2016.

Scott, Jonathan. "The Law of War: Grotius, Sidney, Locke and the Political Theory of Rebellion," *History of Political Thought*, vol. 13, no. 4, 1992, 565–85.

Shah, Niaz A. *Islamic Law and the Law of Armed Conflict: The Conflict in Pakistan*, New York: Routledge, 2011.

Self-Defense in Islamic and International Law: Assessing Al-Qaeda and the Invasion of Iraq, New York: Palgrave Macmillan, 2008.

Sharkey, Noel. "Ground for Discrimination: Autonomous Robot Weapons," *RUSI Defence Systems*, vol. 11, no. 2, 86–89.

Shaver, Robert. "Grotius on Scepticism and Self-interest," *Archiv für Geschichte der Philosophie*, vol. 78, no. 1, 1996, 27–47.

Shue, Henry. *Basic Rights: Subsistence, Affluence, and U.S. Foreign Policy*, Princeton: Princeton University Press, 1996.

"Civilian Protection and Force Protection," *Ethics, Law, and Military Operations*, ed. David Whetham. New York: Palgrave Macmillian.

"Do We Need a 'Morality of War'?" in *Just and Unjust Warriors: The Moral and Legal Status of Soldiers*, eds. David Rodin and Henry Shue, New York: Oxford University Press, 2008.

Fighting Hurt: Rule and Exception in Torture and War, Oxford: Oxford University Press, 2016.

"Last Resort and Proportionality," in *The Oxford Handbook of Ethics of War*, eds. Lazar and Frowe.

"Proportionality in War," in *The Encyclopedia of War*, ed. Gordon Martel, Chicester, West Sussex; Malden, MA: Wiley-Blackwell, 2012.

Shue, Henry and David Rodin ed. *Preemption: Military Action and Moral Justification*, Oxford: Oxford University Press, 2007.

Silverman, Adam L. "Just War, Jihad, and Terrorism: A Comparison of Western and Islamic Norms for the Use of Political Violence," *Journal of Church and State*, vol. 44, no. 1, 2002, 187–209.

Solis, Gary D. *The Law of Armed Conflict*, 2nd ed., Cambridge: Cambridge University Press, 2016.

The S.S. Lotus, (France v. Turkey) (Judgment), 1927 P.C.I.J. (series A) No. 10.

Statman, Daniel. "On the Success Condition for Legitimate Self-Defense," *Ethics*, vol. 118, no. 4, 2008.

Straumann, Benjamin. *Roman Law in the State of Nature: The Classical Foundations of Hugo Grotius' Natural Law*, trans. Belinda Cooper, Cambridge: Cambridge University Press, 2015.

Stepp v. Commonwealth, 608 S.W. 2d 371 (Ky. 1980).

Strawser, Bradley. "Moral Predators: The Duty to Employ Uninhabited Aerial Vehicles," *Journal of Military Ethics*, vol. 9, no. 4, 2010, 342–68.

Stilz, Anna. "Authority, Self-Determination, and Community in Cosmopolitan War," *Law and Philosophy*, vol. 33, 2014, 309–35.

"Nations, States, and Territory," *Ethics*, vol. 121, 2011, 572–601.

"Territorial Rights and National Defense," in *The Morality of Defensive* War, eds. Fabre and Lazar.

Suárez, Francisco. "A Work on the Three Theological Virtues: Faith, Hope and Charity," in *Selections from Three Works*, 2 vols., eds. Gwladis L. Williams, Ammi Brown, and John Waldron, Oxford: Clarendon Press, 1944 [1621], pp. 797–865.

Syse, Henrik and Endre Begby eds. *The Ethics of War: Classic and Contemporary Readings*, Oxford: Blackwell Publishing, 2006.

Tadashi, Tanaka. "*Temperamenta* (moderation)," in *A Normative Approach to War: Peace, War, and Justice in Hugo Grotius*, ed. Onuma Yasuaki, Oxford: Clarendon Press, 1993, pp. 276–307.

Tadros, Victor. "Duty and Liability," *Utilitas*, vol. 24, no. 2, 2012, 259–77.

Terry, Fiona. *Condemned to Repeat? The Paradox of Humanitarian Action*, Ithaca: Cornell University Press, 2002.

Thomson, Judith Jarvis. "Self-Defense," *Philosophy and Public Affairs*, vol. 20, 1991, 283–310.

Tierney, Brian. *Liberty and Law: The Idea of Permissive Natural Law, 1100–1800*, Washington, DC: Catholic University of America Press, 2014.

Tooke, Joan D. *The Just War in Aquinas and Grotius*, London: S.P.C.K, 1965.

Tuck, Richard. *Natural Rights Theories: Their Origin and Development*, Cambridge: Cambridge University Press, 1979.

"Grotius, Carneades and Hobbes," *Grotiana*, vol. 4, no. 1, 1983, 43–62.

"The 'Modern' Theory of Natural Law," in *The Languages of Political Theory in Early-Modern Europe*, ed. Anthony Pagden, Cambridge: Cambridge University Press, 1987, pp. 99–122.

Philosophy and Government, 1572–1651, Cambridge: Cambridge University Press, 1993.

The Rights of War and Peace: Political Thought and the International Order from Grotius to Kant, Oxford: Clarendon Press, 1999.

"Introduction," in *Hugo Grotius, The Rights of War and Peace*, 3 vols., ed. Richard Tuck, ix–xxxiii, Indianapolis: Liberty Fund, 2005.

Uniacke, Suzanne. "In Defense of Permissible Killing," *Law and Philosophy*, vol. 19, 2000, 627–33.

"Self-Defense, Just War, and a Reasonable Prospect of Success," in *How We Fight*, eds. Helen Frowe and Gerald Lang, Oxford: Oxford University Press, 2014.

"2015 Global Terrorism Index: Deaths from Terrorism Increased 80% Last Year to the Highest Level Ever; Global Economic Cost of Terrorism Reached All-Time High at US$52.9 Billion," *PR Newswire*, November 16, 2015.

United Kingdom Ministry of Defense. *The Manual of the Law of Armed Conflict*, July 2004, as amended by Amendment 3, September 2010, Oxford University Press, 2005.

United Nations' Fact-Finding Mission on the Gaza Conflict, also known as the Goldstone Report, "Human Rights in Palestine and Other Occupied Arab Territories," available at www2.ohchr.org/english/bodies/hrcouncil/docs/12session/A-HRC-12-48.pdf.

United Nations General Assembly, Articles on the Responsibility of States for Internationally Wrongful Acts, in Report of the International Law Commission on the Work of Its Fifty-third Session art. 25, U.N. GAOR, 56th Sess., Supp. No. 10, at 43, U.N. Doc. A/56/10 (2001), annexed to G.A. Res. 56/83 (December 12, 2001).

United Nations General Assembly, Reports of the International Law Commission to the General Assembly, 21 U.N. GAOR Supp. No. 9, pt. II, U.N. Doc. A/6309/Rev. l (1966), reprinted in [1966] 2 Y.B. Int'l L. Comm'n 172, at 247, U.N. Doc. A/CN.4/SER.A/1966/Add.l.

United Nations Humans Rights Office of the High Commissioner, *Conscientious Objection to Military Service*, New York: United Nations, 2012.

United States Conference of Catholic Bishops, "Statement on the Catholic Conscientious Objector," October 15, 1969.

United States Department of Defense, *Law of War Manual*, 2015.

United States White House, Office of the Press Secretary, Executive Order, *United States Policy on Pre- and Post-Strike Measures to Address Civilian Casualties in U.S. Operations Involving the Use of Force*, July 1, 2016.

United States v. Peterson, 483F.2d 1222 (1973).

US v. List (American Military Tribunal, Nuremberg, 1948), 11 NMT 1230.

US v. Von Weizsaecker et al (Ministries Case) (Nuremberg, 1949), 14 NMT 314, 329, in *The Trials of War Criminals Before Nuremberg Military Tribunals under Control Council Law No. 10*, vol. 14.

van Sliedregt, E. "The Curious Case of International Criminal Liability," *Journal of International Criminal Justice*, vol. 10, 2012, 1171–188.

Vattel, Emer de. *The Law of Nations*, eds. Béla Kapossy and Richard Whatmore. Indianapolis: Liberty Fund, 2008 [1758].

War in Due Form, London: 1758.

Vitoria, Francisco de. *De Indis et de Iure Belli, Relectiones*, ed. Ernest Nys, New York and London: Oceana Publications and Wiley & Sons, 1964.

Political Writings, eds. Anthony Pagden and Jeremy Lawrance, Cambridge: Cambridge University Press, 1991.

Voltaire. *Political Writings*, ed. David Williams, Cambridge: Cambridge University Press, 1994.

Waldron, Jeremy. "Deep Morality and the Laws of War," in *The Oxford Handbook of Ethics of War*, eds. Lazar and Frowe.

"Justifying Targeted Killing with a Neutral Principle," in *Targeted Killings*, eds. Finkelstein, Ohlin, and Altman.

Walzer, Michael. *Just and Unjust Wars: A Moral Argument with Historical Illustrations*, 5th ed., New York: Basic Books, 2015 [1977].

"On Humanitarianism: Is Helping Others Charity, or Duty, or Both?" *Foreign Affairs*, vol. 90, no. 4, July/August 2011.

"Response to McMahan's Paper," *Philosophia*, vol. 34, 2006, 43–45.

"Responsibility and Proportionality in State and Nonstate Wars," *Parameters*, Spring 2009, 40–52.

"Terrorism and Just War," *Philosophia*, vol. 34, no. 4, 2006, 3–12.

"The Moral Standing of States: A Response to Four Critics," *Philosophy & Public Affairs*, vol. 9, 1980, 209–29.

Warner, David. "The Politics of the Political/Humanitarian Divide," *International Review of the Red Cross*, no. 833, March 1999, 109–18.

Weatherall, T. *Jus Cogens: International Law and Social Contract*, New York: Cambridge University Press, 2015.

Weigend, T. "Perpetration through an Organization: The Unexpected Career of a German Legal Concept," *Journal of International Criminal Justice*, vol. 9, 2011, 91–111.

Wenar, Leif. *Blood Oil: Tyrants, Violence, and the Rules that Run the World*, Oxford: Oxford University Press, 2015.

Whetham, David. "The Just War Tradition: A Pragmatic Compromise," *Ethics, Law, and Military Operations*, ed. David Whetham, New York: Palgrave Macmillian. 2011.

Williams, S. *Hybrid and Internationalized Criminal Tribunals: Selected Jurisdictional Issues*, Portland, OR: Hart Publishing, 2012.

Wippman, David. "Introduction: Do New Wars Call for New Laws?" in *New Wars, New Laws?* eds. David Wippman and Matthew Evangelista, Ardsley, NY: Transnational Publishers, 2005, pp. 1–30.

Whitman, Walt. "The Wound Dresser," *Leaves of Grass*, New York: The Modern Library Publishers, 1921, pp. 263–65.

Witt, John. *Lincoln's Code: The Laws of War in American History*, New York: Free Press, 2012.

Wolff, Christian. *Jus Gentium Methodo Scientifica Pertractatum* (1749), H. Drake (Oxford: Clarendon Press, 1934) para. 9, quoted in Charles Beitz, "The Moral Standing of States Revisited," in *Reading Walzer*, eds. Yitzhak Benbaji and Naomi Sussmann, Abingdon: Routledge, 2014.

Wright, Jason D. "'Excessive' Ambiguity: Analyzing and Refining the Proportionality Standard," *International Review of the Red Cross*, no. 94, 2012, 819–52.

Yoo, John. "Using Force," *The University of Chicago Law Review*, vol. 71, no. 3, Summer 2004, 729–97.

Index